EDWARD GLOVER, M.D., LL.D.

*Selected Papers on
Psycho-Analysis, Volume II*

THE ROOTS OF CRIME

Other books by the same author

WAR, SADISM AND PACIFISM
THE DANGERS OF BEING HUMAN
PSYCHO-ANALYSIS
THE PSYCHOLOGY OF FEAR AND
    COURAGE
FREUD OR JUNG
THE TECHNIQUE OF PSYCHO-ANALYSIS
ON THE EARLY DEVELOPMENT OF MIND

SELECTED PAPERS ON PSYCHO-ANALYSIS VOLUME II

THE ROOTS
OF CRIME

EDWARD GLOVER

INTERNATIONAL UNIVERSITIES PRESS, INC.
New York, N. Y.

First Published in this form 1960
Copyright © 1960 by Imago Publishing Co., Ltd.
All rights reserved

Printed in Great Britain by The Whitefriars Press Ltd.

ACKNOWLEDGEMENT

Acknowledgement is made to the Editors of the Journals in which various articles have appeared, as follows: *The International Journal of Psycho-Analysis. Journal of Criminal Law, Criminology and Police Science, The British Journal of Delinquency, Modern Law Review, The Medico-legal Review, The Journal of Mental Science.* Acknowledgement is also made to International Universities Press and I.S.T.D. Publications.

Full reference is given in the title footnotes.

NOTE

Abbreviations used in this volume are in accordance with the *World List of Scientific Periodicals* (Oxford, 1950). Numerals in bold type refer to volumes; ordinary numerals to pages and dates. Further abbreviations are *C.P.* = Freud, *Collected Papers* (5 vols.), Hogarth Press, London, 1924–50; I.S.T.D. = Institute for the Study and Treatment of Delinquency.

CONTENTS

Section		Page
	Preface	ix
I	*Introductory*	3
	The Roots of Crime	3
II	*Historical*	27
	Outline of the Investigation and Treatment of Delinquency in Great Britain	27
	Part I '1912–48'	29
	Part II '1949–55'	60
	Part III '1956–59'	68
III	*Diagnosis and Treatment of Pathological Delinquency*	79
	Part I Diagnosis	82
	Part II Treatment	97
IV	*The Criminal Psychopath*	117
	Part I Diagnosis	118
	Part II Etiology	132
	Part III Treatment	148
	Appendix—Aichhorn on Treatment	164
V	*Sexual Disorders and Offences*	173
	Part I The Social and Legal Aspects of Sexual Abnormality	175
	Part II The Problem of Male Homosexuality	197
	i. Diagnosis and Classification	197
	ii. Etiology	214
	iii. Prognosis and Treatment	230
	Part III The Psycho-pathology of Prostitution	244
VI	*Clinical Research*	271
	Part I Team-Research on Delinquency	272

Section			Page
	Part II	Recent Advances in the Psychoanalytical Study of Delinquency	292
	Part III	Psycho-Analysis and Criminology: a Political Survey	311
VII	*Socio-legal*		327
	Part I	The Concept of 'Recidivism'.	327
	Part II	The M'Naghten Rules.	339
	Part III	The Prevention of Pathological Crime	347
	Part IV	Psychiatric Aspects of Capital Punishment	352
VIII	*Obiter Scripta*		363
	Index of Authors		399
	Subject Index		401

PREFACE

When the social historian of the future looks back to the first half of the twentieth century with the detachment that comes with the passage of time, it will by then be apparent that amongst the revolutionary changes to be credited to that period, two at least were of vital importance to the development of humanism: the liberation of psychology from the fetters of a conscious rationalism, and the subsequent emancipation of sociology from the more primitive superstitions and moralistic conceptions of crime. It will also be apparent that this twin movement towards a new liberalism owed its impetus to the researches of a late-Victorian scientist, Sigmund Freud, who first uncovered the unconscious roots of that uniquely human reaction which goes by the name of 'guilt' and which is responsible for a brood of moralistic concepts, including those of sin, punishment, expiation and the sacrifice of scapegoats.

We need not assume, however, that our future historian will be living in a crime-free age. To be sure he may have ceased to employ the moralistic term 'crime' and have substituted more dispassionate and illuminating characterological labels for criminal offences. But even if our current calendar of crimes were to become obsolete, there is every likelihood that its place would be taken by a new set of misdemeanours; such is the strength of the unconscious 'need for crime' and of the social compulsion to punish infractions of social codes. Indeed since crime is the co-efficient of friction between man and his society, the Law will always be faced with fresh tokens of this perennial conflict.

Nor is there much prospect that for some centuries possibly millenia ahead we can afford to dispense with what we now call criminal conduct. For as long as society gives assent to the waging of wars, it is essential that it should be able when the necessity arises to loosen in otherwise law abiding individuals those tendencies which when encountered in current life we are accustomed to call criminal psychopathy. The history of civilization is, after all, the history of guilt. We cannot expect to eradicate in the individual tendencies to behaviour which society is prepared to condone and even belaud when it suits its own group purposes.

Nevertheless, meagre and timid as our present advances in

psychological criminology may be, they do represent a resounding victory over superstition, similar in kind to that early nineteenth century advance in psychiatry which finally gave the quietus to the view that insanity was due to the possession of the victim by evil spirits which had to be exorcised by flogging. In fact current advances in criminology are due not so much to a change in spirit of the community, which given the freedom would still be capable of applying lynch law to the more horrifying forms of crime, as to the application of a dispassionate consulting-room logic. No doubt in his turn the sociologist will be given greater authority to tackle the problem of 'natural crime' but in the meantime the only indisputable proposition regarding 'crime' is that when it can be traced to *pathological* sources the primitive impulse to punish the wrongdoer is a form of malpraxis which is calculated to encourage the 'disease' or at least to render it intractable.

In the meantime it is necessary to chart the existing sphere of influence of what is sometimes called, rather portentously, *forensic psychiatry*. Psychiatry has in fact established a professional enclave in the territories of criminology, a bridgehead that may lead ultimately to an infiltration of the whole area with a new 'social psychiatry'. At present, however, forensic psychiatry has done little more than extend the accustomed range of psychiatry to include certain pathological forms of asocial or anti-social behaviour which are still designated by the community as criminal. This new territory has been provisionally delimited but is very far from being fully explored. Only a very small nucleus of trained investigators has been formed, scarcely sufficient to deal with the very fringes of the subject. The situation is indeed not unlike that obtaining in the case of the study and prevention of war. We maintain a War Office to organize the conduct of war, but, excluding, as we may well exclude, the ambivalent activities of Foreign Offices, no single country has ever set up a Peace Office to discover and alleviate the tensions that lead to explosions of war-making. The League of Nations never considered such a possibility and its successor the United Nations is so busy with the phenomena of disunion that it has neither the time nor the inclination to initiate any fundamental researches on the causes of war. In the case of crime we maintain the most elaborate and expensive police and penal organization to attack and so control criminal conduct but it is only beginning to dawn on the authorities that a much more widely ramifying organization is necessary to discover and alleviate the tensions that lead to criminal behaviour.

Already the shape such an organization must take has been indicated by experience gained at delinquency clinics, where it has been found necessary to employ multi-disciplined techniques in the diagnosis and to a certain extent in the treatment of pathological delinquency. This multi-disciplined approach has also been found necessary in the case of sociological investigations of crime; and special investigators are now beginning to approach the subject from a great number of social angles. As a matter of interest, a movement is already afoot the aim of which is to delegate the supervision of juvenile delinquency to educational authorities; and it may not be long before the Ministry of Health is compelled to extend its authority in a like direction.

All this has some bearing on the form and content of the present collection of essays. My own interest in pathological crime was first aroused about 1911 by contact with James Devon, an enlightened prison medical officer whose pioneering views are to be found in his book *The Criminal and the Community* (1912). Shortly afterwards I was seconded from hospital to act as *locum tenens* for a provincial surgeon who was also visiting medical officer to a local convict prison in Scotland, and for a few weeks observed the prison system at its then best and worst. But it was not till the early twenties that I had the opportunity of making psycho-analytical observations on some juvenile and adult delinquents. Apart from such direct experience psycho-analytical practice brings the observer in constant contact with the manifestations of unconscious guilt in both normal and neurotic persons, some forms of which, paradoxically enough, give rise, as Freud first pointed out, to an unconscious need for punishment and hence to criminal conduct. As a matter of interest my observations began in the year before Freud in 1922 adumbrated his concept of the 'super-ego' or 'unconscious conscience' a formulation which, provided it is not bowdlerized too much by psychiatrists and social workers, is destined to revolutionize not only psychology but moral philosophy and sociology, to say nothing of our current social conceptions of right, righteousness and morality.

About seven years later, on the initiative of Dr. Grace

Pailthorpe, a psycho-analytical pioneer on the mentality of prison inmates, I was co-opted to a committee for the investigation and treatment of crime, and in 1931 became involved in the founding of the *Institute for the Study and Treatment of Delinquency* and of the *Psychopathic Clinic* with which at first it was exclusively preoccupied. At that time it was the only psychiatric clinic in the world to concern itself exclusively with delinquent study and therapy. Soon the inevitable happened. Crime being a social phenomenon calls also for the attention of a variety of trained social workers and observers, or social psychologists as they are now called. And so, willy-nilly, a multi-disciplined approach to crime had to be organized. As Chairman of the Scientific Committee of the I.S.T.D., I have since then been closely involved in multi-disciplined research projects, and have inevitably formed some opinions as to the relative merits in the study of crime of psycho-analysis, psychiatry, normal psychology, social psychology, sociology and statistical psychology.

I do not conceal my view that the most fundamental approach to crime, pathological or otherwise, is that of psycho-analysis. And I believe that all other psychological and social approaches can be measured by the degree to which they take cognizance of psycho-analytical principles. The trouble about psycho-analysts is that they have so far produced only the broadest generalizations regarding group psychology and yet are inclined to look down their noses at any detailed social approach which does not render at least lip-service to psycho-analytical concepts. This is the more unfortunate since society has a vested interest in crime and insists on applying current social values whether the psycho-analyst likes it or not. In other words society, although prepared to tolerate the existence of private mental illnesses in its midst is not prepared to tolerate criminal acts and cannot wait till science points ways and means of coping with anti-social conduct outside the range of penal method. For this reason alone psychology and sociology were bound sooner or later to join forces on the common ground of social expediency.

For these amongst other reasons the present volume has been strongly influenced by two needs, first of all to present psycho-analytical views on pathological crime in a form which, I hope, will appeal to readers who are interested in social developments;

and, second, to orientate in the psycho-analytical approach such workers in delinquency as are devoted to other forms of scientific discipline. It is not intended to provide an elaborate résumé of psycho-analytical theories of, or observations on crime, which latter, incidentally, are sparse enough and sometimes undisciplined enough. At the same time it may be of service to those psycho-analysts who are unfamiliar with the peculiar psychological and social conditions and difficulties existing in the criminological field. To be sure I have no great faith in the fertility of existing forms of 'combined' scientific effort, laudable as that approach may seem to be. For it has always appeared to me that the strength of a research team is the strength of its weakest link. Certainly so long as the existence and power of unconscious motives is disregarded, we cannot learn any more about crime than an apparent commonsense dictates. But crime and commonsense are refractory bedfellows and however speculative and uncontrolled some psycho-analytic views on crime may be they do at least promise to uncover the fundamental flight from reality that leads to pathological and possibly all forms of criminal conduct.

We must realize of course that penal codes, being in the last resort an expression of current social and moral values sharpened by the need for social safety must of necessity express also the age-old prejudices, fears and penchant for punishment which bedevil social progress. Society, it has often been said, gets the crime it deserves; and it cannot be denied that its stability owes something to the scapegoat system whereby the criminal is made to pay for the unconscious criminal tendencies that lie dormant in the community. These, however, are matters that may be left to the researches of the social anthropologist. The object of this book is more immediate and practical, namely, to support and conceivably augment the authority of the clinical psychologist in the study, treatment and ultimately prevention of pathological delinquency.

London, 1959   EDWARD GLOVER

I. INTRODUCTORY

THE ROOTS OF CRIME

SECTION I

INTRODUCTORY

THE ROOTS OF CRIME *
[1922]

The recent expansion of public interest in crime and criminology has been so rapid that it is difficult to realize how backward was the general reaction to these problems in the period following the First World War, now almost forty years past. Lecturers on the psychology of crime were apt to be regarded either as cranks or woolly-minded reformers out of touch with the depraved nature of the criminal. Added to which psycho-analysts were generally thought to be in any case more than a little peculiar. It was therefore both surprising and gratifying to be invited to address a congress of magistrates on the psychology of crime; for magistrates in those days were by nature and training extremely conservative and indeed almost allergic to the idea that any crime could be a manifestation of disorder in human relations.

Even at that time, however, a good deal of valuable psychological work on crime had already been carried out in Europe and America. Indeed it is worthy of note that, although the facilities for treating delinquent cases have increased very greatly during the past ten years and the literature on the subject has become increasingly voluminous, comparatively few fresh discoveries have been made regarding the causes, treatment and prevention of crime. Most of the work has consisted in the more systematic application to the problem of principles that had already been laid down by psycho-analysts thirty-five years ago. It is partly for this reason and partly to correct the existing impression that we have recently come to know all that need be known about crime, that I have felt encouraged to reproduce a survey dating from the pioneer period of criminal psychology.

* Being a psychological address delivered to a Summer School for Women Magistrates, held under the auspices of the N.U.S.E.C. (National Union of Societies for Equal Citizenship) at Oxford in September 1922.

This is in some respects an unusual occasion. For the first time in the history of British criminology a meeting of Justices of the Peace has invited a psycho-analyst to lecture on the psychology of crime. By so doing the sponsors of this Summer School have given tacit recognition to the fact that crime is not simply an anti-social phenomenon to be dealt with by the judiciary in accordance with fixed penal codes, but also a psychological problem involving close study on the part of all who are concerned with the motivations of human conduct.

Stated thus baldly, there would appear to be no obstacle to a harmonious exchange of views between psychologists and magistrates. Unfortunately the matter is not so simple. In the first place, psychology is one of the few sciences concerning which the lawyer, the magistrate, the clergyman and, for the matter of that, the man in the street claim to speak with the authority of personal experience. However much they may differ amongst themselves, they do not take kindly to the view that psychology is a scientific discipline calling for prolonged training. Not only so, the magistrate, whatever his private views on the subject of crime, is called on to administer penal codes based on fixed ideas regarding the nature of wrongdoing and the virtues of punishment. Thirdly, psychologists themselves are divided on matters both of theory and of practice. Most important of all, the subject of crime, like that of politics, religion or sexuality, is calculated to arouse the strongest emotions, prejudices, preconceptions and not infrequently superstitions. It does so because in the last resort crime is a moral issue, involving conceptions of good, evil, sin, righteousness, wrong-doing, redemption, absolution, expiation, deterrence and punishment. Under these circumstances it is desirable to bear constantly in mind that when we speak of crime, we are dealing with matters that awaken discordant echoes in the mind of everyman, however law-abiding he may have been from his eighth birthday onwards.

Another difficulty is not far to seek. The Justice of the Peace is a servant of the community, charged with the duty of preserving the peace. His main concern is to enforce one side of the unwritten social contract, namely, to preserve the community from the assaults and depredations of individuals or gangs. Stealing and acts of violence constitute an overwhelming majority of criminal offences. The psychologist, on the other hand, whatever the nature of his theories, is concerned with the individual; and in the case of the medical psychologist or psycho-analyst this general interest is subject to an overriding concern with disease and a professional obligation to treat mental disorders to the best of his ability. From this point of view it is scarcely to be expected that psychology and the Law should always see eye to eye.

On the other hand, there can be no doubt that the Law is compact with the social wisdom as well as the social prejudices of the past. That part of the doctrine of 'criminal responsibility', for example, which determines the age limit above which the Law takes cognizance of anti-social conduct is based on the simplest of psychological considerations. The thefts of infants are by general consent overlooked by the police and the occasional murderous assaults of 4-year-olds on younger siblings are not stigmatized as criminal. In fact up to the age of 8 – and the age limit is higher in some other and more enlightened countries – children belong to a privileged class as far as crime is concerned. Just as absolute monarchs and dictators are above the Law, young children may be said to be beneath its notice.

At this point, without quoting a single case or using a single technical term, we could arrive at a simple generalization regarding the treatment of some forms of crime, a conclusion based immediately on legal precedent and ultimately on a consensus of public opinion. We could say that any adolescent or adult offender whose 'mental age' as ascertained by reliable tests is under 8 should be immune from the punishments of the Law. Expressed in more technical language, this means that mental deficiency is sufficient ground for abrogating penal sanctions and substituting, when the need for social safety demands it, a form of medico-psychological care, and where feasible, treatment. A little imagination would soon raise this 'mental age' to at least 16 years. For unfortunately quite a proportion of the adult population, though apparently sound in mind and 'responsible' for their actions, are actually backward in mental development, although not 'certifiable' as mental defectives.

But if innate mental defect is a sufficient reason for suspending the penalties of the Law, we are under obligation to consider the relevance of *acquired* mental disorder or indeed of physical disorder that gives rise to mental deterioration. This was first brought home to me by an early hospital experience. During a toxic delirium a patient sprang out of bed and, in spite of resistance on the part of his victim, forcibly appropriated the hot water bottle from the patient in the next bed, after which he dived back under his own bed, where he drummed his feet violently. Despite enforced restoration of the stolen article, he repeated his offence with increasing violence and had to be given a sedative. Needless to say, although caught redhanded in robbery with violence, this unrepentant recidivist was not reported to the police. Going on the assumption that his criminal conduct was a manifestation of delirium, I became an accessory after the fact and treated the symptom medically. Next morning his temperature fell.

It is only fair to the Law to recall at this point that almost eighty years ago, in 1843 to be exact, the principle was laid down by a Commission of Judges that a person who commits murder when suffering from 'such a defect of reason, from disease of the mind, as not to know the nature and quality of the act he was doing; or, if he did know it, that he did not know he was doing what is wrong' should not suffer the capital penalty, but be detained at Her Majesty's pleasure in a criminal asylum. The M'Naghten Rules, from which this is quoted, arose out of a case in which a victim of persecutory delusions (a form of paranoid insanity) murdered someone whom he conceived was scowling at him. Although hedged by a number of 'safeguards' intended to maintain the standards of 'criminal responsibility', these Rules recognized the fact that crime can in some instances be due to, or a consequence of, disease of the mind, a proposition having the incontestable if unwritten corollary that, when such is the case, the appropriate course is not to punish the malefactor but to treat the disease, with due regard of course to the need for public safety. That, despite the passage of time and the great advances in mental science, the principle has not been extended to lesser forms of crime and to forms of mental disease less grave than the insanities is due largely to the concern of judges and other authorities lest the door should be opened through which the 'responsible' criminal might escape punishment. Indeed my main object on this occasion is to consider how far this principle and its corollary might be extended to criminal offences other than murder without jeopardizing the public safety and to the benefit of those who commit what we might from now on describe as 'pathological crime', meaning thereby the commission of offences due to mental or physical disorder.

At this point it would seem logical to require a definition of mental disorder, and in particular some indication of the relative frequency of those disorders which are responsible for criminal behaviour. I believe, however, that there is some advantage to be gained by postponing this act of definition, substituting instead a brief outline of man's mental development; in other words, considering the raw material from which criminals of any sort, 'pathological' or 'responsible', are recruited. By so doing we may succeed in side-stepping the moral implications of the term 'crime', replacing these, for the time being at any rate, with psycho-biological reflections.

The first of these reflections is simple enough. It is that *crime is part of the price paid for the domestication of a naturally wild animal*, or, to put it more cautiously, that crime is *one* of the results of unsuccessful domestication. For we have reason to know that there are other consequences of unsuccessful domestication, such, for example, as the neuroses, which in the majority of instances present no anti-social features. In more formal language, crime is one of the results of a conflict between the primitive instincts with which man is endowed and the altruistic codes inculcated by adult society either in its own interests or according to its moral prejudices. Hence as a preamble to considering the psychology of crime we must consider not only the nature of these instincts, but the manner in which domestication is achieved; in other words, how the individual is 'brought up'.

It is at this point that the discoveries of Freud become pertinent to our discussion. As the result of psycho-analysis mostly of adult cases of neuroses (anxiety-hysteria and the obsessional states) and of dream life in normal and abnormal persons, he has found what might indeed have been surmised from psycho-biological reflections, namely, that the mental development of every child is influenced at all points by the existences of primitive untamed instincts which sooner or later give rise to head-on clashes between those with antithetical aims. Powerful, sexual instincts, for example, exist from infancy onwards, and comprise a number of primitive components. During the first year or two oral sexual impulses and, throughout the period of house-training, excretory sexual impulses (anal and urethral) govern the libidinal life of the child. Genito-sexual impulses of a powerful kind do indeed exist from birth, but they are not focused until the age of about 3 to 5 years, during which period they are directed to the parents or such other adult figures as happen to play an intimate part in the child's life and environment. Each of these libidinal components is associated to a greater or lesser degree with the sadistic and masochistic impulses that are also a feature of infantile instinct life. The child in short passes through different phases of a 'polymorphous' infantile sexuality (oral, excretory, genital, exhibitionistic and sadistic) which may, however, clash in a struggle for primacy. The central genito-sexual phase however, being biologically dominant, ultimately gains precedence over the others, giving rise to what is known as the Oedipus complex, a nexus of, for the most part, unconscious sexual wish-phantasies (both heterosexual and homosexual) directed towards parents or their substitutes (infantile incest).

With the infantile heterosexual drives are associated equally powerful reactions of rivalry and hostility directed against the parent of the same sex (or in the case of infantile homosexual attachments, against the parent of the opposite sex). These hostile drives are considerably reinforced by the cumulative hatred and sadism towards environment engendered by any of the numerous frustrations of instinct which the growing infant has to endure, some of which are inevitable, but many others the result of rigid, capricious or thoughtless upbringing. So that already by the age of 3 to 5 years the child has many objects to which he can attach those instincts of destruction and mastery which sooner or later give rise to hate and sadism.

Expressing these more technical discoveries in social terms, we can say that the perfectly normal infant is almost completely egocentric, greedy, dirty, violent in temper, destructive in habit, profoundly sexual in purpose, aggrandizing in attitude, devoid of all but the most primitive reality sense, without conscience of moral feeling, whose attitude to society (as represented by the family) is opportunist, inconsiderate, domineering and sadistic. And when we come to consider the criminal type labelled psychopathic it will be apparent that many of these characteristics can under certain circumstances persist into adult life. In fact, judged by adult social standards the normal baby is for all practical purposes a born criminal.[1]

[1] At the close of this lecture, the lady Chairman and magistrate, Mrs. St. Loe Strachey, remarked: 'But, doctor, the dear babies! How could you say such awful things about them?'

We shall shortly have to enquire how the child succeeds in mastering these primitive impulses and in becoming a reasonably well-behaved, law-abiding and well-disposed minor. In the meantime we must be ready to answer the question that may arise in the mind of the busy magistrate: what, he may reasonably ask, has this apparently macabre account of the early mental development of children got to do with the calendar of offences with which he has to deal, with stealing, for example, or common assault. Setting aside for the moment the offence of stealing, there are two types of case in which the answer is obvious. Crimes of violence are on the face of it an indication either that the infantile hostility and sadism of the offender is specially reinforced or that his system of control of hostility and destructiveness is inadequate. And it is only commonsense to enquire in cases of *unnatural* violence whether the upbringing of the child has been such as to promote this pathological type of discharge, whether the violence of the offender can be traced to an excess of infantile sadistic impulse and whether there is any prospect of modifying it without recourse to penal measures.

In another type of case the answer is even more obvious. During the war years 1914–18 the average number of sexual offences in England and Wales ran to just over 11,000. Of these, offences connected with prostitution accounted for over 8,000. Of the remainder, 1,100 were cases of indecent exposure, almost 1,000 were heterosexual offences, mainly assaults, and over 200 unnatural offences of a homosexual nature.[1] Even if we exclude prostitution and heterosexual offences on the assumption that the offenders may not have been pathological types (an assumption,

[1] [Note 1959] For purposes of comparison we may note that according to the Criminal Statistics for England and Wales, the number of sexual offences in 1957 totalled 21,125, of which 15,486 were offences by prostitutes. Of the remainder 2,266 were homosexual offences tried either at Quarter Sessions, Assizes or Summary Courts (the last accounting for 889) heterosexual offences (mainly sexual assaults) totalled 3,820, to which might be added a small proportion of bigamies. Cases of indecent exposure amounted to 2,310. The number of homosexual (indictable) offences known to the police was 6,327, of heterosexual offences 11,759. Allowance must of course be made in the first place for increase in population and in the second for the assiduity with which the police follow up cases of homosexuality. This varies from time to time. (*Criminal Statistics: England and Wales, 1957*, H.M.S.O.)

incidentally, that is quite unjustified since a considerable number of such offenders are both mentally and sexually immature, deficient and infantile in type) we are left with two substantial groups of sexual perversion or deviation which are criminal offences, namely homosexuality and exhibitionism. We may also note that many more cases of perversion are known to the police but not proceeded against, and that in the case of homosexuality, the offence is sometimes associated with acts of violence, seduction of minors or public indecency. Exhibitionistic offences are essentially contraventions of public decency associated occasionally with acts of molestation. We must not forget, however, that the range of sexual perversion is as wide as the range of those infantile sexual instincts which Freud describes as polymorphous. The adult sexual perversion is in short a recrudescence or persistence of infantile sexuality in an adult setting, which may either wholly or partly replace normal adult heterosexual impulse. In this sense it constitutes a disorder of adult sexual life.

Now while it may be freely admitted that if a perversion is accompanied by acts of assault, seduction of minors, or public indecency, it is clearly a criminal offence, it does not follow that sexual disorder is in itself criminal, unless of course we concede to the state mandatory rights over the sexual mores of the community and are further prepared to adopt the old ecclesiastical view that immorality, sin and crime are synonymous. When further we realize that the penalties inflicted by the law do not succeed either in deterring sexual offenders or in reducing the total number of fresh offences, that indeed, as in the case of exhibitionism, they appear to 'harden' the offender, we have more than a little justification for the demand that, provided they do not infringe the rights of other individuals or of the community, sexual perversions should be treated in the first instance as forms of mental disorder having a specifically sexual expression. And that indeed is what a considerable number of sexual offences are. Not all of them, of course, for we have reason to know that, in the case of the homosexual, for example, the individual may present no mental symptoms and indeed follow ethical and social standards much higher than those of the so-called normal person. The relative proportion of 'responsible' and of 'pathological' types has not been ascertained; but there is sufficient evidence of the 'disordered' nature of many sexual perversions to make a preliminary medico-psychological examination a pre-requisite of disposal. A still more reasonable method would be to exclude all such offences from the criminal code unless they also involve infringements of the social code[1] such as violence, seduction or public indecency.

At this point it would be well to take stock of our position. What I think we have established is that where criminal acts are an expression of or an immediate consequence of such pathological conditions as insanity, mental deficiency (or backwardness) or sexual disorder the appropriate course is to examine, diagnose and if possible treat them as forms of mental disorder rather than have automatic recourse to penal measures which in any case do not appear to be either curative or deterrent. We have also considered whether crimes of unnatural violence might not be due to forces beyond the conscious control of the individual. To this latter category it would be reasonable to add offences, usually of violence, which result from physical disorders such as encephalitis lethargica ('sleepy sickness') or epilepsy, or are found to follow concussion, head injuries or war wounds, or for the matter of that gross organic deformities. To be sure, these 'organic' groups are very small.

Our next step is a more difficult one. We have yet to consider whether in certain instances, such for example as stealing, the commonest of crimes, where the offender *appears* to be in other respects a normal and responsible person, aware of the legal or even the moral wrongness of his act, he may nevertheless be suffering, whether he knows it or not, from disordered mental functions. Incidentally it is at this point that the sympathetic magistrate is inclined to call a halt, fearing no doubt that if matters were left to the psycho-analyst the legal doctrine of 'responsibility' which he regards as a bulwark of social safety would be so undermined that wrongdoers would escape the punishment they

[1] [Note 1959] The Departmental Committee on Homosexuality and Prostitution appointed in 1954 recommended *inter alia* that homosexual behaviour between consenting adults in private be no longer a criminal offence (para. 62). During a parliamentary debate in 1958, the Home Secretary confirmed an earlier decision not to act on this recommendation. [See also pp. 63 and 69.]

deserve.[1] The issue is one that cannot be burked. To the natural social and moral bias of the magistrate is opposed the equally natural bias of the psycho-analyst that behaviour is determined in the long run by factors that are in many instances beyond the individual's conscious control. So we must now consider what these factors are and how far they promote either a state of law-abidingness or a tendency to break the law. For it is obvious that in order to understand criminal conduct we must also be able to explain the remarkable fact that the vast majority of any community are within reasonable limits law abiding.

To begin with we must keep constantly in mind that as Freud has shewn, by far the largest part of the mind is and remains unconscious; secondly that part of the function of this unconscious mind is to control the primitive impulses which would otherwise disturb normal development and adaptation. This control is achieved for the most part by means of a number of unconscious 'mechanisms'. Thirdly, the ego, which is also for the most part unconscious, regulates these unconscious mechanisms through a process of 'unconscious censorship'. Censorship is set in action either when the primitive instincts give rise to anxiety in the ego or when they arouse unconscious reactions of guilt due to the threatened infraction of behaviour codes which go to make up the unconscious 'ego-ideal' as it is called. In other words, *conscious* conscience is not the main regulator of moral and ethical behaviour. Morality and social behaviour depend primarily on the smooth operation of unconscious codes, which have been laid down during the process of upbringing.[2]

---

[1] During the discussion of this paper Lord Olivier, one of the earliest Fabian–socialist peers and one time Governor of Jamaica, rose to protest. 'Never,' he remarked, 'have I listened to such outrageous nonsense regarding the motivation of theft. Quite obviously,' he added, 'the motivation of offences against property is economic in nature and the offences will disappear when a reasonable economic organization of society is established.' To add point to his protest he then stalked out of the meeting.

[2] [Note 1959] Only a few weeks after this lecture was delivered, Freud at the International Psycho-analytical Congress at Berlin produced his final formulations regarding the structure of mind. In this essay (later expanded as *The Ego and the Id*, London, Hogarth Press), he outlined the structure and function of *unconscious* conscience, using in place of the term 'ego-ideal' the designation 'super-ego', and described the process by which early parental controlling influences are unconsciously incorporated

I am well aware that in asking you to accept these fundamental propositions I am putting a certain strain on your good nature and commonsense. Not only so, I must advise you that these propositions strike to the roots of the doctrine of 'criminal responsibility'. On the other hand I can offer you some reassurance. My thesis is not that all crimes should be considered from this angle, only that such crimes as can be shewn to be due to disordered functions of the mind or body should in the first instance be treated as disorders.

If, however, you should ask how it is that we remain unaware of the existence of the unconscious conflict, I can only add to your difficulties by asking you to believe that this is due largely to the existence of an unconscious mechanism which Freud calls *repression*. When this controlling mechanism operates in a healthy manner we remain totally unaware of the existence of any impulse that runs counter to the ego-ideal. There are of course other mechanisms which are of special interest to the student of criminology. The paranoid murderer whose case I have mentioned *apropos* of the M'Naghten Rules, formed the conclusion that society was conspiring against him. This delusional belief was due to the action of an unconscious mechanism called *projection* whereby the hostility which existed in his unconscious mind was felt by him to be directed by the environment against him, thereby 'justifying' his murderous 'counter-attack'.

Another important mechanism is that of *displacement*. As a general rule this unconscious transfer of an interest from an earlier and more primitive object to a later substitute object is of great social value: but if, for example, hostility is transferred from infantile objects to persons or institutions in the present day, you can see that otherwise inexplicable anti-social behaviour may well be an outcome. In a recent case of aggravated assault, it transpired that the young man had occasional compulsions to attack elderly men with pointed grey beards. His father who was much older than his mother had a pointed grey beard.

in the child's mind to form a special mental 'institution'. The phenomenon of unconscious guilt was then attributed to conflict between this super-ego and the ego, aroused by instinctual strivings (arising in what he called the 'Id') that run counter to the super-ego. In course of time the term has gained currency, even amongst those who do not otherwise favour psycho-analytical theories. All modern psycho-analytical research on behaviour, criminal or otherwise, is based on this central formulation.

Sometimes indeed the displacement is quite mystifying as when it is complicated by the operation of an unconscious and extremely archaic process of thought known as *symbol-formation*. We all know of course that we may react to the appearance of the Union Jack as if we were in the actual presence of the Sovereign himself. But in the case of unconscious symbol-formation the transfer of interest is quite *unconscious*. We may for example react to food, money or even clothes as if these were objects of love. Depressed persons often refuse food for this reason or contrariwise eat voraciously to cure their depression. Miserliness is appropriately described as a 'love' of money. So that when, for example, we find children developing a persistent habit of stealing money or sweets or fruit, our first enquiry should be whether or not they have been or at any rate have felt deprived of affection at home.

Let me describe briefly by way of illustration one of the first cases of juvenile delinquency which came my way. A little girl who up to the age of 4 years had been regarded by her parents as a good-tempered and well-behaved child began to steal cucumbers from fruit-shops with open windows. This habit manifested itself shortly after the birth of a baby brother. She was severely scolded by her mother and abandoned the habit, remaining (with the exceptions mentioned below) an exemplary child, rather distant in her relations to her parents, until five years later when she was expelled from a boarding school for stealing small sums from lockers. This money she did not 'convert to use', hiding it in her own locker where it was easily found by the matron. Less attention was paid at first to a concurrent habit of stealing pencils, particularly those with a coloured butt. Improbable as it may seem, only a few analytical interviews were necessary to establish a connection between the thefts and the birth of her baby brother. She was seriously upset by this event, and experienced acute jealousy not merely because of the appearance of a rival baby who threatened her favoured position with her parents, but because he was a baby boy who, she thought, owed his popularity to the possession of a penis. Not long after the cucumber episodes she broke her system of amenable conduct by making a determined attempt to murder him in his cradle by striking him with a hammer and on one occasion when the nurse was absent tried to twist off the baby's offending organ between her finger and thumb. Otherwise she remained a 'good' child. Unconsciously, however, the hostile jealousy and envy remained unchanged. Her compulsive thefts were in fact symbolic actions. Stealing first cucumbers and later on coloured pencils represented the desire to deprive the rival of his sexual organ and, by collecting the pencils, to compensate herself for what she took to be a sign of girlish inferiority. She wished to gain what she thought she had lost, viz. her parents' love, by turning herself into a boy equipped with a store of male genital organs.[1] The desire for 'lost' love was also responsible for the thefts of money. She was aware of the desire to be loved and admired by all the other children at school, yet this was combined with hostility to them as well as to her parents. When in fact her thefts were discovered she became the 'black sheep' of the school and, until the position was explained to them, her expulsion had caused acute mortification and embarrassment to her parents. Actually no very lengthy treatment proved necessary, and after a special holiday in the country with her parents, she was transferred to another school where so far her behaviour has been uneventful.[2]

I trust I have not alienated your sympathies by this unvarnished account of what might well have been a preamble to a confirmed delinquent habit, to say nothing of a ruined social life. But I think you will agree that had the matter been reported to the local police, the majesty of the law governing juvenile delinquency would have been invoked and the child would have appeared in a juvenile court where in the absence of psychological evidence she would at best have been put on probation as a young pilferer. And you may perhaps think that if a sufficiency of clinics existed to deal with the psychological disorders of children a good deal could be done in the way of prevention of delinquency. Following this line of thought you might even be disposed to consider whether

---

[1] The importance attached by psycho-analysts to the factor of unconscious symbolism in theft arouses considerable scepticism amongst lay readers. Those who find the interpretation (pencil = penis) far fetched may be interested to know that when finally pressed regarding her interest, the little girl remarked: 'When I take pencils they give me a feeling of power in my middle.' And in fact she had on occasion inserted the stolen pencils *per vaginam* when urinating, thereby combining a masturbatory impulse with a masculine penis phantasy.

[2] [Note 1959] Following a successful college career she married, raised a family of five children and expects shortly to become a grandmother.

in the case of some adults similar unconscious mechanisms might sometimes be responsible for their criminal behaviour.

As a matter of fact popular opinion is, somewhat tardily it is true, moving in this direction, as witness the increasing use of the term *kleptomania* to designate compulsive recurrent tendencies to steal objects, frequently of no particular monetary value or practical use to the offender. In one instance a clergyman was in the habit of stealing brooches from little girls, which objects he secreted in a locked drawer in the vestry. Needless to say, he was a confirmed bachelor. These compulsive thefts are often heralded by states of confusion or clouded consciousness and the whole condition has a close resemblance to a common neurosis, the obsessional neurosis, with this difference, however, that whilst the obsessional neurotic carries out compulsive acts of a trivial or apparently senseless nature which incidentally hurt no one but himself, the compulsive criminal acts in an anti-social manner and if detected will suffer social and penal consequences to himself usually out of proportion to the gravity of the offence. Incidentally it is important to note that in these kleptomaniac cases, the personality and character is otherwise intact and the offender may be in other respects a responsible and law-abiding, even superior, member of society.

This example of what might be called 'neurotic theft' leads us to consider yet another type of 'pathological criminal' who although usually regarded by his fellows as an 'unprincipled' law-breaker is not simply a persistent offender but suffers from a deep derangement of his character and personality. The type was first recognized in 1836 by a Bristol physician – Dr. Prichard – and for many years was described as 'moral insanity' and still later as 'moral imbecility'. In more recent times the condition has gone by the name of *psychopathy*, and denotes a person who from childhood onwards has exhibited psycho-pathological traits, in particular an incapacity to stand frustration leading already in childhood to tantrums (behaviouristic explosions), which are essentially anti-social demonstrations. Later he may become a liar, cheat or impostor, has frequent clashes with the law and exhibits no sign of guilt for his misdemeanours. His emotions are extremely unstable and frequently his sexual life is abnormal. In extreme cases he may be guilty of crimes of violence, which in rarer instances may go so far as murder, occasionally with a sexual background. Despite this history of criminal conduct he may appear extremely plausible and exercise a certain amount of charm, so that he has little difficulty in maintaining an aspect of 'normality' and is usually taken by his fellows to be normal.

It is here that the most acute difficulty arises between psychology and the law. Owing to his superficial 'normality' and the striking absence of any conscious guilt, the psychopath is usually regarded just as an 'incorrigible' rogue, a view which the magistrate or judge tends to share, with the somewhat illogical consequence that despite his 'incorrigibility' he is considered to be worthy of such condign punishment as the law may allow for his particular offence. Yet in many cases it is possible to show that his mental abnormality is almost as grave as that of an insane person, in particular his absence of reality feeling or judgement and the frequent senselessness and peculiarity of his behaviour. No doubt there is an overlap in some such cases on the one hand with the group of deliberate and responsible criminals and on the other with normal persons in whom the same tendencies exist under cover. But these are complications which can only be settled by expert examination.

Indeed we do well to remind ourselves that psychological research into criminal conduct is still in its infancy. What we must do at the earliest possible moment is to apply to the special problems of anti-social behaviour the principles established by Freud to mental function as a whole. Freud's work on unconscious guilt alone is sufficient to revolutionize the whole system of penal method. To be sure little systematic work has so far been done on the subject, and psycho-analysts have few opportunities to study directly the criminal population, but, as has been suggested, there is sufficient latent criminality in the ordinary law-abiding individual to give the analyst occasion to study the tap-roots of crime in the course of his everyday practice. Sometimes indeed the results are disconcerting, as when Freud, seven years ago, published a note on *criminality from a sense of guilt.* In this short paper he remarks how often children behave in such a way as to induce punishment followed by a state of mental quiescence. And he maintains that in certain criminal cases the same unconscious course of psychic events takes place, namely, that an excess of unconscious guilt due to repressed infantile wishes can lead to outbreaks of anti-social behaviour which in turn lead to the application of penal sanctions; or in other words that, however paradoxical it may appear, an exaggerated unconscious infantile morality can lead to adult crime. Disconcerting or indeed implausible as such discoveries may appear they are borne out by a study of the masochistic systems of self-flagellation, mortification of the flesh, religious asceticism, suicidal compulsions and many other anthropological and clinical data; the difference being that whereas the self-injurer himself inflicts the punishment, the moral sadist, by virtue of his anti-social conduct not only attacks society but induces society to punish him. It is not unknown for offenders to ask the magistrate to punish them.

Running a close second to the factor of unconscious guilt comes that of *unconscious anxiety*. It is a commonplace of child psychology and for the matter of that of adult psychology that a sudden attack of conscious anxiety may lead to explosive violence, as witness the behaviour of an anxious mother who, when her little child just escapes being run over in the street, will celebrate her relief by shaking or smacking him. And during the late war some cases of shell-shock were found to be prone to outbursts of undirected violence. This is of course an attempted abreaction reinforced by the hostility consequent on being compelled to experience unendurable strain. These reactions are, however, not limited to cases where the anxiety factor is manifest. Discriminating child-nurses are well aware of the fact that a naughty child is often an anxious child, and adult anti-social conduct can frequently be explained in the same way. This accounts incidentally for some of the anti-social manifestations of 'neurotic delinquency', and in the case of 'psychopathic' crime it is often easy to demonstrate that the psychopathic outbreak follows a period during which the individual has been subject to increasing stress, either of real or morbid anxiety, which, however, is not recognized as such by the offender; or again of unconscious anxiety tensions which by definition he cannot recognize. As a matter of interest, study of the reactions of the law and of the general public suggests that one of the motivations of punishment is precisely the anxiety and guilt aroused by criminal conduct.

But there is little prospect during this half-century that cases of criminality due to unconscious guilt or anxiety will be scheduled in a reformed set of M'Naghten Rules, as 'pathological criminals'; I mention them here, at the risk of alienating your sympathies, in order to broaden the concept of crime by suggesting that some anti-social acts may have an individual function to perform similar to that of neurotic or even psychotic symptoms amongst the law-abiding. To this it may be added that the existence of crime in the community may indeed serve to strengthen the law-abidingness of the ordinary citizen by providing him with a vicarious outlet or scapegoat for his own repressed criminal tendencies. You may perhaps have noted that bedtime readers of detective fiction may themselves be notably law-abiding in spite of a fascinated interest in murder and its, usually, successful detection. I recognize, however, that speculations of this sort, however interesting to the anthropologist, are likely to be anathema to the Justice of the Peace, already overburdened by the task of social defence. So I propose to return once more to the safer ground of clinical observation.

In addition to the larger groups of 'pathological' crime there are a number of other types which qualify for the designation and deserve our attention. Take for example the relation of crime to *alcoholism*. In this connection I am not concerned with the common view that the consumption of alcohol may loosen inhibitions and thereby be responsible for sporadic crime, or with the legal ruling that intoxication is not an extenuating circumstance. I am concerned with the cases in which alcoholism and crime are combined symptoms of inner mental disorder. Interestingly enough, it is usually the 'projecting' type who commits offences in a state of intoxication. The inturned alcoholic is more likely to damage himself than to become anti-social. And the same applies to the drug-addict. Both groups incidentally are prone to sexual disorder or inhibition and their married life is of precarious stability.

There are of course many other pathological conditions in which episodic criminal reactions are a sign of a more generalized state of disorder. To quote again from the insanities, incipient *schizophrenia* is sometimes *heralded* by antisocial conduct in persons who have previously been apparently normal and actually law-abiding. But I think we may rest the case for psychological diagnosis on the categories we have already isolated: – insanity, mental deficiency, sexual disorders, physical disease either of the central nervous system or other vital organs, criminal compulsions of a pseudo-neurotic type, psychopathy, alcoholism and numerous other disordered states in which unconscious causes may play a significant part in the criminal act. To which may be added a great variety of behaviour disorders of childhood which may present anti-social features or give rise later to acts of delinquency.

It remains to examine briefly how far these views affect the problems of treatment and prevention. But first of all we must eliminate a certain prejudice regarding this matter of treatment. To many it may seem incongruous that 'crime' should be treated by 'scientific' methods. Yet in the same breath they may agree that it is appropriate for a probation officer or prison chaplain or prison visitor to apply respectively friendly, moral and social 'treatment' to regenerate the criminal. Scientific methods merely seek to regulate treatment according to individual needs, and to supplement 'natural' methods with modern psycho-therapeutic procedures.

It must be confessed, however, that in the case both of treatment and of prevention the answer must in the meantime be rather speculative. The existing range of psychological methods of treatment includes only those which have so far been applied to non-criminal mental disorders. They run from methods of suggestion to deep analysis of unconscious factors and will require modification to meet the needs of anti-social types. But whatever may be the variety of technique employed the outcome depends ultimately on the handling of what are called 'transferences'. These are states of potential rapport (either friendly or hostile) derived from unconscious reactions to parents that are laid down during infancy and childhood. The positive (friendly) transferences are more frequently observed in the neuroses: negative transferences are a feature of anti-social cases; hence the difficulty in bringing influences to bear on the latter.

On the other hand although the number of 'pathological' criminals treated by psychotherapeutic measures is so far very small, the results are definitely encouraging and go to show that the essence of the matter lies as much in the attitude of the psychotherapeutist as on that of the 'case', a lesson which should not be lost on a penal minded society. Indeed we may anticipate with some certainty that the number of 'cures' or 'improvements' amongst criminals treated psychotherapeutically will correspond fairly closely to that obtained in the case of the mental or physical disorder of which the criminal conduct is a manifestation. In view, however, of the fact that anti-social impulses are frequently associated with abnormal character traits, we ought to expect that treatment will be longer (particularly in psychopathic cases with a deficiency in conscience formation) and perhaps less successful than in the case of the neuroses. Even a neurotic 'character' is more difficult to resolve than a pure neurosis occurring in a person of normal character. And of course the results will vary according to the severity and chronicity of the mental disorder from which the individual criminal suffers; psychotic and psychopathic cases and long established sexual perversions are likely to be the least favourable. On the other hand it is already beyond question that the younger the case the more favourable the outlook and the easier the treatment.[1]

Herein lies the key to the problem of prevention. If the contention advanced here is accurate, viz., that a factor of early predisposition, due in part to the influence of 'upbringing', is even partly responsible for later 'pathological crime', we have a clear pointer towards policies of prevention. These should be directed to eradicating such individual or environmental factors as can be proved to predispose to the disorders of which the criminal

[1] [Note 1959] It is of some interest to compare these sketchy formulations with the developments that have taken place in the intervening thirty-five years. Since the Second World War treatment of juvenile delinquency is now available at most of the child guidance clinics scattered throughout the country and most psychiatric centres are now prepared to deal with selected cases of adult delinquency. The *Psychopathic Clinic*, founded in 1931 by the *Institute for the Study and Treatment of Delinquency*, was taken over by the Ministry of Health in 1948; it is now known as the *Portman Clinic* and carries an annual case-load of over 900, of whom 500 are new cases. Every variety of psychological treatment either of individuals or groups, is employed and, although complete psycho-analysis is rarely carried out, an analytic approach is commonly applied in short treatment. The average duration of treatment necessary to bring about satisfactory changes is surprisingly short, running to about twelve sessions spread over a few weeks or months and ranging from a few advisory interviews to courses of about 150 sessions. The results as checked by after-histories are very satisfactory and the treatment of young psychopaths, at one time the bogey of the psychotherapist, is undertaken with considerable confidence. Although institutional treatment (in prisons, Borstals, remand homes, etc.) still lags behind the general effort, a satisfactory beginning has been made in many areas. More significant still, both the Home Office and the public at large, have at last come to recognize the necessity of such therapeutic effort.

conduct is a manifestation. Of course we must qualify our optimism to the extent that constitutional, innate and possibly hereditary factors play a part in forming this predisposition, also that deep unconscious (individual) influences contribute largely to outbreaks of anti-social conduct; but this does not absolve us from the professional, if not indeed the ethical and social responsibility of eliminating such faults in upbringing as can be eliminated. We must see to it that from birth onwards all measures of upbringing calculated to promote aggressive anti-social responses in later life are reduced to a minimum, that the child is brought up in an atmosphere of security and affection, that its sexual education is sane, candid and realistic and that an example of law-abidingness is shown by its parents in their private domestic lives. Parents must not expect that beating a small animal will enable it to be considerate of the hurts of others; nor that conscience can be promoted by severity, neglect or capricious attention. It is here indeed that the major advisory function of child psychiatric departments such as was recently set up by the *Tavistock Clinic* lies.[1] As in the field of organic medicine prevention is better than cure and in the long run cheaper.

But here we begin to stray from the province of individual psychology to that of group psychology. Allowing for constitutional factors, each community produces the criminals it deserves. To meet this situation a new science of familial sociology is required. But it must be a sociology that is not led astray by the worship of false gods. Political economists are still addicted to the psychological heresy that man is a rational animal guided in all matters by economic and self-aggrandizing motives. Whereas if anything is patent about the practice of crime, it is that on the average it does not pay. It is in fact one of the distressed professions, at most following the will o' the wisp of magical sustenance. 'Table, cover thyself' is the motto of the phantast, and the most self-aggrandizing burglar who models his economic career on the infantile plan of taking what he needs, if necessary by force, has sooner or later to realize that he has chosen an arduous, unremunerative and in the long run self-punishing career.

But this again is to stray from my terms of reference. Sociologists

[1] [Note 1959] *The East London Clinic* was founded in 1926 and there are now about 700 Child Guidance Clinics operating in England and Wales.

may, if they wish, generalize about crime; and no doubt in the foreseeable future, society will sanction the application of sociological principles to the whole problem. In the meantime the medical psychologist is bound by professional usage to confine himself to research on and treatment of crime that can be traced to mental or physical abnormality. For the moment at any rate his authority lies solely in these fields. As a private citizen he may think what he likes about crime in general and about the most appropriate (or inappropriate) ways in which to handle it; he may believe that the difference between normal and anti-social behaviour (pathological or otherwise) can only be understood by investigating normal as well as abnormal development both conscious and unconscious; he may further believe that the closer the comparative examination is carried, the closer will be found the kinship of normal individuals to criminals. But in his professional capacity he will be well advised to stick to his last, maintaining without reserve that amongst the inalienable rights of individuals in a civilized society comes that of securing treatment for the disorders from which they may happen to suffer. Grant this premiss and the first step has been taken to reduce the prejudice, moral obloquy and physical or mental mishandling with which for untold centuries the problem of crime has been greeted or respectively treated.

To all this the overburdened magistrate may respond somewhat plaintively with the question: how are we to know when a case is to be regarded as pathological or otherwise? Admittedly in the absence of means of examining all criminal cases it is not easy to give a satisfactory reply. Even the most pathological of criminals may not to superficial observation appear so very different from his more law-abiding fellows. But there are a few working rules which may assist the magistrate in this dilemma. If, when listening to the account of the offence, he should find himself wondering why the accused should have committed such an inexplicable or irrational or unnatural action, or again why anyone with apparently law-abiding antecedents should have committed any offence, he has good reason to remand the case for investigation. Moreover, he will do well to consider all juvenile offences as behaviour problems rather than criminal acts. Finally he can make full use of the information supplied by discerning probation officers. These are of course merely rough guiding rules and it is to be hoped that in course of time they will be supplemented by a more accurate sifting system. However that may be, it is comforting to think that, as the present occasion demonstrates, we are about to witness the development of a new tradition in judicial practice, namely, to regard crime as, in the first instance, a problem in human behaviour having its roots in early life. For we have good reason to suspect that, as von Behring once said of tuberculous disease of the lungs, crime is 'the end of a song sung to the child in its cradle'.

II. HISTORICAL

OUTLINE OF THE INVESTIGATION AND
TREATMENT OF DELINQUENCY IN
GREAT BRITAIN
Part I '1912–48'
Part II '1949–55'
Part III '1956–59'

SECTION II

HISTORICAL

OUTLINE OF THE INVESTIGATION AND TREATMENT OF DELINQUENCY IN GREAT BRITAIN

Tracing the history of criminology over almost half a century the present alignment of forces stands out unmistakably: on the one hand, the organized and mostly conservative traditions of the Law, the Judiciary and the Home Office, and on the other the less organized but more dynamic tendencies of modern psychology, both individual and social. The individual psychologist has adopted a somewhat restricted approach, attacking the problem of crime from the point of view mainly of mental pathology, *the sociologist has perforce widened this range by investigating the environmental factors which appear to promote* any *form of criminal behaviour. Both groups are of course interested also in the treatment or disposal of convicted criminals, the individual psychologist seeking wherever possible to substitute therapeutic for penal measures, and the sociologist to modify penal measures by the appropriate application of social remedies both within and without penal institutions.*

The upshot of what has been a protracted struggle between the traditional and the scientific approach is that on the one hand the legal, judicial and penal functions of the state have been to a slight extent leavened by scientific method and on the other the various branches of psychology and sociology have gradually combined to establish a multi-disciplined approach to crime which will form the basis of all future criminology.

The situation is not without its problems. Taking the prevention of crime as a test case it is clear that this does not fall within the scope either of the Judiciary or of the Home Office, though it might well be advanced by enlightened legislation. But enlightened legislation depends on the application of principles formulated by a multi-disciplined criminology, for this latter, private grouping has at present the closer access to the resources of medical, educational and social psychology. Should then the State kill two birds with one stone by creating a Ministry of Criminology which might end the existing antithesis between traditional State interests and a privately organized and multi-disciplined criminology? Failing this expedient should the State itself pursue a multi-disciplined approach, enlisting the services of its own Ministries of Health and Education, possibly creating one of Social Welfare? Should the Home Office shed some of its arbitrary functions? For it is clear that not only preventive measures but the actual handling of, for example, juvenile delinquency would be more appropriately the concern of the educational authorities acting in combination with the services of Mental Health. Or should criminology continue to draw its inspiration from those cultural institutions within the community, whose scientific incentive unlike that of Governmental departments owes little or nothing to expediency? These are a few of the questions which must sooner or later be answered. In the following surveys an attempt is made to follow the development of a scientific criminology in this country, in which, however, the importance of individual psychology and in particular of psychoanalysis is intentionally underlined. For the real revolution in criminology originated in the field of dynamic (or clinical) psychology.

PART I. '1912–48'*

To understand the present position of criminological science in Britain, it is necessary to be familiar not only with the various movements which have concerned themselves with delinquency in this country but with the various 'theories of conduct' by virtue of which these movements have regulated their policies and efforts. Otherwise it is scarcely possible to estimate the significance of any given criminological policy or to measure the impetus it carries. At the time of writing, for example, the British House of Commons is about to pass into law a *Criminal Justice Bill* which has been eulogistically hailed as an extremely progressive measure, a milestone of social progress. To the casual reader of the provisions of this Bill it might indeed appear that at long last society represented by the State is prepared to recognize the validity of the psychological approach to the problem of delinquent behaviour. This is very far from being the case. There is no sign that those who framed the *Bill* have been converted to a psychological point of view, or that they are prepared to strike to the roots of the problem. On the contrary the new *Criminal Justice Bill* is largely a measure of prison reform, a tribute to the devoted efforts of penal reformers but, so far as psychological methods of prevention, treatment and 'after-care' are concerned, a timid, unimaginative and cheese-paring measure.

Of the various criminological movements and hypotheses some are sufficiently familiar to the student of delinquency to call for no detailed consideration here. For example the theory of an *unwritten social contract* whereby the community is ready to protect the individual from injury or unwarranted interference at the hands of other individuals and groups (including sometimes the State itself), provided always the individual in question is prepared to obey social law, is generally accepted as a rational basis of criminal law. When, however, we inquire what steps society will take should the individual refuse to obey social law, we find that these rational contracts are but a screen for a more primitive and irrational *moral*

* First published in *Searchlights on Delinquency*, London, Imago Publishing Co; New York, International Universities Press, 1949.

hypothesis. In its more sophisticated form this maintains that law breaking is a kind of *sin* calling for appropriate forms of *punishment*. One need hardly add that this moral code is derived from animistic and early religious systems which nowadays seek to conceal their retributive aims on the ground that punishment is an effective deterrent to evil-doers, a theory which still flourishes and will continue to flourish in the face of repeated statistical rebuttal.

At this point a *humanitarian movement*, recruited largely but by no means exclusively from Christian denominations, steps in to mitigate the severity of talion law. Though meliorist in aim this movement does not question the moral hypothesis of wrong-doing; only accidentally, as it were, does it find itself committed to a tentative scientific approach. Seeking for effective arguments against the severities of penal law, advocates of penal reform have found that the theory of deterrence is a rationalization of revenge-impulses that can be easily exploded. But they have not pursued this tactical advantage to press for still more scientific investigations in particular of the causes of crime. Indeed until comparatively recent times penal reformers looked somewhat askance at the efforts of psychologists to revolutionize the approach to criminal behaviour. Nevertheless their arguments gained in popular force and, as has been suggested, found their final expression in the present *Criminal Justice Bill*. Indeed it is interesting to speculate on the future of this movement. It can of course continue to press for prison reform or indeed abolition. For the rest it must either divert its energies to more scientific channels of approach or remain aloof from the psychological movement, a rather puzzled spectator of more radical procedures.

The history of the *psychological movement*, or rather revolution, in criminological theory and practice will presently engage our attention: for the moment it is sufficient to say that whilst recognizing the practical utility of the social contract, it insists that society should underwrite a charter of individual privileges and liberties including the right of every individual, whether law-abiding or criminal, to secure treatment of whatever disease he may suffer from.

Nor does the psychological movement deny that a moral hypothesis of crime however diluted will continue to influence for good or ill individual and social reactions to delinquency. It maintains, however, that the legitimate spheres of moral influence lie in *prevention and after-care*, subject always to the proviso that such influence is appropriate to the case and does not override more important prophylactic and therapeutic considerations. Indeed it goes further to insist that *for its own psychological good*, society must treat the delinquent with more understanding and human kindliness.

On the fallacies of deterrence and on the superstitious elements in criminal law the psychological movement is adamant. Those few psychologists who dally with penal measures on the score of expediency merely take advantage of their professional position to gratify (wittingly or unwittingly) their own moral prejudices. There are always moralists in any psychological field; as witness, the exhortatory group of psychotherapists who are ready on the slightest sign of refractoriness or recidivism on the part of their patients to bully their charges in the same fashion as physiologically trained child-minders. Nor do they stop short of excommunicating their patients, i.e., summarily discharging them as incurable. Even psycho-analysts are not immune from this form of super-ego (moral) disorder.

Surveying 'movements' in this rather shorthand fashion, it is possible to 'place' various aspects of present day criminology, a process which, however, involves tracing them to their origins. Thus, for example, the long drawn out controversy between the law and psychology as to the conditions governing criminal responsibility (known as the M'Naghten Rules in this country) is due to the terrified obstinacy with which judges have hitherto defended the unwritten social contract. Fearing that the law would be hopelessly weakened if any other than psychotic factors were to be adduced in extenuation of crime, and convinced, not perhaps unnaturally, that if final authority were delegated to psychiatrists the latter would either be hoodwinked by malingerers or give rein to a sentimental humanitarianism to say nothing of professional and scientific arrogance, judges have ridden roughshod over perfectly valid scientific discoveries such as the nature of psychopathy, have treated psychiatric witnesses for the defence with gross contempt and discourtesy and have stiffened the legalistic backbone of Home Office authorities and Home Secretaries to the point where these naturally timid and conservative creatures have preferred administrative traditions to a courageous recognition of the psychological facts.

To take another example, this time from the chapter of the *disposal* of delinquents: the probationary system in this country is a legacy from the earlier religious and humanitarian movements, one to which the official police system of supervision has contributed not a little. The forerunner of the present probation officer was the court missionary; and the supervision exercised by such of these as did not choose to apply moral pressure at first smacked of the old ticket-of-leave system. Indeed these disciplinary rigidities, though greatly softened by more adequate selection and training of probation officers, still linger, thereby stultifying to some extent the more understanding techniques now generally employed.

A more complicated trail has been blazed by the Borstal institution. Sprung originally from the military prison system, it nevertheless fell heir to some of the traditions of the old poor law institution and 'reformatory'. Gradually, under the influence of Home Office enthusiasts, it took over some pedagogic techniques, in particular the 'house master' system of the public (boarding) school and finally graduated to the position of elder and sterner half-brother to the approved school. Under the new *Criminal Justice Bill* it will continue to play a corrective function for delinquents under 21, a rôle which in the case of those over that age will some day be played by the new detention centre. This last is a euphemism for a 'reformed' type of prison, as yet merely projected. There are none such in existence. So Borstal is a derivative from the older moralistic penology, modified by penal reform influences and by the 'segregation' techniques of pedagogy (empirical educational psychology). For psychologists the Borstal system will remain a form of disposal to be sparingly recommended in a small minority of cases and only then if more suitable and humane resources have failed.

On the other hand it has to be admitted that the summary given above does not do justice to the more complicated sources of interest in criminology and penal method. The 'movements' described omit, for example, all reference to a special group whose members have played an honourable part in the development of enlightened handling of crime. This group is constituted of persons who either by reason of their sublimated interest in anti-social conduct or because of their sublimated interest in youth and its problems or more rarely because they are interested in psychological puzzles turn a generous and patient mind to the delinquencies of the young. (Relatively few respond with equal understanding to adult criminal conduct.) Many of them had evinced earlier an active interest in boys or girls or youth camps, and thereby acquired an empirical knowledge which stood them in good stead when they were caught up in delinquency work. They are a small but enthusiastic band, some of whose members, fortunately for offenders, sit on the magisterial bench, others adorning the Probation Service, others again contributing an influence for good on the staffs of approved schools *et hoc genus*. Less active members are content to exert their influence through some of the many societies for penal or social reform whose interests are bent towards juvenile delinquency.

The Development of Forensic Psychology

Having surveyed very roughly the field of criminological endeavour, the task remains of outlining the *history of the psychological movement in British criminology*. This involves a two-fold approach; cataloguing the various sections in which some branch or other of psychological thought has obtained expression; and at the same time considering the part played by psycho-analysis, either directly, through the research and therapeutic work of trained analysts, or, indirectly, through the influence it has exerted on persons who, though not themselves analysts, have nevertheless been in a position to develop methods of disposal based on the discoveries of Freud. It is when surveying the second of these approaches that we are able to assess the importance of the work done by Aichhorn.

It would take us too far afield, and without adequate recompense, to enter in detail into the question of historical priority of interest amongst non-analytical psychologists. And it is scarcely worth the trouble because, not to put too fine a point on it, pre-analytical psychology was neither a rich nor a very fruitful clinical field. For yet another reason we need not concern ourselves with earlier approaches which, although of scientific intent, were non-psychological in nature. For although the methods adopted, for example, by followers of Lombroso in this country had scientific intent, their best service lay in indicating the desirability of using other scientific methods.[1] Similarly the publications of early non-

[1] Lombroso's most valuable contribution to criminology was the theory that punishment should fit the criminal not the crime.

psychological psychiatrists impress us nowadays more because of their lack of psychological understanding than because of their contributions to the descriptive aspects of delinquency.

Two exceptions to this apparently sweeping generalization exist. In the first place the attention called by some earlier psychiatrists to the anti-social behaviour of psychotic types and of mentally deficient children and adolescents certainly prepared the way for later and more comprehensive groupings of delinquent conduct. And secondly the approach of some exceptional and imaginative medical criminologists was a stimulus to an oncoming generation of workers who were to have at their disposal more powerful instruments of investigation. In this sense the work of Devon, a Glasgow prison officer, on the *Criminal and the Community*[1] deserves to be singled out.

For all practical purposes the development of modern methods of dealing with delinquency ran parallel with the development of normal and abnormal psychology, although interestingly enough, in both instances a considerable time-lag developed between the establishment of psychological principles and their specific application to delinquency. *Clinical* progress in normal and abnormal psychology was stimulated respectively by work done in the field of educational and industrial psychology and in the field of psycho-analysis. But whereas psycho-analysis represented a complete break from existing methods of mental observation and description, educational psychology was based on laboratory studies in mental measurement. For convenience in description it is desirable to outline first the relation of psycho-analysis to delinquency in Britain.

As has so often been the case the application of psycho-analysis to a new field was the result of some stimulating suggestions thrown out by Freud in the course of wider researches. It is no exaggeration to say that his brief article 'Die Verbrecher aus Schuldbewusstsein' (*Criminality from a Sense of Guilt*)[2] laid the foundation not only of a psycho-analytical science of delinquency, but of those freely modified techniques practised by psycho-therapists who were not themselves Freudian and who in fact had only the slightest familiarity with work done by psycho-analysts on the

[1] Published 1912.
[2] 'Some Character-Types Met with in Psycho-analytic Work' (first published 1915), *C.P.*, 4, London, Hogarth Press, 1925.

subject. But in a very real sense all Freud's early contributions, e.g. on unconscious conflict, guilt, and self-punishment, on the libidinal and aggressive vicissitudes of childhood, on sexual perversions and on unconscious character formation had prepared the ground very thoroughly for research into delinquency. Everything was ready for sweeping advances in the subject save the appearance of psycho-analytical workers ready to specialize in it.

It is all the more interesting to note that this accession of specialized psycho-analytical workers was not forthcoming. Indeed even at the present time when psycho-analytical *principles* and *points of view* are freely applied in delinquency, there is an astonishing dearth of psycho-analytical workers in the field. The number of regular analyses carried out on anti-social types in this country is woefully small. Psycho-analysis is a lengthy procedure and it is difficult to persuade young practitioners to devote a substantial proportion of their time to work that is technically difficult, unusually thankless and not particularly remunerative. In fact in the early nineteen-twenties the subject was almost totally neglected. Actually the first public lecture to magistrates on psycho-analysis and crime was given by the present writer in 1922. The clinical material was drawn from some psycho-analytical observations of juvenile delinquents, and the theory was extended to the subject from orthodox Freudian principles. Naturally enough the effort fell distinctly flat and at the time probably did more harm than good.[1] Apart from sporadic efforts of this sort active interest in the subject was promoted mainly by Freudian sympathizers who like Hamblin Smith found that psycho-analytical theories of mental function shed a dazzling light on criminal conduct.[2]

But fresh incentives were soon forthcoming from a number of directions. Rumours of the work of Alexander and Staub in Berlin, of Aichhorn, Reich and Reik in Vienna began to reach this country; from America had already come the linguistically more

---

[1] See Section I, Introductory.
[2] Hamblin Smith's book, *The Psychology of the Criminal* (New York, McBride), which was the result of twenty-seven years' work on criminals was the first purely medico-psychological approach to the problem in this country. It was published in 1922, the year that Pailthorpe commenced her psycho-analytical investigations in Birmingham prison under Hamblin Smith's direction. (*v. inf.*)

accessible publications of Healy, Bronner and the Gluecks. In Britain itself two additional factors were operative, the expansion of child analysis and the publications of Sir Cyril Burt on backward and delinquent children.[1] It is only proper to add that although Sir Cyril Burt had from the beginning exhibited a friendly interest in psycho-analytical developments and applied some psycho-analytical principles in his delinquent studies, his original work was derived from a combination of acute clinical observation and steady application of observational methods (both individual and social) developed by 'normal psychologists'.

It is pleasant to be able to record that the next important step in the direction of specialized work in delinquency in this country was taken by a psycho-analyst, Dr. Grace Pailthorpe. Supported by the Medical Research Council, she carried out investigations on female prisoners and inmates of preventive homes. These observations were based on her psycho-analytical knowledge, and her results were published first in the form of an official report and afterwards in her book *What We Put In Prison*.[2] More important, she immediately busied herself organizing a private committee whose object it was to see whether the methods she had found so useful in investigation could be applied to the treatment of offenders who had not been in prison. Dr. Pailthorpe, being prevented by illhealth from developing her project, invited the present writer to continue this work. The first practical step was to organize a clinic for the study and treatment of delinquency. With the assistance of the late Dr. David Eder, a pioneer psycho-analyst who had also done pioneer work in founding school clinics, of Dr. J. A. Hadfield, a medical psychologist from the staff of the Tavistock Clinic who has taken an active part in the Mental Hygiene movement in Britain and of Dr. E. T. Jensen, a physician who has devoted much interest to the subject of delinquency, a small clinic was set up in 1932 in a room lent by the West End Hospital

---

[1] Sir Cyril Burt's L.C.C. Report on *The Treatment of Backward Children* was published in 1918; *The Dreams and Day Dreams of a Delinquent Girl* in 1921; *The Causes and Treatment of Juvenile Delinquency* in 1922; *The Young Delinquent* in 1925; *The Subnormal Mind* in 1935 and *The Backward Child* in 1937.

[2] Dr. Grace W. Pailthorpe commenced her investigations at Birmingham prison in 1922 and continued them for a period of five years at Holloway. Her report (*Studies in the Psychology of Delinquency*, London, H.M.S.O.) was published in 1929 and her book in 1932.

for Nervous Diseases, which also provided facilities for physical examination. From these slender beginnings was developed the first *specialized* Institute for the Scientific Treatment of Delinquency now known as the I.S.T.D. London.

But this is to anticipate. In the meantime we can review the general state of psychological research in delinquency from 1930 to the present day, and trace its various tributory sources. We have seen that an occasional *prison medical officer* of exceptional understanding took an objective interest in the subject. This state of affairs has changed very little. The number of psychiatric minded prison officers has increased but only marginally. Training in psychiatry (though not in psycho-analysis) is now an essential qualification; but as a whole the prison service was, and psychologically speaking still is, a backwater. This is not to underestimate the importance of the prison work done by Hubert and backed by Norwood East.[1] Hubert was a psycho-analytically oriented psychiatrist, not a regular prison officer. Even more valuable work may be expected from prison psychiatrists such as Mackwood, Young, Frost and others provided of course they are given a free hand by the authorities.[2]

Home Office Influences

In a review of this kind it is essential to estimate the part played by the *Home Office* and by *Home Secretaries* in either advancing or retarding the progress of psychological research and the expansion of psychological methods of dealing with delinquency. To begin with, the Home Office shows all the characteristics one has come to expect from Government departments, run by permanent officials with the support of Home Office specialists and a few privately appointed specialist advisors. The Home Office is naturally dominated by an administrative valuation of the social contract. It is also conservative, acutely suspicious of anything new or revolutionary and devoid of social imagination. Its attitude to

[1] Sir Norwood East was originally a prison medical officer, later H.M. Commissioner of Prisons and subsequently Lecturer to London University on Crime and Insanity.

[2] No special mention has been made in this review of *police-surgeons* for the simple reason that the psychological tasks required of them are negligible. An exception is provided by Baldie, a medical psychologist of Adlerian outlook who combines specialist work on delinquency with the duties of a police surgeon.

psychology, in particular psycho-analytical psychology, has been cautious to the point of neglect. Nevertheless it is only fair to say that amongst the junior ranks of its officials some extremely highgrade workers exist whose practical appreciation of psychological factors and policies has been a constant source of support to delinquency workers. The Home Office has of course been influenced by the work of various Royal Commissions it has itself appointed; but here again a retarding influence generally makes itself felt. Royal Commissions have never included a psychoanalyst, rarely a medical psychologist of first hand experience in the subject. Bowing to public pressure representatives of penal reform societies came to be admitted and now that, as the result of the war, psychiatry has increased in social influence, a gradual psychiatric leavening of Home Office policy may be expected. But on the whole it will be more influenced by 'rational' views of conscious psychology, will rarely be in advance of public opinion and will be more concerned to preserve the traditions of the police service, an organization which though not exactly militaristic is essentially authoritarian, based on the assumption that the social contract must be enforced rather than accepted. Indeed the bias of the Home Office towards the social side of the contract is greatly to be regretted. Whoever controls the Home Office is in a position effectively to thwart or to fulfil the aspirations of the most ardent reformer, or most devoted scientist.[1]

NORMAL PSYCHOLOGY

Next in order of strategic importance comes the influence of what might be called normal psychology. This is exerted in the main from university and teaching colleges and training centres and is directed mostly through the channel of educational psychology, e.g., regional directors of education and experts in mental measurement. It impinges on the problem of delinquency directly through the study of behaviour patterns, both normal and abnormal, during school age and adolescence and indirectly through the, as yet, only slenderly equipped system of child guidance

[1] From a long line of psychologically unresponsive Home Secretaries, Sir Samuel Hoare (now Lord Templewood) stands out as a distinguished reformer. The present *Criminal Justice Bill* is largely a resuscitation of the measure framed and piloted by him just before the war but abandoned because of the national emergency.

clinics. Here the educational psychologist and to a considerable extent the psychiatric social worker operate with techniques fostered during training in normal psychology. Normal psychology has also many techniques in common with sociological research, and has naturally contributed a good deal to the statistical investigation of individual factors (backwardness, mental defect and capacity for adaptation) and of environmental factors (including many familial and economic conditions that exert a psychological influence on behaviour). As we have seen one British representative of this school and method (Burt) gained an international reputation for pioneer work in delinquency and amongst those adopting mainly sociological techniques the name of Hermann Mannheim ranks high. Jennings White is also a prominent worker in the combined tradition. Carr-Saunder's approach is largely biometric and sociological. Nowadays students of normal psychology too numerous to mention busy themselves with social and individual aspects of the subject. This increased activity became particularly noticeable during and after the Second World War when evacuation of children from danger areas led to a mass break-up of the family and offered an unique opportunity of studying environmental factors of great psychological consequence for delinquency work.

As to the research value of these methods: whilst it would be premature to say they have outworn their usefulness (for it is always possible for the normal psychologist to apply statistical tests to some of the findings of dynamic unconscious psychology), it can be said that, lacking any training in, or understanding of, unconscious psychology and debarred by their rules of 'controlled' research from applying psycho-analytical methods of interpretation to their data, normal psychologists can contribute little of value to the *individual and etiological aspects of delinquency*. This valuation does not apply so much to the social investigations of normal psychologists although from the clinical point of view, there is something 'distant' (impersonal) even about valid sociological explanations of crime.

Psychiatric Contributions

Until comparatively recently the contributions of *psychiatry* to research on delinquency have stood in barren contrast to the immense clinical resources of the science. Admittedly formal psychiatry[1] has always had a voice in the matter of criminal responsibility, e.g., testifying in Courts of Law to the presence or absence of insanity in cases of criminal violence. Otherwise the contributions of psychiatrists to the science of delinquency have usually been indirect. Thus they have been able to classify those symptoms of the psychoses, of organic reaction types, and of convulsive states which are responsible for some forms of anti-social or criminal conduct. But these observations do not in themselves constitute research into delinquency, for unless the unconscious etiological factors in e.g., the psychoses, are fully understood (a feat so far compassed only rarely in Britain), it is not possible to make any useful correlations between the conduct of psychotic and non-psychotic types of delinquency respectively. Exceptionally, the work of the psychiatrists Macniven and Dillon has been characterized by understanding of the psychodynamics of delinquency.

On the other hand, psychiatric work on psychopathic states has been a valuable stimulus to research on what is certainly a key problem in delinquency. D. K. Henderson of Edinburgh who combines extensive psychiatric experience with unusual opportunities of studying criminal conduct has produced comprehensive and illuminating observations on this condition. Similarly in the field of mental deficiency, the work of Burt has been amplified by psychiatric studies from Earle E. Lewis and other medical workers. Unfortunately the tendency of workers on mental deficiency is to be content with the demonstration of innate defect and to ignore those psychological factors affecting behaviour that are either associated with or a consequence of mental defect. Further progress in this direction will depend on careful psycho-analytical observations. In the meantime the therapeutic amelioration of psychological complications of deficiency goes by default. Institutional and pedagogic procedures have secured too exclusive priority in this field.

Another psychiatric channel of influence is constituted by the *Child Guidance Clinic* which, for good or ill, has fallen under the sway of the psychiatrist. Here the educational psychologist now plays an auxiliary rôle, sharing with the psychiatric social worker

[1] In this country the term ' psychiatrist ' has until recently connoted a specialist in the psychoses, not as in the United States a specialist in **general medical psychology.**

an uneasy equality of status. This has led in some cases to some intriguing professional situations. Under present training conditions, the educational psychologist and psychiatric social worker are trained in the principles of normal psychology and given a smattering of psychiatry; but a number have of their own choice acquired a good working knowledge of clinical psychology, sometimes of psycho-analysis. It is not uncommon therefore to find psychiatric social workers who have a better understanding of the facts of unconscious conflict than their psychiatric directors. Excellent medico-psychological work in this field has been done by, amongst others, E. Miller, Maberly, Pearce (all medical psychologists of repute) and Paterson Brown (a psycho-analytically trained child psychiatrist). The work of so-called 'play-therapists' will be considered below.

Psycho-Analysis

As has already been indicated the direct application of psycho-analytic techniques to the clinical aspects of delinquency is in absurd disproportion to the overwhelming indirect influence of *psycho-analysis*. In the course of their regular practice many analysts are faced with delinquent problems but this work has never been organized.[1] Nor with the obvious exceptions of young juveniles and of 'neurotic' types of adult delinquency is the classical technique of psycho-analysis altogether adapted to meet the crises that arise with classical cases of delinquency. The most active (medical) psycho-analytical workers in the general field of antisocial behaviour are Pailthorpe, Carroll, M. Schmideberg, K. Friedlander and M. Franklin. The work of Schmideberg with advanced cases of the 'Dartmoor type' has broken new ground in the psycho-analytic handling of delinquents. But it has involved several modifications of the customary techniques which she has described in various papers on the subject. K. Friedlander has produced a standard work of psycho-analytical reference on juvenile delinquency.[2] Amongst lay psycho-analysts who have also

---

[1] Exceptionally Dr. David Forsyth published a lengthy study, 'The Case of a Middle-Aged Embezzler', 1938.

[2] *The Psycho-Analytical Approach to Juvenile Delinquency*, London, Kegan Paul, 1947, New York, Int. Univ. Press, 1947. A book by Schmideberg entitled, *Children in Need*, is about to be published by Allen and Unwin [published 1948].

extensive pedagogic experience Barbara Low has played a prominent part in delinquency work and in the education of public opinion.[1]

It has been suggested that in an indirect way all psycho-analytical work has a bearing on anti-social conduct. And it follows that the more direct work done on the mental development of children the more we shall understand the problems of delinquency. It is only proper therefore to record the increasing influence of child psycho-analysis in this country. The founder of child-analysis in Britain was the late Mary Chadwick who produced also several studies of anti-social behaviour amongst juveniles. Unfortunately a split on the theory and practice of child-analysis has developed in Britain. On the one hand we have the classical approach of the Viennese school (where child-analysis was first developed), guided in this country by Anna Freud, and on the other a new metapsychological system developed by M. Klein. Amongst psycho-analytical workers on delinquency Friedlander follows the classical approach, Bowlby the Kleinian theory.

Inevitably developments in the psycho-analysis of children have given rise to a flattery of imitation amongst non-analytical psychologists. The application of *play-technique* to the needs of child analysis (incidentally, Klein's most useful contribution to the subject) has led to the formation of all sorts of groups of child-therapists. And nowadays there are few psychiatric centres or child guidance clinics which do not include a lay 'play-therapist' on their staff. This form of activity has, except in instances where the 'play-therapist' is analytically trained, nothing to do with child-analysis. Play-therapy of some kind or another has now become part of the ambulant treatment of juvenile delinquents.

Equally naturally the differences between Freudian, Adlerian and Jungian *'schools' of clinical psychology* have been accurately reflected in the approach to and treatment of delinquency. In their several ways Adlerians and Jungians are at home in the handling of anti-social conduct which they feel assured can be very convinc-

---

[1] Space does not permit an adequate acknowledgment of the work done by various educational journals and child-parent magazines in advancing modern ideas on delinquency in this country. In this connection the work of Leon Radzinowicz and J. W. C. Turner, editors of *English Studies in Criminal Science* (London, Macmillan, 1941, including a volume on *Mental Abnormality and Crime*, 1944), is deserving of recognition.

ingly explained in terms of their respective theories. Inevitably the 'eclectic' finds an opportunity for applying his compost of theories and methods particularly to the problem child. Indeed at the present rate of diffusion of clinical theories, it would seem that for some time ahead such psychiatric and child guidance centres as are not run by formal psychiatrists will fall under the direction of eclectics, a state of affairs which bodes ill for any radical progress in research.

Winding up this survey of the more direct approaches to the problem we may note that following the *anthropometric* work of Goring in this country[1] contributions to this method of approach have been made by Burt and later by Norwood East. The *relation of physique to character* has also been followed up but the consensus of opinion is that conclusions based on a study of these constitutional factors should be treated with considerable reserve. And the same may be said of *endocrine investigations* in delinquent types. In any case the psychological influence of these factors on the *development* of mind and character in the child has been very generally neglected.

Attitudes of the Judiciary

In an earlier part of this review attention was drawn to the usually retarding influence of the Home Office on the development of modern techniques of investigation and treatment of delinquency. It is pleasant therefore to record that in other official administrative departments psychological methods are acquiring increasing influence and prestige. Seventy per cent of the cases now sent to the I.S.T.D. are recommended by *magistrates* acting in concert with their own probation officers. Amongst magistrates dealing with adult offenders, C. Mullins stands out as a pioneer who has done more than any other to apply scientific procedures of examination and treatment.[2] In the field of juvenile delinquency similar recognition is due the magistrates Basil Henriques and John Watson. The contribution of Mullins deserves all the more

[1] Published 1913.
[2] Mullins drew freely on the medico-psychological services of A. Court, a general practitioner who undertook psychiatric training and carried out his examinations of delinquent cases mostly in private. This raises the interesting possibility that, given the appropriate training, physicians in general practice could function as experts in delinquency. The advantages of such a system particularly in rural districts are obvious.

recognition in that he is a firm believer in endopsychic as distinct from environmental psychological factors. Most supporters of a psychological approach are essentially environmentalists and consequently pin their faith for the most part on correction of environmental factors either familial or social. From the therapeutic point of view their faith has of course justified itself, but regarded from the point of view of etiological investigation the approach is a blind alley.

By way of contrast the Higher Courts are notoriously barren of psychological understanding, a fact which any medical psychologist giving evidence for the defence either in mitigation of sentence or on appeal against sentence pronounced can readily attest. It would take us too far afield to discuss the factors responsible for this state of affairs. No doubt the age of the offender and the nature of his offence contribute to this refractoriness on the part of recorders and judges by mobilizing their defences against the 'licence' of others. The fact is, however, that with the exception of an occasional recorder ready to listen to a commonsense and plainly expressed statement of the probability of 'cure' by scientific treatment, judges at Quarter-Sessions and High Courts of Assize are still critical to the point of open hostility of the evidence of any but prison medical officers or psychiatrists for the Crown.

The Probation Service

Returning to the activities of the Lower Courts it can be said without fear of contradiction that the *Probation Service* is by far the most enlightened of all the penal services. Despite their extremely curtailed and inadequate training, many probation officers have followed the example of psychiatric social workers by acquiring, often at great inconvenience, a working knowledge of the psychological and sociological approaches to crime. Next to psychiatric social workers and educational psychologists, probation officers provide some of the staunchest supporters of institutes such as the I.S.T.D. They are of course handicapped in their individual efforts at re-education and rehabilitation by the excessive caseloads they have to carry and perhaps more decisively, by their divided loyalties. To be a servant of the Court and at the same time to act as counsellor and friend to the offender is a dual rôle calling for unusual qualifications. Certainly no trained psychotherapist would relish being put in this emotionally ambiguous situation.[1] Nevertheless we must be grateful for attenuated mercies. There are few psychological workers in the field who have not had occasion to be thankful for the co-operation of an understanding probation officer. As their training is gradually shorn of irrelevant and tedious studies and extended to include clinical instruction in the psychology of delinquency, the status of probation officers will rise rapidly. Already it is an open question whether they should not be recognized as a special branch of the association of psychiatric social workers.

Institutional Facilities

Much less satisfactory is the psychological status of workers in the various institutions of disposal, e.g., *remand homes and centres, approved schools and Borstal institutions*. Like most institutions these suffer from their divorce not only from ordinary social contact but from the more positive transference influences existing in the family. They are also hampered by their traditional link with poor law institutions, 'reformatories' and prison services. It is true that the educational and pedagogic standards particularly of approved schools and Borstal institutions have steadily improved but this does not compensate for the lack of psychological training and distrust of non-disciplinary methods of personal supervision, exhibited in most of these institutions. The position of voluntary institutions run by religious bodies and social welfare organizations is little better, if at all. By way of contrast some individual efforts in this field are of a promising order, witness the contributions of pioneers like Wills (*The Hawkspur Experiment*)[2] and Otto Shaw. It is in this particular department of re-education and rehabilitation that the influence of Aichhorn's work has made itself most felt in this country: although undoubtedly some of the credit should go to the experimental school methods practised by A. S. Neill. So far, however, most institutions are psychologically backward and conservative to the point of timidity.

[1] The psychiatrist reporting to the court from the I.S.T.D. is not a servant of the court. There is a pretty general feeling amongst clinical workers that he should not hold a court position. Even if, under a State Medical Service, he should become a civil servant, he still need not be attached to the court.

[2] Published 1941.

To sum up: modern ideas concerning the handling of delinquents in Britain are derived from the work of normal and educational psychologists, of sociologists, of psychiatrists and of medical psychologists including psycho-analysts, not to mention some workers in more circumscribed fields. These ideas are given practical application in the I.S.T.D., in psychological clinics like the Tavistock Clinic, in the psychiatric centres of teaching hospitals, in child guidance clinics, sometimes at welfare centres and more rarely at special schools and institutions. They have influenced the work of magistrates, probation officers, psychiatric social workers, educational psychologists and a number of free lances both medical and lay. It should be noted, however, that the I.S.T.D. is the *only specialized clinic dealing under ambulant conditions with offenders of all ages*. In all other cases delinquency work is, as it were, a by-product of other clinical activities, not a special department. Nor do these other centres so far afford facilities for the *specialized* training of delinquency workers.

Translating this into round figures and dividing the specialty into separate sections dealing respectively with diagnosis, treatment and research, the *strength of the psychological movement in delinquency work* can be estimated as follows. There are now a few dozen medical psychologists and psychiatrists throughout the country capable of making an *experienced* diagnosis of anti-social conditions. At a sanguine estimate two-thirds of these are capable of giving the skilled attention necessary for radical treatment. On the other hand, empirical treatment can be given by most medical psychologists and by quite a respectable number of psychiatrists. The number of educational psychologists sufficiently experienced to rate as delinquency workers is about double that of medically qualified specialists in delinquency. Psychiatric social workers suitable for delinquency work are relatively scarce although the number is growing and will continue to do so. The number of first-class probation officers is roughly the same as that of experienced educational workers. Play-therapists are rapidly increasing but their work on the whole is of poor quality and the technique employed of a hit or miss variety. For the rest a few magistrates, a few prison doctors, a few sociologists, a few school-masters and a few institution superintendents are sufficiently experienced in clinical psychology to rate as trained workers in their own particular branch.

Research

When it comes to *research work* the outlook is at first sight much less encouraging. The indirect influence of both conscious and unconscious psychology has already been assessed; but it must be admitted that amongst medical workers directly engaged in treating delinquency the number capable of doing fruitful research can be counted on the fingers of two hands. The number of lay workers in normal psychology capable of contributing to research is much greater. But against this must be set the fact that the theories on which most normal psychologists base their approach are essentially empirical theories of preconscious and conscious mental function. As has been indicated, psycho-analysts are in a specially favourable position to tap the theoretical resources of unconscious psychology, but unfortunately the number of psycho-analysts who can be said to specialize in delinquency work in this country can be counted on the fingers of one hand. Moreover the great majority of all trained workers are centred in London and its environs, an area which, assessed on a population basis, should absorb only a quarter of the total number existing or required. As a matter of interest the further North one goes the more barren are the psychological resources of the land. Scotland, for example, is still in the backwoods and the North of England is little better. Eire is worse.

Fortunately the outlook is not so gloomy as this survey would indicate. So long as a handful of investigators exists and so long as incentive to fresh research comes either from other scientific institutions within the country or from other countries, research will not come to a standstill. It may well be retarded either because those qualified to conduct research are up to their ears in diagnostic or short-term therapeutic work, or because, as seems to be the case at the moment, some psycho-analysts and medical psychologists appear to be flirting with more superficial techniques, e.g., group-therapy or 'psycho-sociological' approaches, or, again, because pioneer efforts and organizations may be partly blanketed by the development of a State Mental Service with its paralyzing system of organization by a hierarchy of officials. But it will survive.

Diagnostic Techniques

Outlines of research into delinquency can be considered under two headings, the *development of techniques* and the *application of existing theories* of mental function having a bearing on the phenomena of delinquency. For a number of reasons it is desirable to commence with techniques.

Delinquency work calls for highly specialized techniques differing in many respects from those applied in the case of psycho-neurotic and psychotic conditions. Also it necessitates a particular form of 'team work' which, in the case of classical psycho-analysis, for example, is either undesirable or positively detrimental to progress. Admittedly much of the team work that has been developed in psychiatric centres and child guidance departments is a tacit confession of the weakness of whatever individual methods are employed. A psycho-analyst is his own social worker, although in fact he very rarely makes contact with relatives or friends of the patient and practically never sees home conditions at first hand. His social work is done, as in the case of the psycho-neuroses it certainly should be, through his patients' associations and his own interpretations. But owing to a number of conditions both individual and social this exclusive approach is usually waived in delinquency work. To make this point clear some detailed reference must be made to the experience of the I.S.T.D.[1]

The first concern of the I.S.T.D. is to make a *thorough examination* and the second to arrive at a *provisional diagnosis*. The diagnosis should be sound enough to permit of a satisfactory *recommendation of disposal;* the examination should be comprehensive enough not only to exclude diagnostic error but to permit of subsequent statistical and other forms of *research*. But since the cases investigated are usually on remand from a Magistrate's Court, have frequently been investigated by a probation officer, possibly also examined at a remand home, and since part of the disposal recommended may take the form of probationary supervision or change of social conditions, it is rarely possible, even if it were desirable, to undertake immediate and exclusively individual forms of contact. Only when persons not officially charged present themselves voluntarily for private treatment can exclusively analytical policies of treatment be followed.

The actual procedure adopted is as follows: the psychiatric

[1] See also Edward Glover: *The Diagnosis and Treatment of Delinquency: Being a Clinical Report on the Work of the I.S.T.D. during the Five Years 1937–1941*, London, I.S.T.D. Publications, 1944. [See this volume, Section II, Pts. 1 and 2.]

social worker who first contacts the case proceeds to compile a *dossier of social information*. This is drawn from the probation officer's report, the remand centre's report (if any), reports from school authorities, employers or any other social agency that may be concerned in the case. This is amplified from personal interview with the patient, parents or guardians and from the results of a home visit. The educational psychologist then investigates the patient's mental and adaptation capacity, and an organic physician makes a routine physical overhaul and arranges for any specialized examinations or anthropometric survey that may appear desirable to him. Armed with this information the psychiatrist then takes over the case, and having carried out whatever investigations he deems appropriate, makes a provisional psychiatric diagnosis. The whole case is then reviewed by the director responsible for making reports to the court. Certain cross-references may still be made but as a rule it is then possible to send in a report indicating the diagnosis and recommending methods of disposal. These latter have usually been canvassed beforehand with the probation officer in charge of the case. Incidentally the clinic's dossier is strictly confidential; under no circumstances whatever are court or other authorities given more than a 'report' which is itself marked 'confidential'.

The forms of disposal recommended vary in the degree of 'supervision' involved. In a great majority of instances the maximum restriction suggested is that of probationary supervision with or without treatment. Should treatment be recommended, it is usually 'ambulant', the patient continuing to live at home, and follow his usual occupation, attending the clinic as directed. Changes in home, school and social conditions and/or conditions of employment may be recommended. In rarer cases removal to a foster-home may be suggested or the patient may be boarded out at a progressive school or camp. Still more rarely an approved school may be indicated or a Borstal institution. Only in the very rarest instances is a sentence of imprisonment supported. Special educational measures may be carried out particularly in the case of backward children and special courses of training indicated. Contacts are also made with clubs or other social groups. Any recommendations made by the organic physician are followed up and advisory relations are established with the parents. A follow-up lasting five years is aimed at but not always achieved.

From the research point of view the first concrete results of this comprehensive investigation were (*a*) greater clarity concerning the incidence of different types of disorder, (*b*) a fuller understanding of the nature of 'mixed types'. Of course the cases are already 'selected' by court officials but allowing for this fact the percentage distributions are of considerable interest. Thus on the average of five years' work 2·8 per cent were found to be mentally defective, 7·7 per cent 'borderline' defective, 1·1 per cent psychotic, 4·3 per cent borderline psychotic and 29·2 per cent psycho-neurotic. During these years psychopathic character types were unfortunately pigeon-holed with sexual perversions, an unsatisfactory overlap which cannot be rectified until a fresh investigation of all such cases is undertaken. The combined group totalled 36·8 per cent of all cases. Behaviour problems numbered 5 per cent, alcoholic types 0·9 per cent and organic types 2·1 per cent.

The principle of arriving at a final diagnosis only after 'treatment reports' and 'follow-up records' are collected has been laid down but so far shortage of staff has prevented a comprehensive reinvestigation of all cases on these lines. The groups calling for most careful screening are the psycho-neurotic and psychopathic groups. Most of the mixed types were distributed between these two groups according to the predominating clinical characteristics present; but when the material is reinvestigated these mixed types will be isolated and subdivided. Final subdivision of psychopathic types has not yet been attempted. It is probable, however, that the psycho-neurotic group is inflated. Certainly if a wider selection of cases were made by the courts the proportion of 'behaviour problems' and of mild psychopathies would rise considerably.

The immediate research project favoured by the directors of the I.S.T.D. is to establish more exact correlation between, on the one hand, the social and legal diagnosis and on the other the scientific (mainly medico-psychological) diagnosis. This will involve the break-up of various categories of offence, in particular of pilfering (the commonest type recommended to the clinic) and their re-classification in terms either of etiological or of clinical factors. At the moment it is scarcely possible wholly to convert clinical (mostly descriptive) classifications into etiological classifications. Nor is the procedure entirely justified. But there is no doubt that it would solve the problem of the mixed type, that bugbear of the statistician.

From the sociological point of view, work is in progress on conditions calling for purely social measures of disposal; e.g., probation, foster-homes, approved schools, etc.; and this involves also an assessment of the unconscious factors contributing to the therapeutic success of such disposals. Similarly an assessment of the unconscious factors activated by 'bad' upbringing, insecurity in the family, illegitimacy, etc., is overdue. It is already clear, however, that a purely sociological and statistical approach leads to the establishment of descriptive rather than dynamic criteria. As in the case of the legal diagnosis, psychological investigation of sociological (environmental) factors ends in their breakdown in terms of unconscious significance. As has been indicated, it is in this department of research that Aichhorn's work has achieved its most decisive impact.

In this connection it is necessary to remind the reader that the I.S.T.D. is not a purely psycho-analytical institute. Although its foundation was largely the work of psycho-analysts, and although psycho-analysts have up to the present played a large part in its direction, it is a medico-psychological institute. Its diagnostic and therapeutic services are representative of all medico-psychological approaches (including for the moment psychiatric methods). Although therefore psycho-analytical concepts and the pioneer work of psycho-analysts like Alexander, Staub, Reik, Reich and Aichhorn have influenced the approach of most medical psychologists, they are by no means accepted in their entirety, even in the diagnostic field. On the contrary the work of Healy, the Gluecks and in this country Burt and Henderson is still in greater favour. This is particularly clear in the case of psychopathy, and is moreover not altogether without justification. Alexander's 'neurotic character', based on psycho-analytical reflections on the functions of the ego and super-ego, does not satisfy the needs of a psychopathic classification and Reich's *'triebhafter Charakter'* (which may be loosely translated as 'impulsive character'), though clinically closer to a psychopathic standard, is from the psycho-analytical point of view, neither very sound clinically nor very illuminating theoretically. Psycho-analysts on the whole fight shy of 'psychopathic' criteria, and although no doubt the issue will be decided when they condescend more to clinical classifications than to unconscious concepts, that time is not yet. Psycho-analytical characterology is still in its infancy.

Therapeutic Techniques

Yet another factor influences the theoretical views of clinical psychologists, namely, their experience of *their own therapeutic results*. The results of other psycho-therapists are naturally never so convincing and in any case cannot always be checked.[1]

Now the individual psychological treatment given at the I.S.T.D. varies widely. Some of it is of necessity advisory and is given during periods of 'observation'. But even when immediate psychotherapy is recommended, it ranges from hypnosis and suggestion, with or without the use of narcotic adjuvants, through every variety of psychological 'influence', with or without some form of 'analysis', to pure Freudian, Jungian and Adlerian techniques. Actually, owing to shortage of psycho-analytical volunteers, classical psycho-analyses constitute only a minute proportion of the treatments given. It is consequently reserved only for cases in which it seems clearly indicated or in which the difficulties appear to be too great to admit of the recommendation of other and shorter methods. Short treatment is the rule and although some cases are given as many as 300 sessions (eighteen months steady analysis), the average number of therapeutic sessions for all cases fell during the war to ten, the usual range being five to fifty. Under more settled circumstances the average of all cases, i.e., including a few long analyses and many 'incomplete' cases, will run at about twenty sessions.

Despite this fact the *therapeutic results* obtained at the I.S.T.D. are in many respects striking. The standards laid down are exacting. 'Cure' is presumed only when the delinquent has displayed no abnormal conduct for a period of five years after treatment and when in addition the therapist is satisfied that the underlying causes have been resolved. Other apparent cures are for the time being merely rated as 'improved'. Many cases discontinue treatment and others are prevented from completing it for reasons beyond their control. Two statistical facts have emerged from a survey of these results: (1) that, allowing full correction for spon-

[1] It is one of the virtues of the clinic system and in particular of the 'follow-up' method that it is possible to some extent to check the psychotherapist's assessment of his own work.

taneous cure, the number of permanent cures reaches 32 per cent (2) that except in cases psycho-analysed the cure does not depend on the length of treatment. As has been said, most treatments are short; but even including cases that have abandoned treatment within a few days or have not attended as long as might have been desired, the percentage of major and lasting improvements reaches an astonishing figure. Indeed it can be said that if suitably selected cases of delinquency are given adequate treatment, and if the patient carries this treatment through to the end about 90 per cent become non-delinquent.

As far as psychotherapy is concerned this latter figure must, however, be scaled down for two reasons; first that an allowance must be made for spontaneous remission or cure, and, second, that in most cases other therapeutic measures, either individual or social, are put into effect. Except in cases undergoing a full analysis, probationary supervision is usually carried out in addition to which changes are effected either in family, school or social environment. These are recommended by the psychiatrist and brought about through the personal influence of the psychiatric social worker and the educational psychologist. So far no exact 'ratio of benefit' has been arrived at but taking a conservative view and avoiding over-sanguine and sensational estimates it seems likely that as far as psychotherapy is concerned it can be depended upon to bring about 'cure' in at least 30 per cent of cases and major amelioration in about double that figure.

Further research will afford more precise information on these points. In the meantime we are entitled to draw certain conclusions from the existing findings. For instance, although most medical psychologists are agreed that anti-social cases are by no means easy to treat and require various modifications of the customary psycho-therapeutic techniques, it cannot be denied that 'team-influence', that is to say, the combined efforts, both personal and indirect, of a number of workers on any one case, brings about remarkable improvement in a short space of time. And although no psycho-analyst would dream of suggesting that radical alteration of unconscious mechanisms can be effected by short treatments, he is forced to account for this rapid improvement. If he likes, he can do so simply by saying that the result is a transference manifestation. But in that case he must account for the fact that a 'distributed transference' (which psycho-analysts are generally at pains to avoid) so far from hampering progress in short treatment, apparently accelerates it. Indeed he might well speculate whether the form of group therapy most appropriate to regressive types of anti-social behaviour is one in which a single patient is the centre of a group of therapists rather than, as in the case of ordinary group therapy, one of a group of patients sharing a single therapeutic leader. Anyhow it is undeniable that the work of the I.S.T.D. has led to a revision of the customary standards of prognosis. The chronic psychopath may be a tough therapeutic nut to crack but when treated with patience, imagination, skill and an unruffled understanding of his compulsive recidivism the outlook is much more favourable than is generally supposed.

Theory and Practice

Considerations of this sort show how essential it is for successful research not only that clinical data should be constantly screened for their theoretical implications but that existing theories of etiology and therapeutic technique should be repeatedly tested in this, for all practical purposes, fallow field. And since in the writer's view the theory that can be most fruitfully applied to delinquency work is the theory of psycho-analysis it seems appropriate to conclude this review with a brief outline of the theoretical and practical problems arising from the psycho-analysis of delinquency in Britain.

There are two ways by which progress in any branch of psycho-analysis can be achieved, first, by direct psycho-analysis of clinical material and, second, by correlation of existing theories with the results of direct analysis. In the case of delinquency work corroborative evidence can of course be obtained from yet other branches of analysis, e.g., the psycho-analysis of normal or neurotic children and adults, or psycho-analytical interpretations of anthropological material. Unfortunately no anthropological work on crime has been done by any analyst in this country, and the branch of child analysis is riven with dissension on both theoretical principles and technical procedures. For purposes of correlation one is therefore compelled to fall back on the generally accepted theory of psycho-analysis derived mainly from the study of psycho-neurotic adults. It is then possible to enquire how far psycho-analytical observations of delinquent cases corroborate, amplify or correct this general body of knowledge.

Studying the various contributions to research on delinquency in this country from this angle, one is struck by the fact that during the past fifteen years very little has been added to early analytical formulations on the subject. Nor have investigations of delinquency added much to the general theory of psycho-analysis. Indeed it would appear that they have merely corroborated pre-existing analytical theories. This is no doubt a tribute to the validity of the theories but it can also be explained, in part at any rate, by the factor of case selection. Delinquency comprises a number of conditions varying in severity and duration and derived from different levels of developmental structure and function. So far psycho-analysis has been applied mainly to delinquent children in the latency period, to psycho-neurotic types of adolescent and adult delinquency and to some forms of super-ego disorder giving rise to delinquent character and conduct. Under these circumstances it would be natural for a correspondence to exist between the findings in delinquency and those arrived at in the study of psycho-neuroses.[1]

This factor of selection has given rise to some divergences in therapeutic method between psycho-analytical workers in delinquency in Britain. There are some who, following the tenets of Anna Freud and the orthodox child analysts believe that, owing to retarded or abnormal development of the super-ego, treatment of delinquency, particularly of the psychopathic type, must follow the lines employed in their psycho-analysis of young children, i.e., it must be divided into two phases, one in which the super-ego and consequently the ego, is strengthened and a later phase in which psycho-analysis proper is employed.

On the other hand some analytical workers, including the present writer, take the view that, given suitable elasticity of approach, psycho-analytical technique can be successfully applied even in refractory cases of delinquency provided always the patient for one reason or another (the existence of some marginal degree of conflict, or even a desire to escape further penal measures) is pre-

---

[1] It can be argued of course that these are the types of delinquency most suitable for psycho-analysis and that only the analysis of cases in which a favourable 'therapeutic situation' can be developed is likely to lead to new discoveries. This argument not only begs the question of suitability but disregards the fact that legitimate conclusions have been drawn from analytical observations made in refractory cases of every kind.

pared to 'try' treatment if only as a last resource. According to this view the key to the situation lies in the maintenance by the analyst of a supporting attitude together with an immediate and rapid exploration of spontaneous negative (hostile) transferences and catharsis of the early traumata that so often induce or increase these hostile and aggressive reactions.

The policy of the I.S.T.D. is in effect a compromise between these points of view. Its workers have established that, provided measures of re-education are 'dosed' in accordance with psychological principles, they lead to increased stability of mental function. In fact most of the social devices employed by the I.S.T.D. are directed towards this end. *These auxiliary measures are, however, applied simultaneously with analytical (or other) techniques.* This is rendered possible by the 'team method' already described. In other words, the team as a whole mobilizes transferences through its *actual behaviour* towards the delinquent, whilst the therapist proceeds with his *analytical work*. In practice this constitutes a departure from classical analytical therapy but not from understanding of the dynamics of transference.

From this divergence there arises an issue of considerable moment to research on delinquency. While it is true to say that the importance of disorders of super-ego development can scarcely be overestimated, it is also true that exclusive preoccupation with this aspect of delinquency deflects attention from research into the reality function of the ego. The psychopathic delinquent, for example, suffers not only from an apparent deficiency in guilt sense but from abnormalities of reality function. As a result partly of predisposition and partly of traumatic infantile experiences, he has lost or has never acquired a normal faculty of anticipation, popularly described as a realization of consequences. This 'immediacy' of response to excitation is certainly derived from early instinctual experience. In this respect as well as in the repeated and violent crises of uncontrolled behaviour, psychopathic delinquency is closer to a traumatic neurosis than to a psycho-neurosis or psychosis. There is indeed every probability that study of psychopathy will shed more light on ego development than do the more dramatic forms of psychotic abnormality.

If this view be correct it follows that the rôle of unconscious conflict and of unconscious fantasy formation in delinquency differs from that observed in the analysis of the psycho-neuroses where a fault in repression permits the development of compromise symptom-formations. Not only are the pathogenic fixation points in delinquency earlier in the developmental sense but one faulty fixation is followed by another, with the consequence that the ego itself is in a *constant traumatic state of dysfunction*: this is disguised only so long as his environment provides the potential delinquent with a degree of support and gratification which, judged by normal standards, would be regarded as excessive.

In this connection it is of interest to note that the split amongst child analysts in this country reflects divergences of view on this very matter. The orthodox Freudian school is interested in the phase of early ego development that antedates super-ego function: the Klein school of child psychology seeks to find super-ego explanations of function during the first year of life, at a time, that is, when, according to the classical Freudian view, libidinal function is mainly auto-erotic and the organization of the mental apparatus mainly narcissistic. It is the writer's view that the Klein school has been carried away by the superficial resemblances between psychotic and infantile function respectively and has thereby been led to a fallacious postulation of psychotic ego-super-ego-object 'positions' in the first years of life.

Another important source of confusion lies in the emphasis laid by different groups on the respective importance of aggressive and of libidinal impulse in infantile development. The orthodox school maintains the overriding importance of libidinal development whereas their opponents, believing in the existence of complicated object relationships in the first year of life, stress the overriding importance of aggressive impulse. Now it cannot be denied that destructive, sadistic and perverse sexual urges play an important part in delinquent disorders. But this does not justify the theory of super-ego conflict in the first year. On the contrary it suggests that the early increase in aggressive impulse occurring in children who later become delinquent, acts as a traumatic source of over-stimulation long before there is any question of super-ego formation or of the existence of that ambivalence which gives rise to neurotic conflict. Incidentally ambivalence is too frequently regarded as a purely psychopathological factor. Actually its development at an appropriate stage, i.e., when the ego is able to withstand frustration, is to some extent a guarantee against later outbreaks of delinquent conduct.

The foregoing are merely samples of research problems the solution of which will be arrived at by adequate research on delinquent states, in particular on psychopathic types of delinquency. In the meantime we may sum up the position in this country by saying that psycho-analytical research in delinquency is not only held up by the absence of a sufficiency of workers but obstructed by theoretical confusions and fallacious reconstructions of mental development. The outcome will depend largely on whether a sufficiently strong team of psycho-analysts, trained in the accepted theory and practice of psycho-analysis are able to devote special attention to the study of psychopathy.

Training

But when all is said the paramount need of criminological science in this country is a sufficiency of trained workers in every branch of the subject. No psychological training is demanded of magistrates or of the personnel of foster homes, remand centres, approved schools, Borstal institutions. It should be an obligatory condition of appointment that such training is undertaken and proficiency in it secured. The psychological instruction of probation officers should be greatly extended and their professional status raised to that of psychiatric social workers. The training of psychiatric social workers should be shorn of many pedantic and old-fashioned courses and should be reinforced by a thorough grounding in clinical psychology and psycho-analysis. Their status should be raised to that of a lay psychiatrist. Psychiatrists including prison medical officers should undergo an obligatory course of orientation in psycho-analytic theory; but of course society will always demand the service of a special group of psychiatrists who can take care of advanced cases without necessarily understanding or exploiting too much the unconscious factors leading to permanent breakdown.

Finally the training of psycho-analysts themselves needs reorganization. The scientific attainments of psycho-analysts in this country and the scientific disciplines practised by them are not of a high order. Roughly speaking only a half are given a thorough training in classical Freudian analysis. Moreover research workers require special training in the techniques of research and in the objective appraisal of evidence. It is unreasonable to expect that therapeutic practitioners should produce good researches. The study of delinquency is a special study calling for special training and experience. Indeed it should be a binding condition for all research workers that they should be specially trained, first, in the special techniques of diagnosis, prognosis and treatment and subsequently in the special disciplines of research.

PART II. '1949–55'*

Some few years ago I published a survey of the development of criminology in Britain from early in the century,[1] in the course of which it became clear that, although at first a number of independent agencies, religious, humanitarian, reformist, administrative, sociological and medico-psychological, had been groping vaguely towards an objective science of criminology, it was not until 1930 that the systematization of scientific methods of approach was signalized by the founding of the Institute for the Study and Treatment of Delinquency. Shortly afterwards some hospital psychiatric centres began to pay special attention to cases of delinquency and in a number of child guidance clinics the handling of delinquent juveniles began to play a significant part in their therapeutic programme. Other social agencies, e.g. youth centres, were of course also interested in the problem but more as a special focus for social therapy than a source of scientific information. Anyhow by 1948 it seemed that the stage was set for considerable advances in criminology provided only a sufficiency of trained workers supported by adequate funds could be found. It is therefore of some interest to enquire what progress has been made in the last six years.

Before coming to conclusions on this matter it is desirable to consider what were the main driving forces or incentives giving impetus to recent criminological work. These were in fact twofold. In the first place, psychiatry, sociology and educational psychology had, for various reasons connected with wartime necessity (treatment of psychiatric casualties, study of war-time conditions such as evacuation disorders, selection of wartime personnel, etc.) entered into a provisional working partnership and their combined activities had received a good deal of official administrative support. The expansion following on this support

---

* First published in the *Journal of Criminal Law, Criminology and Police Science*, **46**, No. 2, July–August 1955.

[1] Edward Glover: 'Outline of the Investigation and Treatment of Delinquency in Great Britain 1912–1948', in *Searchlights on Delinquency*, Imago Publishing Co., London, 1949. [See Part I.]

and the consequent increase in prestige both of psychiatry and of social psychology has continued apace although, to be sure, psychiatry has now lost a good deal of the popular acclaim it received in wartime and for a few years afterwards. The rapprochement between these cognate sciences has not, however, been damaged thereby, and it was natural that, when delinquency problems began to loom largely in the public eye, recourse should be had to team methods of approach.

The second and perhaps the more powerful impetus can be traced to general anxiety both in administrative circles and throughout the country following rumours of post-war waves of criminal violence, which, however exaggerated, were found to be based on sound statistical evidence. This anxiety was fostered by newspaper campaigns; and it is interesting to observe the changes which can be brought about by journalistic and popular clamour. Needless to say, in the long run these tended to become reactionary and obscurantist in tone, but in the first instance they added force to the demand for an objective criminology. This manifested itself in various directions. The Criminal Justice Act of 1948 reflected, although in an etiolated form, some current views on disposal and treatment of criminals. Also, at the instigation of the Home Office, official calls were made for municipalities to set up committees to deal with local problems of crime; newspapers and film companies gave an increasing amount of space to criminological articles and problems, and generally a not-too-hostile reception was accorded the view that juvenile delinquency in particular called for combined efforts in a social and psychological direction.

Recently this attitude has been tinged with a certain vindictiveness in the popular reaction to violent crimes committed by adolescents and adults, which again was encouraged by journalistic activities and reflected in them. Reinforced by such influential figures as the Lord Chief Justice, the clamour is now more definitely directed towards increased severity in the handling of such criminals. Not long ago an elder statesman, Lord Samuel, added strength to this movement by his somewhat antiquated moralistic animadversions on the subject of homosexual offences. It remains to be seen how far this retrogressive tendency will hamper the existence and patient expansion of measures based on a more objective and dispassionate attitude.

Some indication of the confusion of counsel existing on criminological policy was afforded by the Parliamentary reaction to the Report of the Royal Commission on Capital Punishment.[1] The work of this Commission was of course seriously handicapped by the Prime Minister of the time (Mr. Attlee) who, when appointing the Commission, expressly excluded from the terms of reference the propriety of abolishing the penalty. Nevertheless, and despite many timidities and inconsistencies, some of which are inherent in the examination of such an emotionally explosive issue, the Report, to which incidentally Professor Thorsten Sellin contributed weighty evidence, in effect constituted one of the most damaging indictments of capital punishment that has appeared in the criminological literature of this or any other country. Nevertheless the immediate public response, as indicated in public opinion polls, suggested that over 75 per cent were in favour of retaining the capital penalty; and in fact, when the issue was left to a free Parliamentary vote, the abolitionists were defeated by a narrow majority.

Incidentally it is significant that the evidence on prevention and prediction put before the Commission by the I.S.T.D.[2] was totally neglected in its Report. On the other hand the Commission's searching investigation of the validity of the M'Naghten Rules, although so far shelved by Parliament, will no doubt lead to some modification of existing rigidities in the judicial assessment of criminal responsibility. And the recommendation to establish institutions for supervision and research relating to cases of criminal psychopathy is likely to hasten the appearance of the earlier projected Eastes-Hubert Centre, and in general to strengthen the hands of modern criminologists. In short, progress in criminology depends to a considerable extent on the degree to which permanent officials in the Home Office and other administrative bodies or research foundations can leaven the policies likely to be fostered by elected representatives whose personal views may be influenced in a retrogressive direction by vigorous expression of public prejudice.

A further test of the strength of this prejudice will be afforded by the deliberations of the recently appointed Departmental

[1] *Report of the Royal Commission on Capital Punishment*, London, H.M.S.O., 1953.
[2] *Memorandum Presented by the I.S.T.D. to the Royal Commission on Capital Punishment*. London, H.M.S.O., 1953.

Committee on Homosexuality and Prostitution. Due largely to the publicity given in the press to certain sensational cases of homosexuality, a wave of public reaction reached the bar of the House of Commons and led to the appointment of a Committee which is conspicuous for the absence of all but one accredited expert on the subject. Hence the sanguine hopes of some sexual reformers that homosexual acts between consenting adults, provided they do not offend public decency, shall not be considered criminal, do not seem likely to be fulfilled.

SCIENTIFIC PROGRESS

To turn from general considerations to an assessment of progress in a scientific direction, it is of interest to enquire how far the Criminal Justice Act of 1948 has given official impetus to institutional effort. Study of the Prison Commissioner's Report[1] indicates that apart from increase in the number of open prisons, open Borstals, and classification centres, a beginning has been made with the organization of two special types of centre, recommended in the Act, namely, attendance centres and detention centres. Attendance centres, of which there are now some twenty in operation, run either by the police or by children's training committees, are intended to provide an alternative form of disposal for young offenders who do not require institutional treatment but are considered to need something more drastic than probation. The hours of attendance are limited to twelve and preventive, deterrent and reformative elements have all a place in the system.[2]

The detention centre, of which at the time of writing there are only two in existence, is intended to provide an alternative to imprisonment for offenders under 21 who do not yet require the prolonged residential training which is provided by an approved school or a Borstal, but who have not responded or are unlikely to respond to probation and for whom a fine would be inappropriate. Junior (14–17) and senior (17–21) centres are projected. The régime is 'strict and rigorous', the working week extends to

[1] *Reports of the Commissioners of Prisons*. London, H.M.S.O., 1952 and 1953.
[2] See John Spencer: 'A Note on Attendance Centres', *Brit. J. Delinq.*, 1, 230, 1951; also Roy Braithwaite: 'Attendance Centres for Young Offenders', *Brit. J. Delinq.*, 2, 242, 1952.

forty-four hours, and includes constructive occupation and whole or part-time education.[1]

Limited in scope and technique as they are, such official additions to the range of penal institutions do not give a complete idea of the expansion of modern and liberal methods in prisons, approved schools and Borstals. The reports of the prison commissioners are increasingly concerned with various forms of treatment and rehabilitation, and there is no doubt that a new tradition has been established which is likely to lead to a marked increase in the psychiatric and social work carried out in both open and closed institutions. Here again it may be said that advances in institutional criminology lie in the hands of permanent officials of the Home Office who by an enlightened interpretation of Acts and Regulations can add immeasurably to the strength of crimino-therapy, to say nothing of research. A recent study of prediction methods in Borstal undertaken on behalf of the commissioners by Dr. Hermann Mannheim, Reader in Criminology at London University, and Mr. L. T. Wilkins of Government Social Survey, is an apt case the report on which will shortly be published.

A similar tendency can be found in institutions existing outside the penal system. In a number of psychiatric hospital centres the previously unorganized and haphazard arrangements for dealing with delinquents have developed into special delinquent departments and an increasing number of special institutions for the treatment of maladjusted children are now run on modern multi-disciplined lines. But of course these are still few and far between.

Confirmation of this tendency in criminological work comes from a new quarter. Recent developments at the Institute for the Study and Treatment of Delinquency have provided means whereby modern developments in delinquency research can be estimated with some accuracy. The first of these was the founding of the *British Journal of Delinquency*, now in its fifth year of publication. The policy of this journal is to publish the best original articles available, to record in its 'Notes' various developments in criminology throughout the country and through its 'Research Calendar,' 'Reviews' and 'Abstracts' to keep readers abreast of current work.

[1] See also M. Grünhut: 'Juvenile Delinquents under Primitive Detention', *Brit. J. Delinq.*, 5, 191, 1955.

A number of impressions can already be recorded. To begin with, although the scientific standard of most articles is by no means all that might be desired, an increasing number of contributions are submitted from a number of different fields, and amongst these numerical priority must be given to articles dealing with the population of prisons, Borstals, approved schools, institutions for maladjusted children, youth centres, etc.

Secondly, it is clear that group surveys supported by reliable statistical methods are increasingly popular; also that there is an increasing tendency to organize team-methods of research. And although it cannot be said that the conclusions are very penetrating and although there is a certain sameness about them, it is all to the good that this spadework should be completed as early as possible.

On the other hand, there is a remarkable sparsity of what might be called purely clinical investigations of different types of delinquency, in particular of psycho-analytical studies. This is the more regrettable in that, in the writer's opinion, progress in delinquency work will in the long run depend more on detailed case-studies of different types of delinquency than on team surveys, however broad the scope of the latter may be and however impeccably they are carried out. One of the main drawbacks to this more general type of survey is precisely that it deals with vaguely specified groups, such as prison populations, without any special check on the types of offence. The result is of course broad conclusions which are not very likely to advance our knowledge or to sharpen our therapeutic instruments.[1]

The second source of information, particularly on the value of team research, has been made available through the foundation by the I.S.T.D. of a scientific society which so far goes by the name of the Scientific Group for the Discussion of Delinquency Problems. This now comprises about 200 experts drawn from the fields of psychiatry, psycho-analysis, general and educational psychology, social psychology and sociology, social work, penal administration, organic medicine, in particular neuro-physiology, genetics, statistics and the law.

It is of some interest to note that the first task of this new society

[1] See Edward Glover: 'Team Research on Delinquency: a Psycho-analytical Commentary', *Brit. J. Delinq.*, 4, 3, 173, 1954. [See this vol., sec. VI, part I.]

was and is to survey the different disciplines with a view to finding common definitions and factorial values that can increase the efficiency of team research. Needless to say this is by no means an easy task and it is doubtful whether it can be achieved by general discussions in a large group. A recent interesting account presented to the group by Drs. Grey Walter and Sessions Hodge[1] of the uses of the electro-encephalogram in the clinical study of different delinquent types showed very clearly that a prerequisite of coming to terms whereby the issues can be fruitfully discussed is to submit the operative concepts to a preliminary 'mixed' commission of enquiry.

Judging then by these two means of studying a cross-section of current research, work on delinquency seems about to show a snowball development. This must, however, be qualified by the consideration that a good deal of the work is mediocre and does little more than confirm ideas that have already been accepted for about twenty years. There is too little discrimination of terms, or, what amounts to the same thing, too easy acceptance of general captions, such as that of the 'broken home'. There is too little detailed clinical work, and too little exploration of specific criminological mechanisms in the clinical fields. And there is too marked a tendency to substitute various 'tests' for proper psychiatric examination. Finally there is too little scientific imagination used in exploring unfamiliar avenues, such as the relation of anti-social behaviour to psycho-somatic discharges.[2]

Incidentally, one of the less welcome consequences of the rapid increase in volume of delinquency work, particularly in the field of psychiatric social work, is a tendency on the part of social workers, fostered, no doubt by the misguided enthusiasm of those who train them, to apply all sorts of interpretative techniques in their work with parents. A good deal of this interference, although not exactly bogus, is based on a remarkable and rather smug overestimation of the virtues of pseudo-analytical therapy. It is hard enough for a trained analyst applying his elaborate and lengthy

---

[1] R. Sessions Hodge, V. T. Walter and W. Grey Walter: 'Juvenile Delinquency: an Electro-physiological, Psychological and Social Study', *Brit. J. Delinq.*, 3, 155, 1953.

[2] See Edward Glover: 'On the Desirability of Isolating a Functional (Psycho-somatic) Group of Delinquent Disorders', *Brit. J. Delinq.*, 1, 104, 1950. Reprinted in *On the Early Development of Mind*.

techniques to the treatment of selected favourable cases, to obtain satisfactory results. What happens when half-boiled social workers, half-trained in analytical techniques, apply them indiscriminately in the delicate task of social guidance can but be left to the imagination.

One last matter may be noted. It concerns the allocation of research funds to the specific purposes of delinquency research. During those earlier years when it was comparatively easy to obtain research grants for any sociological effort supported by university centres, it was practically impossible to obtain support for researches in delinquency, which apparently were felt to be without the scope of social and psychological research, or possibly not respectable enough. In the past few years, owing largely to the increase of popular interest in 'crime waves' previously noted in this survey, this policy has changed. Recently some substantial grants have been made for work on delinquency. But these have been mostly in support of general surveys which are unlikely to do more than underline conclusions which are already a little shopsoiled. It is practically impossible to obtain grants for detailed clinical research without which the larger conclusions cannot be given point. Foundation executives appear to be remarkably conservative in reaction to pioneer work on delinquency, a fact which stands in interesting contrast to the readiness with which they will support the most recondite researches in natural science. There will never be any effective progress in delinquency work until this timid and shortsighted policy is reversed.

PART III. '1956-59'

In the few years that have elapsed since the last survey[1] the prediction that criminology would undergo a snowball development has in most respects been fulfilled. The retrogression of public opinion noted in that survey has been arrested and the general public is more reconciled to the spread of criminological influences in Courts of Justice, penal institutions, psychiatric centres and in social and educational institutions dealing with pre-delinquent and delinquent populations. The alarm created by 'crime waves' has also abated to some extent, but is easily aroused by newspaper comments on current increases in crimes of violence, especially amongst juveniles.

At the same time it would be a mistake to assume that the hard core of public resistance to the scientific study and treatment of crime has substantially decreased. What has happened is that the increase in the number of criminological workers at influential centres has at last succeeded in creating a new tradition; and the more enlightened members of the public, following and spreading this tradition, have succeeded in driving some of the obscurantist and anxiety-ridden opposition of the general public underground.

Interesting exceptions are afforded by the fate of the Royal Commission's Report on Capital Punishment and by the reactions of the public and of the Government to the Wolfenden Report on Homosexuality and Prostitution. Although the former report was one of the most enlightened and educative documents produced on capital punishment, the Government announced (November 1955) that it was not prepared to accept any of its major recommendations, and later (February 1956) introduced a bill to retain the death penalty which was defeated by 292 to 263 votes. A later motion by Mr. Chuter Ede, a former Home Secretary, calling for the abolition or suspension of capital punishment was carried. Facilities were then given to Mr. Silverman's private bill to

[1] Edward Glover: 'Delinquency Work in Britain', *J. Criminal Law, Criminology and Police Science*, **46**, No. 2, July-Aug. 1955. [See Section II, Part I, this volume.]

abolish or suspend capital punishment (introduced November 1955). This bill was carried in the House of Commons (March 1956) and rejected in the House of Lords (July 1956). Still later (1957) a Government sponsored measure, the Homicide Act, was passed, modifying the conditions of application of capital punishment, abolishing the doctrine of 'constructive malice', amending the law regarding 'provocation' and suicide pacts, but retaining the death penalty for a list of 'capital murders'.

Controversy over the findings of the Wolfenden Report on Homosexuality and Prostitution has continued to rage. The most publicized recommendation, viz. that homosexual acts committed in private between consenting adults should not be regarded as criminal offences, constituted a remarkable advance. Violent and sometimes abusive opposition in press and public discussion was, however, soon apparent and it surprised no one when the Government officially refused to legislate in the directions proposed (December 1957). The subject was debated in the House of Commons late in 1958 when it was agreed to take note of but not to implement the recommendations of the Committee. The Wolfenden findings on prostitution were not remarkable for deep insight into a problem concerning which, in any case, little constructive evidence was offered. Its recommendations were in effect confined to raising the fines for street solicitation, with the threat of a sentence of three months' imprisonment for the third offence. It was also suggested that the penalties for procuring should be increased and it would appear that the Government will embody these recommendations in an appropriate Act. One cannot but view the outcome of the Royal Commission and of the Departmental Committee with mixed feelings. On the one hand it is clear that public opinion is not yet ripe for fundamental changes (although, to be sure, the recommendation regarding homosexuality would merely have meant a return to conditions existing before 1885): on the other hand, despite the mobilization of deep emotional prejudice by both reports, and the legislative anticlimax to which they gave rise, their ultimate effect will be in all probability in the direction of full abolition of the death penalty, and a more humane, even enlightened court attitude to homosexuality. The problem of prostitution will remain unaffected.

Home-Office Developments

Perhaps the most significant developments in criminology of the past three years have originated in and from the Home Office itself. First comes the foundation of a Home Office Criminological Research Unit which has already embarked on a number of researches carried out either directly through the Home Office or indirectly through University and other centres. Now that the citadel of penal administration, for so long impregnable to the impact of modern ideas, has been breached, or perhaps it would be fairer to say, infiltrated, the possibilities of administrative penal changes 'from within' the Law have been greatly increased.

The second development, initiated by the present Home Secretary, Mr. R. A. Butler, has taken the form of inviting the University of Cambridge, through its Law Department, to form an Institute of Criminology. The formation of such a body was one of the original aims of the Institute for the Study and Treatment of Delinquency, which owing to the shortage of personnel and lack of funds could not be implemented.

The effect of these developments on the advancement of research will of course prove the ultimate test of their utility. In neither case is the situation free from risks, particularly of slanting research too directly towards institutional case-material. It should be realized that both recognition of the causes of delinquency and the institution of effective measures of prevention, depend not so much on the study of convicted criminals, as on the investigation of borderline cases and of the pre-delinquent phase existing in childhood from which organized delinquency arises. This can be achieved only in non-penal organizations. It is of course natural for the Home Office to focus attention on the population of penal institutions from prison via Borstal to the approved school, but it misses the main point of research which is to establish causes and develop treatment along whatever lines are called for.

Regarding the organization of a criminological institute, it is not quite clear why this was centred in the Law Department of an academic institution. It would have seemed more appropriate to organize it in London, which not only covers the most substantial proportion of metropolitan population and is therefore the main centre of criminal activities but provides the most extensive criminological sources in the country. The value of the new institute will obviously depend on the degree to which it enlists the co-operation of extra-mural (non-legal) sciences.

In spite of these new developments in policy, or rather, just because of them, it will be noted that the Home Office has landed itself, in principle, in an embarrassing dilemma. As far as disposal (treatment) in particular of adolescent delinquency is concerned it is lending itself increasingly to the idea of 'short and sharp' correction, the indeterminate sentence and other measures which are at least as punitive as they are corrective. Yet its nascent interest in psycho-social measures of 'disposal' and in research certainly opens the door to non-penal policies. In view of its long attachment to obscurantist systems of disposal it is difficult not to feel unsure of the whole-heartedness of the Home Office conversion. *Timeo Danaos et dona ferentes* is perhaps an unduly suspicious judgement to pass on the present administrative situation; but at least there is as yet no sure sign that supporters of scientific and humanistic criminology can afford to relax either the direct or the indirect pressure they have brought to bear on Government Departments in recent years.[1]

[1] [Note 1959] A recent White Paper emanating from the Home Office and reflecting, *inter alia*, some of the views of the present Home Secretary (*Penal Practice in a Changing Society*, H.M.S.O. Feb. 1959) indicates the fundamental ambivalence which underlies Governmental policies regarding the future development of criminology, and which has indeed been sharpened by the modern leaning of the Home Office towards penal reform. For while the Paper officially concedes what indeed ought to be self-evident propositions, viz., that 'research [on the causes of crime] is not necessarily best conducted by official agencies', and that 'the outlook, training and environment of the academic (*sic*) worker give him advantages in some kinds of research over the staff of a Government Department', it immediately hamstrings its own efforts and limits the efforts of those non-penal research centres it is ready to support, by saying that it will further only those outside researches that employ 'suitable' methods. The Paper states plainly that it 'does not seek to deal with those deep-seated causes which, even were they fully understood, would be largely beyond the reach of Government action'. A more deplorable and stultifying policy in research it would be difficult to conceive.

Not only so, the list of the researches carried out or sponsored by the Home Office Research Unit is concerned for the largest part with investigations of the effect (or possible effect) of existing (or projected) methods of handling criminals in prisons, borstals, approved schools, or under probation. It is nowhere admitted that the very need for such investigations is a tacit confession of the partial or total failure of these

INSTITUTIONAL FACILITIES

Apart from this it is to be noted that the number of prisons and Borstals has steadily increased. These institutions have decreased in size and more 'open' prisons have been instituted. With the rise of population, however, there is more overcrowding. The building of the long projected Eastes-Hubert Institution for the treatment and supervision of criminal psychopaths has at last commenced.

These changes would not of themselves necessarily constitute advances were it not for the concurrent development of staff training. This has been signalized by the better staffing of the Imperial Training School at Wakefield and by the development of the so-called Norwich Scheme for improving relations between prisoners and prison staffs, which it is hoped will bring about a gradual transition of the disciplinary officer from a custodial to a more rehabilitative function. Research on prediction, selection and classification of offenders is preceeding apace and has been given point by investigations on sentencing policy,[1] on variations in the use of prison sentences and on alternatives to short prison sentences (London School of Economics). As judged by the articles submitted to the *British Journal of Delinquency* a steadily increasing amount of investigation (psychiatric, psychological, educational and statistical) by prison, Borstal and approved school staffs, is being carried out. In approved schools the classification system has grown with the opening of another very institutions, the probation system always excepted, to achieve at the same time radical and humane treatment of criminal behaviour. Added to which the sections on penal method contain observations on 'preventive detention' and the 'indeterminate sentence' which breathe a totalitarian spirit regarding the relation of society to the individual, all this of course under the guise of penal reform.

This apparently ineradicable ambivalence of State Departments to individual crime pervades the whole of their administrative policies from diagnosis to treatment. Granting the inalienable right of society to protect individuals and groups from the attacks and depredations of criminals, there is no justification for covering the punitive aim of penal measures with the rationalisations of 'reform', even if these reformist aims are congenial to sociologists, psychiatrists or psycho-analysts. Diagnosis and treatment are scientific procedures in which penal motives have no part or place.

[1] Mannheim, Spencer and Lynch: 'Magisterial Policy in the London Juvenile Courts', *Brit. J. Delinq.*, **8**, 1–13, 2–119, 1957.

classifying school at Redhill. More psychiatric social workers are being appointed at these schools and more use is being made of local psychiatric specialists.

Probation Services

Improvement in the training of probation officers (including some psycho-analytical courses) and the increased use of group discussions led by psychiatrists promise greater understanding on the part of probation officers of their own motivations and their attitudes and feelings towards their charges. A recent article by Wilkins[1] suggests that although so far the results obtained by probation (as judged by reconvictions) are not strikingly different from those in which probation is less frequently exercised, nevertheless a larger proportion of offenders who are now sent to prison or Borstal could be put on probation without any change in the reconviction rate as a whole, a finding which adds considerable force to the recommendations of those who, working at the Institute for the Study and Treatment of Delinquency (I.S.T.D.) and out-patient psychiatric and child clinics have consistently supported the adoption of 'ambulant' treatment of selected delinquents in place of sending them to penal institutions.

Out-Patient Treatment

Actually the effective range of 'ambulant' treatment has extended still farther and we may assume that within a reasonable period it will be possible to arrange for such out-patient treatment at most psychiatric centres and child guidance clinics. It would no doubt be more suitable to organize non-penal delinquency centres throughout the country, but in the meantime more rapid results will be obtained by using existing organizations. There should, however, be closer liaison between child guidance centres and educational organizations. This would accelerate the adoption of a nation-wide 'screening' system which by assembling cases of general behaviour disorder would succeed in netting those predisposed to criminal conduct.[2]

[1] L. T. Wilkins: 'A small Comparative Study of the Results of Probation', *Brit. J. Delinq.*, **8**, 201–9, 1958.
[2] See also Section VII; Part III, p. 347.

Research

In addition an increasing number of psychiatrists, working independently of penal institutions, are taking an interest in clinical researches on criminology; and the proceedings of the *Scientific Group for the Discussion of Delinquency Problems* (founded by the I.S.T.D.) have served to encourage this interest. The work of Mannheim and Wilkins constitutes an outstanding advance (especially in the use of more refined statistical techniques), as does that of Radzinowicz (sexual offences, a predominantly legal study), of Grünhut (on juvenile offenders), of Gibbens (a psychiatric study of prostitution) and of Wortis (depression and crime). In fact, judged by the contributions to the *British Journal of Delinquency*, there are few aspects of criminology that are not dealt with in an increasingly competent fashion by accredited workers.

The Future

The rapid growth of a multi-disciplined approach to delinquency and the relative increase in facilities for research and treatment indicated above are of a most satisfactory nature. And there can be no doubt not only that criminology is becoming a more organized science but that from the point of view both of study and treatment it is creating a body of specialized workers. It will not be long before a standard of specialized training is demanded in all branches of the work. Even magistrates are now becoming accustomed to being lectured on the subject, and may in the foreseeable future have to submit with a good grace or even as a condition of employment to what would once have been regarded as the ignominy of training courses.

Undue optimism for the future should, however, be tempered by three considerations. The first of these is obvious enough, viz. that the increase in facilities is only relative. Under existing conditions only the fringes of the problem can be dealt with; and until more workers are trained in scientific method, no very radical changes can be expected.

The second consideration is more fundamental. Scientific work on delinquency has been so long in arrears that most of the present research consists in making up for lost time, carrying out psychiaric, sociological and penological surveys which of necessity deal only with the more superficial aspects of the subject or, with the application in diagnosis and treatment of a few general principles that were discovered and have been applied for many years in cognate sciences, particularly psycho-analysis and social psychology. All this spade-work is of course essential and no doubt researches on crime will for some time to come be of this general nature. They cannot, however, be expected to strike to the roots of the problem or to give birth to radical changes in method. However reformed by the extension of diagnostic and therapeutic facilities, prisons, Borstals, approved schools and even remand homes are still penal institutions; a probation officer, however much a friend, is still an officer of the law backed by the penal authority of the court, and criminals, even when pathological types are isolated and given special attention, are still criminals in the eyes both of the law and of the general community. All investigations carried out in penal institutions must suffer from the existence of a penal setting however much this is disguised by efforts to treat or to rehabilitate prisoners or Borstal boys.

Thirdly: although it is essential to investigate crime by a combination of various disciplines, the strength of a research team is the strength of its weakest link.[1] This link can be recognized by the degree to which it relies on descriptive criteria, i.e., collecting, classifying and drawing conclusions from data of observation. In the writer's opinion progress in criminology will depend ultimately in the application of psycho-analytical methods of observation and interpretation not only to criminal data but to data drawn from 'normal' groups. However subject to methodological and subjective error, this is the only procedure by which the wells of human motivation can be tapped. At present, it is true, the number of direct psycho-analytical investigations of criminals is still very much in arrears; and recourse has had to be had to psycho-analytical interpretation at second-hand. On the other hand it may be expected that the psycho-analysis of normal persons from infancy onward and of disordered characters who present occult delinquent reactions will materially advance our knowledge of 'open' offenders.

This applies with equal force to problems of prevention and

[1] See Glover: 'Team Research in Delinquency: a Psycho-analytical Commentary', *Brit. J. Delinq.*, 4, 173–88, 1954. [Section VII, part I, this volume.]

treatment. Without direct knowledge of unconscious phenomena such as transference and counter-transference, and without some capacity to recognize unconscious etiological factors, all treatment of offenders is little more than empirical. In any case, treatment in penal institutions merely tells us something of treatment under penal conditions. Moreover, without knowledge of the unconscious processes involved in upbringing we cannot develop a *science of upbringing* to supplant the existing system of trial and error, and consequently cannot produce reliable blueprints for the prevention of crime. We have not yet applied fully the actual psychoanalytical information which exists concerning the development of unconscious guilt and its influence on human conduct, and much may be expected from a fuller application of this knowledge. But we need to know much more. To give but one example, we need to have precise information regarding that elusive problem, 'the option of disease'; we need to know what determines the unconscious choice of neurosis, psychosis, character distortion, sexual perversion or delinquency. And in each case we must be able to recognize the precise point (or points) of fracture of the mental apparatus. This alone will call for the most recondite and painstaking researches into the different phases of mental development. Our existing discoveries are merely signposts to fresher and deeper researches. Of their nature the sociologist, the laboratory psychologist, the statistician and their acolytes merely stand at strategic outposts of descriptive research. Invaluable and essential as their work may be, they cannot be expected to solve the problem of human suffering or the seeming paradox that the criminal who inflicts suffering on society is himself a victim of unconscious suffering. Medical psychology stands or falls by the study of mental suffering, and fallible as it may be, the only systematic science that seeks to uncover the unconscious dynamic sources of mental suffering happens to be psycho-analysis. Despite the recent multiplication of applied methods, passing under new and sometimes rather pretentious labels, there is little really 'new' in criminological research, or at any rate little that was not already known to psycho-analysts thirty-five years ago.

III. DIAGNOSIS AND TREATMENT OF PATHOLOGICAL DELINQUENCY

Part I   Diagnosis
Part II   Treatment

SECTION III

DIAGNOSIS AND TREATMENT OF PATHOLOGICAL DELINQUENCY

[1937-59]

When the Institute for the Study and Treatment of Delinquency was founded in 1931, its first objective was the organization of an out-patient clinic – the Psychopathic Clinic. Essentially a medico-psychological venture, it at the same time constituted a proving-ground for the hypothesis that the old system of penal administration is out of date, in so far at any rate as pathological cases of criminality are concerned. In short it supported the thesis implied in the system of probation that selected cases of criminality can be treated at liberty. It differed from the probationary system in so far as it abandoned entirely the criminal implications of probation and substituted instead the concept of behaviour disorders which could be treated along medico-psychological lines.

Naturally the first concern of the staff was purely therapeutic. But it soon became apparent that the possibility existed of developing a systematic classification of pathological delinquencies. When after some years the intake of offenders began to follow a standard pattern it was decided to initiate a five-year survey of the clinical material. This commenced in 1937. It was unfortunate that the last two years of the survey coincided with the development of active hostilities in the Second World War. Nevertheless allowing for this disturbing factor, the results of the survey were significant enough. They were first published as a chapter of Studies of Criminal Science *and subsequently as an I.S.T.D. pamphlet. The present outline of diagnosis and treatment is based largely on this early observation, amplified by subsequent experience and by some considerations of the principles involved. It remains to be seen whether the conclusions arrived at regarding pathological cases can be applied also to the handling of a proportion of so-called 'responsible criminals'. Such a policy would call for more extensive social and sociological investigations than are possible at a special *out-patient clinic. It seems probable, however, that the next fifty years will witness the most profound and far reaching changes not only in the handling of crime but in the attitude of the responsible ministries to the problem. At the very least the responsibility for the treatment of juvenile criminals will be less the concern of the Home Office (except in so far as public safety must be maintained) and more the duty of the Ministries of Health and Education.*

To the lay observer of human behaviour the diagnosis of delinquency would seem to call for no exhaustive effort. Delinquent conduct, he might well assume, is clearly enough specified and differentiated in legal codes which represent in the long run a consensus of social disapproval of activities that are or appear to be detrimental to the legitimate interests of other individuals or groups. Contrary to this apparently reasonable social assumption the clinical psychologist maintains that in certain cases infractions of social codes are in the nature of medico-psychological 'symptoms', the origin of which cannot be determined by superficial or individual inspection and rational assessment of their social or individual purpose. In so doing he challenges to some extent the generally accepted validity of the doctrines of criminal responsibility *which maintains that man is a rational and responsible animal whose actions are or ought to be invariably governed by 'free will' and who deliberately breaks the law solely from conscious motives of self indulgence, gain, aggrandizement or aggression. To be sure the clinical psychologist is ready to agree that the concepts of rational man and of criminal responsibility will suffice in a majority of instances, such for example, as breaches of traffic regulations, where the assumption of conscious ego-centric motives of convenience or laziness appears to account adequately for the conduct in question. Even so he would be prepared to maintain that where offences of this usually trivial nature, e.g. neglect of lighting-up regulations, are repeated frequently enough and in the face of repeated legal sanctions or where they give rise repeatedly to serious consequences, such conduct cannot be accounted for solely by deliberate ego-centric motives.*

As a matter of historical interest the rationalistic concept of criminal responsibility received its most damaging blow at the hands of legal authorities themselves long before present day clinical psychology was even conceived. For the commission of judges who promulgated the M'Naghten Rules in 1843 gave expression in effect to the enlightened view that the crime of murder may in certain cases of insanity call for psychiatric assessment and a priori for treatment rather than for the automatic application of penal sanctions.

A second factor leading to weakening of the rational doctrine of criminal responsibility is of more recent origin, namely the observation and classification in clinical terms of behaviour and character disorders, *e.g. hysterical conduct, obsessive (compulsive) conduct and persecutory types of character reaction, none of which are governed either by free will or reason. To be sure character disorders did not at first include criminal behaviour partly because at first the medical psychologist was apt to take the social concept of criminal responsibility at face value and to regard the criminal as merely perverse; but it soon became obvious that in principle at any rate some forms of social or sexual aggression in otherwise sane offenders were also psycho-pathological in nature.*

These two developments constitute the thin end of the psychiatric wedge which the modern clinician seeks to drive more deeply into the matrix of criminal conduct. How far he will succeed is an open question. Nor indeed is the clinician concerned to answer it. Whereever society may ultimately draw the line, the clinician will continue to be guided by his own empirical standards, maintaining only that where crime is an expression of or a reaction to mental disorder, the rôle of society is limited in the first place to that of maintaining social safety and in the second to the provision of treatment suitable to the psycho-pathological state. Whatever policy society may adopt, he will therefore continue to maintain that the prerequisite of a rational criminology is accurate diagnosis.

PART I. DIAGNOSIS

The first step towards accurate diagnosis is accurate examination. In principle, legal diagnosis is concerned with the classification and evaluation of behavouristic *end-products;* clinical diagnosis seeks to correlate these end results with the *state of the individual's mind*. This involves an entirely fresh classification of criminal conduct or at any rate of such criminal conduct as can be proved to be due to mental disorder. Psychiatry in other words has extended its frontiers by establishing an enclave in rational criminology.

Regarding the technique of clinical diagnosis it may be said at once that its accuracy depends not simply on the recognition and classification of different types of 'criminal conduct'. That course would land us once again at the dead end of legal diagnosis. Simple theft, for example, may be committed by persons in whom no mental abnormality can be detected; or, on the other hand, it may be a manifestation, *inter alia*, of an obsessional (compulsive) state, of sexual fetishism, of alcoholism, of the climacteric or of larval insanity. In short, mental diagnosis involves first and foremost an examination of the various parts and functions of the whole of mind, whether normal or abnormal.

It is here that the science of psycho-analysis has rendered considerable service to psychiatry. For not only has it shown that by far the larger part of mind is unconscious but by setting out a theory of mental structure, dynamics and economics, it permits a *balanced survey of the total function of mind*. This indeed is the essence of psycho-analytical examination, one which calls, however, for a close acquaintance with a great variety of norms. By this, means alone can pathological crime be placed in its proper perspective.

CLINICAL EXAMINATION

Space does not permit an exhaustive account of the *routines* of examination[1] but the following may be regarded as its essential

[1] An outline of the methods and rationale of psycho-analytical examination is given in the author's textbook *Psycho-Analysis*, Part III, 2nd ed., Staples Press, 1947.

aims; viz: to establish the nature of the individual's instinctual life, to trace the development of his ego and in particular of that specialized part of the ego which subserves the moral faculties (described by psycho-analysts as the super-ego), to estimate the force of his reality feeling, and the degree to which it has influenced the moral faculties (an approach incidentally that calls for a parallel assessment of intellectual capacity), to recognize the prevailing mental modes or mechanisms by which the mind seeks to control stresses of excitation, and to establish what major emotional and instinctual stresses have set the mental apparatus out of gear, an approach which includes the recording of physical illnesses or deformities that may have exacerbated mental stress. Then, and then only is the psychiatrist in a position to evaluate the criminal behaviour and correlate it with the individual's general state of mind.

As a matter of interest the clinician's tendency to concentrate on 'symptoms' to the neglect of the patient's general state of mind is responsible for much of the scepticism with which modern clinical approaches to crime have been met. For while the layman is prepared to admit the existence of the classical mental disorders, he tends to resist any attempt to include criminal conduct amongst them. This difficulty can be resolved by adopting a *general functional approach*. For it will soon become apparent that this approach is in fact more obviously appropriate to the diagnosis of delinquency than to that of insane or neurotic conduct.

To make this point clearer we need only paraphrase in more popular terms the diagnostic factors indicated above. In examining instinctual factors we are concerned to establish *primary motive*, in considering the moralistic and realistic aspects of the ego, we are concerned with *moral character and common sense* respectively, in examining mental mechanisms we are ultimately studying *psychic patterns of behaviour* and in evaluating conditions of mental stress past and present we are concerned with what the law regards as *extenuating circumstances;* motive, moral character, commonsense, social responsibility, established habits of behaviour and extenuating circumstances of stress are even more essential to the appraisal of criminal conduct than in the diagnosis of neurosis or insanity.

Nevertheless when examining some types of criminal behaviour it is impossible to overlook their close resemblance to symptoms of classical mental disorder, e.g. the resemblance of kleptomania to the compulsive rituals of an obsessional neurosis; and as we shall see it is convenient to classify such types of crime in accordance with these resemblances. But in a substantial proportion of pathological crimes the disorder can be traced to a cumulative series of disturbances of the different departments and functions of the mind, which have not been encapsulated in the form of classical mental disorders but have expressed themselves mainly in characteristic behaviour which runs counter to the social standards of the community. In other words, they are character disorders.

Here we must pause to bear in mind certain practical considerations. A comprehensive mental examination of the type described takes time; a period of two to three weeks may be required to complete even a cursory survey of any one person's mental state and social reactions. And Courts of Summary Jurisdiction from which about 63 per cent of the Portman Clinic cases are recruited do not favour lengthy periods of remand: higher courts in any case cannot wait, for this would involve remand until the next sessions. Fortunately for the case-load of delinquency clinics it is possible to focus the examination on essential points, the nature of which depends on the three main sets of observation: (1) that every mental disorder can be traced to a combination of three factors, namely, *constitutional, developmental* (or predisposing) and *immediate* (or precipitating); (2) that the closer delinquent acts resemble the symptoms of classical mental disorder the more certain they are to merit the rating of 'pathological crime' and (3) that the onset duration and distribution of criminal episodes enables one to estimate the intractability of delinquent acts. In other words the general examination of the delinquent mind includes also a *case history;* and a careful case history at the same time sharpens and shortens diagnostic work.

Constitutional Factors

Regarding the first set of factors we may note that apart from congenital conditions which can be detected by inspection or other varieties of physical examination (e.g. deformities, hormonal deficiencies and the like) and from unmistakeable cases of mental deficiency the *constitutional* factors that operate in delinquent cases can only be inferred from close study of mental patterns particularly during the first post-natal years. This is true also of many forms of mental deficiency which although innate often cannot be detected or distinguished from neurotic disturbances until the child is of an age when mental tests can be applied with accuracy. The main factors include excess or deficiency of various instinctual drives, particularly the infantile component-impulses of sexuality and of infantile forms of aggression, a low threshold for stresses (e.g. following frustration), anxiety readiness and marked psychic tendencies on the one hand towards regression and on the other to deal with tension by violent reactions directed towards the environment. There are no doubt many other constitutional contributions which will be recognized in course of time. In the meantime it is to be observed that no one of the above list is specific to delinquency, and that even if all such factors can be found acting in summation we are not yet in a position to distinguish during early childhood between potential delinquent psychopathy and potential schizophrenia. The most that can be achieved by examination of constitutional factors is to narrow the grounds of probability (e.g. a passive instinctual type is unlikely to become a delinquent), to refine to some extent the prognosis of whatever disorder may be found and to provide some criteria for the selection of particular techniques of treatment. Constitutional factors should, however, never be allowed to bias the observer against treatment. For even in outspoken cases of mental deficiency complications of a purely psychological nature are certain to develop and often include delinquent reactions; these it should be the aim of psycho-therapy to reduce by one technique or another.

Developmental Factors

Under these circumstances a heavy onus lies on the observer to recognize the *predisposing or developmental factors* that are liable to lead in the long run to delinquent conduct. It is in this particular field that progress in the understanding of pathological delinquency mainly lies. These predisposing factors may be classified broadly in a number of ways, depending on whether or not the observer recognizes the existence of unconscious processes. Assuming that he does so we can then distinguish between on the one hand *central or endo-psychic* factors the most important of which are unconscious and on the other *peripheral or environmental factors*. In point of fact no such arbitrary distinction is satisfactory, since *there is a constant interaction between these two sets of factors which influences the organization of unconscious and conscious reactions to environment.*

It is essential to underline this last point since a good deal of modern work on delinquency, although useful enough in its way tends to ignore this vital consideration. It is increasingly customary to trace the predisposition to delinquent conduct to faults in 'nurture' or 'upbringing'. Here the stress laid on the 'broken home', and 'separation anxiety', on the 'affectionless child' who has responded in a negative or hostile way to lack of familial affection, and the importance attached, logically enough, to the influence of illegitimacy, parental neglect, physical or mental cruelty and the like. All this is sound enough but it is little more than a development of 'familial sociology' and *neglects the decisive importance of the unconscious (endopsychic) reaction of the child to these familial conditions.* The influence of a cruel, neglectful or unaffectionate parent depends, for example, not just on the traumatic effect of these conditions but mainly on the type of endopsychic reaction to a cruel neglectful or affectionless *parent.* Subjected to these conditions the child develops a warped and sadistic super-ego which the delinquent seeks to deal with by a process of eversion by which its secondary sadism is directed to the external 'environment'.

It follows from this that the examination of developmental factors turns in three main directions, (*a*) exaggerations or deficiencies and frustrations of the instinctual inheritance, in particular the balance of sadistic and masochistic impulse manifested in successive phases; (*b*) obstacles to the development of a sound reality ego, and faulty organization of unconscious and conscious moral faculties or instances (the different facets of the super-ego) and (*c*) the overstress of projective mechanisms which when combined with an exaggerated sadism tend to drive the delinquent to anti-social (anti-environmental) conduct. Naturally these three sets of factors act in combination but in view of the infractions of social codes inherent in delinquent conduct *it seems justifiable to give priority to warping, deficiency and eversion of the super-ego which is the organ of moral and ethical communication with the external world.*

Next to the examination of abnormal super-ego processes, comes a contrasting examination of disturbances of *reality testing,* a function which is carried out by the reality ego. Where the balance is in favour of reality estimations we may expect such manifestations as control and discretion in the matter of primitive instinctual satisfaction. On the other hand there can be no doubt that whatever warps reality estimations of the expediency of legal codes (a different matter from moral and ethical estimations of the rights of society and of other individuals which lie within the province of the super-ego) contributes to the predisposition to pathological delinquency.

Ideally speaking these investigations should include a period of psycho-analytically directed observation or of frequent consultations with the offender. As has been indicated the exigencies of court procedure do not favour such a logical procedure. Fortunately it is possible with increasing experience to elicit within a few consultations information which permits plausible deductions as to the nature of early abnormal mental function. And this when confirmed by the subsequent life history of the delinquent permits a reasonably accurate diagnosis of pathological delinquency.

Precipitating Factors

Regarding the *immediate* (or *precipitating*) factors, it is naturally of importance to take into account the severity of any immediate stress. Fundamentally, extreme stresses are in the nature either of instinctual frustrations or situations that set up violent excitation within the mind. These two types are easiest to observe in childhood, where either family prohibitions set up tension, or where lack of adequate gratification (love and affection) produces a head of frustration; or again where situations (scenes) of family violence or sexual activity set up high degrees of excitation (with conscious or unconscious phantasy). During the school period these primary forms become more elaborate, and include fresh varieties derived from strains in educational adaptation. In adult life an apparently immense variety of possible stresses exists. These can be classified in large groups, e.g. stresses in love, in domestic life, in work and in social contact. It is one of the tasks of forensic sociology to classify these multifarious precipitating factors in terms of frustration or situational stimuli (e.g. gang influences); but in the last resort they should be estimated in terms of the inner (endopsychic) reactions they produce. In particular the offender's inner *estimation* of environmental stresses should be recognized, e.g. where he reacts to unavoidable stresses as if they were deliberate persecutory activities on the part of external individuals or of society as a whole.

It should be remembered, however, that not all immediate factors are decisive in inducing a delinquent outburst: precipitating stresses may be traced over a considerable period *acting in summation*. Not only so, not all precipitating stresses should be taken at face value. An apparently economic factor for example may operate because of the psychological deficiencies associated with the poor economic background. This can frequently be observed where the pilferer does not convert the stolen property to use and where the act of stealing is more important than what is stolen. This tendency is reinforced in obsessional types of stealing where the factor of unconscious symbolism links not only the present with past emotional stresses but determines the nature of the object stolen. This accounts for the apparently 'useless' nature of many acts of compulsive theft.

The Offence

Such considerations lead naturally to a study of the *history of the offence*, an investigation which should reach back to the character tendencies existing between infancy and the age of legal responsibility. It should be recognized not only that the narcissistic organization of the young child makes him react in egocentric and destructive ways but that during this phase reactions that would later be called delinquent are not *organized*. They are more sporadic, seemingly capricious and immediate. In fact there is considerable justification for regarding these earlier years as constituting a *pre-delinquent phase*, a view which adds considerable point to early preventive measures. Nevertheless the later organized patterns can frequently be recognized during this period. In fact the general outline of a delinquent system can often be prognosticated during early childhood.

Examination of later phases of development up to mid-adolescence takes three directions: first to trace the emergence of *delinquent* from a *pre-delinquent* system; second, to follow the continuity, or sometimes spread of the delinquent system and its organization; and third to correlate attacks of delinquent conduct with important changes in the emotional milieu or important fluctuations in the instinctual forces. The best example of the former is delinquency following the birth of a rival sibling and of the latter phases of delinquency during the earlier pubertal years. Naturally the same estimations are made in the case of adult delinquency, although it is to be noted that as a rule the essential character of the offence does not change much between 18 and 40 years of age, and that in consequence precipitating factors do not feature so obviously in adult as they do in juvenile cases.

Classification

With this information in hand, we are ready to venture a *diagnosis* and thereby to commit ourselves to a *system of classification* during which the legal diagnosis arrived at by the Court is translated into terms of mental or physical disorder. This task of classification is a difficult one and can be best approached by isolating in the first instance those offences which are associated with classical disorders or which share some of the clinical or œtiological pattens of classical mental disorders.

Before doing so and above all before venturing on rough statistical assessments of incidence it is well to be familiar with the types of offence actually recommended by courts and other agencies to delinquency clinics. Statistics on this subject must, however, be read in the light of the fact that cases sent to clinics for examination mostly by Courts of Summary Jurisdiction have already undergone a process of rough *selection* by the Bench acting in conjunction with the probation officer. With this reservation we may note that in the first five year survey of the Psychopathic Clinic (the forerunner of the Portman Clinic) covering 700 cases for 1937–41, the legal diagnosis ran as follows: Theft, 45 per cent; Sex Cases, 25 per cent; Beyond Control, 7 per cent; Embezzlement, False Pretences, Forgery, $4\frac{1}{2}$ per cent; Behaviour Problems, $2\frac{1}{2}$ per cent; and a variety of offences none of which exceed 1 per cent, viz. Shop-Lifting, Attempted Suicide, Wandering, Violence, Persistent Cruelty, Breaking and Entering, Found on Enclosed Premises, 'in Need of Care or Protection', Wilful Damage, Truancy, Receiving, Drunk and Disorderly, Insulting Behaviour, Abandoning Child, Indecent Conversation on Telephone. The remainder were non-delinquent.

Comparing these records with the Report of the Portman Clinic for 1957 (550 cases) we find the following percentages: Theft,

31 per cent; Sex Cases, 28 per cent; Behaviour Problems, 16 per cent; Breaking and Entering, 5 per cent; Beyond Control or 'in Need of Care or Protection', 10 per cent; Truancy, 3 per cent; Other Cases (running to 1 per cent or under) were: Drug Addiction and Alcoholism, Attempted Suicide, Shop-Lifting, Taking and driving away car, Receiving, Drunk and Disorderly, Loitering with Intent, Gambling, etc.

Isolating the juvenile cases recorded in the 1937–41 Survey the percentages were: Theft, 50 per cent; Sex Cases, 16 per cent; Beyond Control, 16 per cent; Behaviour Problems, 10 per cent; Breaking and Entering, 4 per cent. Cases running to less than 1 per cent included: 'In Need of Care or Protection', Truancy, Receiving, Being on Enclosed Premises, Damaging Property. In the case of all groups of juveniles the age incidence lay in a great majority of cases between 14 and 17 years. The distinction between 'Beyond Control' cases and Behaviour Problems is intended to signalize the fact that the former group have been so charged in a Juvenile Court, whereas the latter did not come under court jurisdiction. The 'Need of Care or Protection' category usually includes cases which have been described earlier as pre-delinquent.

Medico-psychological Diagnosis

Isolating in the first instance cases in which the offence can be directly attributed to classical mental or physical disorders and therefore deserve specific clinical rating in symptomatic terms, we can single out from the 1937–41 Survey the following two groups:

GROUP A
(1) Cases of Organic Origin . . 5 per cent
(2) Psychotic . . . . . 2 per cent
(3) Borderline Psychotic . . . 4½ per cent
(4) Mentally Defective . . . 3 per cent
(5) Borderline Mentally Defective . 8 per cent
(6) Alcoholic . . . . . 1 per cent
(7) Sexual Disorders . . . 25 per cent
(8) Psycho-neurotic . . . 29 per cent

Total 77½ per cent

DIAGNOSIS AND TREATMENT OF PATHOLOGICAL DELINQUENCY

Cases in which character disorder of one kind or another is the main feature were as follows:

GROUP B	(9) Psychopathic Personality	13 per cent
	(10) Behaviour Problems	5 per cent
	Total	18 per cent

Isolating the *juvenile* cases for the same period, the two groups work out as follows:

GROUP A	Organic	1 per cent
	Mentally Defective	5 per cent
	Borderline Defective	11 per cent
	Borderline Psychotic	5 per cent
	Psycho-neurotic	37 per cent
	Sex Perversion	1 per cent
	Total	60 per cent
GROUP B	Character Cases (including 'behaviour problems')	22 per cent
	Psychopathic Personality	13 per cent
	Total	35 per cent

Between juvenile and total statistics the main clinical differences are, as might be expected, absence of organized psychoses, the small proportion of perversions ultimately diagnosed in spite of the large number recommended because of sexual offences and the relative increase of character disorders.

If these figures are entirely reliable in the diagnostic sense, they would suggest that a classification in terms of classical mental and physical disorders is, to say the least of it, applicable in about two-thirds of the offenders sent for examination by courts. Unfortunately the matter is not so simple. When two sets of factors operate in any one case the final diagnostic grouping is effected in terms of the more important set. In borderline mentally defective cases and in borderline psychosis, the abnormal character deficiency is probably just as decisive as the defective or psychotic organization.

In this connection the grouping 'psycho-neurotic' requires careful scrutiny. In arriving at this diagnosis two standards are adopted: either the patient has suffered or still suffers from a psycho-neurosis (anxiety states, conversion hysteria or obsessional neurosis) to which the delinquent act, however important socially, is psychologically regarded a secondary reaction; or, the delinquent act itself is hysterical or obsessional in character (e.g. compulsive violence or stealing). The decision can often be arrived at only after an examination of unconscious mechanisms, whereby etiological factors of a psycho-neurotic type can be singled out. The best example is that of kleptomania in which the delinquent act is identical with an obsessional act in all but two respects, viz. that society is attacked in some way or another and that the punishment courted is not as in the case of the pure psycho-neurotic an 'unconscious self-punishment' for unconscious guilty phantasies but a real punishment inflicted by society for an actual crime.

Judged by these standards it is probable that about one-half of the psycho-neurotic delinquencies could be described as delinquency due to 'psycho-neurotic character' and allowing similar correction for borderline defectives and borderline psychotics, we could reduce the relative size of Group A (symptomatic forms) in all cases to just over 50 per cent and increase Group B (the character group) to 40 per cent: in the case of juveniles the respective figures would run Group A, 33 per cent and Group B (character cases) 62 per cent. These are of course unchecked approximations but would seem to correspond to the psychological probability that in juvenile phases the pre-delinquent and delinquent manifestations lie more in the sphere of character and temperament and that in adult delinquency the response is organized more frequently in symptomatic form.

Delinquencies can also be classified in accordance with their association with critical phases of development. A 'pubertal type' of delinquency (12–, 14–17 years) can readily be recognized, in which sudden changes of character occur leading to social violence (Beyond Control) combined sometimes with compulsive sex offences. Even with a minimum of treatment such cases tend to recover their balance in mid-adolescence; the delinquency in other words is transitory in nature. The same standards apply to the solitary middle aged shop-lifter, often a lonely spinster approaching the climateric who reacts to an increasing sense of inadequacy by impulsive theft, intended symbolically to compensate her for her many frustrations. And many cases of compulsive and impulsive theft occur in middle-aged men (45–60) who react to unconscious anxieties regarding the wane of their powers with anti-social episodes.

It would seem therefore that although the most generally favoured classification of pathological delinquency is in terms of character disorder it is not possible to apply this system to all types. On the other hand a good deal more could be done in the direction of character pathology provided it were possible to make effective distinctions between different types during the developmental phases of childhood. Although this field of study has not yet been very effectively explored, we have already reached the stage when it is increasingly possible to distinguish the potentially psychopathic child from most types of child character disorder with the exception of the schizoid type.[1] Recent work on prediction[2] suggests that in course of time not only will it be possible to distinguish during middle childhood individuals who are likely to become delinquent but to isolate more accurately the reactions that characterize the pre-delinquent phase. There is indeed no reason why it should not be possible to predict also the type of delinquency likely to be manifested; but that will require close collaboration between predictors and psycho-analytical investigators who can explore not only the main symbolic interests of the growing child but the type of super-ego that has already been set up.

The Diagnostic Team

Whereas in private analytical practice it is as a rule possible to confine the examination of cases to one person only, the analyst, who operates, as it were, as his own psychiatric social worker, this is for many reasons impracticable at a delinquency clinic. To begin with, the referral is usually from a Summary Court of Jurisdiction, is effected often by a probation officer, the case remains on remand for investigation prior to sentence, and calls for the delivery of a diagnostic report within a period of two or

[1] For wider discussion of character and psychopathy, see Section VI, Part II, pp. 134–8.
[2] E. T. Glueck: 'Predicting Juvenile Delinquency', *Brit. J. Delinq.*, **2**, 275–86, 1952; R. E. Thompson: 'A Validation of the Glueck Social Prediction Scale for Proneness to Delinquency', Ibid., **3**, 289–97, 1953.

three weeks. Each case is therefore seen as soon as possible by a *psychiatric social worker, a psychiatrist, an educational psychologist and an organic physician.* If necessary supplementary examinations are made by another psychiatrist, a vocational guidance officer and, when special examination is called for (e.g. X-ray or electro-encephalograph or endocrinological survey, etc.), a variety of organic specialists. The psychiatric social worker's report alone, requiring as it does contact with family, school or factory conditions and co-operation with the probation officer and any social agencies whose help may have been previously enlisted is a comprehensive process involving a good deal of work and application.

The aim of the educational psychologist is to throw light on the individual's capacity for adjustment to life from a cognitive point of view. He may also help in differential diagnosis, e.g. as between a mental defective and a schizophrenic patient (e.g. small range and childish responses as contrasted with a wide scatter and bizarre replies). Intelligence tests also make it easier to assess temperamental qualities, e.g. powers of concentration, easy discouragement, persistence, etc. Performance tests are sometimes helpful in confirming occupational unsuitability. Their greatest service lies in promoting the elimination of occupations grossly unsuitable from the point of view of intelligence. When called for these examinations can be extended by the use of specific vocational tests. In recent times more attention has been given to various personality ratings which, however, vary a good deal in range according to the techniques favoured by the sponsors of different methods. The prediction tests which have been advanced of late include as a rule a combination of psychiatric ratings, assessment of environmental responses and personality ratings. Questionnaires are also increasingly applied in arriving at personality ratings, the number of items investigated running sometimes into a few hundred units.[1]

[1] The tests at present applied at the Portman Clinic (I.S.T.D.) are the Wechsler Adult Intelligence Scale, the Wechsler Bellevue Intelligence Scale, the Wechsler Intelligence Scale for Children, the revised Stanford-Binet Intelligence Scale and the Progressive Matrices. These are used for intelligence testing. The Wechsler sub-tests (six verbal and five performance) enable the observer to assess not only the subject's potential capacities but his ability to use them; they also indicate deterioration of organic origin.

For school children the Binet test is still in general use at the Clinic,

The Diagnostic Report

It should not be forgotten that in the majority of cases examined a diagnostic report has to be submitted to the court together with a recommendation of whatever treatment the clinic may feel to be appropriate. The main object of this report is, of course, to *guide* the Bench in arriving at a sentence. The sentence is a judicial prerogative which the psychiatrist should at no time seek to usurp even if he could. The court may accept the report in its entirety, and if possible give effect to the clinic's recommendation; or following the principle of 'diminished responsibility' it may accept the report as evidence of 'extenuating circumstances' and so 'mitigate' the customary sentences; or it may discard the report for reasons of its own, e.g. considerations of social safety, need for prolonged 'controlled observation', or in some the impossibility of carrying out the recommendations made, e.g. when psychiatric treatment is not available in the area. Incidentally although they should always be cognizant of the practical difficulties that confront the court writers of reports should not omit to recommend what appears to them the ideal form of treatment.

The main difficulty in preparing such reports concerns the degree of psychiatric orientation possessed by the Bench regarding the nature of behaviour disorders. It goes without saying that the report should be couched in terms that can be understood by the court. But this degree of understanding varies widely, with the result that most reports have to be confined (*a*) to a statement of the diagnosis; (*b*) to some account of the predisposing factors and (*c*) to an assessment of the current offence in terms of likelihood of recidivism or accessibility to (*d*) treatment which is then specified. However relevant psycho-analytical observations might be to the nature of the offence it is inadvisable to include them in the report, since not only are they likely to be incomprehensible to the Bench but to alienate the sympathies of the magistrate. Some at least of these difficulties will be reduced when, as now seems

frequently supplemented by the Wechsler Children's Scale. Standardized attainment tests are also employed. The Burt Tests are generally applied.

Personality testing includes the Rorschach method mainly and the Thematic Apperception Test (T.A.T.) less frequently. (Acknowledgement to S. H. Coates, Clinical Psychologist.)

probable, court personnel undergo training in the subject of behaviour disorder and are orientated regarding the various types of treatment suggested.[1]

[1] See also Peter D. Scott: 'Psychiatric Reports for Magistrates' Courts', *Brit. J. Delinq.*, 4, 82–98, 1953.

PART II. TREATMENT

Since it is misleading to talk of the 'diagnosis of pathological crime', as if all pathological crimes had the same underlying causes, and since it is more accurate to speak of a calendar of pathological states corresponding not only with the calendar of offences but also with sub-groups of the main legal categories (pathological theft, as has been pointed out, can be sub-divided in accordance with a variety of psycho-pathological states varying in severity and depth) it follows that the phrase 'treatment of pathological crime' is equally misleading and that ideally we should speak of the varieties of treatment that can be applied to a variety of pathological crimes (distinguishing at the same time a variety of sub-groups of main categories of offence).

Moreover if at any rate one of the objects of treatment is to prevent the repetition of the offence (and this is the primary concern of the court) it follows that medico-psychological measures cannot be rated as the only form of 'treatment'. In fact it broadens our conception of the therapeutic problem if we realize that *every* court sentence is a form of treatment, that, for example, capital punishment can be described as a technique that effectively cures the patient by killing him, and that probation is an experiment in altering the delinquent's social environment by the forcible introduction into it of an advisory and supervising representative of the court. In short, treatment can be sub-divided into a large group of primitive deterrent measures graded according to the heinousness of the crime (a socio-legal criterion) and a group of measures whose object is so to influence or alter the mental function of the individual that he will no longer be under the necessity to commit the crime. This second group can be sub-divided in a variety of ways; social, educational, ethical, religious, economic and psycho-therapeutic, this last term being used in the specialized sense of planned alleviation or cure of mental disorders, according to their causation.

By so broadening the concept we can apply to each form of treatment a number of distinguishing criteria, e.g. its rationale, effectiveness, consonance with public opinion and correlation with accurate diagnosis. Thus the predominantly penal nature of most legal treatment is on the whole consonant with public anxiety and prejudice, its rationale depends on the effective conditioning of the offender through the induction of frustration, mental pain and anxiety, the effectiveness of some of the most severe measures is, as far as the individual offender is concerned, open to the most serious question, and there is no obligation on the court to do more than diagnose the legal offence (convict the offender). Apart from the application of the M'Naghten Rules in cases of murder and the legal tradition of taking into account 'extenuating circumstances', there is no obligation on the law to secure accurate diagnosis before recommending treatment, and this is the essence of quackery. On the other hand social, religious and educational measures are generally consonant with public opinion, depend on methods of modifying mental function without recourse to punishment or anxiety-induction, are certainly not less effective than penal methods and involve some degree of diagnosis even if, as in the case of religion, it be in terms of the somewhat arbitrary or at least non-medical categories of sin. Psychotherapy is not yet fully acceptable to public prejudice, its aim is not solely to resolve or control the impulse towards a particular offence but to prevent the emergence in action of any other criminal impulses, its rationale as we shall see varies, its effectiveness is certainly not less than that of penal measures and whatever form it may take is based on accurate methods of diagnosis. Good psychotherapy in fact depends on the accuracy of diagnosis, and the appropriate selection of case and technique.

Sample of Clinical Recommendations

Having underlined the necessity for diagnostic discrimination it is necessary to establish that under clinical auspices equal discrimination is exercised in the recommendations for disposal of the offender which are entered in the diagnostic report. Reverting to the clinical five year Survey of the Psychopathic Clinic (I.S.T.D.)[1] we find the following percentage for the years 1940–41 set to the nearest integer:

[1] The forerunner of the Portman Clinic.

Psychotherapy	60 per cent
Psychological Observation	5 per cent
Institutional Treatment	
Mental Hospital (as voluntary patient)	3 per cent ⎫
Mental Hospital (under certificate) .	1 per cent ⎪
Mental Deficiency Hospital . .	2 per cent ⎬ 8 per cent
Approved School, Borstal . .	2 per cent ⎪
Home for Inebriates (1 case) . .	– ⎭
Organic Treatment	3 per cent
Environmental Changes (home, school, work, etc.)	15 per cent
Supervision (social or probationary) . .	7 per cent
Non-delinquent	2 per cent

Dividing these recommendations into (*a*) directly therapeutic measures at clinic or hospital and (*b*) social-educational and environmental measures, we find that the former group comprises roughly 69 per cent of the total cases and the latter (including approved school and Borstal recommendations; home, school and occupational changes; and the 5 per cent put under psychological observation, which acted no doubt as an environmental influence rather than as an organized course of therapy), roughly 29 per cent.

A few other comments on this table are relevant. In roughly half of the cases the diagnosis was effected without much difficulty and the recommendation of treatment was not hard to arrive at. This applies obviously to organic cases, cases requiring hospitalization, sex offences, and to about half of the neurotic types and character disorders. In other instances diagnosis was not easy and the exact recommendation difficult to arrive at. It should also be noted that for one reason or another the ideal recommendation was not always given effect. In two sample years an average of 59 per cent of new cases were recommended treatment: yet only 35 per cent received it. This wastage is accounted for mainly by cases refusing treatment, cases relapsing and sentenced before treatment, and cases referred to other clinics.

VARIETIES OF TREATMENT

The range of psychological techniques employed varied from hypnosis and deep suggestion to (very occasionally) pure psychoanalysis. Techniques of 'open' suggestion were frequently combined with methods of 'indirect' suggestion, e.g. persuasion, exhortation. In a majority of short-term cases 'combined' methods were chosen usually on an eclectic basis. Various types of exploratory approach were exploited in combination with degrees of guidance, persuasion, education and suggestion. These exploratory methods were either Freudian, Jungian or Adlerian in type. The 'short-term' approach involving the application of psycho-analytical principles was essentially a focal anamnesic and thematic approach eked out with periods of free association directed at focal points in the clinical history and intended to place the anti-social reactions in a developmental setting, to reduce the 'negative' reactions and to loosen the more positive transferences of the offender. These are of course to be distinguished from psycho-analysis carried out *secundum artem*. 'Psychological observation' though at first employed as a long-term diagnostic procedure, was found to produce beneficial results and subsequently rated as a 'therapeutic technique' of an environmental type. Many cases, particularly those in the pubertal age group, were given advice and instruction only. Under the age of puberty treatment usually took one or other of the forms of child therapy. These could be distinguished according to whether persuasion, advice, re-education and suggestion were applied over a short term or whether, as in longer treatments, the techniques of play therapy were employed. In recent times a number of additional techniques have been exploited in the psycho-therapy of delinquents. These fall into three main groups, so-called 'hypno-analysis' where mild hypnotic trances are exploited to gain further material which is then subjected to analytic scrutiny and extension, 'narco-analysis' where a variety of narcotic drugs are employed for a like purpose; and various forms of 'group-therapy' by which larger numbers of cases can be dealt with and a direct attempt made to increase positive social feeling and adaptation. In all these types of treatment the exploratory approach adopted depends on the theories, eclectic or otherwise, favoured by the therapeutist.

Although as has been indicated purely 'organic types' of delinquency were transferred to hospitals or other clinics for correction of the physical abnormality or functional disorder, a number of psychological cases also suffer either from physical disorders or sometimes defects which produce unfavourable psychological reactions. Undersized or physically deformed children, children whose pubertal phase is either premature or unduly delayed or who suffer from other endocrinological abnormalities come into this group and treatment of the particular disorder or defect is given concurrently with psychological treatment. Amongst adults similar abnormalities may be noted: e.g. delinquent outbursts during pregnancy. Experiments along these lines are occasionally carried out in the treatment of sexual offences, particularly that of homosexuality, but as a rule a purely psychological approach to strictly selected sexual offenders is preferred.

Rationale of Psychological Techniques

It has been suggested that psychological treatment should be graded according to the diagnosis of the case. To do this effectively it is necessary to establish rapidly a prognosis (e.g. whether the examination suggests that the case is relatively favourable or is likely to be difficult to treat), also to have a clear idea of the rationale and depth of the various types of treatment. Here two awkward factors have to be taken into account, viz., that it is possible to apply most of the types of treatment described above to most forms of mental disorder and that in cases of pathological delinquency sent by the courts a number of practical considerations sometimes limit the choice of treatment. Considerations of time alone, to say nothing of case load, naturally bias the consultant in favour of short methods. Treatment of delinquents is also subject to a number of interruptions, and the sooner effective influence is brought to bear the better. These factors too favour the selection of short-term methods. Nevertheless it is possible to give some rough indications which, ideally at any rate, should govern the selection of treatment. And this in its turn requires some understanding of the main principles governing all forms of psychological treatment. Here again psycho-analysis has performed a major service to psychiatry by outlining the main aims of different psychological approaches, and the main differences that exist between their techniques. Psycho-analysis in other words is not simply a form of mental therapy, it constitutes also a theory of mental organization and function which is concerned to explain both normal and abnormal mental activities.

It goes without saying that the cardinal proposition of psycho-analysis is that the larger part of the mental apparatus is unconscious not only in the descriptive sense but also in the dynamic sense, namely: that it requires special techniques to overcome mental *resistance* before the full instinctual forces, the various unconscious institutions of mind and the mechanisms these latter employ to control, distribute or discharge instinctual forces can be recognized or brought into consciousness. As far as the study and treatment of pathological delinquency is concerned, this central proposition can be extended in a number of postulates having a practical bearing on both diagnosis and treatment. These are as follows (1) that the type of behaviour of both juvenile and adult pathological delinquents, is determined not just by the immediate force of circumstances but by patterns laid down (*and unconsciously maintained*) during the fateful early stages of childhood mental development from birth to, as a rule, the fifth or sixth year, an age limit which interestingly enough is close to that of criminal responsibility in this country. This developmental acquisition of patterns gives substance to the Wordsworthian aphorism 'the child is the father of the man'; (2) that in both normal and abnormal subjects the attitude to personal and social situations is also formed during this developmental (familial) phase which determines the prevailing degree of friendliness or hostility to social figures or institutions; (3) that for the most part these immediate transferences are unconscious but can be evoked most readily by situations calculated to re-animate the original unconscious patterns, e.g. environmental reactions of friendliness or hostility, either real or apparent. In the psycho-therapeutic situation, owing to the physician's attitude of friendly receptivity which is not diminished by the nature of the offence, such potential friendly transferences as exist can be mobilized and so render the patient amenable to such influence as the therapeutist can bring to bear; (4) that mental symptoms can be roughly distinguished in accordance with the degree to which the pathological changes affect the individual's mind or body without seriously affecting his social reactions or alternatively the degree to which, during periods of stress, modifications of environment are attempted. In the pure neuroses for example the changes affect mainly the individual himself: in the psychoses, in disordered character formations and in delinquency an attempt is made to mould the environment to the pattern of the individual's instincts and phantasies; (5) that in cases of pathological delinquency the immediate transferences to environment both individual and social are either of a predominantly hostile type or become negative during occasions of stress.

Building on these assumptions we can then say that *all forms of psycho-therapeutic approach depend on the nature of transferences*,[1] the degree to which they can be evoked and controlled or in the case of psycho-analysis the degree to which, having been evoked in the analytic situation, infantile transferences can be resolved or liquidated leaving the individual free to react on a more realistically adapted level. This enables a somewhat arbitrary and radical distinction to be drawn between techniques such as psycho-analysis in which the main therapeutic device is the evocation, analysis and resolution of the transferences, and all forms of treatment in which either no special attention is paid to the transference situation (it being allowed to operate spontaneously), or, even if it is openly cultivated and exploited, no attempt is made to resolve it.

As a matter of interest, it would be possible to divide the treatment of pathological delinquency into a large group consisting of a great variety of techniques in which transference factors are either spontaneously or deliberately exploited and another extremely small group in which they are analysed. In fact the number of cases of pathological delinquency treated by pure psycho-analysis is extremely small, although in fairness it must be said that this does not invalidate the general conception of delinquency advanced by Freud and by those of his followers who have concentrated on a selected few cases of anti-social conduct. In any case such a grouping would have little practical value for our present purpose. Even if we characterize the larger group as 'transference therapies', meaning thereby that the transference is exploited without ultimate resolution, it is important to distinguish between different forms of transference therapy.

This is the more important in that unlike most other cases of disorder (particularly those seen in private practice) the delinquent is subject from the first to a *number* of transference stimuli, e.g. if he should belong to a delinquent group to gang influences, to familial and social disapproval, to arrest or summons, court proceedings and interviews by the probation officer, before the question of diagnosis, to say nothing of treatment, has ever been

[1] Aichhorn was the first to lay down this law in the case of psychopathic delinquents in *Wayward Youth*, Imago Publ. Co., 1951.

mooted. And during treatment the transference situation usually continues to be complicated by the interposition of probation officers, psychiatric social workers or a variety of social agencies. This situation of 'distributed transference' may have a good effect or it may have a bad one, depending on the balance of friendly or hostile reactions in the offender. In fact it would be possible to arrange 'transference therapies' in series according to this 'transference balance', starting with legal and penal proceedings, social reproach or contumely to which the offender's reaction is in most cases negative and ending with lengthy psychotherapy during which hostility is ventilated and the conduct of the offender is regarded as a problem to be approached with friendly interest, in which case the reaction may in favourable cases be positive.

Even so the sub-division, though important, would be too broad to enable us to distinguish between different types of transference therapy. We are compelled therefore to effect distinctions in a number of other ways. Of these the most important can be described in accordance with the degree of attention paid to (*a*) the nature of the offence (a symptomatic standard), (*b*) the reality organization of the ego and, (*c*) the nature of conflicts and their relation to the presence or absence of conscious guilt, (*d*) the anxiety stresses of the patient (a traumatic standard), (*e*) the capacity for control of impulses and, (*f*) the environmental setting. Most of these approaches vary according to the focal point or level at which they are directed. Obviously the environmental conditions can be of immediate importance or act in summation; the level of the ego or of the moral institutions (super-ego) can also be approached according to their historical or immediate importance. Long-standing and current stresses, both instinctual and emotional, can also be distinguished.

Take for example the impact of the *probation officer* on the delinquent situation. As the representative of the court, the probation officer exercises reality pressure on the ego; as a moral suasionist he seeks to strengthen the offender's super-ego (moral faculties) and in both these ways aims at improving control of impulse. As a friendly social worker he endeavours to eliminate current environmental stresses. The focus of his approach lies mostly in immediate and in that sense superficial factors, but this does not necessarily mean that his influence is superficial, for in the last resort the outcome depends on the nature of the offender's transferences and of the probation officer's countertransferences, both of which operate at a deep and unconscious level.

Pursuing these assessments we can say that all *psychiatric social workers* have in common a concern with immediate familial and social stresses impinging on the reality ego but may according to the nature of their training play a more directly psychotherapeutic rôle of a superficial type. The psychiatrist, again according to his training, may prefer to attack the more immediate factors but is in a position to apply his techniques at any accessible level of the mind. Suggestionists can operate at levels varying in depth but prefer to manipulate the more superficial factors, symptomatic or dynamic. Hypnotists and psycho-analysts have a common interest, viz. in the manipulation of unconscious levels of the mind, but differ entirely in techniques, and in transference exploitation. The characteristic aim of psycho-analytic therapy is to resolve the unconscious resistances which obstruct approach to the root causes of the offender's behaviour.

We are now in a position to summarize the problem of *selection of treatment*. Cases where immediate stress, emotional or environmental, seems to have precipitated the offence, can be dealt with by the psychiatric social worker backed by a few interviews with the psychiatrist; stresses due to faulty education (a common factor in pubertal offences of a sexual nature) may respond to psychological re-education, e.g. of the sexual life. About a half of the psycho-neurotic types respond to analytical or eclectic psychotherapy spread over three to six months; the other half call for deeper investigation of an analytical nature. Cases of a psychopathic type almost invariably call for deep and prolonged treatment and extend the therapeutist's skill and patience to their very limits; and the same may be said of many though by no means all sexual offences. Psychotic cases call for specialized techniques appropriate to the variety of psychosis. Defective types require a combination of special educational techniques combined with supportive techniques of psycho-therapy to deal with the special psychological handicaps that arise from a deficient mentality.

All this, as has been suggested, must be qualified by the facts that the accessibility of patients to treatment is not always easy to assess, and that cases that appear to be of a deep and intractable nature may respond to apparently superficial and comparatively 'short' techniques. In these instances the factor of transference or of summated transferences is probably decisive. Where the immediate effect of short treatment is unsatisfactory in spite of a promising prognosis, it is often possible to change over to more intensive, continuous and prolonged psycho-therapy. But this change is not always easy to effect and can be made more readily in private than in clinic practice. Most court offenders find it difficult enough to satisfy the time requirements of short treatment and are liable to break off more continuous therapy.

Finally with regard to psycho-analytic therapy, it has been noted that the exigencies of a busy clinic practice severely limit the applicability of this type of treatment even where the case may appear to be otherwise suitable. But there are other difficulties to overcome. On the whole cases of delinquency start treatment in a state of negative transference, which is only partly masked where the factor of social anxiety has paved the way for a reassuring contact. And in a considerable number of instances the social complications that spring from delinquent crises disturb the analytical situation. Psycho-analysis of delinquent conduct is in fact most suitably applied in cases not sent under court compulsion, i.e. in private and voluntary treatment.

Reviewing the problem of selection of cases and of treatment, it becomes obvious that in the early days each therapeutist began by applying to delinquent cases the psycho-therapeutic methods with which he was most familiar and which he had applied with some success in the treatment of neuroses and characterological disorders. To begin with he was not familiar with or did not understand either the mechanisms peculiar to delinquent conduct as a whole or the special mechanisms characteristic of each type of delinquent disorder. Once he gained this experience he was faced with the problem of cutting his therapeutic cloak to suit the cloth. This is particularly true of psycho-analytic therapy. For the difference between an obsessional and a psychopathic delinquency is almost as great as the difference between a neurosis and a psychosis and calls for variations in technique. It remains to be seen how far special techniques can be devised to meet special cases. It can of course be agreed that all psycho-therapy rests on certain basic principles, and therefore does not alter much. Time alone will tell whether special 'focal' therapies can meet all the requirements of an omnibus group such as anti-social behaviour.

The Duration of Treatment

It follows from these considerations that in surveying the course of clinic treatment, wide variations in its duration will be found. Reverting to the first five-year survey it is to be noted that the average annual number of sessions per case over the 1937–1941 period ran to ten (The Portman Clinic figures for 1957 give an average of eleven). The range varied according to the nature of the treatment. With cases requiring short psychological treatment, advice, or social handling, the number of sessions varied from five to fifty interviews approximately. These might, however, be scattered over a period of a few weeks to six to twelve months. Cases calling for more intensive psychotherapy attended from 50 to 150 times over a period of one to two years. No exact figures of the distribution between different types of therapy were available; but the exigences of staffing reduced the numbers receiving extended treatment to a comparatively low level.

Results of Treatment

Although it is not hard to obtain reasonably accurate tables of diagnosis and prognosis in clinic practice, it is extremely difficult to discover the efficiency of treatment with satisfactory accuracy. This is particularly true of a delinquency clinic where, as will be seen, the 'wastage' of cases suitable for treatment is extremely high. On the other hand it is possible to set more precise, if not so fundamental standards in the case of delinquency work, since the primary object of treatment laid down by the court is to liquidate the symptoms (i.e. the delinquent conduct). This symptomatic test can be applied in two ways, first, by setting a minimum period of abstention from delinquent conduct, and, second, by noting whether or not the causal factors have been eradicated. Thus in the table that follows the category 'cure' or 'recovery' means that the fundamental causes of the delinquency have been discovered and dealt with, leaving the individual non-delinquent, e.g. a mental disease of which the delinquent symptom is symptomatic or an unusual traumatic environmental factor in an individual who otherwise would have remained normal.

The term 'improved' is intended to indicate that the patient reached a stable non-delinquent state although the causes of his delinquency had been of such a nature that it would not be justifiable to establish recovery until after a period of years (fixed provisionally at five).[1] This non-delinquent state is not simply a behaviouristic standard; it implies also a considerable improvement in the patient's mental stability. Most delinquent cases treated fall in this group.

The 'unimproved' group includes only cases whose lack of response to treatment is due to *intrinsic* difficulties.

The following table taken from the I.S.T.D. survey covers three consecutive years and deals with a total of 187 cases discharged. It gives no indication of the relation of the particular offence to the variety of treatment employed, as on attempting to break down the figures in this way, the numbers in the various sub-groups were too small to apply statistical checks. On the other hand the diagnosis and results provide dependable indications and the table is produced here to give a very rough idea of the overall results; as follows:

	Per cent
Recovered	15·5
Improved	44
Unimproved	4
Discharged self	22
Discharged for other reasons	9
Transferred elsewhere after some treatment	2
Relapsed	3

With regard to the groups 'discharged self' and 'discharged for other reasons', these can be sub-divided into three sub-groups according to the operation of unconscious, conscious and environmental factors. Of the first group 'unconscious gain through illness' and strong aggressive drives leading to lack of positive

[1] Regarding the dependability of a five-year after-history it is interesting to observe that, according to the Reports of the Prison Commissioners, the percentage of those discharged after a first prison sentence for serious ('finger printable') offences who were given a subsequent sentence of imprisonment within a period of ten to twenty years is not substantially greater than that recorded after five years, except in the case of offenders in the age group 17–20 and, though to a lesser extent, in the group 20–29. In both these instances the increase is greater where offences occurring previous to the first imprisonment have been proved. In the higher age groups the increment after five years is negligible, whether or not previous offences have been proved.

rapport with the therapeutist are the best examples. One conscious factor may be described as 'lacking awareness of the need for treatment'. A neurotic or early psychotic case is usually well aware of his need for help: but a delinquent does not find it at all easy to grasp the connection between disordered conduct and mental health. For the matter of that, he often is unaware that his conduct is disordered, although he may agree tranquilly with the view of society that it is 'bad'.

Environmental factors re-enforcing non-co-operation are of two kinds. As in ordinary psycho-therapeutic practice there is a good deal of opposition on the part of parents, relations and friends; this may be strong enough to make the patient discontinue attendance. Again some patients who may have shown signs of improvement are often compelled to discontinue owing to circumstances beyond their control, e.g. place of work, place of residence, extended hours of employment. Now the 'cured' and 'improved' group are judged solely on combined medical, psycho-therapeutic and social standards. If cases who discontinued treatment but made no further appearances at court were also regarded as improved, as they may very well be, the number included under 'unimproved' and 'discharged self' would be correspondingly reduced.

With regard to relapses, as reported in after-history, it is to be noted that the figure is small and includes some cases who although originally constant offenders did not relapse for one to two years. And this is to a certain extent a sign of improvement. Incidentally the difficulty in obtaining reliable after-histories in delinquency work is unusually great. Although some patients may themselves be the first to make contact, it is often inadvisable to 'follow-up' too vigorously. The patient may be sensitive about his past misdemeanours or be anxious lest they should 'leak out', with untoward social and economic consequences. These in addition to such factors as change of residence tend to make statistical follow-up unrepresentative. It may be said with confidence, however, that *recidivism among those who have completed treatment is rare*, also that when the treatment is not fully completed but the patient becomes apparently non-delinquent few relapses are recorded. Combining these groups under the heading 'satisfactory results', but excluding cases discharging themselves whether improved or not, we can get a rough idea of the more positive results of treatment. In the five-year survey the annual percentage of cases which, whether they completed treatment or not shewed a 'satisfactory' result (i.e. cured or rendered non-delinquent) was as follows:

1937, 54 per cent; *1938*, 59 per cent; *1939*, 49 per cent; *1940*, 21 per cent; *1941*, 15 per cent.

These figures should be corrected for the facts that in the last two years of the survey, owing to war conditions, a larger number of cases were discharged with treatment uncompleted, and that owing to staff exigencies the majority of the others were given short treatment only. The average of satisfactory results for 1937–39 alone was over 54 per cent: for the whole five years 39 per cent: these cases were rated as non-delinquent and likely to remain so. If we were to exclude cases which for one reason or another did not complete treatment, a practice which is usually followed in clinic reports, the percentage of satisfactory results would be much higher.

Correction for Spontaneous Recovery

On the other hand, although the practice is seldom followed in clinical reports, it is essential to make allowances for the factor of spontaneous recovery, which is observed in every form of psychological disorder. Some writers, for example, have estimated that the number of spontaneous recoveries in schizophrenia is as high as 35 per cent, and in the cases of psycho-neurotic disorders the spontaneous remissions rate has been estimated as between 7 per cent and 33 per cent. On clinical grounds, however, it is probable that the spontaneous remission rate is rather lower in delinquency than in psycho-neuroses. It is no easy matter to recognize and eliminate these 'abortive' types of delinquency except perhaps in the group of 'pubertal delinquents'. But even if, to be on the cautious side, we allow a 20 per cent rate of spontaneous recovery, the rate of satisfactory results for the first three standard years would be 40 per cent of those treated, and the overall average including two atypical war years would be 32 per cent.

The Factor of Distributed Transference

It should not be forgotten that in delinquency work, psychological treatment is usually and often of necessity combined with various forms of environmental handling. With court cases where clinic treatment is combined with probationary control this latter takes two forms. The probation officer maintains a degree of advisory supervision but combines this with activities calculated to smooth over social difficulties. In non-court cases a varying amount of social influence is brought to bear by club leaders, hostel wardens and other social workers. And of course the clinic's psychiatric social worker plays an important part in organizing suitable environmental conditions, and in dealing with difficulties at home or school. She also acts as a liaison officer between all the parties concerned. The educational psychologist also plays his or her part in re-education. Generally speaking the more effectively these various influences are applied the better the results of treatment. It cannot therefore be said that satisfactory results are due *solely* to specialized psychological techniques, and allowance should be made for this in estimating results. It is naturally impossible to distinguish between the factors in summated treatment. Some information might be gained by comparing the results obtained by social treatment only with those in which psychotherapy was carried out with a minimum of social work. So far comparisons made along these lines are not very dependable. Even where social work is combined with a few psychiatric interviews, the influence of the psychiatrist is and of course always should be paramount.

Comparison with Prison Sentences

The argument is sometimes advanced that the numbers of prisoners who are not convicted a second time is also large. For example a Prison Commission Survey of persons committed to prison for the first time *serious* ('finger-printable') offences during the years 1930–34, and 1940–43 shewed that after five years, 74 per cent of all cases had not again been received in prison. Where no offence prior to the first sentence had been proved the percentage rate for all cases reached 85; where previous offences were proved it was 64. The lowest rate appeared in the age group 17–20: where no previous offences were proved 75 per cent, and

49 per cent where they were proved. In the age group 20-29 the respective figures were 83 per cent and 57 per cent: in the group 30-39, 88 per cent and 70 per cent: for those 40 and over, 92 per cent and 78 per cent.

There is, however, no effective basis of comparison between the percentage of cases not returning to prison and the percentage of a selected group of cases suffering from pathological delinquency who are cured of their disability and rendered non-delinquent; and in any case the standard of recovery under clinical treatment is, both clinically and socially, immensely more stringent than the criterion of absence of a recorded second prison sentence. Moreover the pathological offenders selected for clinic treatment would if sentenced to imprisonment tend to be refractory to prison routines and so to swell the hard core of prison recidivism. This is particularly true of the psychopathic offender. In fact the most important check on the efficiency of psycho-therapeutic treatment can be effected not by comparing clinic statistics with prison statistics, but by comparing them with the results of psychotherapy in the non-delinquent psycho-neuroses. Admittedly it is hard to obtain satisfactory statistics on this latter subject. But generally speaking the figures of the five-year survey indicate that the results of psychotherapy of pathological delinquents is only slightly lower than in the case of treatment of the psycho-neuroses.[1]

Questions of statistical comparison aside, the point of fundamental importance is that clinic results are obtained under ambulant conditions, i.e., the offenders are, subject to a varying degree of probationary supervision, at liberty, living in their own homes and following their usual occupations or in the case of juveniles attending their usual school. From the economic point of view alone treatment at liberty represents a considerable gain; from the point of view of social adaptation it is unmeasurably superior to correction in penal institutions; and from the humanitarian point of view it represents a considerable advance on the moralistic and expiatory traditions on which penal methods have hitherto been based[2] the social implications of which are difficult to over-estimate.

[1] See p. 161 for a comparison of results in psychopathic cases and in cases of psycho-neurotic delinquency.

[2] An interesting parallel argument in support of probation has recently. been advanced by L. T. Wilkins (*Brit. J. Delinq.*, 8, 201-9, 1958) Comparing the after-histories of cases at a court where prison sentences

Results in Cases Treated Privately

For a number of reasons it is not possible to make reliable comparisons between clinic results and those obtained in private psycho-therapeutic practice. Such private records as are published usually concern isolated and specially selected cases or small groups. Even where a small series is published (e.g. Allen's records of treatment of homosexuality[1]) it is still not possible to make valid comparisons. In any case private cases as a rule come voluntarily for treatment which is not restricted in length, hence *coeteris paribus* a higher percentage may be expected to respond satisfactorily. This must, however, be corrected for the fact that a substantial number of cases treated in private are of an intractable nature, e.g. psychopathic offenders. The point is well worthy of investigation provided suitable methods of comparison can be established.

As will be gathered from the above account and from the sketchy almost speculative nature of the statistics on which some of the impressions are partly based, an immense amount of work remains to be done before we can claim to have established adequate, systematic and controlled psycho-therapeutic measures for the treatment of delinquency. And the same can be said of existing methods of diagnosis. Careful sub-division must be effected of a great variety of character disorders, which should also be more precisely distinguished from symptom constructions; equally careful classification and subdivision of offences is essential; research must be carried out on the effects of different types of psychotherapy and if possible of new techniques or combinations of existing techniques, to say nothing of appraisement of various types of social and occupational therapy, of educational devices and of many other measures both individual and social. The findings arrived at by means of these researches must be correlated

predominated with those of cases at a court where probationary supervision was favoured he points out that, although no striking differences in results could be established, nevertheless it followed that many cases given a prison sentence could have been put on probation with equally satisfactory results.

[1] Clifford Allen: *Homosexuality*, London, Staples Press, 1958.

both clinically and theoretically and checked by subsequent after-history (including where possible thorough re-examination). Once this has been done we may be able not only to form more accurate prognoses and thereby guide more effectively the 'disposal' of offenders, but arrive at criteria which sharpen our diagnostic measures and enable us to apply predictive techniques to the pre-delinquent as well as to the 'first offender'.

Apart from all this, a literally enormous amount of research remains to be carried out on the early development of the normal mind. Obviously without a clear grasp of normal phases of mental development we cannot hope to isolate the special characteristics and etiological features either of pathological delinquents, or, more important, of pre-delinquents. Indeed the whole future of criminology may be said to depend on the investigation not so much of delinquents themselves but of those who have entered the transitional phase between reasonably normal adaptation and a final delinquent response. It is in these basic researches that psycho-analysis will be called on to provide more and more information regarding the unconscious aspects of human behaviour, in particular the earlier nuclei of unconscious conscience. For behaviour is after all but one end result of processes which are unconscious in both the descriptive and the dynamic sense of the term. Important as are the advances that have already been made in the clinical psychology of delinquency and immeasurably superior to a purblind penal system as are the existing therapeutic methods employed we must recognize that the science of criminal psychology is still in its infancy.

IV. THE CRIMINAL PSYCHOPATH

Part I   Diagnosis
Part II   Etiology
Part III   Treatment
Appendix   Aichhorn on Treatment

SECTION IV

THE CRIMINAL PSYCHOPATH

[1940-59]

Psychopathy, under whatever caption it may run, has throughout its chequered nosological history been the step-child of psychiatry. This was due in part to the fact that it did not fit comfortably into existing psychiatric classifications, in part to general psychiatric neglect of characterological disorders, and, in the case of criminal psychopathy, to the circumstance that it has always been difficult to distinguish on the one hand psychopathic criminal conduct from that of 'responsible' criminals and on the other the apparently normal conduct of psychopaths from that of law-abiding persons.

At the same time the tendency to equate psychopathy with criminality is a step in the wrong direction. For there are many psychopaths who are even more law-abiding than 'normal' persons and who in fact put themselves in a masochistic and presumably guilt-ridden pillory of self-inflicted mischance. Indeed one of the main reasons why the essential task of sub-dividing psychopathy has given rise to so much difficulty and confusion, is that having its etiological roots in a progressive series of developmental fixations and traumatisms embedded in a constitutionally hypersensitive matrix, psychopathy manifests affinities with the whole range of classical mental disorders, e.g. hysterical crises, obsessional confusions, depressive slumps, hypomanic activities, sometimes megalomaniac but fleeting ambitions, paranoid and schizoid stigmata, to say nothing of a variety of inhibitions and perversions both social and sexual, all of which are inter-woven and held together in a sometimes superficially charming personality-frame which the psychopathic swindler exploits to his frequent undoing. Psychopathy is in short one of the great groups of character disorder vying with schizophrenia for pride of pathological place. This at any rate is the thesis maintained in the present section.

PART I. DIAGNOSIS

Psychopathy is without question the most interesting and at the same time one of the most baffling of problems in clinical psychology. In the first place a substantial number of psychiatrists do not believe there is any such condition. Many other clinical psychologists who, somewhat reluctantly, recognize its existence, nevertheless regard the psychopathic group as a dumping ground for unclassified mental disorders. Psycho-analysts view the term with an equally jaundiced eye, and indeed rarely use it, preferring their own characterological nomenclature, which however is, as we shall see, still far from adequate. Even forensic psychiatrists (or, as one might say, 'clinical criminologists') although readiest of all to accept the term, are not agreed as to its exact connotation. In some European countries the more violent forms of criminal psychopathy are included under the heading of *l'état dangereux*, a somewhat timid and purely social designation. An Austrian, and in his earlier days psycho-analytical psychiatrist, Wilhelm Reich, preferred the term 'triebhafter Charakter', a phrase difficult to translate except perhaps as 'instinct-ridden character'. Incidentally, this qualifying term is no more specific than *l'état dangereux*. A schizophrenic or paranoiac can be in a dangerous state at times; a sexual pervert is certainly 'instinct-ridden' and the more sadistic types can on occasion be dangerous enough. Nevertheless neither psychotics nor pure perverts can be called psychopaths. Indeed one of the distinguishing features of the psychopath is precisely that, however inadequate functionally his reality sense may be, he is *not* insane. And while a psychopath may also be a pervert, most sexual perverts are *not* psychopaths. The homosexual for example may, outside the range of his perversion, have an even higher ethical and social sense than the majority of so-called 'normal' people; to say nothing of psychopaths.

This may sound a discouraging preamble to the study of 'psychopathy'. Even more discouraging to the forensic psychiatrist is the fact that many magistrates and most higher judges view the term with profound suspicion, regarding it often as a piece of psychiatric flummery designed to frustrate their prerogative of sentencing confirmed offenders. Added to which the general public, although now glib in the use of the term, has, naturally enough, not the remotest idea of its exact connotation, accepting instead the purely journalistic view that it describes homicidal maniacs with a perverted sexual tendency.

To the commencing forensic psychiatrist it may seem curious to include in a scientific survey any reference to popular opinion. Quite the contrary; one of the first lessons he must learn is that criminological diagnosis has been from the first and still is profoundly influenced by a popular consensus of opinion which is sooner or later embodied in criminal codes. And as many psychopaths give a superficial impression not only of 'normality' but of an extremely frank, plausible and at times charming disposition, it is not at all surprising that both judges and the commonalty should regard with suspicion any attempt on the part of 'experts' to find extenuating circumstances for psychopathic conduct.

Fortunately the diagnostic situation is not quite so black as these circumstances might suggest. To be sure the differential diagnosis of psychopathy is difficult enough. But this is due mainly to three facts, first, that clinical diagnosis reflects the current state of psychiatric opinion; second, that psychiatric classifications of mental disorder are so far of the most rudimentary order, and third that, historically, psychiatrists were concerned mainly with grave mental disorders such as the insanities, had little interest in character disorders, and still less in those character disorders that are responsible for criminal behaviour. Added to which, it is scarcely possible to develop an all-embracing and at the same time comprehensible classification of mental disorders without an equally extensive and equally comprehensible theory of mind. Few psychiatrists possess such a theory. It is for this reason in particular that the psycho-analytic approach to psychopathy, although at present far from adequate, is the most promising. For psycho-analysis does at least possess a theory of mind that bridges the apparent gulf between abnormality and normality and takes into account the decisive importance of unconscious factors in all mental development. That it has so far neglected the problem of psychopathy is due largely to the facts that criminal psychopaths rarely come of their own free will to the psycho-analytic consulting room, and that when they do come their successful analysis is not easy to achieve.

Classifications of Psychopathies

With these reservations in mind we may attempt to outline the main features of what for lack of a more precise term we are compelled in the meantime to describe as psychopathy. But first of all we must get our definitions in order. On this subject there exists an extensive literature which it would be tedious to review and which on the whole does little to relieve the student of the many uncertainties with which he approaches his subject. Controversies have centred round such problems as whether the condition exists and if so whether it is due mainly to constitutional or to psychogenic factors, and if the latter whether they are conscious or unconscious in origin: whether the instinctual inheritance is too strong or the ego too weak; what is the nature of the fault in the psychopath's moral faculty. As regards descriptive features it is perhaps sufficient to say that since Prichard in 1835 described what he termed 'moral insanity' many attempts have been made to expand his definition and just as many to prune the expanded versions.

In fact Prichard's description is as useful today as it was when he isolated 'moral insanity' from other mental disorders such as 'intellectual insanity'. It runs as follows:—

> '... a form of mental derangement in which the intellectual functions appear to have sustained little or no injury, while the disorder is manifested, principally or alone, in the state of the feelings, temper or habits. In cases of this nature the moral and active principles of the mind are strongly perverted or depraved: the power of self-government is lost or greatly impaired, and the individual is found incapable, not of talking or reasoning upon any subject proposed to him, but of conducting himself with decency and propriety in the business of life.'

When one reflects that the psychiatry of the early nineteenth century was a little more rudimentary and confused than it is today. one cannot but admire Prichard's clinical acumen. By using the qualifying term 'moral' he grasped the essence of the matter, namely, that the 'moral faculties' of the criminal psychopath are subject to pathological development or change. True, modern psychiatry has dropped the term moral 'insanity' and such later modifications of it as moral 'idiocy' (Naecke, 1907) or moral 'imbecility' (still recommended by Mercier as late as 1913). But that only goes to show how unimaginative modern psychiatric terminology can be. For although the criminal psychopath is not insane and, despite somewhat erratic use of his sometimes notable intellectual gifts, far from imbecile, he certainly suffers from stunting of his moral faculties both conscious and unconscious. Moral obliquity is in fact the hallmark of the psychopaths who engage the attention of the courts.

But however accurately observed were Prichard's original studies it soon became clear that the condition was capable of clinical sub-division. A good example was the distinction by Kraepelin of a number of distinct types of psychopath, viz. the excitable, the unstable, the impulsive, the eccentric, the anti-social, the quarrelsome and the liars and swindlers. This clearly suggested the existence of a general category of which the 'criminal psychopath' represented only one element. Sir David Henderson,[1] a distinguished Scottish psychiatrist with an extensive first-hand knowledge of the subject, divides the general group into three sections, as follows:

(1) *Predominantly aggressive:* these states are intermittent and transitory included amongst the groups are persons who attempt to injure themselves (impulsive suicides, for example), those who attempt to injure others, alcoholics and drug addicts, epileptoid cases, and active sex-variants.

(2) *Predominantly inadequate:* these too may be aggressive but to a lesser degree than in the previous group. If delinquent, they indulge in thieving, lying or swindling and are more persistently abnormal than the aggressive type. They may, however, lean towards neurosis (hysterical, neurasthenic), or psychosis (cycloid or schizoid). They follow the line of least resistance and may be regarded as charming companions.

(3) *Predominantly creative:* includes those geniuses who manifest also states of mental unbalance, heightened sensitivity, and disordered mental equilibrium. The same applies in a lesser degree to cases of heightened ability or 'talent'. All these types are linked by 'an instability, queerness, explosiveness, intuitiveness and egocentricity which form the picture of psychopathic states.'

Regarding this classification, two preliminary comments may be

[1] D. Henderson: 'Psychopathic States', *Brit. J. Delinq.*, **2**, 84–7, 1951.

made. In the first place the criteria of classification are mixed. The first group is isolated on instinctual criteria, the second on standards of ego-efficiency, and the third on the capacity to sublimate instinct. In the second place Henderson, although specially interested in criminal psychopathy, does not isolate a special group of this sort, preferring to distribute anti-social manifestations amongst the first two of his groups. These formulations may be compared with the system advanced by Partridge,[1] who substituted for psychopathy the term 'sociopathy' comprising deviations in social relations with individuals and groups.

When considering these and other classifications in order to obtain an accurate picture of the 'criminal psychopath' it is essential to keep constantly in mind that the main feature of criminal psychopathy, viz. moral obliquity, is estimated by social rather than clinical considerations. The lack of 'moral fibre' is measured by the degree to which the criminal psychopath ignores and contravenes social codes. On the other hand it cannot be denied that the anti-social psychopath, despite his apparent lack of social conscience, may nevertheless have a system of private values that does not differ greatly from that of 'normal' persons. Moreover the 'normal' person may on inspection be found to have a number of anti-social traits which, however, do not bring him in open conflict with the law.[2]

Even more important is the fact that a group exists whose members although showing many of the general characteristics of the criminal psychopath (e.g. urgency to gratify instinctual demands and weakness of the ego), are in the social sense law-abiding and therefore *appear* to have developed a social conscience.

This difficulty can be overcome only if we divide a general state of psychopathy into two sub-groups, viz. a condition of 'private' and (in the social sense) 'benign' psychopathy in which the condition affects the individual's private life and character and a (again socially speaking) 'malignant' or 'criminal' psychopathy

[1] Partridge: 'Current Conceptions of Psychopathic Personality', *Amer. J. Psychiat.*, **10**, 53–79, 1930.

[2] Anthropologically speaking, it can be maintained that not so long ago in the history of mankind what we now call psychopathy was a feature of 'normal' social life. Indeed during wartime it is still incumbent on the combatant to behave like a psychopath practising without conscious guilt, homicide, wounding, destruction of property, robbery with violence and other habits which are forbidden in civilian life.

where the condition gives rise to serious and persistent anti-social manifestations. The 'private' psychopath has often an exaggerated and sensitive conscience and is prone to disordered reactions which are closely akin to melancholic depression. It is incidentally the lack of this working distinction that has led to so much confusion within the group and also to unnecessary overlapping of psychopathy with other mental disorders.

To those who object, not entirely without reason, to the use of social terms such as 'private', 'benign', 'malignant', etc. and who prefer their main classifications to be based on etiological considerations, it might appear desirable to substitute such terms as 'masochistic' psychopathy and 'sadistic' psychopathy respectively; for certainly there is a strong streak of masochism in the make-up of the 'private' psychopath and a marked degree of sadism in the actions of the 'criminal' psychopath or, alternatively, one could use structural instead of dynamic labels and speak of 'ego (subject)' psychopathy and 'object' psychopathy according to whether the psychopathic impulses are on the whole turned on the ego or directed mainly to its objects.

This preliminary sub-division does not, however, resolve all our difficulties. Even the criminal psychopath in whom disorder or stunting of unconscious conscience (super-ego) is a leading feature presents other important symptoms of mental disorder which are not actually anti-social. In other words psychopathy is in the clinical sense a *cluster-formation*, a syndrome comprising a variety of elements. Our first concern in classification must be to establish whether the *combination* of elements is specific enough to justify a special group designation, and second to see whether sub-divisions can be effected in accordance with the loading of different elements. In this connection there is a rough guiding rule in classification, namely, that however various the symptoms of any specific state may appear they should on the whole serve the same general psycho-pathological function. The elements of the syndrome should not be too grossly *antithetical* in function. Descriptively speaking, there is a world of difference between the symptoms of conversion hysteria and those of anxiety hysteria (phobia); yet they serve the same function and have closely similar unconscious causes. On the other hand, although some criminal psychopaths may occasionally exhibit symptoms of depression and in fact may sometimes *end* by committing suicide, it is desirable either to regard such cases as constituting a special sub-group of depressive psychopaths or, if the depression should be a leading feature, to transfer these particular cases to a borderline psychotic group. For on the whole depressive aspects are antithetical in function to the characteristic projective (e.g. anti-social) aspects of criminal psychopathy in that the depressive turns his sadism on himself.[1] To regard suicidal tendencies as psychopathic stigmata is simply to overload the group with cases that are more appropriately placed under the heading of depressive psychoses.

A similar argument applies to the inclusion of alcoholism and drug addiction amongst the signs of psychopathy. Although the criminal psychopath is sometimes addicted to drugs and, though less frequently, to alcohol, most alcoholics and drug addicts are far from being psychopaths. Actually, addicts have closer affinities with the psychoses and the neuroses (with depressive states and the obsessional neuroses). Their psychological make-up places them in the group of 'private' or 'masochistic' pathological disturbances in which the conflict both conscious and unconscious affects mainly their own personalities and at most their familial relations. To be sure, addicts with larval paranoid tendencies may be given to violent conduct: but this is certainly not true of the depressive and obsessive types of addiction which are generally inhibited. As however, alcoholics and drug addicts are neither psychotics nor obsessional neurotics it is convenient to isolate them in a special group, labelling them in accordance with their main clinical manifestation, namely, the chronic habit of taking pharmacotoxic substances. In other words they are psychopathic only in the etymological sense of the term, viz. that their minds are disordered, but not in the special sense with which we are now concerned.[2]

---

[1] This argument is not entirely foolproof, as in certain psychotic conditions, e.g. manic-depressive insanity, the manic and depressive phases stand in antithetical relation; yet despite this clinical alternation they belong correctly to a special group which is in fact often described as 'alternating' insanity. Nevertheless, there is no great justification for including suicidal tendencies as a leading feature of criminal psychopathy. At best they are signs of the co-existence of depressive formations.

[2] In any case addictions can also be divided into 'benign' and 'noxious' types according to the harmfulness of the substance taken: See Edward Glover 'On the Etiology of Drug-Addiction'. *Int. J. Psycho-Anal.*, **13**, 3, 1932, published in *On the Early Development of Mind*. Imago Publishing Co., 1956.

Least of all is there any justification for calling sexual perversions by the term 'sexual psychopathy' or even for regarding them as stigmata of psychopathy. This only confuses the term psychopathy and has no particular merit in itself. In fact the tendency arises from that period of psychiatric investigation when sexual disorders were regarded as signs of degeneration. The group of sexual perversions, deviations or inhibitions deserves a distinguishing caption of its own (with due subdivision of course) just as the terms ego disorder, character disorder, neurosis or psychosis. The psychopath may be perverted, but the pervert is not a psychopath, quite the contrary.

Summing up the problem of defining and classifying psychopathies, it may be said that although the tendency to include under this heading symptom formations which overlap with those of other psychiatric groupings gives us some hint as to the wide ramifications or affiliations of psychopathy, it certainly does not conform to one of the prerequisites of a good classification, viz. that the symptoms or combination of symptoms described should provide a specific diagnostic formula for the general condition and for the main subdivisions of it.

Clinical Features of Psychopathy

Adopting this criterion and excluding those symptom formations which could be more conveniently transferred to another psychiatric grouping, it is possible to assemble a number of stigmata of criminal psychopathy, none of which, however, is specific to psychopathy but which in summation provide a near-to-specific syndrome. When itemizing this reaction syndrome, it is convenient to divide the manifestations into special groups dealing respectively with (i) instinct, (ii) emotional set or temperament, (iii) general character, (iv) general behaviour, (v) working capacity, (vi) reality sense, (vii) moral sense, (viii) individual and social attachments and (ix) anti-social reactions. This subdivision is only for convenience in presentation and not only involves a good deal of overlapping but much repetition of qualifying terms. Incidentally, it is of interest to note how commonly the anti-social characteristics of psychopathy are described in derogatory terms, a fact which suggests that the moral obliquity of the psychopath exists in almost direct ratio to the moral (or social) indignation of the observer, an observation which, incidentally, applies only too often to psychiatric descriptions of the sexual perversions. Psychiatrists cannot altogether dissociate themselves from the ethical implications of their diagnostic terms.

Psychopathic traits, then, can be classified as follows:

I. *Instinctual Characteristics*

Judged by his behaviour the psychopath manifests a general tendency to crude gratification of primitive forms of instinct. These gratifications are irregular in incidence and give the impression of being compulsive episodes. There is also a distinct lack of capacity to control any form of instinctual expression; delay in gratification is badly tolerated.

(*a*) *Sexual instincts:* so-called sexual excesses are frequent: the psychopath tends to be promiscuous and there is a significant interest in homosexual forms, also in sadistic practices: sexual attachments are fleeting and jilting of sexual objects is commonly practised.

(*b*) *Aggressive instincts:* behind an apparently friendly façade the psychopath is aggressive in reaction both in minor and in major social contacts: there is a barely concealed negative attitude particularly to persons of the same sex which often takes an explosive form in outbursts of hate: he is also an aggressive rebel against all forms of authority.

II. *Emotional Set and Temperament*

General tendencies to irritability and excitability combine to create the impression of emotional instability and sensitiveness. Emotional discharge tends to be explosive occurring at irregular intervals. There is, however, only relative quiescence after discharge: hence the impression that the psychopath is perpetually dissatisfied and emotionally disturbed. In spite of his emotional sensitiveness an outstanding shallowness or retardation of positive (friendly) feeling exists which may go so far as to suggest a complete absence of capacity for positive affective contact.

III. *General Character*

Despite a superficial bonhomie and an apparently plausible disposition, the psychopath is outstandingly selfish, egotistical, stubborn and deceitful, with an insatiable appetite for prestige which, however, is irregularly pursued. Setbacks in these capricious efforts only serve to accentuate a general sense of grievance and injustice. He blames others for his misfortunes and is generally defiant, difficult and disharmonious in his relationships.

IV. *General Behaviour*

During psychopathic episodes this is infantile and ill considered to the point almost of irrationality. He acts apparently without thought and his compulsive behaviour is notably foolish and senseless. His psychopathic explosions are stereotyped in character but at other times he is given to eccentric and unpatterned behaviour. He has a penchant for causing trouble in any setting in which he may find himself, although he seldom remains for any length of time in any given setting however favourable it may appear to the observer.

V. *Working Capacity*

The psychopath suffers to an outstanding degree from lack of capacity to concentrate and consequently is incapable of sustained effort or application. This creates a false impression of slackness and lack of drive. He seldom is able to follow regular occupations and throws them up either after a brief trial or when they threaten to be successful. Industrially regarded he is a recalcitrant with a perpetual antagonism to authority: he is given to fomenting trouble for the sake of doing so.

VI. *Reality Sense*

The psychopath may give the superficial impression of shrewdness, particularly regarding the faults of others and his reality sense may appear to be normal. His intelligence may indeed be superior. Yet in fact his insight during episodes is purely 'immediate'. Apparently he cannot foresee consequences, or profit by experience. These tendencies are, however, more apparent than real. He *can* foresee consequences but owing to his need for immediate gratification or **for** emotional discharge this foresight has no restrictive effect on his action.

VII. *Moral Sense*

His psychopathic conduct creates the impression that he is callous, inconsiderate, thoughtless, without conscience or sense of guilt. Hence the general view that he is unprincipled and without moral sense. This latter generalization is however too sweeping, for despite his apparent lack of remorse during episodes, the psychopath may at other times subscribe to quite conventional forms of moral judgment.

VIII. *Individual and Social Attachments*

In addition to his incapacity to form deep personal attachments and his penchant to cause suffering to those who are attached to him, the psychopath is essentially a non-conformist, who in his reaction to society combines hostility with a sense of grievance. Both his individual, his familial and his social allegiances are shot through with negative feeling. If unmarried he constantly exploits women who become attached to him: if married he exploits and neglects his wife and children.

IX. *Anti-Social Reactions*

The psychopath's disorders of social conduct are recurrent, episodic and characterized by the tendency to 'take gambles' (the psychopath is often an actual gambler). His crimes can be classified according to the degree of open aggression and destructiveness manifested. He may be a confirmed liar, cheat and swindler living often on false pretences eked out by petty theft and defalcation which he sometimes achieves by means of impersonation. Or he may be given to crimes of violence or passion of a peculiarly vicious nature, up to and including sadistic murder or plain homicide. He is a recidivist *par excellence* and is not deterred from psychopathic conduct by any form of punishment.

To sum up, the criminal psychopath is a constitutional 'sensitive' peculiarly intolerant of frustration; inclined to sexual 'excess' or perversion, deeply aggressive and openly negativistic; selfish and egotistical, with an immediately ineffective reality sense, incapable of sustained effort; callous, inconsiderate, unprincipled and lacking in moral sense; incapable of deep attachments; given to periods of anti-social conduct; recidivist and refractory to punishment. His psychopathic outbursts are irregular in incidence, stereotyped and on the whole compulsive but even in quiescent periods his character is disharmonious and often eccentric. At the same time he wears the mask of friendly normality.

But although it would seem that we have satisfied the prerequisite of recognizing a clinical group of disorders, viz. the isolation of a specific syndrome or cluster formation having a number of leading features, it would be a serious error to limit our diagnostic efforts to recognizing these pathological features. If psychopathy consisted solely of these abnormal manifestations, the victim of the disorder would be so profoundly disturbed as to justify his certification. The most important feature of psychopathy is the existence of symptomatic processes in a personality that in many respects does not differ from that of a 'normal' person. This gives rise to a dynamic antithesis – a contrast that adds force to the pathological outbursts. This incidentally is also true of some of the neuroses. The force of an obsessional compulsion, for example, depends to some extent on the contrast between the compulsive systems and the general character of the patient which is in many respects inhibited or at any rate free from compulsive reactions. Similarly with the psychopath. The 'normal' aspects of his character are such that he frequently passes amongst his fellows as a stable and even attractive personality. It is the interaction of these normal phases with abreactive periods of psychopathic tension that gives a clue to the dynamics of psychopathy. The neurotic preserves his reality sense by encapsulating his neurosis, the psychotic lends his whole personality to unreality, the psychopath walks on a razor edge between reality and unreality. His outbursts preserve the normal facets of his personality from destruction: his normal aspects add 'discharge-value' to his peculiarities. The essential nature of psychopathy is indicated not through the contrast between his psychopathic behaviour and social standards of behaviour but through the contrast between his psychopathic explosions and his own normal behaviour.

Another comment on the clinical aspects of psychopathy is pertinent. The composite picture of psychopathic character presented above is, of course, the clinical picture of *adolescent and adult psychopathy*. A few enquiries will readily elicit the fact, however, that many of these pathological features were present during the pre-pubertal period and from closer investigation amongst the family it emerges that the psychopath has been a problem child since infancy. During this earliest period, however, it is not possible to apply with such accuracy the test of moral obliquity. Signs of profound disturbances are present but it is difficult to distinguish these from the infantile prodromata of an adolescent or adult schizophrenia, a circumstance which may account to some extent for the fact that many observers stress the schizoid aspects of adult psychopathy, or indeed include the schizoid character amongst the psychopathies.

The general picture of the *child-psychopath* is one of consistent intolerance of frustration leading to frequent outbursts of a tantrum type. Nursery life is a recurrent series of crises, and house-training and discipline is badly tolerated. Infantile sexuality is more than usually manifest and sexual orgies of an aggressive type with other children are common. Destructive behaviour is a prominent feature, and usually follows periods of unusual irritability. Untidiness and unpunctuality develop and during the school period the child psychopath is refractory to teaching and any form of regulation, is commonly a truant and soon a pilferer both at home and abroad. Lying and quite senseless prevarication is a common feature. He cheats on every occasion, preferring deceit for its own sake. Although sometimes quick in perception, his application is poor. His personal attachments are notably tenuous, his family reactions negative, sibling jealousy is prominent. A good deal of his behaviour is of a bizarre type, more so indeed than that of the adult psychopath. And despite a long record of childhood scandals, for which he is often severely chastised, he is quite refractory to punishment.

So striking indeed is the history of consistent disordered conduct from childhood to adolescence, that it constitutes a reliable diagnostic sign in adult cases. The other condition in which a history of heightened sensitiveness to frustration and disordered conduct during infancy and childhood can be elicited is schizophrenia. The child schizophrenic, however, does not exhibit such consistent disorder, and often has periods of apparently normal behaviour both in late childhood and early adolescence. Moreover the disordered behaviour of the child schizophrenic though markedly negative, is largely regressive, neither so active nor so destructive as that of the child psychopath; and he shows intermittently much more open anxiety and an apparently normal moral sense.

Some observers have not been able to confirm this feature of the early history of adult psychopaths, and even maintain that an episodic form of psychopathy exists with an uneventful childhood history. These views cannot altogether be disregarded. Particularly about the period of puberty and for a few years after, spells of disordered conduct with anti-social outbursts can certainly be noted; and these bear a close resemblance to criminal psychopathy. But the tendency nowadays is to describe such episodes as 'pubertal behaviour patterns'. This may appear to be splitting hairs. No doubt children with constitutional sensitivity who have managed to weather the early school period without major disorder may not have sufficient stability to be able to weather the pubertal access of sexual excitation and the hostility it engenders. But in the majority of cases pubertal disorder is transient and requires relatively little readjustment. I have never observed an organized form of late adolescent or adult criminal psychopathy in which careful enquiry could not elicit a consistent history of a psychopathic childhood.

PART II. ETIOLOGY

In pre-Freudian days, the science now known as psychiatry was, from the psychological point of view, a sinecure. Diagnosis and differential diagnosis depended mainly on the acuteness of the psychiatrist's clinical perceptions and on his capacity to isolate specific symptoms, to classify them in large groups and then to distinguish in most cases a number of sub-groups. These tasks he carried out largely on a descriptive basis, labelling the condition or group of conditions usually after some prominent symptomatic feature (e.g. alcoholism, manic-depressive insanity) and less frequently hinting in his terminology at the supposed etiology of the condition (e.g. schizophrenia, neurasthenia). In so far as he employed psychological concepts in his work, these were the concepts of a rational and conscious psychology. If he could indicate what appeared to him to be an obvious (conscious) and apparently rational cause of the condition, good and well. But he was under no obligation to explain irrational manifestations, usually contenting himself in such cases with attributing them to constitutional flaws or to faults in the nervous system; hence the original use of the term 'neurosis' as distinguished from 'psychosis'.

With the advent of psycho-analysis this situation underwent a radical alteration. Freud's early work was mainly concerned with the unconscious factors giving rise to those conditions which he specified as 'psycho-neuroses'. When after a time he turned to the etiology of the psychoses, the ground was prepared for rapid advances in the classification of mental disorders. Having isolated specific unconscious factors in a number of these disorders, it became possible to classify the psycho-neuroses and psychoses *in depth*, that is to say, in accordance with the *developmental level* in childhood at which the specific flaws arose which predisposed the individual to later mental disorder.[1] For it was Freud's view that there was no adult neurosis without an infantile neurosis, a formulation which *mutatis mutandis* can now be extended to most

---

[1] See Glover: 'Psycho-analytical Classification of Mental Disorders', *J. Ment. Sci.*, 1932; reprinted in *On the Early Development of Mind* (Chap. XI), Imago Publishing Co., 1956.

mental disorders; e.g. no adult psychosis without an infantile psychosis, or, more germane to our present study, no adult 'pathological crime' without 'infantile pathological delinquency'.

At all times Freud was careful to distinguish both *constitutional* and *environmental* (immediate precipitating) factors, from the *developmental* factors which result from pathological fixation at unconscious infantile levels and give rise to the unconscious *predisposition to illness*. He was never in any doubt that these unconscious (endopsychic) factors played the most important part in late symptom formation. Therapeutically this was a promising view (though Freud was no optimist regarding the effective range of psychotherapy); for it suggested that resolution of these early conflicts would materially advance the prospects of symptomatic amelioration and, in well selected cases, of 'cure'.

The possibility of achieving a psycho-analytical classification of psychiatric disorders *on the basis of their etiology* was retarded by the realization that a number of important disorders could not be pigeonholed under the classical categories and that in fact a good deal of mental suffering could be caused by abnormalities in *character formation*, without apparently any neurotic or other symptom-formations. In fact a large proportion of the analyst's practice was constituted of pathological character formations apparently more difficult to resolve than at any rate the psycho-neuroses. And it became clear that these character cases must also be classified in terms of flaws in the unconscious development of what is sometimes called the 'total personality'.

The first step in this direction was to make a broad distinction between cases in which instinctual stress (the prime motor of mental activity) is dealt with on the whole by modification (either mental or physical) of the individual himself, from cases where on the whole attempts are made to release the tension by modification of environment. These two tendencies were described by Freud and Ferenczi as respectively '*autoplastic*' and '*alloplastic*' and are, of course, *normal processes* without a combination of which life would be either insupportable or indeed impossible. But it was soon observed that *abnormal processes* could be classified in the same way. The *psycho-neuroses*, for example, were obviously autoplastic in nature, modifying the mind to meet conflict by the development of symptom formations, which only to a minor extent affected external relationships. Equally clearly the *psychotic's* hallucinatory and delusional techniques were alloplastic attempts to modify the environmental to his primitive needs.

It was only logical then to enquire whether *character formations*, *either abnormal or normal*, could be subdivided in the same way as neurotic symptoms. The passive, inhibited type was obviously autoplastic in character, the active aggressive type equally obviously alloplastic. The ascetic person is autoplastic: the criminal psychopath alloplastic seeking to bend the environment to his imperious (infantile) will or attacking it in default of satisfaction. The suicide is an autoplast: the murderer an alloplast.

Early Psycho-analytical Characterology

But this is to anticipate. In the meantime we may note that early psycho-analytical classifications both of normal and of exaggerated character traits were strongly influenced by interest in the *development of the libido*. By 1925 a series of distinctive character traits had been isolated and traced respectively to oral, anal (and urethral) and infantile genital stages of development.[1] Of these the traits most relevant to the study of psychopathy were oral impatience, omnipotence and envy and the obstinacy characteristic of the anal type. Even more relevant were some obsessional characteristics described by Freud, viz. quarrelsomeness, peevishness, argumentativeness and pettiness,[2] and the reactions of the 'resistant' types claiming to be 'exceptions' exempt from all restrictions of the pleasure principle. Such types he maintained had suffered libidinal thwarting during the infantile period, adding that women who felt that they had been unfairly injured during childhood (as psychopaths do, not always unjustly), had an unabsorbed castration complex. A study by Jones of the influence of omnipotent father phantasies on the ego was also relevant to the psychopathic character.[3] To sum up, the governing features of

---

[1] Freud: 'Character and Anal Erotism', *C.P.*, **2.** E. Jones: 'Analerotic Character Traits', *Papers on Psycho-Analysis*, Baillière Tindall & Cox, 1923. K. Abraham: 'Contributions to the Theory of Anal Character', *Int. J. Psycho-Anal.*, **4**, 4, 1923 (*Selected Papers*, Hogarth Press, 1927). Edward Glover: 'Notes on Oral Character Formation', *Int. J. Psycho-Anal.*, **6**, 2, 1925 (*On the Early Development of Mind: Selected Papers on Psycho-Analysis*, **1**, Imago Publishing Co, 1956). K. Abraham: 'Manifestations of the Female Castration Complex', *Int. J. Psycho-Anal.*, **3**, 1922.

[2] Freud: 'The Predisposition to Obsessional Neurosis', *C.P.*, **2.**

[3] Jones: 'The God-Complex', *Essays in Applied Psycho-Analysis*, Hogarth Press, 1923.

abnormal character traits were the absence of conflict or of any struggle against regression both of which trends are of considerable significance in psychopathy.

Following Freud's structural formulations which divided the mental apparatus into ego, super-ego and Id, and his later formulations of the relations of the neuroses to the psychoses,[1] psycho-analytical characterology took on an increasingly structural aspect whilst still maintaining that as Freud remarked, the 'illogicalities eccentricities and follies of mankind' enable abnormal types to 'spare themselves repressions.'

The earliest general formulation regarding character deviations was that of Alexander[2] who under the caption 'The Neurotic Character' described persons who live out their impulses, are often asocial and 'driven by a demoniac compulsion'. They make life their neurosis. They differ from neurotics in not seeking for substitute gratifications of primitive impulse. The overwhelming power of their Id-impulses produces tendencies alien to the ego. Also their gratifications are alloplastic as distinct from the autoplastic gratifications of the neurotic. Although conscious conflict and insight are absent, conflict does exist, and the neurotic character's behaviour ends in self-punishment. The ego is weaker than that of the neurotic and behaviour is irrational and apparently senseless.

It is clear from this description that, although the range of Alexander's 'neurotic character' is wider than that of the criminal psychopath, it includes traits that are commonly found in criminal psychopathy. This is even more obvious in the case of Reich's 'triebhafter' character.[3] Reich included these special types under the general heading of neurotic characters but distinguished them from inhibited characters in that they are subject to a primitive compulsion to repeat their behaviour, that this behaviour acts out unmodified instincts and that there is no specific 'fixation point' in development, only a specific developmental disturbance of the ego.

[1] Freud: *The Ego and the Id*, Hogarth Press, 1927; 'Neurosis and Psychosis' and 'The Loss of Reality in Neurosis and Psychosis', *C.P.*, 2.
[2] Alexander: 'The Castration Complex and the Formation of Character', *Int. J. Psycho-Anal.*, 4, 1923; 'The Neurotic Character' ibid. 11, 292–313, 1930.
[3] Reich: *Der triebhafte Charakter*, I.P.V., 1925

These 'instinct-ridden' characters manifest open ambivalence, sadistic actions unaccompanied by guilt, and are usually sexually perverted. On the other hand they often present neurotic symptoms and frequently schizoid characteristics.

Looking back, it is apparent that the concepts of 'neurotic character' and 'instinct-ridden character', although pointing in the right etiological direction, were in the clinical sense both confused and confusing, a state of affairs which was not lessened by an early attempt on my own part to isolate yet another set of 'neurotic characters'.[1] Included under this grouping were persons showing incapacity for everyday social adaptation leading to emotionally toned crises; a tendency to breakdown when faced with circumstances calling for decisive action; prone to matrimonial crises; suffering from exaggerated suspicion and a tendency to regard themselves as the victim of conspiring circumstances. The crises usually followed a change in the libidinal milieu and were repetitive in nature, often engineered to meet periodic stresses of instinctual tension. This type of neurotic character brought about situations of self-injury and thereby caused a good deal of unhappiness to his family and circle of friends. But although refractory to customs and conventions *he was not noticeably anti-social in behaviour*, and was prepared to justify his actions with cast-iron rationalizations. He suffered from ineffectiveness in action, and his financial activities usually ended in failure. He changed one ineffective occupation for another and ended by feeling himself to be a martyr. His love life was repetitive and usually ended in disappointment: although sometimes mildly homosexual in adolescence or early adult life, his sexuality was inhibited rather than perverted. He might also exhibit mild neurotic symptoms, occasionally mild hypochondria, and intense but muted envy and jealousy of his familiars. Infantile character reactions mostly of a frustrated oral type were present. Id components were accentuated, ego control relatively ineffective, his super-ego capricious in function, and his sublimations rudimentary and ineffective. In general this type of neurotic character took advantage of rather than attacked the social situation, disguising his solution broadly

---

[1] Edward Glover: 'The Neurotic Character', *Brit. J. med. Psychol.*, 4, 1925, reprinted in *On the Early Development of Mind* (Chap. III), Imago Publishing Co., 1956

speaking under accepted social conventions. His disorder was diffuse and there was a general deficiency of the sense of reality.

The flaw in this description is obvious; it exceeded the limitations of the term 'neurotic' and included some traits that might have been considered signs of a psychotic character (jealousy, hypochondria, etc.). Indeed even in this early paper I felt convinced that it was essential to exclude psychotic types of character from the group.[1] The virtue of the description lay in isolating a special group of neurotic characters from the more violent and aggressive egocentrics and in particular from the criminal psychopath. In fact the group suggested the existence of (in the social sense) a 'benign' or 'masochistic' group of psychopaths who on the whole injure themselves much more than they injure others.

As events proved it became necessary to confine the term 'neurotic' character to (*a*) personality disorders in which mainly *neurotic mechanisms* are exploited in life relations, and (*b*) those which are dynamically '*equivalents*' *of neurosis*, i.e. have similar localized fixation points and perform like defensive functions. In short it is clinically justifiable to distinguish (*a*) hysterical characters (which incidentally may exhibit anti-social crises) and (*b*) obsessional characters (who are rarely anti-social). These are true neurotic characters, and are to be distinguished from (*a*) depressive or cyclothymic characters (seldom anti-social except in the maniacal phase), (*b*) paranoid characters (frequently anti-social) and (*c*) schizoid characters (frequently anti-social). These are true psychotic characters.

These clinical distinctions can be supplemented by the isolation of other groups; for example, the epileptoid character, and the alcoholic character or group of characters. Although it is often difficult to distinguish the hysterical, the paranoid and the schizoid characters from the true psychopath, *none of the above groups are strictly speaking 'psychopathic' characters.* When these neurotic and psychotic characters have been split off from the general group of character disorders, the remaining types will usually be found to qualify for the term general psychopathy, and to be divisible (in the social sense) into benign (or masochistic) and malignant (or

---

[1] Ferenczi always maintained that character peculiarities were 'private psychoses' tolerated by the ego, but this was not a very practical clinical distinction.

sadistic) types, the latter of which comprise the different forms of criminal psychopathy or as Partridge termed it, 'sociopathy'.

With this involved discussion we have completed the circle and are once more confronted with the fact that legal codes compel us to distinguish 'criminal psychopathy' from other disorders and that medical psychology is compelled to admit the clinical justness of the distinction. Under these circumstances the only satisfactory course open to us is to review the situation from the point of view of unconscious etiological factors.

Psycho-analytical Etiology

All psycho-analytical approaches to clinical descriptive psychology, to etiology and to classification of mental disorders are governed by one working formulation, viz. that no psychic event or construction can be described adequately unless it is approached from three points of view: (i) the dynamic or instinctual; (ii) the economic or mechanistic and; (iii) the structural or topographical. Needless to say, this *metapsychological* approach, as it is called, must be supplemented by various other cardinal concepts, including the existence of unconscious forces and mental institutions, the unconscious Id, the partly unconscious ego, and the mostly unconscious super-ego; also the division of the mind into developmental layers or phases which to some extent retain their differing forms of function throughout life. While recognizing the importance of *constitutional factors* in all varieties of mental function psycho-analysts prefer to consider these as operating through the Id, and to describe them in terms of instinctual strength or weakness, of affective type, of sensitiveness to stimulation and frustration, and of tendencies to deal with excitation in ways which are subsequently organized and recognized as unconscious mental mechanisms. In the case of psychopathy, for example, constitutional factors may be assumed to be responsible for the following general reactions: tendencies to irritability, excitability and a-rhythmic responses, sensitivity, intolerance of frustration, flight and aggressive reactions, explosive discharge and swings from active to passive. Anxiety readiness is also a constitutional factor and possibly the degree of guilt-readiness also, although that is by no means so certain. The sexual constitution and the weighting of infantile components are constitutionally determined in the first instance, also the primary force of aggressive instincts. Finally the tendencies of the mind which subsequently develop into unconscious mechanisms are no doubt constitutionally variable. Nevertheless these factors can be assessed only through their metapsychological effects and expressed in terms of the following groups:

I. *Dynamic (instinctual)*

Study of the character traits of criminal psychopaths together with analysis of their private phantasies and dream life indicate that the infantile instincts *mainly* concerned are pregenital, derived from a combination of oral and anal phases together with the characteristic sadistic reactions to frustration at these levels. No one of these traits is specific but it is possible that in this libidinal triad (oral and anal erotism and sadism) we have a combination of instincts which predisposes to psychopathy. In particular the *oral-sadistic* elements are well marked and are characteristic of the *orally dissatisfied type*. This type is extremely ambivalent to objects, has rapid motor reactions to disappointment and equally rapid emotional discharge. A strong need exists for the environment to perform maternal functions. The psychopath expects to get what he wants from society and feels that it is the fault of the community if he is not supported. Any frustration gives rise to a fury of impatience together with envy, grudge and a sense of injustice. The oral sadism is of the biting (cannibalistic) type. The psychopath is given not only to disappointing those concerned with him, but to 'taking from' them with a feeling of justification. These are forms of oral sadistic revenge.

The *anal-sadistic phase* of the criminal psychopath serves to reinforce the foregoing characteristics. Apart from increased irritability the anal libidinal component accentuates earlier reactions to frustration, producing states of defiance and resentment of interference which may lead to outbursts of anger and rage, together with a strong sense of injustice. Advice is usually rejected – a factor to be noted by those who treat psychopaths – and the characteristic of self-willedness produces a sense of compulsion in action.[1] Above all the sadistic reaction to frustrating objects is extremely marked and is reinforced by anal obstinacy.

[1] For a detailed account of anal-erotic characteristics see Jones: 'Anal-erotic Character Traits', *Papers on Psycho-Analysis*, London, Baillière, Tindall & Cox, 4th Edn., 1938.

Frustration reactions at both oral and anal stages are responsible for an exaggeration of the *narcissistic valuation of the growing ego* and this in turn increases the psychopath's sensitiveness and egocentricity. It also interferes with his capacity to make friendly identifications with objects and so reduces to a low level both altruism and the capacity to love. The object is of value only so far as it enhances the patient's ego. Hence the tendency to exploit society which is so marked a feature of psychopathy.

This naturally raises the question of the strength of the *infantile genital impulses* in psychopathy, a matter concerning which there is a good deal of difference of analytical opinion. Some observers believe that the fixations of the psychopath are *exclusively* pregenital and narcissistic. This is not my experience. To be sure the manifest sexual life of the psychopath includes occasional phases of homosexual interest, and even when these are not manifest the factor of unconscious homosexuality is not hard to detect. The phantasies are on the whole of an 'active' type. It would, however, be a mistake to exclude the influence of unconscious heterosexual infantile genital impulse, or, perhaps it would be more accurate to say, of unconscious conflict over infantile genital incestuous impulse. This is responsible for some of the unexpected genital inhibitions of the psychopath and for his more frequent regression to non-genital forms of sexual drive. The trouble about his infantile genital impulses is that they are strongly impregnated with sadism, an analytical observation which can be easily confirmed in the cases of sexual murder, where incidentally the genital or other sexual violations occasionally occur after the murder, not before it.

II. *Economic (mechanistic)*

It should be made clear at the outset that no mental mechanism is specific to psychopathy. The whole rota of unconscious mechanisms (regression, projection, introjection, repression, identification, displacement, reaction formation, sublimation *et alia*) are normal methods whereby the mind deals with excitatory processes and play an all-important part in normal development and behaviour. When the psycho-analyst maintains that paranoia is a 'projective' psychosis, he means that the primary tendency of the mind to deal with painful excitations as if they came from without has been exaggerated to the point where reality sense is disturbed and (e.g.) persecutory delusions are developed regarding the attitudes of external objects to him. The paranoiac is an expert projector: the projector is not necessarily a paranoiac.

Moreover it should be remembered that with the development of the mind the channels along which mental mechanisms operate become increasingly tortuous. This complexity is brought about by the processes of introjection of the imagos of external (instinctual) objects and identification. Not only so, the aims of the instincts directed towards external objects are modified during development. So that what was at first a dynamic defence against painful excitation is increasingly modified and itself develops ultimately into a pattern of object relationship.

Psychopathy is especially interesting in this connection. For outside the paranoias, paranoid characters, and the paranoid wings of schizophrenia and of schizoid characters, there is no psychopathological state in which the mechanism of projection is so consistently exploited as in criminal psychopathy. True, some alcoholics may also tend to pathological use of projection and the hysterical character, within circumscribed emotional limits, is also at times a projector. But their use of projection is more episodic. The psychopath overworks his projection mechanisms not only during crises of behaviour but during the more quiescent phases when his behaviour does not appear to be particularly abnormal. In other words his *Weltanschauung* is essentially projective. And his sublimatory mechanisms tend in consequence to be inhibited. As will be noted under the heading of treatment, displacement is an essential auxiliary to the projective system and gives rise to characteristic negative 'transference' reactions.

Although it cannot be claimed that pathological projection is specific to criminal psychopathy, it is not difficult to distinguish psychopathic projective types from other projective states with the possible exception of the schizoid character. For the criminal psychopath is not only a consistent projector but has been continuously a pathological projector since his earliest childhood. The peculiarly psychopathic nature of his projection can, however, be ascertained only by study of the instincts or component instincts (e.g. reactive aggression and sadism) giving rise to pathological excitation or by examination of the structures of his mind through which these excitations are made to pass.

III. *Topographic (structural)*

In view of the fact that moral obliquity is the hallmark of the criminal psychopath and that the action of unconscious conscience is easiest to grasp by using structural analogies and conceiving of a special scrutinizing ego institution, the *super-ego*, which promotes the activities of conscience, it would seem that structural factors are most likely to provide a specific etiology and a possible subdivision of psychopathic states.

Now the super-ego is laid down as the result of the action of unconscious *introjection* by which the imagos of parents or their substitutes are psychically incorporated in the ego to form a special active imprint (ultimately an institution) which establishes parental influences in the mind. This imprint although including realistic impressions of the regulating and controlling activities and codes of parents is constantly distorted by the operation of the mechanism of projection previously described. The child projecting his hostile reaction phantasies on to the imagos of the parents creates imagos that are more powerful and draconic in morality than the parents actually are. So as he continues to introject parental imagos, the child introjects these distorted elements also, with the result that his unconscious conscience can be more severe (sadistic) and continuous in action than are the realistic interferences of the parents.

These exaggerations are of course quite normal, and are gradually modified as with increasing reality estimations of the actual character and attitudes of parents more lenient imagos are gradually introjected and buttressed by friendly ego-identifications. This process is accelerated by the abandonment, or by the effective repression, of the infantile sexual drives towards parents, the inevitable frustration of which causes marked infantile hostility to objects and thereby encourages excessive projection.

But in such instances we are taking for granted that the actual behaviour of the parents is humane enough, protective enough and consistent enough to promote friendly introjections and identifications and therefore a more lenient super-ego and a more adaptable ego. Now that is precisely what we cannot assume in the case of most criminal offenders and particularly of criminal psychopaths. In recent years a voluminous literature has sprung up regarding the nature of the environmental influences to which the offender is subjected. Emphasis has been laid, for example, on the child's need for consistent affection and security, so much so that the term 'broken home' has been grossly overworked. For a moment's consideration will show that not all children coming from a 'broken home' manifest delinquent tendencies. They may not even show 'neurotic' reactions, although that outcome is common enough. Nevertheless the term has its uses and has in fact been extended to include as many as sixteen varieties, e.g. death of parents, absence of parents, one or other or both, over lengthy intervals, illegitimacy and the like.[1] And the same applies to such concepts as 'separation anxiety', the 'affectionless child' and other environmental concepts.[2]

When we add to this the factors of ill-treatment or unwise treatment (e.g. violent fluctuations in parental reaction which appear inexplicable to the child), discord and open quarrelling between parents, sexual traumas and others undue excitations and a host of other unsatisfactory family conditions, not excluding, by the way, the influence of delinquent parents, it is not hard to surmise that the child's imago of 'bad' parents (which it introjects) is in many instances not without a considerable degree of justification. After all the child has even more reason to believe that these influences are 'bad' than the psychiatrist who castigates them in professional textbooks and nowadays in the popular press.

But although surveys of this important subject are far from complete we are entitled to assume from some of the more convincing studies and especially from psycho-analytical investigations that an emotionally traumatic factor is of considerable importance in psychopathy, inflamed no doubt by constitutional sensitiveness. It must be emphasized, however, that the effect of these infantile environmental traumas is not just an immediate one but *in summation* warps the *development* of the unconscious superego. In other words the *environmental* factor fosters the development of an *endopsychic* factor in delinquency. It is necessary to emphasize this point, for recently a new kind of specialist – the familial sociologist or as he might be called, the child sociopsychiatrist, has taken enthusiastically to studies in which the

---

[1] Batchelor and Napier: 'Broken Homes and Attempted Suicide', *Brit. J. Delinq.*, 4, 99, 1953.

[2] J. Bowlby: *Forty-Four Juvenile Thieves*, Baillière, Tindall & Cox, 1946; and *Maternal Care and Mental Health*, W.H.O. Monographs, 1952.

endopsychic consequences of environmental influences are totally ignored and the environmental factor consequently either exaggerated or misinterpreted, that is to say, taken at its face value.

Here again we cannot claim to have uncovered a specific unconscious factor of *traumatism* in criminal psychopathy, but it does explain to some extent why the mechanism of projection plays such a prominent part in the condition. And it does explain why the immediate precipitating factor in any given outbreak may sometimes be apparently trivial. In these instances it is merely a trigger impulse which touches off an explosion. In the M'Naghten case the homicide conceived that his victim was scowling at him.

The next step is to examine the structure of the super-ego in the criminal psychopath to ascertain whether any particular type can be recognized, or whether any particular layer of the super-ego is pathologically warped. And here we touch on a comparatively unexplored psycho-analytical field. For even in the case of normal super-ego development, we have as yet only the most rudimentary forms of classification. Two main approaches are possible, namely, to isolate super-ego forms associated with maternal and paternal imagos respectively, and to recognize the stage of development of the libido at which traumatic fixations or frustrations have occurred. In this latter sense we can speak of oral, anal or infantile-genital super-egos. In fact it is essential to combine both standards, and when tracing the instinctual components to pay special attention to the factor of sadism.

Now in normal cases it is not hard to observe that the super-ego is based primarily on introjection of the frustrating parent. Thus the original form of super-ego is a maternal super-ego and the original frustrating factor is an oral one. Fortunately this is offset, first, by the more positive relations existing between the child and its mother which ultimately promote friendly identifications and so strengthen the ego, and second, by super-ego elements derived from the parent of the opposite sex who is not yet the more important frustrator. This permits an elastic alternation. For when in due course the frustrating father is introjected to form a sadistic father super-ego, the child can meet this extra strain partly by regression to the maternal super-ego and partly by strengthening its ego.

Examining now the case of the psychopath, it is not difficult to ascertain that both the maternal and paternal aspects of the super-ego are primitive and sadistic in tendency and that the unconscious phantasies of the child are concerned mainly with oral and anal-sadistic images. Moreover, as the child is soon, or soon feels, frustrated by both parents simultaneously and over prolonged periods, it has not the same chance as the normal child of strengthening its ego by friendly identifications. The identifications, exaggerated by unconscious phantasy, tend to be of a hostile type.

This is a psychic situation which threatens all normal development. It is, however, not specific to psychopathy and can be observed also in cases of depression. The difference, however, between the depressive and the psychopath lies in the fate of the sadistic and masochistic impulses. The constitutional masochism of the depressive leads to his anchoring released sadism in the ego, in other words he turns it against himself: on the other hand the constitutionally reinforced sadism of the psychopath leads to his reflecting it against the world of external objects.

The function of projection in psychopathy thus becomes a little clearer. The psychopath's sadism is constitutionally strong; his traumatic experiences tend to focus this on the apparent or actual external causes of mental pain, i.e. in the first instance the parents; his early super-ego forms are sadistic in type and his ego-identifications are if anything even more hostile. All this leads to a sadistic overcharge of the mental apparatus. Little or no equivalent binding force of a loving nature exists to cancel out or offset this sadistic overcharge. So the psychopath falls back on and accentuates the projective system, which in any case plays a part in super-ego formation. *There is no question therefore of the non-existence of the super-ego in psychopathy:* at most one can say that the psychopath on the whole, remains arrested at an earlier form of super-ego formation where the central issue of mental life is the control of sadism, and where projection is part of the ordinary sequence of super-ego formation.

Fortunately for society and for the resources of mental hospitals this super-ego fixation, even in the case of violent criminal psychopaths, is only relative. As has been noted these cases may also exhibit perfectly normal super-ego facets. We are in fact forced to the conclusion that it is misleading to talk at any time of a unified or synthesized super-ego, but must distinguish between those layers or nuclei of it that have undergone arrest at a primitive level and those that have undergone a development that approximates to that of the normal person.

Some twenty years ago I advanced this nuclear theory of ego (and super-ego) development[1] and it still seems to me that this theory explains *inter alia* some of the more baffling contradictions of the psychopath's nature and behaviour. We may then assume that during the periodic crises in behaviour, the more primitive ego and super-ego nuclei command the approaches to consciousness and that the trigger-impulse of the crisis is an endopsychic over-excitation of a sadistic nature, which sets in action the constitutionally reinforced tendency to projection. The psychopath has indeed a super-ego but during crises it operates in reverse action.

To this outline of the three main metapsychological groups of factors in the etiology of criminal psychopathy, it is necessary to add some reflection on the nature of disturbance of *reality-sense*. For as has been suggested, in the sense of effective function the psychopath manifests a degree of disturbance of reality-sense which although descriptively different from that observed in the psychoses has many affinities with the psychotic's reaction to reality. In particular he seems to have little capacity for effective foresight, meaning thereby that though during crises he is aware of possible consequences of his actions, this does not appear to exert any restraining effect on immediate action.

When, however, we come to consider the causes of this disturbance of reality-testing, we are faced with the fact that the problem of reality adaptation is one that is as yet far from being solved. The general contributing factors are, however, not difficult to indicate. They include: (*a*) constitutional factors, (*b*) domination of the pleasure principle during early infancy, (*c*) strength of the impulses of aggression, in particular of those impulses which combine with the libido to form the sadistic group, (*d*) confusion at early developmental levels of internal experience and external perception, (*e*) strength of projective mechanisms, (*f*) inversion of the usual super-ego relations in consequence of which the restrain-

---

[1] 'Psycho-analytical Approach to the Classification of Mental Disorders', *J. Ment. Sci.*, Oct. 1932; 'The Relation of Perversion Formation to the Development of Reality Sense', *Int. J. Psycho-Anal.*, **14**, 486, 1933; 'The Concept of Dissociation', *Int. J. Psycho-Anal.*, **24**, 1, 2, 1943. Reprinted in *On the Early Development of Mind*.

ing effect of positive object relations is limited, not only immediately but in anticipation.

Of these the last is perhaps the most significant. I have on earlier occasions described reality sense as depending on a capacity to maintain psychic contact with instinctual objects, whether or not the instinctual impulses concerned have been, are, or are likely to be gratified. The psychopath's tenuousness of libidinal relations and his overcharge of sadism reduces his positive object contacts to a dangerously weak level. Unlike the psychotic he does not abandon reality estimations, unlike the neurotic he does not retain infantile forms of positive relation but he is unable to appreciate the force of object relations beyond an immediately ideational level. His reality sense during crises is thus of the most fleeting nature. Needless to add this applies only to those phases of reaction which constitute psychopathic crises. At other times his reality sense does not differ greatly from that of a normal person.

It remains to consider how far these etiological considerations affect the general *terminology* of psychopathy or enable us to formulate precise subdivisions of the main group of criminal psychopaths. As I have said we still have much to learn about the layers or nuclei of ego and super-ego formation. But already the combined factors of parental introjection and of libidinal layers of development would permit us to postulate at least six different types of abnormal super-ego in such cases, i.e. paternal and maternal super-egos, subdivided in terms of oral-sadistic, anal-sadistic and genital-sadistic fixations. And doubtless the permutations and combinations would be greatly increased if we took into account the factors of relative activity or passivity and of variations in traumatism. All this suggests that given adequate psycho-analytical research on character formation, we may be able to abandon the characterological term psychopathy and substitute metapsychological labels. In the first instance no doubt structural captions would be the most useful. But in the long run it is probable that diagnostic *formulæ*[1] will replace one-factor nomenclature of all mental disorder. That time, however, is not yet.

[1] See Glover: 'Ego-Distortion', *Int. J Psycho-Anal.*, **39**, 260–4, 1958.

PART III. TREATMENT

A. Rationale

It must be confessed, not without regret, that the treatment of criminal psychopathy has not yet passed the empirical stage. It is true that, due largely to psycho-analytical researches on the normal structure of mind and in particular on the development of unconscious conscience and of social feeling, we know a great deal more about the nature of psychopathy than we did. Nevertheless the hunt for a specific etiology of the condition is as yet far from the kill. And until we are able to establish a specific etiology or, better still, specific etiologies of different sub-groups of criminal psychopathy it is not possible to direct therapeutic methods, whatever their nature and technique, with the necessary precision.

Not that there is anything to be ashamed of in an objective empiricism. The main disadvantage of empiricism is that the observer's awareness of ignorance not only inhibits his readiness to look in the right directions but inevitably tends to bias him in favour of conclusions arrived at by earlier empirical observers, which by that time may be quite inadequate. Thus in the case of criminal psychopathy, the earlier empiricism of the law led to the view that the criminal psychopath was an incorrigible. This of course simply meant that he was incorrigible by the penal methods then employed; in other words, that he was refractory to punishment. Hence the incongruity of the severe sentences inflicted at that time.

This legalistic and somewhat revengeful pessimism was reinforced by the experience of psychiatrists from the time of Prichard onward. They too noted that adolescent and, even more, adult criminal psychopaths were refractory not only to punishment but to existing methods of treatment. With the unfortunate consequence that this refractoriness was attributed to the psychopath's repudiation of law-abiding influences and not regarded, as it should have been, as an essential characteristic of his disorder. However this may be, the tendency in both legal and psychiatric circles still is to regard the psychopath as a penal recidivist and a therapeutic recalcitrant.

An even more unfortunate consequence of this psychiatric pessimism is that, instead of regarding this recalcitrancy as a therapeutic challenge, the psychiatrist, when faced with an obstinate case (and as has been noted, obstinacy is a feature of psychopathy), falls back on institutional recommendations (either of prison or of hospital supervision) long before the more patient resources of individual 'ambulant' therapy have been exhausted. Perhaps this counsel of despair too owed something of its animus to a mute but nevertheless active professional revengefulness .It has always been a cardinal sin for patients to be so ungrateful for professional attentions as to remain refractory to them. On the other hand we must not forget that the professional patience of the psychiatrist is sorely tried by the aggressive obstinacy of the psychopath. So much so, that it is possible to lay down dogmatically the following axiom: *no psychiatrist should ever attempt to treat a psychopath who has neither sufficient understanding of psychopathy nor sufficient counter-transference to endure the psychopath's assaults on his most cherished possession, namely, his capacity to heal.* In other words the prerequisite of any therapy of the psychopath is a capacity to endure repeated disappointment.

Another distant effect of the empirical approach is to be found in the fact that until comparatively recently the psycho-therapeutic methods employed were not specially designed for the psychopathic criminal: they were methods that had been found useful in a number of psycho-pathological states (neuroses, character disorders and sexual disabilities) in which as a rule no special anti-social features are present. It was natural, however, to experiment with these methods in anti-social cases also, ignoring the fact that, as in the case of manifest psychoses, methods of treatment must be adapted to the special necessities of the case.

Fortunately there was some theoretical justification for this apparently unimaginative procedure. This lay in the fact, discovered by Freud, that all forms of psychotherapy, whatever their special technique, depend in the last resort on the method of handling the *transference* – i.e. that state of potential *rapport* existing between psycho-therapist and his patient which is determined by unconscious patterns of infantile reaction (both friendly and hostile) displaced to the current therapeutic situation. In fact all psycho-therapeutic methods can be divided into two main groups, namely, (*a*) methods in which the transference is manipulated, either deliberately or intuitively, in order to bring about an improvement in symptoms or behaviour, and, (*b*) analytical methods by which the transference is first of all used to encourage the unfolding of unconscious factors and then dissolved or 'analysed out' in order to free the patient from an infantile state of dependence.

There are of course other means of distinguishing between therapeutic techniques, but this is not only the most convenient but the most radical criterion. It enables us to say, for example, that even if we use an analytical 'approach' (as in some forms of 'short' therapy) but leave the transference unanalysed, the method, however much it may be guided by analytical information, depends for its result on the factor of unconscious *rapport*. This is more obviously the case where methods of hypnosis, suggestion, re-education, exhortation, moral suasion or ethical influences are employed. These are *rapport* therapies *par excellence*.

We may, however, pause for a moment to contrast the rationale of hypnosis with that of psycho-analysis proper. The application of hypnosis to criminal cases has been from the first a purely empirical device. Apart from securing an outline of the 'symptomatic' history, no particular knowledge of the psychodynamics of the case is called for. In the case of psycho-analysis the aim of the technique is to reduce those specific factors responsible for the 'symptoms' or malfunction. And this presupposes not only an understanding of psychodynamics in general but of the specific etiology of different clinical types of case. Under ordinary circumstances, however, the psycho-analytical technique is the same in all cases, namely, the unfolding of unconscious instinctual life, the reduction of resistances, and defences (by interpretation and by 'working through'), the analysis of unconscious ego institutions, in particular of the super-ego, and the final resolution of infantile transferences.

In recent years a number of special techniques have been developed (so-called hypno-analysis, and narco-analysis, analytically directed group therapy and 'focal' ('sector' or 'vector') analysis) in which analytical methods are either combined with other techniques or trimmed to deal with special 'disturbed' areas of the mind. But as has been suggested these cannot really be regarded as psycho-analyses proper, and as far as results are concerned they should be rated as *rapport* therapies. It is convenient therefore to begin our survey of treatment by a description of psychopathic responses to psycho-analysis.

(1) *Psycho-analytic Therapy*

The first and most practical discovery made in the course of analysing delinquents in general and in particular criminal psychopaths was that treatment begins with the patient in a state of *negative* (hostile) *transference*. Whereas the psycho-neurotic commences his analysis with sufficient free positive (friendly) transference to carry him into the analytic process or situation, *the criminal psychopath begins treatment in a state of hostile defence*. In the case of the neurotic this hostile transference can only be *uncovered* in the middle stages of the analysis and only then after the most searching investigation of transference phenomena. This 'floating negative' of the criminal psychopath is greatly reinforced in that, with the exception of cases seen in private practice, the patient accepts treatment mostly under duress. Treatment may, for example, be made a condition of probation; in which case the patient enters upon it with an additional load of 'negative' displaced from the penal authorities to the psycho-therapeutist. Unless this unsatisfactory situation is fully ventilated at the earliest possible opportunity, treatment is likely either to founder or, if continued, to be undermined by a reinforced drive to sabotage it.

But even if analytic treatment is entered upon voluntarily the need of the psychopath to sabotage the process is still overpowering. His hostile transferences are governed by two special tendencies; first, to *test the analyst's capacity to endure his conduct* and second *to disappoint his therapeutic aims* by a series of relapses or crises. These tendencies are superimposed on a more fundamental characteristic of the psychopath, viz., *to act out his unconscious phantasies in his personal relations*.

In the case of the psycho-neurotic such acting out is confined to the symptom formation, a disguised compromise which gratifies at the same time the repressed infantile phantasies and the need for punishment consequent on super-ego disapproval of them; fluctuations in the unconscious charge are then signalized by symptomatic crises. Outside the range of the symptoms personal relations are not affected notably. During the analysis of such cases, however, and especially when the 'transference neurosis' is established, wishes to 'act out' in relation to the analyst are often uncovered. Failing gratification in this direction, the patient may begin to embark on a series of emotional relations with external persons. Such libidinal 'acting out' must be countered by effective interpretation, if the analysis is to retain sufficient positive charge to continue effective.

In the 'neurotic character' group the place of the neurotic symptom is taken by situations of 'acting out' which involve and often warp the patient's relations with external objects. The analysis begins with this character defence in full operation. On the other hand the reaction to external objects is not manifestly hostile, destructive or anti-social.

In 'neurotic delinquency' the place of the symptom is again taken by character traits affecting external relations. Periodically these take the form of hostile anti-social reactions. The relation to external objects is, however, often disguised by the unconscious symbolic nature of the act; it is in consequence somewhat distant and without much personal animus. This is easily observed in cases of shop-lifting from stores, of factory theft or theft from public corporations.

In 'psychopathic' crime, however, the destructive or injurious personal intent of the crime is much more obvious. Moreover it will be found that throughout his life the criminal psychopath tends to exploit, hurt or disappoint relations, friends and intimates as well as 'strangers'. In other words the acting-out of infantile phantasy is much more personal and direct. We can therefore understand not only why the criminal psychopath starts the analysis in a negative transference but why he persists in trying to exploit his analyst. These attitudes constitute the most profound resistances; yet their resolution is essential to any fundamental improvement in his condition. In most cases this cannot be achieved by immediate interpretation. As Freud pointed out, defences of this sort are essentially 'Id-resistances'[1] and can only be countered

[1] *Id resistance* is a 'push-pull' phenomenon representing not only the forward drive of unmodified instinct but the pull back of the Id from engaging in those modified and more realistic (at the same time ego-syntonic and socio-syntonic) drives which represent adaptation. This regressive pull tends to take with it some of the sublimated energy that is already available to the ego. The combination of these two sets of forces leads to an 'active-inertia' of the Id which, unlike the more specific resistances of the ego and super-ego, cannot be modified by immediate structural and functional interpretation. Id-resistance expresses itself in

by a process of 'working through' as distinct from analysis of unconscious ego and super-ego factors.

And here we encounter one of the main obstacles to carrying through a *classical analysis* of psychopaths. This, it is true, is not exclusively characteristic of the treatment of psychopathy; it is encountered also in the analysis of alcoholics, drug-addicts, and psychotic cases. In the classical analysis of psycho-neurotics, of sexual inhibitions and perversions and of most autoplastic character cases (except occasionally in severe cases of masochistic character) the analyst is able to maintain an attitude of benevolent and expectant neutrality, keeping his own personality literally in the background and refraining from advice, *ex-cathedra* opinion, or other form of personal interference, unless of course the projected activities of the patient seem to jeopardize his ultimate interests (sudden changes of occupation, sudden decisions to marry, and the like).

In criminal psychopathy, as in addictions and the psychoses, such neutrality cannot always be maintained. The wife of an alcoholic may telephone to say that her husband is drunk and incapable in a compromising situation in a hotel and asks for help which cannot be refused. The depressive case may make a determined attempt at suicide and hover between life and death; a crisis from which the analyst cannot stand apart. The masochistic character may embark on actions that are likely to prove seriously detrimental to his career, and therefore call for an embargo from the analyst. The criminal psychopath has an even wider range of acting out. He may repeat any of his favourite crimes and be held on charge at a police station. This may at least necessitate a visit by the psycho-analyst to the station and in all probability a later visit to court to give evidence as to his abnormal condition, and to present a plea for continuation of treatment. Or the patient may become involved in serious difficulties at work which call for the intervention of the analyst with the employer. There is in fact no end to the crises (domestic, emotional, economic, or delinquent) that the psychopath may engineer and during which the analyst is compelled to abandon for the time being all pretence at a neutral attitude and either take active steps to help in the crisis, or,

the 'compulsion to repeat' and can be countered only by long drawn out interpretations of the repetitions under favourable conditions of transference. This is what is meant by 'working through'.

should he have suspected from analytical material that a crisis was pending, to issue strong cautionary recommendations, in other words, to interfere.

The situation is even more complicated should, as often happens in court cases, treatment be *combined with a probation order*. In classical psycho-analysis, the analyst works alone; or rather, he acts as his own social worker, depending, however, on the social information he obtains either at consultation or during the course of 'free association'. The interposition of a probation officer leads to the situation of a 'distributed negative transference' and offers the psychopath an additional means of playing Box and Cox with his analyst. Moreover unless the analyst is attached to a non-penal organization such as a delinquency clinic or psychiatric centre, his position between the patient and an officer of the court is an extremely invidious one and arouses conflict between his professional and his official allegiances. In fact *it is doubtful whether a classical psycho-analysis can be conducted successfully in such circumstances*, a fact which should be made clear to all parties concerned. Understanding probation officers are, however, often ready to waive their official privileges and powers in order to give the psycho-analyst a free hand. The analyst for his part must be ready to accept such deviations from the technique as are necessitated either by the patient's symptoms or (within reasonable limits) by conditions imposed by courts. He can, however, see to it that at all other times he continues to apply the fundamental techniques of psycho-analysis without deviation.

With regard to the detailed technique of psycho-analysis, the uncovering of special defences and the nature of the unconscious content and motivations, it is not possible within the scope of a general survey to extend these in adequate detail. A full account of the interplay of metapsychological factors and of the shifting of psychic balances that occurs at focal points in the development of a single psychopath would literally require a volume to itself.[1] And of course each of the varieties of criminal psychopathy requires equally ample documentation. For present purposes it is sufficient to say that no psycho-analysis of psychopathy can claim to be complete that does not deal adequately with the major

---

[1] It is a thousand pities that more volumes of this sort are not available. The ortho-psychiatrist, Ben Karpman, is one of the few who have not been intimidated by the voluminousness of psychopathic case records.

factors in etiology set out in the previous section of this survey. No doubt in course of time more detailed and precise etiological information will become available. But this will necessitate much more detailed work on the part of psycho-analysts than is at present available.

Briefly the first move is to ventilate the spontaneous negative attitudes that have accumulated before and after conviction. Should analytic material then present itself more copiously, the next step is to bring out and analyse the negative father transference, which (in the case of male psychopaths of course) usually obstructs further progress. If this is successfully or even partly achieved, and allowing for a number of intervening crises, the analysis will begin to approximate to that of a neurosis, but of course a neurosis with many traumatic elements. This centres largely on the analysis of unconscious sexual phantasy, the most difficult level of which is that of unconscious homosexual organization. Behind this lie elements of the Oedipus situation. At this point the analysis of the oral sadistic relation to the mother presents the most difficult phase of the whole analysis. Provided it can be reduced to some extent it is then possible to examine in detail the organization and function of the super-ego. In this connection it may be remarked that although throughout the analysis the reversal of projections is a constant task, the force of these projections will be found to diminish considerably, once the layers of a primitive and extremely pre-genital type of super-ego are uncovered. At all stages of the analysis ample ventilation and resolution of traumatic reactions is necessary. These will be found to be closely associated with the tendency to explode in psychopathic crises, and must be allowed extensive 'working through'.

Naturally the course of analysis indicated above is not necessarily a standard one. Owing to differences in the fixation points of libido, in the localization of super-ego disorder and the amount and timing of frustration, the resistances and consequently the order of emergence of analytic phases vary from case to case. But whatever the order psycho-analytic therapy of psychopathy is governed by two main aims, the reduction of traumatic amounts of unconscious sadism and the uncovering of the channels of ego and super-ego communication along which these charges of sadism are directed towards the external world.

(2) *Transference Therapies*

The reference made above to the difficulties of carrying out a classical analysis with criminal psychopaths, and in particular the complications that arise when a situation of 'distributed transference' exists, may give rise to some confusion. It should not be assumed either that analytical interpretations cannot be applied save in a classical analytical setting or that a system of distributed transference (either positive or negative) cannot be used with effect in the treatment of criminal psychopaths. As for the matter of duress, it should not be forgotten that the classical psycho-analysis of children is usually carried out under conditions of duress, in so far as the minor is made (by his parents) to undergo treatment whether he likes it or not. These confusions in therapeutic classifications can be overcome if we add to our previous transference criterion a standard based on structural considerations. We can then distinguish between psycho-analytical techniques (however modified by clinical necessity) in which the aim is to alter ego-structure through interpretation and all techniques in which the aim is to modify defective ego-structure by stimulating 'new growth'. This latter technique is, incidentally, the basis of re-education or rehabilitation.

Here we have a crucial point in definition which calls for close consideration. If we assume, for example, that in the case of the criminal psychopath either a deficiency or a defect in super-ego formation exists, in all probability both, it is clear that there can be only two main lines of action. One is to submit the super-ego defect to analysis, in the expectation that during the process the deficiency may be made good. The other and non-analytical line of action is to make good the deficiency in the super-ego in the expectation that during the process the defect may be made good or at least counter-balanced. This latter method may be accelerated by timely interpretations of a focal nature, but essentially the method is one of promoting new super-ego growth under transference conditions. The situation merely illustrates the fact that an obstacle to psycho-analytical therapy may prove a signpost to the correct technique of transference therapy. A distributed transference is a stumbling block to pure analysis but it may well be the secret of stimulating new super-ego growth in the criminal psychopath.

At this point a number of intriguing problems arise, the solution of which will depend on more thorough analytic research on ego-structure and on the origins of social feeling in both normal and abnormal persons. For example: although we can be certain that the most profound influences on super-ego development and consequently on social feeling operate during the infantile period (up to the sixth year at the very latest) and that both symptom formations and major character defects can be traced to this early period, the *process of character formation* and the acquisition of more conventional social feeling continues, although of course in a rapidly diminishing degree, up to the age of 40 (at the latest: after that age character changes are of a regressive rather than a progressive nature). The question then arises regarding super-ego adjustment through transference therapy, namely, at what level of super-ego development is new growth stimulated? Does the patient complete an arrested course of infantile super-ego development; or does he erect a buttress of more conventional and superficial super-ego layers?

Theoretically speaking the answer depends on three factors, first, on the capacity of the individual to *introject* new objects and therefore add to the organization of his super-ego; second, on his capacity for empathic identification with objects which adds to the elasticity of the ego; and third, on the nature of the object influences (and therefore imagos) to which he is subjected (introjects). For if these influences are 'good' (in the sense of friendly understanding) he is likely to introject more humane attitudes: if they are 'bad' (in the sense of censorious if not indeed primitive misunderstanding) his newly-formed super-ego layers are likely to be as cross-grained as his infantile layers.

This incidentally is a problem that should be pondered deeply alike by penal authorities, transference therapeutists and indeed by psycho-analysts. The penal officer, however good his intentions, cannot expect to function to the criminal psychopath as anything other than a 'bad' object. The psychiatrist who preaches discipline is in little better case. Even the analyst who sometimes recommends disciplinary control for children on the somewhat specious ground that children are often made more anxious unless controlled by adults, will find that this essentially parental attitude will not go down well with criminal psychopaths. Aichhorn,[1]

[1] A. Aichhorn: *Wayward Youth*, Imago Publishing Co., 1951.

that doyen of criminological pioneers, was in no doubt on this point. Although fully oriented in psycho-analysis he was, and never claimed to be anything else than, an educational psychologist; or, as he would have been described in modern terminology, an exponent of rehabilitation. To Aichhorn (who, although he did not make use of the term, was in the habit of treating violent psychopaths) the therapeutic agent was first, last and all the time the positive transference. To be sure, he never allowed his charges to fool him and could give them apposite interpretations of any violent, undisciplined or deceptive conduct they might manifest; but these interpretations were invariably directed by understanding rather than by censoriousness.[1] When his charges proceeded to destroy their temporary dwelling place, Aichhorn proceeded, quite undiscouraged, to establish a new home and continue his work.

Indeed in the absence of precise psycho-analytical information on this particular issue, we are compelled to fall back on discoveries made in course of empirical treatment, particularly at outpatient delinquency clinics or psychiatric centres where the factor of penal handling is eliminated (except in so far probation orders include a warning, really a threat, of penal action should the conditions of probation be broken) and where other forms of interference are at a discount. The first of these was that a number of cases of delinquent conduct (excluding for the moment psychopaths) cleared up within the few weeks necessary for a complete psycho-physical overhaul. Of course the occasional therapeutic effect of a single psychological examination had long been noted in cases of neurosis and other mild patholgoical states; and it is generally held that these rapid changes were due either to a reduction in floating anxiety or to positive transference (*rapport*) or to both. In view of the fact, however, that most delinquents start treatment in a predominantly 'negative' mood, the observation calls for special scrutiny.

No completely satisfying explanation of this therapeutic phenomenon, or of that fact that in cases who embark on treatment a comparatively short period seems to produce the desired effect, has yet been found; but it seems probable that the mobilizing of a *number* of potential transferences is responsible for the success of a therapy that is anything but radical. The average duration of

[1] See also pp. 164–9.

treatment at the Portman Clinic for example, runs to eleven sessions. During this period, however, a number of influences have been mobilized, including various examinations by psychological and organic specialists, a full psychiatric overhaul, and of course various interviews with the social worker, who acts as a liaison worker between the psychiatrist and those social, educational, ecclesiastical and industrial agents who may be interested in the case, and, should probation have been ordered by the court, with the probation officer also.

Now these constitute a *ring* of transference situations surrounding the patient; hence the treatment may be described as, in the best sense of the term, group or team treatment. It differs from the customary group treatment in that there is one patient and a group of therapeutists or well-wishers; whereas in ordinary group treatment there is usually one therapeutic leader (sometimes but not very frequently an analyst) and a group of patients. After all if one is bent on instigating fresh super-ego formations even in the most superficial sense of the term, it seems likely that a milieu of transferences will be more successful than one transference point in the environment. Moreover, many of the team are actively engaged in helping the patient, whereas in conventional group treatment the most they do is to talk about or discuss the nature of altruism.

In the special case of the criminal psychopath a similar mobilization of a number of environmental agencies is even more desirable: but immediate results should not be too readily anticipated. Moreover since psychopathy is a deep and serious disorder it is essential that one of the therapeutic group should function as an analytical interpreter. Of course the psychopath will immediately engage in a game of beggar my neighbour with the various members of the therapeutic circle, trying to set one member against the other. But that is precisely what one should expect: indeed one of the functions of the interpreter is ultimately to short circuit these manoeuvres. But not before the patient has been allowed to disappoint all and sundry to his immediate heart's discontent.[1]

---

[1] In a brief review of the rationale of transference therapies it is scarcely possible to argue in detail the principles involved in different practices. It is perhaps sufficient to indicate that some acute differences exist in this field. For example, the McCords (W. and J. McCord: *Psychopathy and Delinquency*, New York, Grune & Stratton, 1956) stress

Interestingly enough, in the case of conventional group treatment it has been found desirable to select the members and to exclude those negative and disruptive types whose metier it is to disrupt all groups. And since it is unlikely that a special group of psychopaths, selected precisely because of their disruptive tendencies, will exert an immediately beneficial effect on one another, it seems logical to accept this conclusion and proceed to reduce the number of patients to one or two and increase the number of group-therapeutists accordingly.

B. Results

When one comes to investigate the results of treatment of criminal psychopathy whether analytical or non-analytical, the facts that must be faced that so far only the most general impressions can be recorded and that no satisfactory comparative studies are available. This is not at all surprising. In the first place not all psychiatrists are ready to admit the existence of a special group of criminal psychopaths, or, for the matter of that, the clinical validity of the term psychopath. Secondly, those who do adopt the term vary widely in their diagnostic standards. For example, many of them insist on including under a psychopathic heading sexual deviations or perversions. And this of itself is sufficient to vitiate all comparisons with the results obtained by those who

the importance in 'milieu therapy' of 'permissiveness and unconditional love' on the part of the therapeutist. Schmideberg (M. Schmideberg: review of above, *Brit. J. Delinq.*, 7, 323–4, 1957.) *per contra* emphasizes the need to impart social values, to encourage participation in the affairs of the institution, to teach responsibility and to make the delinquent aware of the consequences of his behaviour. The case must be accepted for what he is but this, she maintains, is not the same as permitting bad behaviour.

'Permissive' systems of treatment must of course be distinguished from other systems advocating discipline in its own right. It should also be distinguished from the psycho-analyst's general policy of non-interference or of expectant neutrality to the behaviour of his patient. Even so the analyst does not refrain from interference when he considers that the patient's condition or behaviour calls for restraining advice or action. And in the case of delinquent conduct it is essential that whatever technique is employed the therapeutist must not allow himself to be fooled by his patient's defensive manoeuvres. Work along these various lines is still in the experimental stage, hence before laying down arbitrary rules we must await the conclusions arrived at from more elaborate, controlled and contrasted investigations.

refuse to include sexual difficulties under this heading. Even where agreement as to diagnostic standards does exist there is as yet no satisfactory classification of cases in terms of the variety of treatment adopted. Finally a strong tradition exists that the criminal psychopath is refractory to treatment and that the main aim of treatment must be to preserve society from his aggressive depradations, a view which, as has been suggested, leads ultimately to the policy of institutional supervision.

In spite of all these difficulties, or rather just because of them, it is important to stress the fact that, taken at the right age, and given the treatment appropriate to his particular type (however lengthy that may be), the criminal psychopath is by no means so refractory as is generally supposed. This is supported by the fact that without any treatment a number of psychopaths begin to stabilize spontaneously, after the age of 40 certainly and often much earlier. This is no doubt due to the fact that after that age many of the unconscious stresses arising from pressure of instinct have lessened. And doubtless the degree of success the psychopath attains in his life and work during remissions contributes a good deal to this seemingly spontaneous improvement.

As a matter of fact a comparative survey carried out by T. Grygier[1] on 2079 cases in different clinical groups treated at the Portman Clinic (I.S.T.D.) indicated that the results in cases of psychopathy compared favourably with those in cases of neurotic delinquency. And although there may be many sources of error, particularly diagnostic error, in such surveys, the results are sufficiently striking to offset the standard pessimistic view. There can also be no doubt that the earlier the diagnosis is made the more effective treatment is likely to be. Indeed we may look forward to the time when with adequately organized psychiatric services and diagnostic sifting systems the treatment of psychopaths will be embarked on, if not always during early childhood, at any rate not later than puberty. Admittedly this point of view requires the most careful corroboration which so far it has not received.[2] But the necessary effort will be fully justified; for if

---

[1] Glover and Grygier: 'Projected Researches on the Alleged Preventive Effect of Capital Punishment and on the Methods of Prevention of Crimes of Violence', *Brit. J. Delinq.*, 2, 144–9, 1952.

[2] Unfortunately the records of treatment of juvenile psychopaths are even more inadequate than those of adolescent and adult psychopaths.

preventive treatment can be successfully effected, the status of ambulant treatment will be immeasurably increased, and the need for institutional or prison disposal correspondingly reduced.

Comparison of the virtues and defects of different forms of therapy are at all times invidious, and in the case of criminal psychopathy would certainly be premature. For, as has been pointed out, we simply do not have adequate data on which to found them. Given the appropriate case any form of psychotherapy will obtain its quota of satisfactory results. But we cannot be sure which case is appropriate for a given type of treatment, until we know more of the etiology of different types of criminal psychopathy. Nor is it altogether satisfactory to have a sliding scale of therapies in reserve to meet the needs of specially refractory cases. The analysis of cases that have already run the gauntlet of transference therapies (including 'short-cut' analyses) is by no means easy. These, however, are difficulties that may well be resolved by future research, in particular by the study of incurable cases. For we learn more from failures in psychotherapy than from successes. What, I think, stands out from a survey of criminal psychopathy or indeed from psychopathy in general is first, that it represents one of the great groups of mental disorder deserving of a central position in all psychiatric classifications, and second, that it is as worthy of unremitting therapeutic attention as any other psycho-pathological group.

Whether the *term* 'psychopathy' will retain its present heuristic utility is much more open to question. It has of course as good a claim to general recognition as the currently accepted term 'schizophrenia'. And interestingly enough psychopathy is a much better illustration of a 'split mind' than is schizophrenia itself. But there is good reason to suppose that with increasing knowledge of metapsychology, the disorders of character will be more accurately sub-divided and given labels more appropriate than is

Diagnosis even of convicted child psychopaths (8–14 inclusive) is more uncertain. And in any case the most important cases are to be found in the earlier age groups (infancy and early childhood). Actually most of these are lost in the records of child guidance clinics, where they are frequently disguised under non-specific labels: e.g., behaviour problem, schizoid character, etc. Not only so the terms 'delinquent' or 'predelinquent' are applied in such early groups without adequate discrimination. Indeed little improvement in records can be expected until standard criteria of diagnosis and differential diagnosis are established.

the case at present. It is possible, for example, that psychopathy could be adequately represented under the heading of super-ego disorder with of course due sub-division in accordance with the particular variety of super-ego disorder and the most important levels of instinctual fixation with which it is associated. In the meantime there is no satisfactory alternative to the term provided always we contrive that from time to time it is scaled of whatever irrelevant clinical accretions it may have acquired.

APPENDIX

AICHHORN ON TREATMENT*

To describe a book as a 'classic' is often tantamount to passing a death-sentence on it. This is even more true of a scientific text-book than of a literary work. For whereas the latter may, despite the intimidating label, continue to be read by generations of reluctant students and teachers, the scientific classic commonly ends by being decently interred in footnotes and lists of references, only the title and one or two hackneyed quotations being handed on from article to article or from text-book to text-book by writers who have never even seen the original, much less read it. For this among other reasons the second English edition of Aichhorn's classic calls for re-assessment in the light of modern researches on delinquency.

Actually the quality of the book and the qualities of its author can be inferred from the title originally chosen for it, *Verwahrloste Jugend*, which curiously enough emerges in translation as 'Wayward Youth'. It would be interesting to know what exactly the author meant by *verwahrlost;* for although, when Aichhorn first wrote, the word was already in current use in the literature of delinquency[1] its meaning was somewhat ambiguous. It could indicate either an environmental or an endopsychic factor in anti-social conduct. Actually the term connotes specifically 'uncared for', 'abandoned' or 'neglected', as in the case of 'waifs and strays' spoiled by a state of neglect or squalor, whereas 'wayward' can be read as 'childishly self-willed' as well as 'capricious', 'froward' or 'unruly', incidentally a by no means inappropriate part-description of the psychopathic type, which could be better rendered in German by *widerspenstig*. However ambiguous its scientific connotation, the expression serves to indicate the

---

* First published in *Brit. J. Delinq.*, 2, 167, 1951: review of *Wayward Youth*, by August Aichhorn, London, Imago Publishing Co., 1951.

[1] See, for example, Hans Gruhle, 'Die Ursachen der Jugend-Verwahrlosung und Kriminalität' (1912), and Gregor and Voigtländer, 'Die Verwahrlosung . . .' (1918). Already in 1901 Krohne had written on institutions for 'verwahrloste' Jugendliche.

characteristic approach of its author who broke through the conventional implications of the words 'criminal' and 'delinquent' to discover the psychological characteristics of the individual offender and who maintained in effect that anti-social conduct represents the coefficient of friction between parental influences and the instincts of the child.

Add to this the fact that Aichhorn, after exploring the resources of academic psychology, found in Freud's theory of unconscious conflict the solution to many of his problems, and it might appear, as indeed the publishers suggest, that Aichhorn was simply the first to apply psycho-analysis extensively to the study and treatment of delinquency. This, however, would do less than justice to the individuality of Aichhorn. It is of course true that in the earlier days of psycho-analysis a number of pioneers sought to exploit the new theory in investigations of the social and cultural activities of man. It became the fashion indeed for newcomers to win their spurs in the field of applied psycho-analysis. Aichhorn did not belong to this band of knights-errant. He was not an analyst exploring the field of delinquency, but a student of human nature who turned to psycho-analysis for help in the understanding of delinquent youth. He was first and last a pedagogue, a teacher moulding his charges by precept and example.

That he was an educationalist rather than a clinical research scholar is evident on the very first page where he defies all standards of classification by including under the term 'wayward' not merely delinquent and dis-social children but also so-called problem children and others suffering from neurotic symptoms. This is essentially the view of the enlightened pedagogue whose professional interest is first aroused by the discovery of 'problem children' who prove refractory to the routines of school life. In one sense it is a pre-requisite of understanding delinquency, since to isolate delinquency from the behaviour problems and neuroses of the non-delinquent is to strangle research at birth. Nevertheless we are now at the stage when, having discovered the common sources of behaviour problems, we must establish a specific etiology for each distinct variety. Aichhorn had certainly not reached this point when he first wrote this book; and it would have been more appropriate had he contented himself with the title 'Delinquent Youth'.

This pedagogic angle of approach becomes more manifest

throughout the book. Following the lines laid down in the psychoanalytic theory of the neuroses, Aichhorn drew a distinction between 'manifest delinquency' and 'latent delinquency'. Delinquency is manifest when it develops into dis-social behaviour: it is latent when the same state of mind exists but has not yet expressed itself. From this generalization Aichhorn drew a number of practical conclusions; for example, that the task of re-education is to weaken the latent tendency and that the removal of dis-social symptoms is not necessarily a sign that the latent conditions have been liquidated. But putting these considerations aside for the moment, we may note that his first attempt at classification was a very modest one, namely, into borderline neurotic cases with dis-social symptoms and dis-social cases in which that part of the ego giving rise to the dis-social behaviour shows no trace of neurosis. This, however, does not reflect Aichhorn's flair for differentiation; the different causal factors he enumerates and illustrates by simple yet convincing case-histories could well form the basis of an etiological classification; e.g., traumatic types, faulty identifications with one or other parent, too strong love relations with parents or siblings, pathological regression of libido, jealousy of siblings, pubertal stress, sensitiveness to frustration with consequent weakness of reality sense, various types of unconscious guilt, and faulty super-ego formation. In short, as far as etiology is concerned, Aichhorn followed the broad lines of a developmental approach, with the consequence that his therapeutic endeavours were concerned with the correction, mostly through environmental influence, of the faulty stage of development responsible for the delinquency, the immediate manifestations of which were of less concern to him either in theory or in practice.

Many of these views are now accepted as a matter of course by clinical workers, but in their time they represented remarkable advances in our understanding of delinquent states; and in fact they do not preclude the possibility of formulating detailed classifications. It must be admitted, however, that Aichhorn was to some extent handicapped by following too exclusively the patterns of symptom formation that had already been established for the beuroses. A broader psychiatric approach would have served him netter. Indeed, it is significant that the term psychopathy is never mentioned although many of the cases he described would qualify for this special designation. Of the relation of some delinquencies to the psychoses little or nothing is recorded. Further, although it is true that the symptoms of delinquency must be distinguished from the underlying disease, still they provide valuable information regarding etiology and useful indications for treatment.

As far as therapy is concerned it is no exaggeration to say that Aichhorn's book is not only a mine of information but a source of inspiration and encouragement to all who undertake the arduous and delicate task of handling delinquents. Here again Aichhorn acknowledged his debt to psycho-analytical concepts. 'What', he asked, 'helps the worker most in therapy with the dis-social?' His own answer was 'The transference! And especially what we recognize as the positive transference.' In both out-patient and institutional work his approach was governed almost exclusively by the necessity of stimulating and developing the transference in the interest of re-education. Working often by sheer intuition and seizing every favourable situation, whether fortuitous or specially designed, he sought to modify the pathogenic situation and at the same time to bring about increased stability and synthesis of the ego. 'With the worker's help, the youth acquires the necessary feeling relative to his companions which enables him to overcome the dis-social traits.' The source of the new character formation is the worker himself. 'The word 'father-substitute', so often used in connection with remedial education, receives its rightful connotation in this conception of the task.'

To appreciate Aichhorn's contributions to the problem of treatment, it is necessary to recall the strenuous opposition that was once, and in many quarters still is, offered to any course that smacks of 'mollycoddling' the offender or depriving him of the alleged benefits of a rigid discipline. The story of his early experiences with a selected 'aggressive group' deserves to be engrossed on vellum and presented to every official connected however remotely with the handling of delinquents, to say nothing of a multitude of penal reformers. Indeed it should be read with especial care by psycho-analysts themselves. For although Aichhorn's work was at all times governed by psycho-analytical precepts, he was careful to insist that it was in no sense a psychoanalysis. As Freud remarked in his foreword to the book, 'Psychoanalysis could teach him little that was new of a practical kind, but it brought him a clear, theoretical insight into the justification of his way of acting and put him in a position to explain its basis to other people.'

This is perhaps the most valuable of Aichhorn's contributions to the subject. Psycho-analysis, originally a technique for the treatment of the psycho-neuroses, encounters peculiar difficulties when applied to graver disorders. No very satisfactory technique has for example been evolved for its use either in the psychoses, where the essential factor of 'accessibility' is greatly diminished, or in the psychopathic disorders, where negative transferences so often obstruct the therapeutic approach. It is significant indeed that the conventional analyst reacts to any suggested modification of his classical technique with a mixture of outraged virtue and uneasy aggressiveness. Yet it is clearly as impossible to apply the classical technique of psycho-analysis to a violent or perverted psychopathic recidivist as to a melancholiac in a state of catatonia. The crises that may occur during the treatment of delinquents and the situations in which the therapeutist may be compelled to participate in many cases preclude the leisurely and for the most part passive chair-and-couch methods of formal analysis. Aichhorn showed, however, that knowledge of unconscious mechanisms and conflict is essential to the regulation of environmental therapy and influence; and in this book he quotes sufficiently extensively from his own records to give the reader some idea of his methods.

To be sure, there are occasions when his approach seems to be somewhat naïve, and when some of the set-backs he describes might well have been anticipated by him. But perhaps a modicum of naïveté is an asset to the born therapeutist, if there be such a creature. It is possible too that Aichhorn exaggerated the importance of playing the rôle of 'father-substitute'. The transference is after all to a large extent a repetitive phenomenon, and in neurotic cases its most effective analysis depends on the therapeutist *not* playing the part assigned to him by the patient. But Aichhorn's work, as has been said, was re-education, not analysis; and its success indicated that playing the rôle of the friendly parent can bring about astonishing readjustments provided it is accompanied by a clear understanding of the patient's unconscious motivations and tricks of defence. In these days when psychiatrists are, sometimes justly sometimes unjustly, accused of all sorts of sins of omission and commission in their handling of delinquents, it is useful to be able to recommend for general reading a book proving convincingly that sympathy and understanding are not necessarily the step-children of folly.

To which it may be added that *Wayward Youth* should lie, open, on the desks of all who seek to understand or treat delinquents.

V. SEXUAL DISORDERS AND OFFENCES

Part I   The Social and Legal Aspects of Sexual Abnormality

Part II   The Problem of Male Homosexuality
      i   Diagnosis and Classifications
      ii   Etiology
      iii   Prognosis and Treatment

Part III   The Psychopathology of Prostitution

SECTION V

SEXUAL DISORDERS AND OFFENCES
[1940-59]

Study of criminal offences provides a remarkable confirmation of Freud's classification of instinctual forces into two main groups, libidinal and aggressive or reactive. For in principle the majority of offences (including even many apparently trivial infractions of by-laws) can be divided into (a) acts of violence, injury, damage, depreciation or neglect either physical or mental directed against the physical or mental functions, interests, rights and possessions of other individuals or of groups both organized or unorganized; (b) acts infringing such sexual mores, either of individuals or of groups, as are laid down by law. Needless to say some offences, e.g., sexual violence, belong to both divisions.

But although the right of the civilian to commit mental or physical acts of aggression outside the family circle and sometimes within it is nowadays denied by general consent, the position of sexual offences is still in the highest degree anomalous. For, as we have seen as recently as 1958, it is possible for a law abiding Departmental Committee to recommend that acts of homosexuality committed by consenting male adults in private should no longer be regarded as offences in this country. To be sure even this marginal amount of tolerance is qualified in many directions. For despite the refusal of society to stigmatize as offences Lesbian activities or prostitution, both of which involve a good deal of perverse sexual practice, this latitude is due more to prejudice than to reason. Indeed when closely examined sexual prejudice is seen to run much deeper than Ecclesiastical Law which is usually blamed for it, reaching back to the draconic moralities that animate and govern the sexual habits of primitive societies and in the last resort to unconscious moralities that dwell in the more archaic layers of the unconscious mind.

Naturally all this puts the great majority of forensic psychiatrists in a professional dilemma. At the behest of courts they may be called on to treat conditions which they do not regard as criminal, and in many instances, perhaps a majority, must therefore be content with inducing in their patients a degree of control or discretion. This may in part account for the slow rate of progress of research on sexual offences. Two of the following papers were written in the early 1940's; yet after the lapse of fifteen years it cannot be said that our knowledge has advanced very much. The series of papers on male homosexuality was compiled from lectures delivered between 1940 and 1959.

PART I
THE SOCIAL AND LEGAL ASPECTS OF SEXUAL ABNORMALITY*
[1945–56]

INTRODUCTION

Although the twin-science of forensic medicine testifies to the close bonds that unite medicine and the law, these professions have, I venture to say, more in common than even members of the Medico-Legal Society may suspect. To begin with, both are concerned with the diagnosis, prevention and treatment of disorder. A conviction for theft, for example, is an act of legal diagnosis, differing only in depth of understanding from the medico-psychological diagnosis of kleptomania: in principle a sentence of imprisonment is as much a form of treatment as the hospitalization of the insane: a probation order is a preventive measure of the same order as placing a case of infectious disease under quarantine. The main differences between the law and medicine are these: medical science is concerned for the most part with the health of the individual, the law for the most part with the well-being of the community; medical science is concerned with causes as well as with effects, the law, except in the case of the criminal irresponsibility of the insane, is concerned with effects: finally, the law still nourishes a primitive and mostly superstitious belief in the virtues of punishment: medical science has abandoned the view that illness is reprehensible or that it serves the sufferer right.

I have emphasized these common interests and divergencies because the subject we are about to discuss calls not only for the most dispassionate scrutiny but for a clear understanding of the different psychological and sociological premises of the two sciences. Regrettable as the fact may be, it has to be admitted that the problem of sexual disorder is calculated to arouse in both medical and legal practitioners not only conscious passion and prejudice but unconscious reactions of a more profound and in-

* This brochure was originally delivered as a lecture to *The Medico-legal Society* on May 24th, 1945, and was published in *The Medico-legal Review*, **13**, 3, 1945. It was reprinted as an I.S.T.D. pamphlet in 1946. A second revised edition was published in 1956.

tractable nature. A great deal of the aversion from and punitive attitude to homosexuality, for example, is derived from unconscious sources. It is only fair to record, however, that in sexual matters the practitioner of the law is more objective than the medical practitioner. Why this should be so I do not pretend fully to comprehend but I suspect it to be due partly to the medical practitioner's lack of psychological understanding and partly to the emancipation of civil law from ecclesiastical control. However that may be, psychologists have good reason to be grateful for the comparative immunity of the legal profession from official sexual prejudice. Against this, however, must be set the rather old-maidish and obscurantist attitude of many police and court officials who, despite an intimate contact with what used to be called the seamy side of life, do not appear to have acquired much human understanding in the process. In short, we might as well begin with the frank admission that few, if any, of us can approach the problem of sexual disorder with that complete emotional detachment that is the pre-requisite of successful research.

Infantile Sexuality

Perhaps the most dramatic example of sexual prejudice was observed when, over half a century ago, Freud began to formulate his theory of infantile sexuality. In its simplest terms this laid down that sexual impulses do not, as had previously been taken for granted, first spring into activity at puberty but exist from birth; that during the first five years of life sex instincts are not unified but manifest themselves in a number of independent infantile 'components' or, to use the technical term, that the infantile sexual impulses are 'polymorphous'; that in so far as these component-impulses are directed towards external persons (infantile 'love-objects', as the technical phrase goes), these objects are found within the family circle, primarily the parents; that, owing to the emotional conflict aroused by familial sexual impulses, the greatest part of infantile sexuality is and remains unconscious; and that, roughly speaking, between the age of five and the onset of puberty a sexual *latency period* exists during which, in the majority of instances, the earlier infantile impulses disappear from sight. When, in addition to all this, Freud made it clear that the early sexual components are not just babyish, and therefore presumably negligible, forerunners of adult (genital) sexuality, but powerful sexual urges aiming at gratifications which if sought by an adult would be branded as *sexual perversions*, a storm of disapproval broke. In Britain this was at first not quite so violent as on the Continent, not because the British were less prudish, but because for some time few of them were aware of Freud's existence. When his ideas finally percolated to this country the reaction was not only just as violent and abusive but was expressed also in that most devastating of British penal judgements, the stigma of 'bad form'. And although the more violent abuse has died down, the prejudice against the concept of infantile sexuality is still strong enough to hamper understanding of sexual problems.

Interestingly enough, the final confirmation of Freud's theory came not from doctors or lawyers or biologists, but from those sympathetic and observant mothers whose simplicity of approach saved them from being squeamish about the facts of life. It was then established that most little children, if unhampered by the panicky regulations of anxious parents or prudish nannies, display quite openly during the first five years of life most of the sexual activities described by Freud. Not all of these activities, of course, for a large part of the infant's sexual life is of such a primitive and phantastic nature that it cannot pass the censorship of the unconscious to gain expression in thought or action. Let me give a simple example of parental observation. Recently a rising five-year-old of my acquaintance, a bright, healthy and attractive little boy, full of animal spirits, began to arouse his parents' concern in various ways. His conversation was increasingly garnished with references to the posteriors of all and sundry, which were alluded to with obvious relish and not a few sly smiles as 'bottoms': he also began to display his sex organ in and out of season, but with obvious unfailing pride: he took frequent occasion to urinate in the front garden overlooking the public highway: finally he was observed acting out a little exhibitionistic scene to the huge delight of his little sister, who evidently regarded him not only as a first-rate comedian but as a conjuror of considerable merit.

No doubt there are still some who would react to this observation by laying their tongues to the nearest terms of abuse: they would roundly characterize his conduct as disordered if not a sign of degeneracy. Others, less violent in prejudice, would no doubt be content to say that he was 'a nasty little boy', who ought to have been soundly spanked by his 'over-indulgent' parents. But with these myopic and prejudiced judgements I am not for the moment concerned. The relevant point is this: had the boy been 15 years old instead of 5, he would in the eyes of the law have been regarded as a sexual pervert and, if detected, would have been hauled before a juvenile court charged with indecent conduct. Fortunately in this case no such outcome is to be anticipated. A little understanding on the part of the parents, including the satisfying of his unspoken but urgent demand for sexual information, some smoothing out of the unconscious love rivalry activated by the birth and continued existence of his little sister, whom he consciously adores, and the problem will be happily solved. In a comparatively short time he will pass into the smooth waters of the latency period and when he comes to the age of 15 will be able to tackle the immediate problems of adolescence, in all likelihood without even a memory of his childish escapades to disturb his growing adult interests.[1]

Admittedly it is dangerous to generalize from particular instances. No doubt there are many young children whose sexual activities are either so compulsive or so peculiar as to suggest that some disorder of the sexual instinct already exists at that early age and that it requires expert psychological attention. Nevertheless, it is generally true to say that the child who is sensibly and reasonably brought up, whose thirst for sexual information is adequately satisfied and whose early sexual activities are treated with polite and friendly understanding, is much less likely to get into trouble in later life than the child whose deep anxieties and guilts are aroused by threats, warnings and punishments for which there is not the remotest justification, and which are, in fact, merely a sign that the parents have never satisfactorily overcome their own sexual difficulties.

This conclusion has an important bearing on the social and legal aspects of adolescent or adult sexual abnormality. For if the sexual difficulties of later life can to a considerable extent be prevented by proper upbringing, it is reasonable to enquire whether measures of psychological understanding and treatment would not produce better results than the moral opprobrium and punishment inflicted on sexual offenders under our present legal code. We

[1] [Note 1959] As a matter of interest the after-history of the boy fulfilled this prediction: the infantile perversion soon disappeared and he is now a healthy and sexually normal adolescent.

might be tempted to ask whether the law itself unwittingly encourages the commission of sexual offences, not only by inflicting drastic penalties, but, quite simply, by paying too much attention to them.

But it would be imprudent to attempt to answer these questions before we have a clear idea of sexual development. Briefly, the sequence of events is this: the sexual impulses, although biologically destined to serve the purposes of reproduction through the genito-sexual organs, do not derive their strength exclusively from the reproductive systems. All the organs and tissues of the body are invested with charges of sexual energy. *Body-libido*, as it is called, is, however, obviously concentrated in certain zones, and as the infant passes through its stages of development, one or other of these zones seems to exert a primacy over the rest or, if you prefer the term, a priority of urgency. On closer examination, this primacy is seen to be both natural and appropriate. Thus the *oral* or mouth zone of the *libido* is naturally most important and biologically most useful during the sucking period. Following this the excretory zones of infantile sexuality, the *anal* and *urethral* zones, assume priority. This coincides with and follows the period of excretory 'cleaning' through which every little human is made to pass, in company with any kittens and puppies that may be undergoing domestication at the same time. It is only after the excretory phases have been passed that true infantile genital interests establish their primacy. Throughout both oral and excretory phases, the *skin* has important erotic functions to perform and in the anal stage we observe a form of zonal (skin) priority, when the buttocks first come to exercise charm and provide sensual gratification. Libidinal satisfaction is, of course, provided also by the other sensory organs, of sight, hearing, smell and taste.

But infantile sexuality is not limited to sensory experience. Although most of the sensual zones contribute to *auto-erotic* satisfactions (*i.e.*, the desire to obtain gratification by masturbating them can be satisfied by the child without any reference to external love objects, as is seen in the earliest form of auto-eroticism, namely, thumb-sucking), there are certain impulses which are directed towards external persons, in particular those familial objects (father, mother, brothers or sisters) who play an active part in the child's life. The discovery of the Oedipus situation, as the genital love of small children for their parents is called, aroused in its time a storm of moral indignation, but nowadays it is not difficult to prove that the first *heterosexual* and *homosexual* strivings of the child are directed inevitably towards family figures. But even under the most favourable conditions we see only a small part of these sexual urges. The externally directed genital impulses of the small child are not only completely frustrated but arouse unconscious anxiety and guilt. The only outlet these frustrated impulses can obtain is in the form of *unconscious phantasy*, that is to say, active wish-formations which cannot pass the barrier of repression to reach consciousness. The unconscious sexual phantasies of the child make up in variety and intensity what they lack in gratification. They are encouraged also by a factor of infantile sexual *curiosity*. This too is subject to frustration, though not to the same extent as the actual sexual impulses. Children are good observers, and in their biological studies very frequently make sexual discoveries of an accuracy that is embarrassing to their less downright parents. Nevertheless, many of their inferences are inaccurate and are expanded in the unconscious into complicated systems of sexual theory, which if reactivated in later life contribute a good deal to the formation of sexual as well as psychoneurotic disorders. Typical phantasies are that mothers make babies by eating food or that babies are born through the abdominal wall or through the anus or that the mother deprives the father of his sex organ during a violent act of intercourse and subsequently incubates it inside her abdomen until it develops into a baby. These unconscious phantasies are commonly discovered in the gastro-intestinal neuroses, in frigidity, impotence and homosexuality.

Apart from these purely sexual manifestations, two forms of infantile impulse exist in which sexual instincts are fused with impulses of aggression, in particular, the impulse to inflict or endure injury, pain or humiliation. In the active, or *sadistic*, group the subject treats the sexual object with varying degrees of aggression: in the passive or *masochistic* form, he endures injury at the hands of the sexual partner. Manifest forms of sadism and masochism are commonly associated with beating activities or scenes of punishment in early childhood but, as with other varieties of infantile sexuality, the largest part of sadistic and masochistic impulse remains unconscious in a state of repression. Repressed sadism or masochism is strongly reinforced by any emotional situation of frustration giving rise to anxiety, envy, jealousy or hatred. These repressed sado-masochistic components have an important bearing on the degree of cruelty and aggression practised by the grown-up and naturally are mainly responsible for crimes of sexual violence. As will be seen later, they are also an important contributing factor in the various delinquencies in which apparently non-sexual acts of violence or destruction are observed.[1]

Adolescent and Adult Perversions

If now we turn from the study of infantile sexuality to examine the *sexual perversions of adolescence and adult life*, we find that these disorders, although more systematized than the infantile components of sexuality, are of the same nature. For the sake of convenience we may confine ourselves to the forms most frequently dealt with by the courts, namely, exhibitionism and homosexuality. Of the former it need only be said that it does not differ in any descriptive respect from the exhibitionism practised by small children. The main point to note is that what was once a *component* of the child's sexuality has in classical instances come to monopolize the *whole* of the adult's sexual interest: the normal adult genital aim has disappeared or has failed to make an appearance at puberty. To be sure these are extreme cases and in many instances sufficient genital interest remains to lead to marriage. This, however, is liable to be set aside in periodic outbursts of infantile exhibitionism.

Homosexuality, on the other hand, is a much more complicated problem. Its main characteristic is that a love object or sexual object of the same sex is chosen. To take extreme examples: the male homosexual may either choose an object who plays a passive feminine rôle or he may himself play the passive rôle to an active partner. In a great number of cases the rôles are interchangeable. Further distinctions can be made in accordance with the type of sexual activity favoured. Oral-genital perversions (fellatio) or

[1] An undue amount of attention, in both professional and lay circles, is paid to those cases of murder and manslaughter in which a factor of sexual jealousy or of manifest sexual perversion plays a leading part. Undoubtedly these are the most striking forms of sadistic aggression, yet statistically regarded, the group is a very small one. By far the commonest form of sexual aggression is an 'assault' in which the sadistic aim may be either a primary or a secondary one.

anal-genital perversions (sodomy) are commonly observed; or, again, both partners may practise some of the numerous forms of mutual masturbation. In fact, there is hardly a component of infantile sexuality that cannot be pressed into the service of adult homosexuality. By the same token there are only two important forms of adult love practice that cannot be directed by the homosexual towards his love object, viz. normal coitus and, in the case of the male homosexual, manipulations of the female breasts. Although his sexual impulses have been arrested at or have regressed to a stage somewhere between self-love and love of a woman, he is in many respects much nearer to adult heterosexual love than is the exhibitionist. And since he can put the whole of his imaginative powers and cultural achievements (which are often of a high order) as well as his talent for warm friendship at the service of his love feeling, the erroneous impression is sometimes created that the homosexual has reached a higher level of sexual development than the more normal and heartier heterosexual!

Into these fascinating problems I have no time to enter. Nor can I afford the space to catalogue the different varieties of sexual perversion, for information regarding which recourse must be had to standard text books on the subject. The points I wish to emphasize so far are these: the sexual perversions (for the term sexual 'abnormality' includes many conditions that are not the concern of the law) are derived and built up from infantile sexual components: they are in the nature of *regressions* to earlier systems, which regressions however are, in classical instances, so organized that they take the place of normal sexual activity: their development can in many cases be prevented by adequate measures of upbringing: *if despite the most understanding efforts of parents or child-minders abnormal sexual conduct should, nevertheless, manifest itself at puberty or in later life, these manifestations require suitable psychological observation and treatment. No other form of handling has the slightest chance of resolving sexual disorder. To be sure it is sometimes possible by means, e.g. of hormone treatment to reduce or counterbalance sexual excitation and thereby render sexual control more effective. It is also possible to castrate the male offender, as is actually done in some otherwise civilized countries on the Continent. But these measures do not resolve the difficulty in the psychological sense of the word: they merely bludgeon the offender's sexual system into inactivity*.

The social implications of these formulations are easier to grasp if we realize the fact that the sexual disorders of adolescents and adults have a definite function to perform. They are not simply chance disturbances of normal function. Paradoxical as it may seem, they constitute spontaneous attempts *to cure earlier disordered functions*, a characteristic they share with all other forms of psychological illness. In the case of common neuroses (hysteria and the obsessions) this has been proved beyond a shadow of doubt. The symptoms of adult neuroses are essentially attempts to find a compromise between unconscious stresses of infantile instinct and the restraining forces which exist in the mind, and which are, although to a much less extent than is usually supposed, reinforced in adult life by social and penal codes. Adult neuroses are without exception superimposed on infantile neuroses. Similarly, in the case of adult perversions. They are built up on the pathological sexual conflicts of infancy. We have already noted that in these conditions the gratification of normal heterosexual and reproductive impulse is either partly or totally inhibited; but the meaning of this inhibition can be grasped only if we realize that the normal heterosexual impulses of infants are incestuous, and that these normal incestuous impulses, together with all the rivalries and hostilities they engender, are normally controlled by the development of an unconscious incest barrier of anxiety and guilt. If an infant counsel's opinion could be taken on the morality of adult heterosexual impulse, adverse judgement would be given in no uncertain terms. According to the infant any form of normal adult sexuality is not only dangerous, but highly immoral. Here we have a most peculiar and disconcerting paradox. In the unconscious of the sexual pervert, his renunciation of adult sexuality is a moral act. His regression to infantile sexuality, though by no means guilt-free, is the lesser of two evils. As I have said, the outbreak of a neurosis in adolescence has a similar function. But here the regression is not a manifestly sexual one: the neurotic regression takes disguised forms the meaning of which neither the individual nor his familiars can understand. Hence, although the neurotic may be bullied by his family, his friends, his family doctor and himself, he is not regarded by society as a criminal. The sexual pervert who flaunts his perversion or involves others in his practices is regarded not only as a delinquent but as a peculiarly disgusting species of criminal. Yet in the sense of primitive unconscious morality, both the neurotic and the sexual pervert are more 'moral-minded' than the normal heterosexual adult.

This close, if partly antithetical, relation between the mechanisms of neurosis and of sexual perversion suggests what is, in fact, the case, that the symptoms of sexual disorder are by no means limited to manifest sexual activities or phantasies. This fact can be readily established by studying transitional forms of perversion in which the techniques of perversion-formation and of neurosis-formation are combined. One of the best examples is the case of *fetichism*, in which sexual interest is *entirely diverted* from the body of the sexual object to some article of clothing; for example, to corsets and other forms of underclothing, to shoes, hats, waterproof coats and so forth. Admittedly a certain amount of fetichism adds relish to the normal desires of normal people, but in the abnormal case it completely replaces adult genital drives. The disguised *displacements* of interest characteristic of the neurotic reinforce the pervert's *unconscious denial* of adult sexuality. To be sure, fetichism adds to the individual's range of sexual promiscuousness. The fetichist has only to make a collection of shoes or corsets, for example, to possess a number of inanimate love objects greater and more readily accessible than those animate love objects traditionally pursued by Bluebeard, Don Juan or the sailor who has a wife in every port. But like most forms of maladaptation, fetichism can exact a heavy price in unhappiness, conflict and inferiority feeling, and in certain cases is associated with alcoholism, always a sure sign of unconscious conflict and sexual maladaptation.

This displacement of compulsive sexual interest to non-sexual objects suggests the possibility that some apparently non-sexual compulsions, for example, pig-tail cutting, ink-splashing, railway strap-cutting, cushion slashing, minor forms of arson, and many other delinquent forms of conduct are also pathological expressions of unconscious conflict, in which primitive sexual urges and reactions of a sadistic type operate in disguise through the archaic unconscious mode which is called *symbolic thinking*. And we would not be very far wrong if we surmized that many neurotic compulsions to collect unusual articles have a similar motivation. I should like to illustrate this by reference to a case in which the factors of perversion and obsessional compulsion led to a conviction for delinquent conduct. For reasons of discretion which you will readily understand I have disguised all non-essential particulars, publication of which might lead to identification of the sufferer. The case was that of a man close on 28 years of age who worked on the land near a Midland factory town. He had been arrested for stealing a leather dog lead. Preliminary reports showed that he had suffered from a mania for collecting leather articles, especially those with a shining or reflecting surface, and he was sent for further investigation. It then transpired that the interest in leather articles had first manifested itself at the age of 4, when he secreted his sister's leather music case and stroked it in private. A few years later he experienced some fascination in watching the reflection of light from the leather uniform equipment of soldiers drilling in the park. But this was only a temporary homosexual deflection; at puberty his compulsion was again definitely associated with leather garments, bags, shoes, or buckles worn or carried by girls. From puberty onwards he made a habit of collecting such objects with or without payment. These he hoarded in a garret. He practised other and more innocent collecting habits and, had the examination stopped at this point, his peculiarities would doubtless have been regarded as a form of obsessional (i.e., neurotic) collecting, giving rise on occasion to kleptomanic activities. Psychiatric examination proved, however, that he was a true fetichist, obtaining sexual satisfaction from observing and manipulating leather articles. As a child he had exhibited a number of neurotic symptoms, but his adult mental organization was of a more unstable pattern, showing some reactions of a schizoid type, i.e., he exhibited some traits closely resembling some of the symptoms of adolescent (schizophrenic) insanity. In short, socially regarded he was a true kleptomaniac: from the psychological standpoint he was a sexual pervert with marked mental instability.

To complete this brief clinical survey of the problem I would remind you that although by far the greater proportion of sexual disorders do not concern the law, in that they consist mostly of sexual inhibitions of a purely private nature, impotence, frigidity and the like, there are certain cases of sexual disorder which, although in no sense perversions, nevertheless come under the attention of juvenile courts. Since the passing of the Juvenile Delinquency Acts, the law has thrown its net wider than ever before and has set up two categories which include a number of cases of sexual maladaptation. These are respectively children 'in need of care or protection' and children and adolescents 'out of control'. If time permitted, it would be interesting to study the social implications of these two categories. The distinction between the two groups is, for example, a tacit admission of the *duties* of the State in certain cases. But although the term 'out of control' suggests that a factor of social expediency is the final diagnostic standard, the sexual cases included in both groups prove that psychologically there is no very accurate distinction between them. A great number of 'out of control' cases are simply pubescents who for one reason or another (usually lack of proper sexual upbringing) have been unable to weather the storm of oncoming adult sexuality and have manifested this weakness by a certain amount of refractoriness to social conditioning. It is, by the way, a good rule to regard most outbursts of sporadic violence or anti-social conduct as a sign of weakness rather than of strength. On the other hand, amongst cases 'in need of care or protection' come a number of minors who, because of bad family conditions and/or 'bad' company, are thought not only to need care or protection but to require preventive supervision lest they should take later to disorderly forms of conduct. This apprehension is not entirely without foundation. Amongst these two groups are to be found those 'larval' prostitutes who, having tasted some of the rebellious joys of impulsive conduct, may come under the influence of older and more experienced 'professionals', and graduate as confirmed prostitutes. But these cases are in a small minority. By far the largest proportion of these groups are simply cases of pubertal and adolescent maladjustment readily amenable to psychological guidance or treatment.

The Extent of the Problem

Two points remain to be considered: the extent of the problem of sexual disorder and the possibilities of successful treatment. As to the prevalence of sexual disorders I regret to say that such official records as exist are of little scientific value: they record merely the number of charges and convictions. In any case there is little or no discrimination between different types coming within the larger 'diagnostic' groups. Indeed it is significant of the moral bias of the law that a substantial group of homosexual offences are pigeon-holed under the euphemistic caption of 'unnatural offences'. Even if we were to add the number of 'suspects' known to the police, we would still have no accurate measure of the problem. It is obvious that, in the case of homosexuality at any rate, few persons of discretion need come in conflict with the law, particularly in the larger cities where homosexual groups can afford their members protection from blackmailers and police alike. Naturally this does not apply to cases in which it is an essential condition of satisfaction that the sexual object should be a stranger. Moreover, even amongst the cases charged, a high proportion have evidently some unconscious need for punishment, since they take the most absurd and unnecessary risks, leading sooner or later to detection. All we can say of the incidence of sexual disorder is that it is certainly much greater than either court statistics or private medical records would suggest.[1] The 'successful' pervert is rarely caught and rarely consults a medical psychologist. As a matter of interest, during the year 1954, only 7,647 cases were charged with sexual offences throughout England and Wales. Of these, 2,298 were cases of indecent exposure; 2,625 were homosexual offences and 2,274 were heterosexual offences (assaults, 'defilements', etc.). The number of offences by prostitutes was 11,518. In passing we may note that, although prostitution is not generally regarded as a sexual abnormality, there is conclusive evidence that a large number of prostitutes, both young and experienced, not only suffer from emotional and intellectual backwardness, but exhibit many signs of unconscious mental conflict.[2]

By way of comparison, of an annual average of 523 cases recommended to the Portman Clinic (I.S.T.D.) during the years 1952-3-4, 24·28 per cent were sexual offences. It should be realized, of course, that the cases sent to the Portman Clinic (I.S.T.D.) are already selected by the courts or other interested parties. The distribution was as follows :

---

[1] According to the *Kinsey Survey*, 37 per cent of the total male population of the U.S.A. have at least some overt homosexual experience between adolescence and old age. Fifty per cent of all single males of 35 and under have overt homosexual experience after adolescence. (*Sexual Behaviour in the Human Male*, by Kinsey, Pomeroy and Martin. Philadelphia: W. B. Saunders. 1949, pp. 650–51).

[2] See *The Psychopathology of Prostitution*. (pp. 244–67).

Annual averages for the years 1952, 1953, 1954

Offence	7–14	14–17	17–21	21 and over	Total
Exhibitionism	1	5	4	36	46
Homosexuality	1	5	7	54	67
Heterosexual offences	0	5	2	7	14
	2	15	13	97	127

The Possibilities of Treatment

Coming now to the results of psychological treatment of sexual offenders, it may be of interest to record first of all the after-history of the case of leather fetichism already described. This was highly satisfactory. It was originally recommended that the patient should undergo prolonged and intensive psychotherapy, but owing to extrinsic causes it was impossible to carry out this recommendation. Nevertheless, the careful exploration of his case brought him under favourable psychological influences – a fact of some significance in estimating the importance of a psychological examination. Shortly afterwards he made a successful marriage and as far as can be ascertained has remained free from his pathological compulsions up the present time. It must be emphasized, however, that by no means all sexual disorders are amenable to psychological treatment. The most favourable group is naturally that of 'pubertal sexual stress': in these cases the most dramatic changes can be brought about by simple sexual instruction and enlightenment preferably combined with advisory contact with the parents. Apart from this it is generally true to say that the younger the case the more effective the result of psychological treatment. Where the sexual perversion has been fully organized and practised over a prolonged period, the outcome is much more uncertain. Only in cases where there is a definite 'will to recovery' can favourable results be anticipated. Even so, there is no certain guarantee of 'cure'. On the other hand, there are a number of sexual perverts who, after passing through a lengthy phase of perverse practice, become spontaneously heterosexual. This happens usually between the ages of 34–44. Apart from this, the *general mental condition* of many advanced cases is such that psychological treatment is called for irrespective of whether the sexual compulsion is likely to be resolved or not. Some recent investigations carried out at the Portman Clinic (I.S.T.D.) by the Research Fellow, Mary Woodward, on the records of 113 homosexual offenders discharged during the two years 1952–53 illustrate the points mentioned above. Almost 9 per cent of the cases were under 17 years of age and 48 per cent were aged from 17–30 years. In 40 per cent of the cases homosexuality was more dominant and in 25 per cent heterosexuality was more dominant; 35 per cent were equally attracted to both sexes. In 38 per cent of the cases homosexuality had manifested itself before the age of 15, and in another 23 per cent between 15 and 19. The condition was accompanied by manifest signs of mental disorder or defect in 46 per cent of the cases. The prognosis was good in 31 per cent, fair in 32 per cent, doubtful in 23 per cent and poor in 14 per cent. The greater the degree and organization of homosexual activity the worse was the prognosis. Of the cases treated (mainly by psycho-therapy) 44 per cent had no homosexual urges at the end of treatment; 26 per cent, retained their homosexual urges but achieved discretion or conscious control; just over 7 per cent were unchanged. Bisexual cases did much better than exclusively homosexual cases: 51 per cent of the former, but none of the latter, lost their urges.[1]

Particularly in homosexual perversions it is necessary to estimate the respective significance of constitutional and of developmental factors. The stronger the constitutional factor the less likely is resolution possible by psychotherapeutic means. In any case it is unreasonable to expect that, even in favourable cases, the improvement will necessarily be immediate or permanent. It is in the nature of compulsions that even under treatment they are repeated at often regular intervals. *It is too readily assumed by the courts that because an offence is repeated during treatment the case is therefore to be written off as a failure suitable only for condign measures of punishment.* It is no more reasonable to expect magical

[1] From the Appendix to a memorandum presented to the Departmental Committee on Homosexual Offences and Prostitution by a Joint Committee of the I.S.T.D. and the Portman Clinic (I.S.T.D.) 1955, published later as a pamphlet entitled *The Problem of Homosexuality*, edited by Edward Glover, I.S.T.D. Publications, 1957. See also Mary Woodward: *Brit. J. Delinq.*, 9, 44, 1958.

cures of sexual disorders by psychological means than to expect immediate recovery from chronic rheumatism on the administration of appropriate drugs.

Here then is a convenient point at which to consider the medicolegal aspects of sexual abnormality. And here too it is necessary to remind the reader that, since the calendar of criminal offences is drawn up by law and presumably embodies the moral and social consensus of the time, any conclusions that are advanced here are liable to be upset by those changes in the moral and social consensus which reach the Statute Book. For example, some weighty evidence has recently been brought before the Departmental Committee on Homosexual Offences and Prostitution[1] in support of the recommendation that homosexuality between consenting adults and between consenting minors should not be regarded as an offence unless it is associated with criminal violence or undue influence. When we speak of the social aspects of sexual disorder we must not assume that these are fixed. The social and legal reaction to homosexuality, for example, is a combination of those early moral and religious codes which in their time formed the basis of ecclesiastical law, with the popular prejudices that have been embedded for many centuries in our criminal code and common law. Public opinion on this matter is of three orders: the prejudiced and intolerant reaction of those who have a violent aversion to homosexuality, the more complaisant attitude of those who are tolerant of it and the neutrality of a large middle group whose members tend to treat the matter with passing levity. Yet although, as we have seen, roughly one half of the cases examined belong to the group of 'pathological' cases, we cannot ignore the fact that the others are so constitutionally predisposed or organized that neither therapeutic nor punitive measures will alter this disposition. In such instances it is clear that there is no answer to homosexuality save increased tolerance on the part of the intolerant group which has so far played an undue part in the shaping of our law. Should then the recommendation put before the Departmental Committee ultimately be given legal sanction, the considerations advanced below would require appropriate revision; although of course the needs of the 'pathological' group would still call for organized and extended measures of treatment.

With these general reservations we may return to the question of

[1] loc. cit.

recidivism. If recidivism is to be expected during the treatment even of favourable cases, it is clear that the law must display some of the patience expected from every physician who deals with chronic ailments. The principle of exercising discretion, however, must be formulated in such a way that the psychologist's efforts are encouraged without weakening the social proscription of the offence. The possible complications arising in this connection are interestingly illustrated by a recent case in which the carrying of firearms proved to be part of a compulsive system. Actually the habit was part of a childish ritual to which no social risks were attached. The patient never carried ammunition and would not have hurt a fly. Psychologically speaking it would have been desirable to permit this patient to continue the practice for some time. Yet, as you can well imagine, no court could have been expected to countenance such enlightened and, in this particular case, safe procedure.

I have singled out this point because I do not wish to give the impression that psychologists ignore the difficulties with which those who make or administer the law are faced. Psychology and the law, although they have much more in common than either physicians or lawyers suspect, are bound to come to loggerheads sometimes. And for the simple reason that whereas the therapeutic psychologist is concerned primarily with the mental disorder of his patient, the law is concerned to protect the rights of society as a whole, that is to say, rights of any person or institution with which the patient may come in contact. Obviously this is a situation calling for concessions on both sides. Successful psychotherapy of delinquents includes recognition by the patient of the reasonableness of social order (provided always it is reasonable and not a product of superstition); successful administration of the law involves some recognition of its own psychological limitations. There are, of course, occasions when compromise is not possible; in the case of persons who have periodic impulses to make sexual assaults on strangers it is obvious that, unless they can be rapidly cured, society must be protected by segregating the offender, even if it were desirable that his treatment should be carried out under ambulant conditions, i.e., living at home and voluntarily attending a psychological clinic. These and similar dilemmas frequently arise during the work of the Portman Clinic (I.S.T.D.). The policy in such instances is first to state what, from the psychological point of view, would be the ideal course, and then to make practical suggestions as to how the various compromises might be effected. The final decision obviously is a matter for the court. It must be recognized that the aims of the law are not and never can be identical with those of medical psychology. The law court cannot become the exclusive preserve of the medical psychologist for the simple reason that it is itself a product of the inevitable and unending conflict between the instincts of the individual and the needs of the group.

It follows from these considerations that the problem of treatment or prevention of sexual offences must be approached from two angles, from the point of view of sexual pathology and from the point of view of social expediency. As I have already pointed out, by establishing the category 'in need of care or protection', society had admitted its responsibilities for one particular social group. There is no good reason why this 'protecting' principle should not be applied to pathological groups. And since it is well established that in a large majority of instances outbreaks of sexual disorder can be prevented by proper upbringing, it is clearly the duty of society to use every means at its disposal to provide suitable sexual instruction for parents, child nurses, teachers, club leaders, in short, for all who are in a position to influence the mental development of the child. Next to the actual psychological treatment of young children already showing signs of sexual disorder, this is the best means of prevention. The effect of suitable upbringing and preventive treatment would, of course, be greatly enhanced if all sources of serious mental strain during childhood were reduced. For there is more than a little evidence to show that many non-sexual emotional strains may induce instability in psycho-sexual development.

Society's Responsibility

Regarding the actual handling of sexual offenders, there is one overriding consideration: viz., that sexual disorder is in the majority of instances a form of mental illness. It follows that *every sexual offender without exception should be psychologically examined and given the opportunity of receiving psychological treatment.* As a rider to this proposition I would add that *wherever possible both examination and treatment should be carried out by medical psychologists who are not officially connected with the court.*

Whenever possible, the patient should be allowed to live at his own home with or without probationary control, and, unless his existing occupation is psychologically unsuitable, encouraged to follow his usual employment. Where the treatment recommended is intensive, involving frequent contact with his physician, probationary supervision should be waived. When, in the interests of public safety, temporary segregation is essential, this should be in an institution where expert psychological aid is available. Under existing conditions this would involve residence at an in-patient psychiatric centre but not, of course, in any department where border-line or certified insane cases are admitted. In every case before even temporary measures of compulsory segregation are decided upon, the possibility of partial segregation should be considered. In privately treated cases requiring supervision it is often possible to achieve satisfactory results by 'placing' the patient on parole in a country foster home: but this should be within easy reach of a psychiatric centre. In fact, it is not difficult to draw up an 'ascending scale' of supervision from probationary control up to temporary segregation. Only when all these measures have failed to effect improvement is there any justification for dealing with the offender as a public nuisance. In any case, it should be recognized that imprisonment of sexual offenders is not only a confession of failure on the part of society but in all but habitual and incorrigible offenders an incitement to recidivism. And there is every reason to believe that if, on the first offence, the sexual delinquent were given appropriate treatment, the number of incorrigible offenders would be reduced to a negligible figure.[1]

[1] A full discussion of the uses and abuses of imprisonment as a form of treatment is beyond the scope of this essay. The argument most commonly advanced in favour of the practice is that it has a deterrent effect; but it is also held by some experienced prison psychiatrists that it may render the prisoner more amenable to psycho-therapeutic treatment, either because the offender has been influenced by the shame of imprisonment, or because he has come to realise the full strength of the social authority with which his offence has brought him in conflict. Even some of those specialists who favour the ambulant treatment of delinquency are ready to agree that on rare occasions a prison sentence may be the last effective resource. Some confusion of counsel on this matter can scarcely be avoided since the aims of imprisonment vary widely, from punishment or deterrence to compulsory supervision or segregation in the interests of society. The psycho-therapeutist, although ready to admit the necessity in some cases of segregation and compulsory supervision, main-

Apart from this there is a good deal to be said for reforming the present system of charging sexual offenders. Society is entitled to protect itself against acts of public indecency, but is not entitled to 'punish' psychological disorder. The power of the court over the recidivist could be amply maintained through a 'contempt of court' system. As in the case of prostitutes, sexual perverts could be charged with offences against public decency. But instead of imposing fines or periods of imprisonment the offender could be bound over on set terms of treatment and supervision. The commission of subsequent offences would then constitute contempt of court. The penalties for contempt of court, however, would be suspended until all efforts at treatment had failed.

But even if the most enlightened reforms of this sort were effected, society could not thereby absolve itself from the responsibility of putting its own house in order. The majority of penal codes are based on the tacit assumption that society, like the customer, is always right, that its calendar of offences and *a priori* its moral codes have an absolute authority and justification. This proposition will not bear a moment's inspection. The black market offences which most reflective citizens rightly regard as anti-social are merely an indication that some peace-time incentives are inappropriate in war-time. In peace-time, identical activities are regarded as signs of business acumen and valued accordingly. To come nearer to our subject, it is still an offence to attempt to commit suicide. This is manifestly absurd. Society by lending its authority to the certification of the insane has already

tains that the methods of supervision and segregation should be determined by the psychological needs of the offender. As regards the most common sexual offences, viz., exhibitionism and homosexuality, treatment by imprisonment is more a counsel of despair than a rational method. No doubt many offenders would prefer a sentence of imprisonment to an order for compulsory residence at a psychiatric institution; but that is less a tribute to prison conditions than a reflection on the organization of mental hospitals. No great advances can be expected until psychiatric centres are organized to meet the special needs of non-certifiable mental disorders. In this connection it is interesting to record that of twenty-three scientific experts in the diagnosis and treatment of delinquency who contributed to an I.S.T.D. questionnaire on the suitability of prisons as places where treatment of homosexuality could be carried out, nineteen regarded them as unsuitable, two as suitable, one as suitable 'in certain cases only', and one as neither suitable nor unsuitable. (See Memorandum, loc. cit.)

done all that is necessary to strengthen the hand of the psychiatrist who alone is in a position to deal with the depressive psychoses. The time is now ripe to develop similar lines of policy in the case of sexual offenders. Please do not misunderstand me. I am not recommending the certification of chronic sexual offenders. I am merely suggesting that sexual offences are not to be regarded as outbreaks of the old Adam in us, and therefore a matter for punishment, but that they are mental disorders and therefore the concern of the mental specialist. Society can best protect itself by handing these cases over to the psycho-therapeutist, merely reinforcing his authority in the rare instances where varying degrees of restriction are unavoidable. Admittedly we must also impose safeguards to prevent any abuse of authority by the mental specialist. The safeguards imposed on the certification of the insane can, *mutatis mutandis*, be applied to the treatment of sexual offenders and thereby secure the liberties of the normal subject. In short, the law must recognize its own shortcomings and with a good grace invoke the aid and reinforce the authority of those educational and psychological authorities whose training qualifies them to deal with mental abnormalities.

But the matter does not end here. It is a well-established fact that although many sexual disorders are a sign of emotional backwardness and although some are associated also with a degree of intellectual backwardness, in a great number of instances the cultural standards and ethical codes of sexual offenders are of a very high order. This is particularly true in the case of the homosexual. On the other hand, the moral codes enforced by society also show a degree of backwardness which, if examined closely enough, can be traced back to the superstitious codes, rituals and taboos first imposed by our prehistoric ancestors. Compared with the individual, society normally exists in a state of regression. It is regressive not only in its impulses but in its methods of controlling impulse. Prudery, moralistic indignation and an urge to punish are infallible signs of a backward outlook. By the same token they are signs that we all have within us the urges to sexual misconduct which we are quick to reprobate and punish in others. It would do us a world of good, and at the same time avoid the infliction of untold miseries on, sometimes, highly sensitive individuals, if we could bring ourselves to regard the aberrant sexual behaviour of adults in the same way as tolerant understanding parents regard the first uprushes of infantile love, anxiety, envy, rivalry and hate. By this I do not imply that the individual should not be given full protection from the unsolicited aggression of others, whether that aggression be social or sexual. Society is after all the instrument of man: one of its particular functions is to afford him protection from the egocentricities and eccentricities of his fellow men. But I do very definitely imply that the 'normal' individual, to whom codes of decency are neither a temptation nor a burden, should realize how much he has in common with those who suffer from aberrant impulse. Once he grasps this fact it is not so hard to see that sexual aberration calls for appropriate treatment, not for an immediate application of penal clauses which, more often than not, aggravate the problem instead of resolving it.

PART II
THE PROBLEM OF MALE HOMOSEXUALITY
[1940-59]
i. DIAGNOSIS AND CLASSIFICATION

Although one of the ambitions of the clinical psychologist is to produce a classification of mental disorders in which the various groups can be distinguished and at the same time correlated on the basis of their etiology, there are times when by way of respite from this task he is tempted to the scientifically dangerous courses of generalization. In the light of his experience of the classical symptom-formations (the neuroses and the psychoses), of disorders of character and of a multitude of inhibitions and perversions of sexual and social function, he cannot help wondering sometimes whether amongst the plethora of contributory causes he discovers there is not *one dynamic and decisive psycho-pathological factor* common to all mental disorders.

For a number of reasons the psycho-analyst cannot avoid being pulled in both these directions. On the one hand his theories of mental development which postulate a sequence of infantile phases of libido development together with corresponding phases of development of aggressive impulses and the clinical assumption of a series of 'fixation points' which determine the level of regression of the libido of aggressive impulses and of the ego during illness and consequently the form of symptoms, incline him to look for specific etiologies characteristic of *different* types of mental disorder. And in any case his metapsychological technique of examination whereby he investigates in turn the dynamic, the economic and the structural aspects of any given symptom-formation does not lend itself to the isolation of *one-factor etiologies*.

On the other hand Freud's earlier formulations on mental disorder were based on the assumption of a *kernel complex* of an unconscious nature. Although the existence of this 'Oedipus complex' was established through study of psycho-neuroses and of dreams and gave rise later to the generalization that hysteria had a specific relation to the faulty repression of the infantile genital Oedipus situation, it was not long before the influence of this kernel complex was demonstrated in conditions ranging from slips of the tongue and mild inhibitions to the most grave of the psychoses. This gave rise to a certain stereotyping of etiological factors which can still be observed in present day analytical communications. To be sure, a degree of elasticity was introduced by Freud's distinction of two phases of the Oedipus complex, a positive (heterosexual) and a negative (or homosexual). Still later he strengthened the foundations of a system of differential etiologies by saying that the Oedipus phase could be extended to include all the libidinal and aggressive relations of the infant to its parents. This obviously allowed ample scope for differentiation of mental disorders in terms of the depth and spread of their regression to different phases of Oedipal development.

Nevertheless there were still strong arguments in favour of establishing a one-factor etiology of mental disorder, in particular the desirability of correlating infantile phases of development with phases of *racial development*. To be sure these racial theories were largely hypothetical but it seemed psycho-biologically plausible to regard the infantile Oedipus complex as a repetition in the individual of phases of pre-historic organization when, it was supposed, the incest taboo was first established and consequently when homosexuality offered an outlet to inhibited males. In this respect the genital Oedipus situation could be considered to have greater dynamic influence on mental development and therefore play a more important part in psychopathology than, for example, the earliest oral stages, in that the former represents a characteristically and originally, social human crisis. In other words, what is now an unconscious and extensive complex, was once a social problem or crime giving rise to the most condign social sanctions, and a host of prohibitions or laws.

As a matter of interest the valuation in psycho-analytical circles of the importance of the classical genital Oedipus complex in pathogenesis has varied from time to time, reflecting thereby the degree of importance attached by different observers to early or late stages of libido development and to early and late stages of infantile ego formation. Some observers indeed have discounted the importance of the genital Oedipus situation by rating it as a tertiary phenomenon. But on the whole the balance of analytic opinion remains as originally, i.e. that the Oedipus complex is not only the key to unconscious conflict but, through its repression, the source of sublimation and civilized adaptation, in other words that *all mental disorders have a one-factor etiology*.

On these matters a good deal of latitude and speculation must be allowed. When in earlier times I attempted to isolate the most disruptive unconscious factor in individual development I was influenced by the then existing psycho-analytical interest in libidinal development to nominate on clinical grounds *overcharge of the negative phase of the Oedipus complex* (or, to use a somewhat ill-defined term, of '*unconscious homosexuality*'). Later, following Freud's views on the importance of the aggressive instincts in stimulating unconscious guilt, I was tempted to allot an all round pathogenic influence to the unconscious *sado-masochistic impulses* in which the forces of aggression are mingled with the libido. Nowadays, I would be inclined to combine both factors and to maintain that *conflict over unconscious homosexuality (the inverted Oedipus phase) is still the most perilous and disruptive of all libidinal crises*, but *that this danger is due to lack of success in mastering the sadistic, sado-masochistic or masochistic impulses that are released when the positive Oedipus situation is, from time to time or finally, abandoned in favour of the negative, inverted or homosexual phase.*

But although there are good grounds for assuming that the unconscious homosexual phase is one of the most difficult stages of infantile sexuality, it would be a grotesque misrepresentation of the facts to suggest that it gives rise solely to difficulties and crises. Quite the contrary: unconscious homosexuality is responsible for many important and constructive developments both individual and social. It plays an important part in unconscious ego (and super-ego) development and thereby contributes a number of character formations and reactions which can be uncovered in the unconscious personality or observed in the manifest personality. By thus promoting the development of 'bisexual' character traits it contributes to mutual understanding between the sexes and thereby reduces the sexual antagonism (both conscious and unscious) which otherwise is liable to poison both the sexual and social relations between men and women.

Most important of all, social cohesion and co-operation is immensely reinforced by the sublimation of precisely the unconscious homosexual impulses. It is indeed doubtful whether society could survive without the freed energy derived from the desexualization of these instincts. *For this reason alone the problem of unconscious homosexuality is of vital importance to the clinical criminologist*, and should be also to the forensic sociologist. For it can scarcely be denied that the phenomenology of criminal conduct points to a *weakness in the forces of social cohesion and co-operation* whereby more primitive (narcissistic and ego-centric) impulses are able to escape repression and to obtain relatively unimpeded outlet. We might indeed go so far as to say that a criminal group is one in which the unconscious homosexual impulses have given rise to friction rather than to co-operation.

Definitions and Distinctions

It is therefore essential when approaching the problem of 'manifest homosexuality' to preserve a clear distinction not only between this form of actual sexual perversion and 'unconscious homosexuality', but between 'unconscious homosexuality' and 'latent homosexuality'. 'Unconscious homosexuality' is used, rather loosely, to designate an important phase of mental development, during which the sexual instincts of the child are directed predominantly to family imagos of the same sex. It is dynamically unconscious in the sense that the impulses are held in control by unconscious mechanisms of which the most important is repression. For this reason it is frequently referred to as 'repressed homosexuality' although, as we shall see, this usage is liable to blur the distinction between 'unconscious' and 'latent' homosexuality.

Whether 'unconscious' homosexuality will give rise later to 'manifest' homosexuality depends on a number of factors: (*a*) constitutional, (*b*) developmental and (*c*) precipitating or environmental factors. The developmental factor can in turn be subdivided according to: (1) the quantity and quality of the instincts and the nature of infantile instinctual fixations. Thus a combination of pre-genital and genital impulses directed to the parent of the same sex may if quantitatively reinforced lead to a fixation of instinct at the unconscious homosexual phase; (2) the predominant nature of identifications and introjections which contribute to ego and super-ego fixations or arrests, e.g. a mother identification or a maternal super-ego may contribute to a homosexual predisposition; (3) the amount of control of unconscious homosexual charges of instinct achieved by various unconscious mechanisms in particular, repression, projection and sublimation. Faulty repression or insufficient sublimation will predispose to manifest homosexuality.

Should these various factors operate harmoniously to produce an effective unconscious non-conflicting balance of instincts, no predisposition to manifest homosexuality may be expected. When, however, either the instinctual cathexes or the infantile object choice or the ego-formations are markedly homosexual a *predisposition* is formed which, given any increase in cathexis (charge), will lead to faulty repression or to failure to sublimate adequately, or both.

Even so this may not give rise to 'manifest' homosexuality. For example, an exaggeration of homosexual (non-erotic) character formations may result; or a psycho-neurosis or psychosis may develop: or again abnormal behaviour of an anti-social kind may ensue. Further increase in homosexual cathexis is, however, liable to produce a condition of 'latent' homosexuality, which, given more massive breakdown of repression, will lead to the breakthrough of erotic homosexual impulse, i.e. to a 'manifest homosexual perversion' which either wholly or partly exercises primacy over whatever erotic impulses may be characteristic of the period. This breakthrough may be transient, sporadic or continuous, in which last case we may expect the gradual development of an 'organized' homosexual perversion. It is of course possible to use the term 'latent' or 'repressed' as a synonym for 'unconscious homosexuality', but in that case we should have to pre-empt such terms as 'larval' or 'occult' to designate those homosexual tendencies which unconsciously have already taken a perverse direction and are capable, given a suitable stimulus, of breaking into consciousness.

While in principle this view implies that the *ultimate* determining factors in manifest homosexuality are psychological and developmental, it does not exclude the effect either of constitutional or of precipitating factors, which have to be assessed in each case. It does, however, imply that manifest homosexuality occurring from mid-adolescence onwards is due to a disturbance in the normal unconscious balance of instinct and inhibition. This does not permit us to say that all manifest homosexuality is a *disease*. The standards of disease are clinical standards, and the fact that the vast majority of manifest homosexuals are neither detected by the law nor disposed to seek professional advice (i.e. live on terms with their manifest psycho-sexual system) would prevent any such categorization. In any case it is quite unpermissible to refer to manifest homosexuality as a 'neurosis'. It does not have the structure of a neurosis. At best it might be described as the 'equivalent' of a neurosis, although even that usage is too restricted, for in some cases manifest homosexuality serves to preserve the individual from a psychosis.

Criminological Implications

It follows from these preliminary considerations that the existing standpoint of British law, viz. that 'manifest' homosexuality whether it be practised in public or in private is a criminal offence, is to say the least of it, a socially biased and sectional view of a larger problem which strikes to the roots of human organization, enters into every human relationship, provides the energy for many of man's cultural activities, oils the wheels of human society yet which, under certain circumstances is responsible for many of the day-to-day frictions that disturb friendly communications between men, between women and between men and women, plays a preponderating part in war-readiness[1] and finally is capable of disrupting the human mind, giving rise to a multitude of mental disturbances and disorders from mental unhappiness to persecutory insanity. To amplify this last point: excessive 'unconscious homosexuality' has been advanced by psycho-analysts to account for the systems of paranoia; it plays a part in some forms of schizophrenia and in depressive states; it is an important factor in alcoholism and drug addiction; it is found in psycho-neurotic conflict (in hysteria and the obsessional states); it was discovered to be a source of violent resistance in the analysis of characterological disorders and it gives considerable trouble in the analysis of normal people.[2]

It is therefore not surprising that a sharp cleavage exists between psychiatry and the law on the criminal status of homosexuality.

---

[1] See Glover: *War, Sadism and Pacifism*, Allen & Unwin, 3rd edition, 1947.

[2] See Glover: 'The Etiology of Drug-Addiction', *Int. J. Psycho-Anal.*, **13**, 1932, 13; reproduced in *On the Early Development of Mind, Selected Papers on Psycho-Analysis*, **1**, 1956.

Most psychiatrists experienced in the study of homosexuality hold that manifest homosexuality when practised in private between consenting partners of the age of 18 (some would say 16) is a sexual disorder, not a crime. The psychiatrist agrees, however, that it may be associated with infractions of legitimate social law, as when it involves practice in public (offences against decency), or when it leads to the use of violence, or seduction of minors[1] or again, when it is associated with theft, swindling and blackmail.

At this point an interesting problem in etiology arises. Some of the infractions, e.g. public indecency or seduction of minors are clearly part of the clinical picture of the manifest perversion, involving respectively exhibitionistic mechanisms and a special type of object choice. But it is not so clear that others are on the same etiological level as the *manifest* perversion, as can be shewn by the analysis of some thieves and blackmailers who are not manifestly homosexual but are found to have strong unconscious tendencies. As for the use of violence, study of sadistic crimes shews that the offenders in question are often psychopaths. And psychopathy can very definitely be *traced to unconscious factors*.[2] Moreover it can frequently be observed that the *conscious conflict associated with manifest homosexuality is not due solely to the manifest sexual activity but is derived from conflict over the unconscious homosexual matrix from which the manifest perversion arises.*

These arguments are strongly reinforced by the consideration that, despite prison statistics regarding the criminal habits of manifest homosexuals, the vast majority of homosexuals are not given to criminal conduct. If therefore we confine ourselves to the criminal behaviour *associated* with manifest homosexuality the conclusion would seem to be that this is due at any rate as much to the existence of pathogenic (reinforced) unconscious homosexuality as to the practice of the manifest perversion.

Apart from their criminological implications these considerations have an important bearing on the nature and results of psychological treatment of manifest homosexuals. To this point we shall return; in the meantime we can but repeat one of the main contentions of this essay, viz. that manifest homosexuality is but one end-result of the activity of forces that constitute a sub-

---

[1] See *The Problem of Homosexuality*, edited by Edward Glover, M.D., LL.D., London, I.S.T.D. Publications, 1957.
[2] See Section IV, Pt. II, this volume.

stantial part of the instinctual heritage of the race and give rise to at least as many if not more creative and social processes as they do to destructive and anti-social manifestations.

Clinical Aspects

Having stated categorically the view that manifest homosexuality, practised in private between consenting adults or late adolescents, should not be regarded as a crime, a view incidentally which until 1885 was implicit in the laws of this country (it still applies to female homosexuals) and which if given effect would eliminate from the forensic calendar a substantial number of homosexual 'offences', we must for the time being resign ourselves to the existing ruling of the law that male homosexuality is an unqualified criminal offence, and proceed to a brief outline of its clinical manifestations and variations.

Incidence and Age Distribution

Apart from the fact that statistics on the manifest aspects of any form of sexuality and *a fortiori* of 'criminal' sexuality based on questionnaires and brief interviews or correspondence are notoriously untrustworthy, it would seem that they are used frequently to advance one of the propagandist aims of the homosexual penal reformer, viz. to show that homosexuality far from being a comparatively rare form of 'unnatural vice', is sufficiently common to be regarded almost as a 'natural' form of sexual organization. Certainly if the Kinsey figures are to be relied on, sexuality could be regarded as a continuum from complete heterosexuality to complete homosexuality. And even the more conservative estimates which vary from 2 per cent to 10 per cent of the adult population indicate that the problem is not a negligible one.[1]

[1] It would be superfluous to enter into prolonged discussion of the statistical validity or significance of various assessments of the prevalence of adult manifest homosexuality. Even if we were to strike a mean between high and low estimates or allow for a 50 per cent margin of error in the Kinsey estimates (e.g. that 37 per cent of males beyond the age of puberty have at least some overt homosexual experience ending in orgasm: or that one male out of approximately every four has had or will have homosexual experience or reactions for at least three years between the ages of 16 and 55), the facts would remain, that manifest homosexuality is widely prevalent and that only a small proportion of cases are detected and con-

Such a naturalistic generalization would, however, ignore the facts on the one hand that homosexuality is but one of many perversions and on the other that even the so-called normal forepleasure of heterosexual coitus comprises many activities which if isolated from the end-aim of coitus and magnified could justifiably be regarded as deviations, various forms of kissing, for example, a great variety of manual manipulations, and of course anal intercourse.

What we really need to know about incidence is: (*a*) the type of homosexuality; (*b*) its persistence, e.g. episodic, sporadic, recurrent or organized; (*c*) in each case the age of distribution, e.g. date and duration of first manifestations, of recurrences, duration of persistent forms and; (*d*) in each case the quantitative distribution of sexual interest as between homosexuality and other forms of perversion and between homosexuality and heterosexuality. These are precisely the figures we have not got in a clinically dependable and statistically accurate form. Under these circumstances we have in the meantime no alternative to using the *impressions* formed regarding these matters by experienced clinicians.[1]

In the case of homosexuality, for example, proceeding from the central assumption of 'unconscious homosexuality', the psycho-analyst would expect to find manifest homosexual practices amongst children between the age of 3–4, a scatter of sporadic homosexuality amongst children during the latency period (6–10), an increasing number of cases during pre-puberty (9–11), a peak

victed. The most useful deduction from these figures is that although the number of detected homosexuals depends on the varying activities of the police, nevertheless to the extent that they run obvious risks of detection they constitute a special group either of a compulsive or of a specially masochistic character.

[1] Naturally these vary a good deal according to the diagnostic methods and theories of the observer: on the other hand they have one advantage over more meticulous statistical methods, namely, that the observer as he goes along, discards weak or irrelevant impressions and summates more vital factors; so that after a time he is better able to grasp the essence of a clinical condition than can a statistical machine. Another advantage is that he can deliberately manipulate his impressions in order to seek confirmation of the general validity of *a priori* theories. Although statisticians have always looked askance at the practice, psycho-analysts have always done this; and in fact many of their theories, although based on the discriminating analysis of but a few cases, have proved later to have general validity.

of pubertal homosexuality, either sporadic or continuous, gradually diminishing towards mid adolescence, the appearance of organized adult forms from late adolescence onwards and afterwards a plateau of organized homosexuality, persisting but gradually tapering off to the age of 38–40, after 40 a more marked drop. And that roughly speaking is what the psycho-analytical observer does find. To be sure he has to look for it and in particular to take with a grain of salt the considered denials regarding infantile sexuality which his adult patients will offer him in answer to diagnostic questions. In such cases he must fall back on the information obtained during an actual analysis.

Even with an accurate statistical rating it is necessary to make some clinical reservations regarding age incidence. For example, unless manifest homosexuality during the first five years takes an exaggerated form, liable to canalize later sexual conflicts it can be regarded as normal, or at least as a very uncertain indication that the child will become an organized homosexual in late adolescence or adult life. The same applies although to a lesser degree to manifest homosexuality during the latency period. As for sporadic phases of pubertal homosexuality the after-history of cases of public-school homosexuality also shews that after a few years the manifestations may disappear and give place to normal heterosexual urges. To be sure the history of homosexual episodes or phases cannot be neglected, but its significance can usually be estimated only in retrospect. This clinical correction should be applied to all statements regarding the high rate of manifest homosexuality in the general population. The hard core of manifest homosexuality lies in its organized adult or late adolescent forms.

Classification of Types

The manifestations of homosexuality are subject to the following variations; (*a*) variations in the homosexual impulses of the *subject*, including variations in the *aim* of the impulse, and in the choice of *object*, in the *associated perversions* and in the *degree of heterosexuality* present (if any); (*b*) variations in frequency and in degree of organization; (*c*) variations in the accompanying (non-sexual) mental disorders. To these it is convenient to add (*d*) variations in etiological factors and (*e*) variations in accessibility to treatment. These last two will be dealt with in their appropriate sections.

Before considering the first three of these groups it is necessary to refer to a controversy existing mainly in psycho-analytical circles on the nature of 'bisexuality'. Strictly speaking this matter should be considered under the heading of etiology but as the term is commonly used when describing variations in the subject, aim and object of homosexual impulses it is convenient to consider the point here.

Psycho-analysts generally attach considerable significance to the constitutional factor in all mental disorders, and in the case of homosexuality are accustomed to maintain that man is *constitutionally* bisexual. This does not mean that they discount in any way those *psychological* factors which are responsible for a pre-disposition to *homosexual perversion*. Quite the contrary; they go out of their way to emphasize precisely these *developmental* factors. Some analysts, however, maintain that homosexuality as such is due wholly to psychological causes and that the assumption of a constitutional or hereditary bisexuality is unnecessary if not unwarranted.

The controversy is largely a nosological one based on a restricted view of the nature of infantile sexuality. The essence of infantile sexuality is its *polymorphous* (component) nature, and there can be no doubt that these components are constitutionally determined and consequently vary in strength. And, as will be seen, the aim and range of homosexual activities includes most of the infantile components. The psycho-geneticist maintains, however, that the essence of homosexuality lies in the *choice of an object of the same sex*, and that object choice develops along exclusively psychological lines, starting with early identifications. A third argument is that the term 'bisexuality' is misleading, that the combination of manifest homosexuality with manifest heterosexuality forms a continuum from faintly heterosexual and predominantly homosexual to predominantly heterosexual and faintly homosexual. While therefore it would seem that the ultimate choice of sexual object is psychologically determined, this does not apply either to the infantile components that determine the homosexual aim or to the degree of activity or passivity of sexual impulse in general. These may be accentuated or diminished in course of development but their original force is constitutionally determined. The statement that bisexuality is not constitutionally determined is in any case incapable of conclusive proof – perhaps no great matter, for in psychological medicine, the most that can be done about a constitutional factor is to record it in the case-history.[1]

(a) Variations in Instinct, Aim and Object

Where homosexual impulses alone exist these can be subdivided in rough series into; (1) mainly *active*; (2) mainly *passive* and (3) mixed active-passive. The terms 'active' and 'passive' require careful definition. All instincts have a dynamic force and can therefore be described as 'active': except after gratification they are rarely 'passive' although they can fairly be described as 'quiescent'. 'Active' and 'passive' as used to classify homosexual activities connote respectively 'active' and 'passive' *aims*, corresponding to the 'active' aims of the male heterosexual and the 'passive' receptive aims of the female heterosexual. For this reason although the sexual aims of early infancy are in a general biological sense active and passive without necessarily connoting masculinity and femininity, it is in this last sense that they are most commonly applied to manifest homosexuality: e.g. in the practice of sodomy, where one partner is active and the other passive. Nevertheless many homosexual practices lend themselves to both designations and in fact the commonest forms of homosexuality are mixed active-passive, as in mutual or alternating masturbation. In those cases which, for convenience, we shall continue to call 'bisexual', the same tendencies are found, but where the ('active') heterosexual element is marked there is frequently an increase in the 'active' forms of homosexuality, although this is not without a number of significant exceptions, where the heterosexual component is normally 'active' and the homosexual component predominantly 'passive'. This rather than an equal distribution of manifest impulse is the nearest to a real distinction of clinical 'bisexuality'.

Variation in aim. Further investigation of the erotic aims of

---

[1] Therapeutically regarded the constitutional factor is a bogey, which tends to produce defeatism in therapy. Even in the case of constitutionally backward or defective children it served for a long time as an excuse for therapeutic neglect. Only recently has it been recognised that the *psychological consequences* of mental defect can be as profound and as deserving of treatment as the psychological consequences of a clubfoot or undescended testicle or hypospadias. So in the case of manifest homosexuality.

the homosexual impulses shews that these can also be classified in terms of the *infantile components* activated. These can be arranged in a behaviouristic sequence. Accosting only can be practised or the homosexual activity can be limited to exposure or viewing only; and these in turn can be subdivided into mainly genital forms of viewing, or mainly excretory forms or mixed genito-excretory forms as practised either in public urinals or secretly, as through spyholes drilled in lavatory walls. Next comes sexual petting with or without masturbation. Masturbation can be practised either in mutual form or in one-sided active forms. Next in order come various forms of fellatio which is not only an oral-genital gratification but a homosexual equivalent of heterosexual coitus. Intercrural coitus is also a heterosexual coitus equivalent, as is naturally anal intercourse or buggery. When we recall that buggery exists in a substantial number of heterosexual relationships (some say about 15 per cent), it will be seen that as regards erotic aim there is nothing to distinguish homosexual from heterosexual erotic practices save the absence of vaginal intercourse. Even the rudimentary male nipple can be used as a substitute for heterosexual breast-play (nipple-mouth). In short, as might be expected, the instincts derived from the various erotogenic zones can be marshalled under primacy of homosexual object choice.

In addition to the purely libidinal components, a special group of aims in which libido and *aggressive impulses* are fused to form sadistic (active) and masochistic (passive) impulses. These when associated with homosexuality are of special interest to the clinical criminologist because when strongly charged and uncontrolled by the usual fixed ceremonials (e.g. beating practices, active and passive) they tend to give rise to crimes of violence on the part of the active partner, and in the passive partner tend to incite the active partner to violence.

The next step is to examine the *psychic manifestations* of homosexuality, in particular the capacity of homosexual subjects and objects to fall in love. It is sometimes suggested that the homosexual is incapable of falling in love or that if he does it is only in the most fleeting and inadequate fashion. This if true would be a most significant finding. But in fact it is very far from true. A considerable proportion of homosexuals are capable of falling in love and can manifest the most tender and affectionate forms of idealization of their objects and, unless they become attached to objects of a fixed age group, such as late adolescents, can maintain a high degree of fidelity to them.

It is also held, with more reason, that a higher degree of jealousy exists in homosexual triangles than in heterosexuality (*mutatis mutandis*). Although the figures are not very dependable, there seems to be some basis for this assumption: certainly homosexual jealousy is more disruptive (pathogenic) than heterosexual jealousy.

It is tempting to arrange the erotic and love aspects of homosexuality in series, ranging from exclusively love relationships to exclusively erotic activities, with a variety of intermediate combinations. Unfortunately this does not seem to square with the facts. There is no doubt an approximate series of this sort, but it is not capable of progressive quantitative grading. There seems to be a marked contrast between a love group and a totally erotic group and in the intermediate series in which psychic and erotic elements are combined idealizations are commoner than love feelings. This issue is of considerable therapeutic significance and will be considered later.

Homosexual phantasy. As in the case of heterosexual aims and choice of objects, it is essential to compare the manifest homosexual activities with the conscious homosexual phantasies that are reported. These as a rule show a wider range of interest than the organized activities, and include a number of infantile and pubertal components. Active and passive sadistic phantasies (beating, seduction, etc.) are commonly found and anal elements (phantasies of active or passive buggery) which if practised would give rise to open revulsion. Needless to say the restricted phantasies vary according to the degree of interest in and conscious conflict produced by different infantile sexual components. Of perhaps more significance are the organized and defensive systems which give rise for example to fetichistic and transvestite phantasies. All these extend our diagnostic range and help to assess the amount of unconscious defence against heterosexual interest.

In passing it is worthy of note that in an unascertained but unquestionably large group of homosexuals, the whole homosexual system may be confined to phantasy which is never realized in practice, but may be accompanied by active masturbation. In more inhibited types even the masturbatory outlet is controlled; the individual secures his restricted gratification by cultivating the friendship of objects who arouse his erotic homosexual phantasy.

Manifest homosexual dreaming. In this last group the strength of homosexual phantasy gives rise frequently to manifest homosexual dreaming with or without nocturnal emission. As in the case of heterosexuality, these manifestations have to be distinguished from dreams in which the unconscious erotic content is disguised by the usual dream processes, e.g. symbolism, and are frequently accompanied by intense anxiety instead of erotic excitation. In this connection it is interesting to note that after normal intercourse, many heterosexuals who never experience conscious homosexual impulses may have frankly homosexual erotic dreams, which again have to be distinguished from their disguised homosexual dreams. Incidentally the universality of disguised homosexual dreaming amongst apparently normal heterosexuals has an important bearing on the concept of 'bisexuality' previously discussed.

Variation in object choice. It is a sound generalization that in the field of homosexual activity, indeed throughout all forms of sexuality that call for the existence of a partner, an adequate supply of objects exists to meet the sexual demands of the subject, however recondite these may be. This applies in general to the passive, active, or active-passive types of homosexual object and to the component aims of the impulse – except of course in the more sparsely populated areas, a limiting factor which incidentally applies also to heterosexual supply and demand. As regards both instinct and aim therefore it may be taken that the same groups can be distinguished in homosexual objects, as in the case of variations in subject-impulse.

An interesting variant may, however, be noted here. Some active homosexuals will have nothing to do with objects that are already manifestly homosexual. They prefer a heterosexual object whom they can seduce.[1] In one instance observed by the writer it was essential that the object should be a pugilist or professional footballer who was apparently and in fact a 'normal heterosexual' but could be seduced when intoxicated. The patient picked them up at closing time. This observation merely reinforces the fact that, as well as a sliding scale of manifest bisexuality there is a sliding scale of 'latent' or 'larval' bisexuality. Another case, that of a 'bisexual', maintained that given sufficient time and opportunity

[1] Some observers maintain that unconsciously all do so.

(between six to twelve months of intimate acquaintance) he had never failed to seduce normal heterosexuals, adding, however, that he did not care very much for the practice as the objects were so unskilled.

But it is perhaps more important to consider the part played in homosexual object choice by the age of the object. This is a matter consideration of which has been biased in the past by public prejudice regarding the seduction of minors. That under certain circumstances the subject may show a special preference for objects of certain limited age-groups applies of course to heterosexual object choice also, as witness the seduction of infant males by child-nurses, or the common preference of those who have passed middle age for late adolescent females, or again the less common infatuation of young males for women approaching the climateric. Examination of forms of age selection sheds a good deal of light on the unconscious dynamics of object choice and on the unconscious incestuous proclivities (positive or negative) that determine them. Infantile homosexual seduction is, however, comparatively rare; much commoner is the seduction of pre-pubertal boys and pubertal adolescents. Amongst the voluntary homosexual liaisons of adolescents or adults, the most outstanding group is that in which the subject is attracted to objects of a fixed age, e.g. to striplings of 17, although the range extends commonly to 22. A feature of the situation is that the attachment is abandoned as soon as the object passes the fixed age. In one case the subject made a point of abandoning his objects on their twenty-first birthday.[1]

(b) *Variations in Associated Perversions*

In the case of the homosexual phantasies of non-practising homosexuals it was pointed out that these frequently include a number of fetichistic and transvestite elements. A similar observation can be made regarding the activities of the practising homo-

[1] As a matter of interest the tendency of the subject to become attached to mid-adolescent or late adolescent objects, particularly when the social class of the object is of a lower rating than that of the subject, is often responsible for theft on the part of the adolescent who steals ostensibly in order to find the wherewithal to keep up social appearances. This is the kind of case which might be regarded as the 'legitimate' concern of the criminal psychiatrist who is concerned with the anti-social consequences of the liaison rather than with the liaison itself.

sexual. The nature and significance of the fetich depends on the relative strength of the homosexual component. In complete homosexuals they comprise erotic interests in male clothing (e.g. uniforms, hats, the racing clothes of jockeys), but in 'bisexuals', the fetiches are attached to both male and female garments. Transvestism is common particularly in passive feminine types but is also found amongst active homosexuals. Apart from the obviously homosexual garment fetiches, a number of fetichistic interests exist which are common to both homosexual and heterosexual individuals, e.g. mackintosh fetiches, leather goods fetiches, shoe and corset fetiches and the like.

(c) Variations in Accompanying Mental Disorders

These variations deserve to be grouped for a number of clinical reasons, diagnostic, prognostic and therapeutic. Some analysts have, however, seen no special reason to single them out in this way on the alleged grounds that *every* homosexual presents signs of neurosis. This is certainly not true of the homosexual group as a whole and the suggestion in all probability is due to the particular range of cases observed. It is no doubt common to find neurotic formations in those cases who come voluntarily to private treatment but it is doubtful whether of those private homosexuals who do not come to treatment and are capable of social discretion in their homosexual activities clinical disorders exist in more than a tithe of the cases. The Portman Clinic figures,[1] taken from a sample mostly of selected court cases, gives a better idea of the incidence of clinical complications: – psycho-neurosis, 23 per cent; mild neurotic character, 10 per cent; psychopaths, 10 per cent; psychoses, under 2 per cent; organic brain disease, 2 per cent, low intelligence (I.Q. below 85), under 2 per cent. No abnormality could be detected in 50 per cent of the cases. No mention was made, however, of two inhibitions which may be a marked feature of the homosexual population, although to be sure these are more commonly encountered in private practice, namely, inhibitions in work and social inhibitions. Incidentally although alcoholism is not common in the general group of homosexuals, a good deal of heavy drinking exists amongst young homosexuals from 18 to 23, and again in the over 40's. In the latter case, however, more true alcoholism can be found.

[1] loc. cit.

Finally, although it is difficult to estimate the exact amount of personal unhappiness, thwarted ambition, feeling of failure and inferiority that exists amongst homosexuals, there is some reason to believe that these reactions are slightly more common amongst the homosexual than amongst the heterosexual population. The intensity of this personal suffering, thwarting and inadequacy is sufficiently strong in many instances to deserve the rating of a clinical symptom. But of course the same can be said of those heterosexuals with whom personal suffering or inadequacy happens to be a marked feature of their psycho-sexual relations.

ii. ETIOLOGY

The etiology of homosexuality is a subject beset with peculiar difficulties. In the case of most classical symptom formations (e.g. the hysterias and obsessional neuroses) where the symptomatic processes are localized, and sometimes encapsulated in an ego that otherwise shews no crude disturbances, it is often possible to narrow down the etiological factors to a small group (as a rule not more than six) operating at ascertainable (fixation) points in or (fixation) levels of the mental apparatus, having specific dynamic functions and employing characteristic mental mechanisms. Where, however, the disturbance can be traced to a scatter of fixation points varying in 'depth' (or developmental level of the ego), although the total dynamic functions of the condition can be ascertained and the special mechanisms can be isolated, psychic localization is difficult, unconscious content variable, prognosis uncertain and treatment in the nature of a hazard. This is particularly true of omnibus groups such as psychopathy and schizophrenia. And it is largely true of sexual perversions where the manifest activity represents the peak of a broadly based unconscious construction.

To be sure in the case of sexual disorders, it is sometimes possible to establish an 'equivalence' between the sexual manifestations and some neuroses. Some varieties of impotence and frigidity, for example, have the same etiological basis as cases of anxiety hysteria; and certain varieties of manifest homosexuality can be correlated with obsessional symptoms of a contamination type. Similarly it is probable that the more crude and primitive sexual perversions (e.g. combined sadistic and excretory practices) are of the same developmental level as psychotic, or even psychopathic symptoms. Unfortunately it has so far proved impossible to establish an exact parallel series of on the one hand sexual inhibitions and perversions and on the other non-sexual symptom formations, the reason being that, whereas the more primitive perversions have usually a psychotic connotation, and the milder perversions a neurotic connotation, a comparatively mild type of inhibition or perversion (impotence or fellatio) may also be associated with a psychotic sub-structure. Modifying Freud's generalization we can say in general that whereas in the developmental sense some neuroses, or some forms of alcoholism or some psychoses are the 'negative of a perversion' this is a clinical rule subject to many exceptions. It is in short merely a suggestive pointer to the general etiology of perversions.

To put this in working clinical terms, the main difficulty in establishing the etiology of manifest homosexual perversions is that, since these are derived mainly from a phase of unconscious mental development (so-called 'unconscious homosexuality' or more accurately the 'negative Oedipus complex'), *there are as many varieties of the main group of homosexual perversions as there are roots and ramifications of the negative 'kernel' complex.*

Another difficulty is more of a psycho-biological nature. In the sense of organization, of lien on the forces of sexuality and of potential capacity to establish love relations between adult subjects and objects, manifest homosexuality constitutes the only serious competitor with heterosexuality. And since we have reason to know that manifest homosexuality may not give rise to any indications of conscious conflict, we are compelled to limit our etiological generalizations to; (*a*) such cases as are driven to seek treatment because of conflict; (*b*) cases in which owing to the compulsive force of the perversion the individual is unable to preserve discretion and therefore comes in conflict with the law, where, as in Britain, the law is sufficiently obscurantist and prejudiced as to designate homosexuality a criminal offence.[1]

[1] In point of fact very few analyses of 'undisturbed' homosexuals have been carried out, although occasionally manifest homosexual practices in persons who undertake analysis for other reasons may come the way of the psycho-analyst.

Incidentally this is a difficulty which confronts the clinical criminologist at every turn. Unlike the sociologist who can study crime in the most general and comprehensive terms, the clinical criminologist is compelled to isolate special groups of offender whose behaviour is the result of pathological causes, mental, physical or both. In a private capacity he may disagree with the social designations 'natural' or 'responsible' criminal, but should he be asked by a court to examine and report on an offender who presents no pathological changes to which the offence may be attributed, he is compelled by his professional standards to describe the case under the caption 'no abnormality detected'. If it were possible to examine representative samples of the *whole* homosexual population – including non-conflicted and so far unobserved homosexuals – an as yet unascertained proportion but certainly a majority of cases would be returned under this negative clinical heading.[1]

FUNCTIONAL CONSIDERATIONS

Before embarking on an attempt to sketch the main etiological features of manifest homosexuality, it is essential to consider some of the functional aspects of the problem. It is sometimes assumed not only by the intelligent reading public but by such psychiatrists as are ready to recognize the existence of infantile forms of sexuality, that an adult perversion is no more than a regression to or a persistence of infantile 'perverse' forms. At first blush this seems reasonable enough; but it ignores some important functional aspects of sexuality, in particular its *capacity to still mental pain.* And since the most compelling forms of mental suffering are those associated with *anxiety, guilt and depression*, it is essential to ascertain how far this stilling or neutralizing factor plays a part in perversion formation.

The compensatory and neutralizing relation of manifest sexuality to anxiety is not seriously in dispute. It is apparent at every stage of life from infancy to senescence. Under emotional stress and particularly in states of anxiety the infant can be observed to ply thumb-sucking or any other auto-erotic form of sexual activity up to genital masturbation; the pubescent does likewise; the adult constantly makes use of sexual intercourse or of genital

---

[1] Meaning, of course, in these instances, no abnormality save the sexual practice.

masturbation, either to relieve himself of anxiety and depression or to celebrate their disappearance; the senescent again betakes himself to childlike forms of masturbation or impotent autoerotic practices to allay the anxiety caused by his increasing realization of genital incapacity. The point of importance is the *regressive* nature of most of these reassurance practices, *suggesting as it does that in early development a similar function has been performed by the infantile components of sexuality*. It follows therefore that excess of infantile anxiety is liable to promote a disposition to perversion formation, and that if in later life anxiety is intense enough to give rise to regression, one of the possible results is the eruption of infantile sexuality in the form of a manifest perversion.[1]

Equally important is the action of libido in *neutralizing, suspending or sidetracking the impulses of hostility and aggression*. It is not a coincidence that frustration of libido at each successive stage of infantile development gives rise to impulses in which libido is combined or fused with aggression to form a characteristic 'sadistic' component (e.g. oral sadism, anal-sadism and infantile genital sadism). Given an excess of the aggressive component, the force of repression may be insufficient to deal with any of the sadistic reactions, in which case the ground is prepared for a later sadistic perversion. Over thirty-five years ago Rank[2] pointed out that sadism was the true type of perversion in so far as it excluded guilt. And guilt as we now know is occasioned by conflict over unconscious impulses of aggression. This formulation enables us to extend the sequence of psychic events as follows: frustration, anxiety, hate, aggression towards objects, introversion, unconscious guilt. The disposition towards perversion formation is fostered by the simultaneous countering of anxiety and guilt through exaggeration of the infantile components of sexuality, which help to 'contain' the aggressive impulses at the cost of an infantile canal-

---

[1] This does not of course exhaust the relations of sexuality to anxiety. Two other contingencies may arise, first that dammed up libidinal excitation may under certain circumstances be *transmuted* into anxiety (as in the 'anxiety neuroses') and second that where unconscious libidinal phantasy is contrary to the demands of the super-ego (ego-dystonic) it may provoke anxiety in the ego (as in the psycho-neuroses where unconscious incestuous inpulses provoke the fear of sexual punishment or castration anxiety). This latter situation as will be seen also plays a part in homosexual perversions.

[2] O. Rank: 'Perversion und Neurose', *Int. Z Psychoanal.*, **8,** 397, 1922.

ization of adult sexual impulse and a reduction or suspension of normal heterosexual impulse.

A third factor, although involving more abstruse considerations and calling for detailed research[1] is the *function of perversion formations in preserving reality sense*, when this is threatened by excessive quantities of infantile libido and consequently excessive quantities of infantile anxiety, hate and aggression. This has an important bearing on the vexed question of the 'option of mental disease'. It has always been difficult to determine why one individual develops a neurosis or psychosis, instead of, e.g. a character disorder, a social inhibition, inhibitions in work, a tendency to anti-social conduct, or a sexual perversion. And it is not without significance that whereas the first two of these conditions involve some degree, sometimes a major degree, of interference with reality sense, and the third and fourth involve interference with non-sexual reality activities, sexual perversions, on the whole, limit the interference with reality sense to sexual functions, leaving the individual comparatively free from symptom-formations, character difficulties and inhibitions.

Generalizations of this sort are of course subject to strict qualifications. There are all sorts of mixed types in which manifest perversions are associated with other manifest mental disorders (inhibitions or neuroses) but as has been pointed out these are more common among patients who have open conflict over their sexual organization or are given to compulsive conduct which brings them in conflict with the law. Amongst the more discreet homosexuals the total function of the ego will be found to stand comparison with that of so-called 'normal' persons.

As for the *unconscious option* of perversion-formation instead of anti-social conduct, an interesting hypothesis has recently been put forward by Schmideberg,[2] viz. that 'most acts of pathological delinquency can be classed wholly or partly as perversions or fetiches.' The neuroses and perversions have, she maintains, similar etiologies but branch off, one in an autoplastic, the other in an alloplastic direction.[3] Similarly with delinquent acts. Formula-

[1] Glover: 'The Relation of Perversion Formation to the Development of Reality-Sense' *Int. J. Psycho-Anal.*, **14**, 1933. Reprinted in *On the Early Development of Mind*.
[2] M. Schmideberg: 'Delinquent Acts as Perversions and Fetiches', *Brit. J Delinq.*, **7**, 44–9, 1956.
[3] Definitions of autoplasty and alloplasty, see p 133.

tions of this sort seem to run counter to all the canons of descriptive psychiatry (although it is not uncommon to find fetich-formation and kleptomania in conjunction): they may perhaps discount the relative strength of the aggressive impulses in the contrasting conditions (neurosis and delinquency), but they do support two psycho-analytical contentions, viz., that the key to the classification of mental disorders lies in their etiology and that owing to a developmental 'scrambling' of instincts adult sexual impulse and adult social impulses have an extremely close, if subterranean, relation to one another.

The three functional aspects discussed above represent general forms of *mental defence*, and for this reason each of them has been advanced by enthusiastic psycho-analytical theoreticians as the main or even sole cause of manifest homosexuality. Thus the view is sometimes held that the defensive displacement and libidinization of aggression is responsible for all perversions. On the other hand as originally the aim of infantile libidinal impulses is active even when the object as such is not appreciated, it is scarcely possible to ignore the canalization of active sexual aims in manifest homosexuality, unless of course we take the view that aggression *generates* libido, a view which runs counter to the basic psycho-analytical classifications of instinct. It is indeed a useful discipline preparatory to investigating etiology to remember that whilst defence is a constant feature of mental activity the instincts that give rise to defence have a certain autonomous function, and up to a point play an autonomous part in all mental functions.

Classification of Etiological Factors

As in the case of the clinical symptom formations (neuroses, psychoses, etc.) it is convenient in the case of manifest homosexuality to classify etiological factors into; (A) constitutional; (B) pre-disposing or developmental and (C) precipitating; and to sub-divide the second of these groups in accordance with the principles of metapsychology, into; (1) instinctual or dynamic; (2) structural or topographic factors, e.g. the development of the ego and ego-object relations, and (3) economic or mechanistic. Needless to say, these distinctions are made mostly for convenience in presentation, and none of the categories can be demonstrated in independent action. To say that some instincts are arrested at a fixation point is to combine dynamic and structural criteria, and to imply a developmental relation between instincts and the ego.

A. Constitutional Factors

These have already been considered in Part I and require no amplification at this particular point. We need only assume that constitutionally any or all of the infantile components exist in excess.

B. Predisposing or Developmental Factors

These can be divided into; (*a*) *dynamic*, viz. the instincts concerned and the affects and unconscious phantasies they engender; (*b*) *structural*, the nature of ego and super-ego formations and the fixation points at which infantile libido is arrested; (*c*) *economic*: the mechanisms which in excessive or diminished action contribute to the perversion formation.

(*a*) *Dynamic (Instinctual)*

As has been indicated the range of manifest homosexuality includes every variety of infantile component impulse marshalled under the primacy of homosexual object choice. This fact greatly simplifies the task of recognizing those components which have contributed to the total fixation at a homosexual level, always a difficult problem in the case of the neuroses where the infantile fixations can be inferred only from the results of analytical exploration. The main source of error lies in the fact that owing to the operation of defensive displacement one sexual element may be accentuated for the unconscious purpose of masking another and more guilty element. Nevertheless many analysts maintain that some fixations are common to all forms of homosexuality as when, for example, they postulate an overall *oral-sadistic* fixation. Now this fixation is perfectly clear in the case of homosexual fellatio where the equation of breast-nipple with penis and of mouth with female genital is not hard to establish. But the same importance attaches to *anal* fixations in the case of buggery, to *skin* erotism in sado-masochistic homosexual practices and to infantile *genital* erotism which last is to be observed not only in the common practice of mutual masturbation amongst homosexuals but also in the pursuit of genital orgasm of both parties in most perverse practices.

Incidentally it is important to remember that the genital erotism of infants is not quite the same as the adult genital-(heterosexual) erotism that develops at puberty. It is limited mainly to the function and valuation of the penis – hence the term 'infantile phallic erotism'. Phallic erotism is exquisitely illustrated in mutual homosexual masturbation. In spite of, perhaps because of these differences between infantile and adult genital erotism, the 'phallic stage' exerts a most important influence on homosexuality. This is clear not only from the central significance attached to the erect penis by both parties in homosexual play (however varied or passive their aims) but also from the central rôle of the penis in homosexual phantasy both conscious and unconscious. These phantasies play a double part in stilling genital anxieties. On the one hand they underline the possession by both parties of an undamaged penis, at the risk, however, of guilt at having appropriated the father's potent phallus; and on the other they protect the homosexual at the same time from the fearfulness of the (castrated) female genital and from anxiety regarding the woman's possession of a hidden penis. These phallic interests are of course reinforced in fellatio by oral reactions to the penis – nipple equation. The full force of phallic erotism cannot therefore be estimated until the nature of the object choice has been ascertained and the various levels of libidinal interest established.

The same may be said of that other group of infantile sexual components, the sado-masochistic group. These vary with each stage of libido development and produce characteristic differences in libido rating. Those who emphasize the importance of oral fixations in homosexuality likewise underline the importance of oral sadism (or masochism); those on the other hand who attribute the greatest significance to infantile genital elements favour the importance of genital sadism (or masochism). But in either case it is necessary to establish the nature of object choice. The same considerations naturally apply to those reactions of unconscious hostility which are engendered by frustration, jealousy, etc.

Object Choice. Although at first sight the nature of object choice would appear to be easily ascertainable, since, the earlier component impulses apart, there are not many infantile objects to choose from, the situation is complicated in that object choice is not the first relation to objects. The first form of psychic object contact is in the nature of identification. Hence when considering object choice we must know also what forms of identification (or introjection) have development in the ego and influenced object phantasy. We must know for example whether the homosexual subject forms a *direct* homosexual object choice and whether the attachment is indirect through identification with his father or as the case may be his mother.

With these reservations in mind we may note that while component infantile erotic drives have limited aims (and therefore, from the descriptive but not from the dynamic point of view, limited objects (e.g. mouth sucking nipple or penis)) object choice becomes more complex in course of development and includes a multiplicity of aims, of which in the absence of early fixations, the latest is usually the most dominant. Infantile object choice reaches its most advanced form in the positive infantile heterosexual aspects of the Oedipus complex. And since this constitutes the main source of infantile conflict, the question arises whether manifest homosexuality is to be attributed to an arrest of infantile libido development at the negative (infantile homosexual) phase or whether it performs a mainly defensive function, guarding against re-activation of the positive Oedipus complex.

The answer seems to be that although fixation at the negative Oedipus complex is operative in all cases of manifest homosexuality, *the factor of defence against re-activation of the positive Oedipus situation is of paramount significance.* Expressed in non-technical terms this means that *in cases of manifest homosexuality even where apparently no erotic interest in women has ever existed, the unconscious situation is invariably a triangular one, from which in consciousness the female (maternal) figure is eliminated and denied.*

It is at this point that the most important etiological distinctions of manifest homosexuality can be effected. If, as seems to be the case, the negative Oedipus situation can function as a point of regression in the flight from the positive incest situation, we may expect to find a number of standard types varying according to the particular identifications effected. These will vary from extremes of feminine (mother) identification to extremes of masculine (father) identification. And the same applies to the choice of object. The situation is of course complicated where the primary (parental) Oedipus drive has been displaced in part to what can be called the 'secondary' Oedipus complex, viz. incestuous attachments to siblings. Moreover the existence of cross-identifications has to be taken into account as when an apparently narcissistic identification exists, the object representing also the subject himself. This is particularly true of 'fixed-age' objects. Further distinctions can be drawn in accordance with whether the defence is directed mainly at the libidinal aspects or at the hostility aspects of the problem. Sibling rivalry giving rise to intense unconscious hostility can for example give rise later to a positive homosexual attachment to brother-substitutes. In fact the homosexual situation, containing as it does at least nine variables in object choice cannot be assessed without a close examination of each individual case.[1]

It follows that we should treat with a considerable amount of reserve etiological explanations which accentuate one factor only, e.g. father *or* mother identification. In short it is this variety of combined identification and object choice that gives rise to the greatest difficulty in establishing the function of any one homosexual system. The subject can play the part of father, mother or child to an object who by identification or displacement can also represent the father, mother or child. This double triangular play (father, mother and child in both subject and object) gives rise to a number of combinations of which, however, two (an active set and a passive set) usually exercise a primacy in both active and passive homosexuals. On the other hand successful disentangling of these combined factors is the key to success in the analysis of male homosexuality.

Another reason for caution in assuming one main identification is the high degree of elaboration of *unconscious homosexual phantasy*. Since there is the widest possible variation in these groups of infantile phantasy, it should not be assumed, as is so often done, that all varieties of unconscious phantasy exert an equal etiological influence. There is, however, one exception to this rule, namely, the significance of *procreation phantasies*. To be sure there is a general tendency in homosexuality to deny the possibility of child-production. Homosexuality like earlier forms of

[1] This consideration adds support to the argument of those who emphasize the psychological as opposed to the constitutional nature of homosexuality. For it is obvious that the process of cross-identification in the subject (i.e. mother, father and self) lays the door open to *bisexual play in unconscious phantasy*. In this connection it is not without significance that the commonest form of homosexual activity is mutual masturbation which gives ample scope to this unconscious bisexual play.

component sexuality lends itself to this denial. On the other hand the unconscious wish of the male to produce a child lends itself to a fixed feminine identification, and, incidentally seems to give rise to some of the most violent forms of anxiety.

Affective. Taking into account the strength of early narcissistic organization of the homosexual which at the genital stage gives rise to an unusually intense valuation of the phallus (and this of course is greatly accentuated by the subject's identification of his genital organ with either the penis of the father or the phantasied penis of the mother) it is not surprising that the *castration anxiety aroused by the development of the positive Oedipus complex should be the central etiological factor of homosexuality*. The homosexual organization simultaneously denies the fear of the father's castrating penis and eliminates the horror of the female genital. The factor of guilt is more conveniently described in connection with the structural ego and super-ego factors.

(b) Structural

So far we have considered the importance of identifications or introjections on the unconscious homosexual rôle played by both subject and object. We must now consider the influence of these same processes in *guilt* formation. The function of the super-ego, which is based on the introjection into the ego of father and mother imagos and tendencies, usually instigates the repression of *all* infantile sexuality. Hence the obvious question arises, why does an essentially infantile form of sexuality, viz. homosexuality, escape the action of repression and supplant to a greater or lesser degree the adult functions of sexuality. The simplest answer seems to be that the censoring activity of the super-ego is 'bought off' by a severe repression of the positive Oedipus complex, which, however, enables the regressive activation of the negative Oedipus or homosexual complex.

The matter is, however, by no means so simple. To take one example, the denial of positive incestuous wishes is greatly reinforced by the child's need also to deny what to him is an incestuous activity on the part of the parents, namely, their sexual intercourse and the fact that they are able to produce children. The child's identification with the father in a homosexual situation kills two birds with one stone: it denies the rôle of the mother and it prevents in phantasy at any rate the father taking part in intercourse or procreation. It is this factor of unconscious *denial* which when sufficiently strong interferes with the super-ego's customary control of all infantile sexuality. Or perhaps it would be better to say that the powers of the non-sexual super-ego are depleted by an erotic ego-identification with the father.

To put this another way, in the case of homosexuality the desexualization of infantile impulse consequent on abandoning the positive Oedipus attachment does not follow its usual course of providing 'neutral' energy for purposes of effective displacement, and sublimation and this inadequately desexualized energy when turned aside from positive Oedipus wishes favours a sexual regression to more narcissistic forms of object relationship, such as homosexuality.

As for the influence of maternal forms of super-ego, it is sufficient to note that a similar distribution of maternal influences exists, as between ego-identification and super-ego introjection. The strength of the tendency to identify with the mother imago and to perform in phantasy her maternal functions, diminishes the force of the introjection of the forbidding mother in the form of a super-ego facet. Apparently the maternal super-ego strengthens the paternal super-ego in so far as repression of the positive Oedipus wishes are concerned; but the ego is able to retain both infantile pre-genital interests and a genital organization which depends on the *exclusion of the maternal object*. In cases of homosexual conflict, however, the manoeuvre is not achieved without difficulty. The fear of loss of maternal love combined with the guilt of having destroyed her add force to the super-ego's primitive attitude and at the same time spur the ego to increasing denial of any love attachments to the mother.

(c) Economics

It is evident from the foregoing considerations, and from the broad infantile basis of homosexual attachments that every variety of unconscious mental mechanism is called into play to promote the ultimate perversion. It is not possible therefore to adduce any one mechanism or set of mechanisms in support of an economic etiology, with the possible exception of regression and displacement and faulty sublimation, which are, however, characteristic of mental disorder in general. The question depends on whether the homosexual solution of sexual difficulties produces a working balance of instincts and so adds a strong primary gain to the development of the perversion. Owing to the absence of adequate investigation of 'non-conflicted' homosexuals, no generalizations on this point are so far possible. Yet it seems likely that in such cases and despite the many limitations, disadvantages and indeed social risks of the homosexual situation the primary gain is sufficient to offset secondary loss, inhibition or injury. In so far as social punishment is concerned we may assume that in such cases no effective balance is achieved and that the ensuing failure of successful repression gives rise to typical unconscious guilt, or, as it is better termed, unconscious need for punishment, which, if strong enough, is gratified in the process of detection and subsequent punishment.

C. *Precipitating Factors*

It must be admitted that differences in the classification and evaluation of precipitating factors in manifest homosexuality depend largely on the theories and preconceptions of the observer. Those who believe in the existence of unconscious dynamic factors favour the assessment of precipitating factors in terms of their unconscious dynamic significance. Those who are sceptical about the importance of such factors, are content to emphasize the importance of immediate stress or frustration. This is also true of sociologists, who unless specially trained in dynamic psychology, are unlikely to consider the existence of unconscious frustrations and to prefer such social factors as the influence of male homosexual sub-cultures, or the importance of seduction or even of economic factors which last they hold influence, for example, the choice of homosexual prostitution by otherwise heterosexual 'hard-ups'. It will be found convenient therefore to consider each group in terms of both immediate and unconscious effect.

Needless to say the most fruitful clinical approach to the precipitating factor lies in the study, first, of so-called 'bisexual' cases and, second, of cases in which the predisposition to perversion is so strong as to require little immediate stimulation to render a 'latent' or 'larval' form 'manifest'. It is in these 'marginal' cases that the immediate swing-effect of the precipitating factor can be most readily observed. Needless to add the psycho-analyst holds that this swing-effect does not operate directly but is obtained after passage of the frustrated or withdrawn energy through the dynamic unconscious system. In other words the process is similar to that obtaining in the psycho-neurotic or even psychotic process of symptom-formation where immediate frustration or withdrawal of libido sets up an introversion of instinct and later regression to the fixation point or points of the ensuing disorder.

Stimulation Factors. It is not without significance that the problem of *seduction* of young boys and adolescents has engaged a good deal of attention amongst those who favour the independent action of immediate factors, also amongst those who support 'preventive' legislation on homosexuality. At this point the dynamic psychologist feels compelled to take a very definite stand. Many of the stories of seduction told later by manifest homosexuals are, like the reminiscences of prostitutes and hysterics, extremely unreliable. The fear of seduction is, in the dynamic psychologist's view, a common hysterical fear which has its roots either in the unconscious wish for seduction (passive) or in the unconscious wish to seduce (active). As has been pointed out earlier,[1] the onset of homosexual practices is in any case common in adolescence. And it is doubtful whether in such cases the seduction of heterosexual youths can be regarded as an important factor. It would be much more to the point to estimate the significance of homosexual seduction in young children of the age of 3–9 years. Infantile seduction, though no doubt much exaggerated, seems to act as a traumatic or fixation factor. Incidentally, it need not necessarily be a homosexual seduction. The seduction of infants by nurses or even by mothers is even more liable to induce a revulsion from the opposite sex. Even so, a number of qualifications arise. For example it is not always the elder partner who initiates the seduction. Many young children enjoy a sense of power in seducing even grown-ups. Secondly, an even more important form of 'seduction' is not manifestly sexual; it lies in the conscious or unconscious attitude of the parents who may persistently treat the child as if he were a girl. The mother may wittingly or unwittingly discourage his masculine attributes and the father may cultivate feminine identifications on the child's part. In most cases it is unlikely that the stimulation factor will have persisting effects if the unconscious predisposition to homosexuality has not already been established.

Frustration Factors. There is, however, less doubt about the

[1] See pp. 205–6.

effect of frustration. This can be recognized during the observation of infants or during their analysis of children in later years. For there is not only a natural development of alternating phases of attachment to the mother and to the father, but these swings from female to male parent are readily exaggerated by frustration and disappointment. These early factors, however, do not receive so much attention as later frustrations. The form to which a good deal of sociological importance has been attached is the effect of *isolation* from female society of apparently heterosexual men living in closed male communities (prison camps, or under combatant conditions in the armed services, etc.); or under predominantly 'male' conditions (boarding schools, merchant service, etc.). Although apparently a tension factor, this is highly selective in action, affecting mostly those who are already predisposed to sexual perversion but who, on the cessation of isolation, revert to heterosexuality.

As during early childhood, immediate frustrations of heterosexual libido are liable to provoke homosexual swings in predisposed adolescents and adults. But this alternation is not due to a purely quantitative factor. It occurs more frequently where the damming up of libido follows a traumatic experience with a woman, e.g. humiliation, depreciation, sudden jilting. It is also increased by the factor of aversion from women, as in the case of the more sordid experiences with prostitutes or after venereal infection by women. Such major traumata are not confined to isolated episodes: lesser traumata if repeated frequently enough can end by producing in summation the same effect as major injuries and set up a traumatic regression which may end in manifest homosexuality.

On the other hand in many instances the factor of immediate frustration appears to be absent or to be of such a mild nature as to be unlikely to cause much mental disturbance. This fact brings to a head the question raised earlier, namely, how far the effect of the precipitating factor depends on unconscious factors that have been re-animated by regression. A common example is where the individual turns homosexual after some social injury or slight of an apparently trivial nature; in one instance failure in an army test. This linkage between current and infantile frustrations or depreciations of the ego is effected largely through the influence of *symbolism*. The social depreciation and consequent inferiority feeling of the personality is equated unconsciously with phallic depreciation (threatened castration) with the consequence that a regression takes place to the (in phantasy safer) phallic emphasis of manifest homosexuality.

Economic Factors. The idea that immediate economic factors play a deciding rôle in various forms of sexual perversion, not to mention such heterosexual activities as female prostitution, is one that dies hard. Male homosexual prostitutes frequently aver that their activities are prompted by the need for gain, and it is not perhaps without significance that homosexual blackmailers commonly belong to this group. It is increasingly recognized however, that economic factors require to be estimated in terms of their psychological significance. In the dynamic sense their main impact is to increase the narcissistic sensitiveness and sense of injury of the individual, but this is not a factor specific to homosexuality and in any case is of secondary importance. However defensive a psychic manoeuvre the development of homosexual perversions is, it is primarily due to disturbance of some of the psychosexual life past and present.

Summary

Assembling the various factors that play a part in the etiology of male homosexuality the following list can be compiled: (*a*) *constitutional*: relative excess of some of the various component libidinal impulses from oral to genital and of sado-masochistic tendencies; (*b*) *developmental* fixation of infantile components particularly at the negative Oedipus (homosexual) phase, flight from the positive Oedipus (incestuous) situation, which may reactivate purely narcissistic organizations of the ego, castration anxiety, a fetichistic overvaluation of the phallus, cross-identification with the parents resulting mainly in bisexual phantasies, concentration of super-ego disapproval on the positive aspects of the Oedipus complex; (*c*) *precipitating* stresses or traumata arising from earlier heterosexual experiences or from ego-depreciations which lead to regression of insufficiently sublimated erotic impulse.

iii. PROGNOSIS AND TREATMENT
PROGNOSIS

If we adopt the clinical uses of this term, namely, the prognostication of the future course of a disease, we immediately find ourselves in a dilemma. For *in the case of male homosexuality the clinical term 'disease' would be applicable only to cases in which the sexual perversion is a direct outcome of disordered mental or physical processes of such intensity as to disturb the function of the individual to the point where he requires and seeks medico-psychological attention.* To judge from the incidence of homosexuality in both private and court practice, only a small fraction of the total homosexual population would conform to this mainly therapeutic standard. Yet there are many commentators who, taking dictionary licence, and accepting one of the definitions of disease as 'a deranged, morbid or depraved state of mind or morals' would insist that whether or not homosexuals complain of or in some important respect 'suffer from' their condition, they all are 'diseased' in at least a sexual if not also in a moral and social respect. And of course those who maintain that homosexuality is due exclusively to warping of psychological development would on the whole be inclined to suggest that in *all* cases a factor of early abnormality can be detected.

The dilemma can be made a little clearer if we consider to what extent the term can be applied to *heterosexual* activities. Now it is certainly unusual to talk of the 'prognosis' of heterosexuality. With the exception of conditions such as nymphomania, prostitution or Don Juanism which are sometimes regarded as sexual disorders, and, to the extent that they are responsible for disturbances of individual function, justify the use of a clinical term, 'prognosis' is applicable to heterosexuality only in the general psycho-biological sense of 'prognostication'. Thus, the average intensity, range and fluctuation of heterosexual libido at different ages can be roughly estimated, and these standards can be used for purposes of prognostication. Or, 'patterns' of object choice can be recognized and made the basis of predictions of future conduct. In fact a good deal of marriage counsel depends on accurate prognostication of this kind.

As far as medical psychology is concerned the use of the term as applied to homosexuality is strictly limited. The fact is that ever since the educated public discovered the possibilities of psycho-therapy, psycho-therapeutists have been consulted from time to time by homosexuals who for one reason or another wished to be relieved of their sexual propensities. Psycho-analysts in particular have therefore been legitimately concerned to discover how far the complaints of these homosexuals are accessible to psychotherapy; in other words, what are the most favourable factors on which a recommendation of psycho-therapy can be based. Although therefore they are also interested in general prognostications regarding the course of different forms of sexuality, in the case of homosexuality they restrict the term 'prognosis' to its clinical uses. It is in this clinical sense that the term is used here. *In effect this limits our consideration to cases which come voluntarily for treatment or which, if sent under court orders, have nevertheless a readiness to accept treatment of whatever sort.*

Two further variables should be noted. In the first place obvious differences exist in the type of male homosexuality; and in the second clinical prognosis varies with the efficiency of treatment. Since there are a number of different types of psychological or social therapy, we must therefore expect some differences in prognosis to reflect the therapeutist's convictions regarding the efficiency of the methods he employs. In the past the main difficulty in arriving at agreed prognoses lay in the fact that no adequate or controlled statistics on the subject existed. Nevertheless a number of general impressions gained currency based on the treatment of isolated cases encountered in the course of general psycho-therapeutic practice.

Briefly the results of earlier work led to the practice of giving only guarded prognoses in male homosexuality. Roughly speaking it was thought that, provided they were prepared to co-operate in treatment, young homosexuals (under the age of 30, preferably under 25) of the 'active' genital type were amenable to treatment, particularly if they were bisexual in habit and if they manifested neurotic symptoms. The degree of amenability seemed, however, to vary. Occasional change from homosexuality to complete heterosexuality was observed, more frequently loss of homosexual impulse without change to or increase in heterosexuality and most frequently greater integration of the ego with corresponding increase in power to control homosexual impulse. Contrariwise, the organized and completely passive homosexual over the age of 30 with pregenital interests but without neurotic or personality disturbance was given a poor prognosis even if he were ready to co-operate in treatment. Between these extremes a sliding scale from good to bad prognosis existed. Although these impressions were not correlated with the type of treatment employed, it seemed that the results of different therapies did not vary widely. In more recent times some observers have formed more favourable (in some cases extremely favourable) prognoses; but on the whole the consensus of informed opinion has remained in favour of guarded prognosis, making due allowance for variations in 'accessibility' to treatment, a factor which is increasingly recognized as the most decisive of all.

The earlier absence of statistically significant figures lends increased importance to such systematic surveys as have been conducted in more recent years. The following are the conclusions arrived at by the Portman Clinic (I.S.T.D.) in a Survey of 103 adult and ten juvenile homosexual offenders, all but ten of whom had been convicted of such offences. The overall prognosis was 'good' in 31 per cent of cases, 'fair' in 32 per cent, 'doubtful' in 23 per cent and 'poor' in 14 per cent. Dividing the group according to the Kinsey ratings, it became clear that the best prognosis lay amongst those 'only incidentally' homosexual or 'more than incidentally' homosexual (Good = 44 per cent; Fair = 40 per cent; Doubtful and Poor = 16 per cent). Amongst those 'equally heterosexual and homosexual' and 'predominantly homosexual but more than incidentally heterosexual' the percentages were respectively 40, 28, 31, whereas the 'predominantly homosexual but incidentally heterosexual' and the 'exclusively homosexual' gave percentages of 18, 31, 50. 'Bisexuals' tended to have a better prognosis than those who were exclusively homosexual, the percentage rate for the former being: Good 35 per cent, Fair 32 per cent, Doubtful 22 per cent, Poor 9 per cent.

As regards the *aim* of the perversion there was a statistically significant tendency for the aim of anal intercourse to be given a worse prognosis (58 per cent doubtful or poor) than other types of aim (26 per cent doubtful or poor). Unfortunately no figures were available regarding the prognosis in predominantly 'active' and predominantly 'passive' types.

Interestingly enough, *age* and *persistence* of behaviour (or organization) did not affect prognosis when considered statistically as single factors. Actually there appeared to be a tendency of those aged 30 and over to have a 'good' or 'fair' prognosis more frequently than those under 30. But the impression did not prove to be statistically significant and the conclusion was drawn that age is apparently an important consideration only when other conditions are favourable. The expectation that sporadic cases might have a better prognosis than persistent cases was not borne out by the figures; or, rather, although there was a tendency in this direction, it was not statistically significant.

Finally as regards the bearing on prognosis of various co-existing types of mental disorder, or *complications* as they might be called, the numbers were too small for statistical control. Certain trends, however, could be observed; e.g. cases with organized psycho-neurotic symptoms (conversion hysteria, anxiety hysteria and obsessional neurosis) but not those with mild psycho-neurotic character disorders, appeared to have a good prognosis (eight out of twenty-five), certainly as compared with psychopathic cases (one out of eleven).

When one takes into consideration the fact that a large majority of these cases were 'convicted offenders', a fact which itself indicates either a degree of ego- (or reality-) weakness or a compulsive type of homosexuality or both, the striking feature of this survey is the relatively favourable over-all prognosis of some male homosexuals. As we shall see when considering the results of treatment noted in the same survey, the actual favourable prognoses fell short of the favourable results, a fact which indicates that the prognosis was not exaggerated by personal optimism on the part of the observers. This would appear to support the recent tendency to take a more favourable view of the accessibility of homosexuality to treatment. It does not follow, however, that if and when statistically significant figures can be obtained regarding the prognosis of cases seeking private and voluntary treatment, equally favourable estimates will be justified. On the one hand it is certainly true that the factor of co-operation seems to be more marked in private cases; but on the other a higher proportion of organized cases seek help in private. And despite the equivocal evidence of the Portman Survey, which incidentally was not borne out by the results of treatment, it is hard to believe that organized cases over 30 are as favourable as younger cases of sporadic homosexuality. If that were really the case, it would be difficult to account for the marked preponderance of homosexuals who throughout life live 'on terms' with their sexual perversion.

Bearing in mind that the conclusions are based on the examination and treatment of selected cases of male homosexuality, it may be said that the following groups comprise the cases in which psychological treatment is clearly indicated; (*a*) cases in which conflict exists and a desire to be freed from the habit; (*b*) cases of 'pathological' homosexuality mainly of a 'defensive' type; (*c*) cases in which, owing to age, temptation, seduction and other factors, an individual who might otherwise have developed in a heterosexual direction has become temporarily homosexual or has developed a homosexual organization. To these should be added cases in which the homosexual urge is associated with criminal conduct of a pathological type (violence, rape, seduction, theft or swindling) for these are after all the cases in which the forensic psychiatrist is primarily interested. This is no doubt a conservative estimate and perhaps it would be a better policy to cast the therapeutic net more widely. But if this is done it is essential that in unselected types of case the patient should be clearly forewarned that the treatment recommended is in the first instance 'expectant' and can be discontinued after a probationary period, if by that time no improvement of any kind seems likely.

TREATMENT

In no department of medical psychology does greater uncertainty exist than in the field of psychotherapy. Nothing is harder to secure than accurate, controlled and correlated results of treatment. In the earlier days this was only natural. Systems of diagnosis varied widely, methods of treatment varied equally widely. They still do. Most of the cases were treated in private, and little or no effort was made to check the results by after-history. With the increase in numbers of organized psychiatric centres some of these defects will no doubt be remedied. But on the other hand it is improbable that clinic records will ever be able to compete with private records for depth of diagnosis, accuracy of prognosis and detailed estimations of the progress of treatment. This is certainly true of psycho-analytic and other forms of dynamic approach. To be sure the scope of diagnostic methods employed at clinics will appear to increase, for nowadays the psychiatric clinic is the home of the 'multi-disciplined' approach. Once psychiatrists have been seized of the desire for 'scientific' records there is no limit to their ambitions. But, alas for the prospect, methods of diagnosis must be rated not by their multiplicity but by their depth. And the same can be said of methods of treatment.

Results of treatment can of course be estimated by purely empirical standards. Indeed it will be found convenient to preface consideration of the therapy of selected male homosexuals by summarizing the results of the Portman Clinic Survey of convicted offenders. It should be remembered, however, that; (a) these cases were selected in the first instance according to legal categories of offence and belong to the more compulsive group; (b) the types of homosexuality varied in aim, object and prognosis; (c) the type of treatment varied; (d) the number of treatments and over-all length of treatment varied; (e) the number of interruptions to which treatment was subject varied, owing in particular to the imprisonment of cases who offended again during its early course; (f) the need for institutional supervision of a non-penal type varied; (g) the amount of familial and social contact during treatment varied, as did the amount of follow-up.

Clinic Records

Of the 103 adult and ten juvenile homosexuals discharged during the two years 1952–3, seventy-seven adults and four children were treated. Psychotherapy alone was employed in seventy-four of the eighty-one cases, psychotherapy combined with hormone treatment in five cases and hormone treatment alone in two. The number of visits varied from under five (18·5 per cent of the total) to between fifty and 170 visits (12·3 per cent). The largest group (28·4 per cent) attended between ten and thirty times. In some cases the course was not completed owing to various intrinsic and extrinsic reasons. The total duration of treatment varied from up to five months to as many as five years. The variety of psychological treatment ranged from psycho-analysis alone, psychological analysis or guidance, suggestion or hypnosis, to simple psychological investigation, supervision and advice. Unfortunately these variations in the forms of treatment were not correlated with variations in the type of homosexuality. Psychotherapy mainly was used for cases complicated by psycho-neurosis, and social or hormone treatment for cases complicated by low intelligence.

At the end of treatment thirty-six of the eighty-one (44 per cent) no longer experienced homosexual impulses; twenty-one who had still homosexual impulses had achieved discretion or conscious control (in nine of these the impulse was also diminished); in eight cases no change was noted; and in fourteen treatment was interrupted or discontinued. With regard to the results obtained in various types and degrees of homosexuality it may be noted that none of the nine cases who were exclusively homosexual lost his impulses after treatment, whereas this was the case with 51 per cent of the 'bisexuals'. Of the eight who were unchanged all had a greater degree of homosexuality than of heterosexuality, as had thirteen of the nineteen who still retained the homosexual impulse but with newly acquired discretion or conscious control. No significant differences existed between sporadic and persistent types in the loss of homosexual impulses; but seven of the eight unchanged cases were persistent types. No adequate comparisons could be made of cases with different types of complication. Finally a follow-up of one to three years of as many cases as could be traced revealed that nineteen were known to have made a satisfactory adjustment and thirty-four were presumed on reasonable grounds to have done so; twelve were convicted again for homosexual offences after referral.

In general it may be said of this series that although a considerable proportion abandoned treatment at an early stage, treatment was successful in some measure with those who attended for a longer period. Loss of impulse was found to be more likely in patients under 30 years of age (a result conflicting somewhat with the prognostic findings). Above that age a much longer period of treatment was necessary to secure improvement. The same applied to those cases over 30 who secured control and discretion. The final conclusion is noteworthy: 'Psycho-therapy appears to be unsuccessful in only a small number of patients of any age in whom a long habit is combined with psychopathic traits, heavy drinking or lack of desire to change.'

Next in importance to the satisfactory record of improvement noted in the *Portman Clinic Survey*, and to the fact that these improvements were obtained employing a great variety of techniques, is the remarkable shortness of the treatment and the fact that even a short period of examination, advisory supervision, sexual re-education and social work can secure satisfactory improvement. It would be extremely interesting if these results could be compared with the results obtained in private cases, particularly those treated by lengthy methods such as psycho-analysis. For reasons already indicated such comparisons cannot so far be made in a form that would have statistical significance. In fact the only satisfactory index of the results of psycho-analytical treatment so far available must be inferred from the general prognostic attitude of the psycho-analyst which, as has been indicated, is generally a very guarded one. To be sure even an improvement rate of 33·3 per cent would be quite satisfactory so long as we remember that it would be obtained from specially selected cases. Even so it would not justify more than a guarded prognosis.

'Focal' Treatment

Nevertheless it appears to be the case that we can sub-divide the degrees of improvement into three substantial categories; (a) 'cure', i.e. abolition of conscious homosexual impulse and development or full extension of heterosexual impulse; (b) 'much improved', i.e. the abolition of conscious homosexual impulse without development or full extension of heterosexual impulse and, (c) 'improved', i.e. increased ego-integration and capacity to control the homosexual impulse. And clearly it is desirable to be able to distinguish the therapeutic means by which these degrees of improvement can be effected. This is all the more important in the case of 'short treatment' of say between twenty-five and fifty sessions, where owing to considerations of time what might be called a 'focal' approach is unavoidable. In this form of approach, sometimes described as 'sector' or 'vector' therapy, therapeutic techniques are applied directly to symptom constructions and any accompanying disorders or complications; also direct correlations are attempted between these manifestations and either precipitating factors or major unconscious constellations. In this connection it will be found that the application of psycho-analytical principles will not only serve to guide the focal approach but to account for variations in the degree of improvement obtained thereby.

The first point to be noted when conducting 'focal' treatment is the degree of social anxiety which prevails particularly amongst patients seen in private. In court groups this is not so obvious at first because of the compulsive nature of the activity and, to some extent, because of the reactions of compulsive offenders to legal codes. The fact that homosexuality is treated as a criminal offence acts as an additional if unconscious incentive to the commission of such offences without regard for social consequences. But whether manifest or camouflaged at first by lack of discretion this social anxiety operates in all cases and will be found to exercise a most disintegrating effect on ego-capacities and on the emotional balance of the individual. It is therefore essential to ventilate it at once in all forms of focal treatment excepting perhaps those which depend mainly on suggestion. Naturally this ventilation is greatly encouraged by the therapeutic situation in which for the first time in his life the patient is reassured by an uncritical, sympathetic and receptive environment.

Psycho-analysis has shown, however, that this social anxiety is based on a projected form of unconscious guilt. The penal attitude of society enables the patient to project concealed super-ego reactions on to society or the law. It is at this point that the therapeutist must decide whether to pursue the problem through the regular and prolonged courses of an analysis or whether he will be satisfied with a focal relief. Assuming that he adopts the latter course he will soon find that having uncovered some of the guilt, he will then strike against a core of sexual anxiety and in particular on the multifarious manifestations of the castration complex. And here will be the point that the history of the individual familial relations, his traumas, frustrations, disappointments, jealousies, etc. will come to the surface or should be brought to the surface. Above all it is necessary to demonstrate the defensive aspects of the homosexual situation, for only by uncovering the positive aspects of his original relation to women (mother, sister) and demonstrating the anxieties and guilts (real or phantasied) associated with the hostile aspects of these early relations can a path be cleared for the return of heterosexual libido.

From this point of view short treatment can be regarded as in essence *a process of sexual re-education*. To be sure a good deal of more systematic sexual instruction is also called for, particularly since the unconscious phantasies of homosexuals tend to promote a number of conscious sexual myths of a phobiac nature that inhibit heterosexual impulse. But as in the case of child education the best means of accelerating the education or re-education of homosexuals is to uncover and release inhibiting anxieties, and where possible uncover also the sources of childish guilt. The uncovering of defences is a more elaborate process.

Following these leads we can understand why improvement may stop short at control of sexual impulses. In the group that obtain such control (in the Portman Clinic Series 21 of eighty-one = 26 per cent) the patient, supporting himself the while on his transference relationship to the therapeutist, has achieved a considerable reduction of social anxiety (manifest or occult), a lesser reduction of guilt and has by educative measures been freed of some of his phobiac sexual reactions: his ego- and reality-sense have thereby been greatly strengthened. His defences against, and aversions from, heterosexuality have, however, been left intact, hence he clings to his homosexual impulses even if in a diminished form. Abolition of homosexual impulse depends on a full liquidation of guilt and of heterosexual defences. And this takes time. Incidentally and in view of the substantial size of the group that secure control during treatment it is good practice to inform all prospective patients that such an outcome may prove to be the maximum benefit obtainable.

Insufficient attention is paid to the group of cases which, having carried through the prescribed treatment, are discharged 'in statu quo' in the sense that they continue to practise their perversion and may subsequently be reconvicted. It can of course be argued that such cases should not be regarded as 'failures' unless they have carried out a lengthy analysis: for clearly 'short' treatment in such instances is only a gamble. This is where accurate prognosis is essential. Actually many of them undergo a slight diminution of their compulsive sexuality and a general ego-improvement but this is offset by the reduction of their guilt, with the result that they live 'on terms' with their perversion and continue to practise it under risky conditions. As in the case of all mental disorders, closer investigation of the 'failure' group would lead to improvement in the techniques of focal therapy by highlighting the obstacles to 'cure', and thereby enlarging the 'success' groups.

Psycho-Analysis of Male Homosexuality

In the first two sections of this review emphasis has been laid on the nature and universality of 'unconscious homosexuality' and in particular on the part it plays in preparing the ground for a later 'manifest homosexual perversion'. In this sense it can be said that whatever the clinical condition for which the patient is treated, his analysis will inevitably include an investigation of his infantile homosexual phases and their relation to his positive Oedipus complex. For this reason it can fairly be said that whether or not a psycho-analyst ever treats a case of manifest perversion, he is in pretty constant touch with the *roots* of manifest homosexuality. We can indeed venture the generalization that *given appropriate selection of cases the ultimate success (or failure) of the psycho-analysis of male homosexuality lies in the thoroughness (or inadequacy) with which the analyst explores not only the unconscious libidinal phases of the negative Oedipus complex and the reactive aggression with which these are associated but the effect on ego and super-ego structure of those identifications and introjections that are laid down during both positive and negative phases of the Oedipus complex.*

As, however, the technique of psycho-analysis proper precludes a 'focal' attack on symptom formations or other psycho-pathological manifestations it is not possible to direct analytical attention to any one phase of mental development to the exclusion or neglect of other material. This can be attempted only in the case of short focal treatments. In any case the requirements of psycho-analysis cannot be satisfied by libido-analysis only, or for that matter by the analysis of the unconscious hostility and aggression that run in series with libidinal development. If the course of psycho-analysis can be said to be directed at all, it is directed by the vicissitudes of anxiety and guilt and by the defensive manoeuvres (resistances) which these affects engender. Effective interpretation of resistances may in this sense be said to guide the analysis, but effective interpretation is regulated at all times by *ad hoc* considerations, not by preconceptions of the symptom structure.

The second generalization is obvious enough: it can be arrived at on the strength of the clinical observation that despite the priority of homosexual object choice, homosexual organizations comprise a wide range of component impulse. There is consequently a wide scope for regression to various contributing fixation points. *It follows that there can be no standard course in the progress of analyses of homosexual cases considered as a group.* In this respect the analysis of homosexuals differs somewhat from the analysis of most transference neuroses, where fixation points are more clearly localized at definite ego levels. To be sure the *final* analysis of homosexuality is concentrated at the same levels as are associated with the formation of hysterical and obsessional states, viz. the genital level. To this extent it is still true that the homosexual perversion is the negative of a neurosis, to vary Freud's dictum. But this concentration at the genital level of the patient's development cannot be successful so long as the pre-genital regressions are not fully ventilated. As has been suggested, some hint as to the range of pre-genital regressions can be obtained from study of the phantasy systems and actual practices in vogue. Behind these conscious phantasy systems and manifest practices, however, lie more primitive unconscious systems the analysis of which is essential to the loosening of defensive regression. It is at this point that some of the most intractable resistances are to be found, more particularly since these early unconscious sexual phantasies if powerfully enough charged are capable of disturbing the patient's reality sense to a degree that if persistent would give rise to pre-psychotic reactions. Fortunately these reactions are not commonly encountered in patients who undergo treatment voluntarily. More commonly the patient seeks to terminate his analysis at the point where these resistances accumulate and is content to have secured some control of his more compulsive conduct.

Another factor which serves to tide the patient over such crises is the degree of *transference rapport*. This is, however, by no means a standard factor. As the fixation points in homosexuality vary, so do the transference manifestations vary. Reactions corresponding to hysterical, obsessional, depressive and paranoidal transferences can be observed in different types. No reliable statistics are available regarding this point, but on the whole the obsessional type of transference seems to be that most commonly encountered. And indeed there are some transitional forms in which obsessional reactions and perverse sexuality seem to overlap. In such cases the obsessional ideas though to some extent distorted are manifestly of an infantile sexual type and on the other hand the character and psychic reactions of the patient are distinctly obsessional. This becomes increasingly obvious as the analysis proceeds. The patient converts his associations into a running obsessional commentary on his manifest homosexual reactions and often on his anti-feminist disposition. By so doing he blocks the approach to his underlying hostility to men and attraction to women. Unless this situation is dealt with by effective interpretation the analysis is liable to end either in stalemate or in the acquisition of control only.

In this obsessional type of transference the reactions to the analyst rarely reach the hothouse intensity observed in the hysteric or the fulminating crises of the psychotic type. Manifest erotic transferences are rarely observed and seldom exceed the compulsive expression of phantasy: even in hysterical and psychotic types manifestly erotic transference activities rarely pass the exhibitionistic level.

In the early stages of the analysis there are of course many indications of spontaneous transference some of which can soon be recognized as essentially maternal in origin. There exists in particular a passive receptive attitude to interpretation which alternates with disappointment when this is not forthcoming. But as is only to be expected the first open expressions of activated analytic rapport take the form of father transferences in which the positive element at first predominates. It is essential, however, to uncover the negative elements of the father transference; only when these have been fully ventilated is it possible for the deeper mother transferences both positive and negative to appear. Most analytic failures (in the sense that the patient retains his homosexual system even if only in a less marked form) are due to the failure to uncover and analyse these potential mother transferences, which at first are almost exclusively saturated with pregenital sadistic phantasy. With the successful overcoming of these deeper regressive phases the prospects of a successful outcome are greatly improved. As a rule the first sign of fundamental improvement is the appearance of anxieties which would ordinarily set up neurotic defences. These differ from the earlier manifestations of social anxiety which are encountered at the beginning of the analysis of most homosexuals. These deeper anxieties gradually give place to guilt reactions: and it is at this point that super-ego analysis can be made effective. This calls for persistent ventilation of the projection systems by means of which the patient covers his guilt. During this period the patient may manifest a number of transitory symptom formations of a conversion type or his inhibitions in work and in social contact may be exacerbated. Once these have been worked through, the way is open to analyse the genital kernel of his Oedipus complex which the homosexual has used every unconscious mechanism to conceal.

It will be clear from the foregoing surveys of the etiology, prognosis and treatment of selected cases of male homosexuality that although we now know a good deal about the etiology of this group of conditions, we are very far yet from having overcome difficulties in treatment. This might indeed be inferred from the fact that clinical statistics regarding such cases of male homosexuality as have been treated have not yet been adequately broken down to indicate the relation of different types of treatment to different sub-groups of homosexuality. Until the results of more detailed investigations are available it is not possible to arrive at more than the broadest generalizations on the subject.

Nevertheless it is safe to say that under present conditions of selection success in treatment depends on the following factors, viz. the effectiveness with which the purely psychological disposition to homosexual object choice can be uncovered, the degree in which current ego-difficulties and frustrations can be offset, and the degree of transference rapport that can be established or, in the case of psycho-analytic technique, analysed. The first of these factors depends on the amount of primary gain secured through the perversion, the second on the amount of secondary gain obtained in current life and the third on the degree of potential accessibility of each case. As in all other forms of treatment of mental disorder, the third factor is by far the most important.

As far as the wider issue is concerned, namely, the degree to which unselected cases of male homosexuality are amenable to treatment, the very greatest reserve should be maintained. It is indeed more than likely that the answer to this problem, if it be a problem, is in the development of greater tolerance amongst the sections of the community which at present tend to make a scapegoat of homosexuality. In this sense the treatment of homosexuality as a whole should be directed as much at the 'diseased' prejudices of society as at the 'diseased' propensities of the individual homosexual.

PART III

THE PSYCHOPATHOLOGY OF PROSTITUTION*
[1943-57]

Modern psychopathology (in simpler words, the study of disordered mental processes), unlike organic pathology, is a highly inflammable subject, liable to give rise to acute dissension in the most sophisticated audience. In fact we cannot do better than begin our investigation by facing squarely the emotional difficulties inherent in the study of prostitution. To give a simple illustration: the professor of chemistry lecturing on the properties of a simple salt, whether poisonous or innocuous, knows that his audience will accept with equanimity whatever he may have to say on the subject. The lecturer on prostitution is equally well aware that the subject-matter of his investigation will already have aroused disapproval, conflict or a degree of fascination before its psychological constituents have been even mentioned. A still greater obstacle to objectivity lies in a peculiarity of mental pathology, namely, that its subject-matter, being derived most from unconscious layers of the mind, is unfamiliar and ordinarily inaccessible. It is not open to naked-eye inspection like, say, diseases of the skin, or to simple measures of examination, like most diseases of major organs. Not only so, the normal structures of the mind are also for the greater part unconscious, as are, naturally, our normal instincts, and the inner laws that regulate them. The fact that these structures, forces and mechanisms are not only unconscious but primitive in nature gives rise to a common confusion. It is often assumed that whatever is unconscious is not only pathological, but reprehensible. This confusion can be avoided if we compare the state of modern psycho-analytical knowledge with the state of organic medicine some centuries ago. We are at present at a stage in the develop-

* Published by the I.S.T.D. by permission of the International Bureau for the Suppression of Traffic in Women and Children, this lecture was one of a series delivered on the occasion of an International Meeting convened by the Bureau and held at the London School of Hygiene and Tropical Medicine, 22-23 October, 1943. The complete Proceedings were published in booklet form under the title *The Abolition of Tolerated Prostitution*. London, International Bureau for the Suppression of Traffic in Women and Children.

ment of psychology similar to that existing in organic medicine when Harvey discovered the circulation of the blood, and when what ultimately became bio-chemistry was of the most rudimentary order. We have, as it were, mapped out the main mental organs (or institutions), have isolated the main energies (or instincts) which set them in action, and have studied the main mechanisms by which these instincts are regulated. And because all these are unfamiliar and peculiar, we are inclined to regard the normal structure and function of the unconscious mind as pathological. We talk loosely of repression, for example, as if it were a disease or a bad policy, whereas, in fact, repression is a normal unconscious mechanism without which we could not function adequately. It is not repression that is pathological, but the results of 'faulty repression'. You can well imagine the confusion that would have arisen if early anatomists, discovering the liver, had assumed it to be a malignant tumour.

Infantile Sexuality

I stress this point because, in approaching the subject of prostitution, we must first of all familiarize ourselves with the normal development of sexual instincts. Some of Freud's earliest discoveries lay in this field, and in their time evoked in the scientific world the most lively disapproval, not to say repugnance. This opposition has now largely died down, on the surface at any rate. The main points established by Freud's studies were that sexual impulses, so far from first developing at puberty in a unified form, exist from birth onwards; moreover, they are made up of various *components*, which merge between the ages of 3 and 5 years. About this time they disappear owing to the unconscious conflict they arouse which leads finally to their repression; and a fallow period ensues called the *latency period*. This continues until puberty when the normal and familiar adult sexual impulses appear. This, in brief, is the theory of *infantile sexuality*. Now these component impulses can be classified in various ways. The most familiar division is in accordance with the *body zone* with which the impulses are concerned. For example, the sucking activities of the infant are combined with libidinal pleasure in mouth activity, hence one of the most important components of infantile sexuality is known as an *oral* component. In the same way, we speak of *anal* and *urethral* sexuality, connected with the activities of excretion which together with nutritional activities constitute the main concern of the growing infant. Each of these forms has a phase of *primacy* over the others, but by the age of 3 the main primacy is an infantile *genital* primacy during which the sexual interests of the child begin to correspond to some extent to the sexual drives of the adult.

Infantile components can also be classified in accordance with the *aim* of sexual impulse, e.g. sadism or masochism, or, again, exhibitionism and viewing. In the former case, an element of pleasure in injury is fused with the sexual impulse; if it is active it is called sadism; if, however, the individual obtains sexual pleasure passively through injury by another person, the fusion goes by the name of masochism. The sadist, for example, derives satisfaction from beating his sexual partner, the masochist from being beaten. The same distinction between active and passive is found in the exhibitionistic-viewing couple. The aim of the *voyeur* is active: the exhibitionist's aim is essentially passive. He gets pleasure in being sexually 'viewed', although, of course, he most frequently takes the initiative in the situation. It is obvious that an element of *sexual curiosity* enters into this set of impulses. And, indeed, the child's curiosity is an important element of his infantile sexuality, and can be gratified by any of the sense organs of sight, taste, smell, touch and hearing.

Already at this point it is possible to indicate some of the relations between sexual development and prostitution. To begin with, it is common knowledge that, from puberty onward, normal sexuality can be partly or wholly replaced by the so-called *sexual perversions*, and on examination these are seen to be derived from the various infantile components I have described, e.g. fellatio (a mouth perversion), sodomy, exhibitionism, etc. Of course, perversions are more systematised, and the relation to the sexual object is frequently of a manifestly homosexual pattern. In other words, the perversions are essentially *regressive* in type, i.e. earlier infantile forms are substituted for more developed adult forms of sexuality. Now it is significant that perverse practices play a large part in the activities of prostitutes, either because of the inclinations of the prostitute or in response to the clients' demands. The readiness to satisfy sadistic or masochistic perversions, for example, is part of her stock-in-trade. *Hence one of the first questions to be raised regarding prostitution is whether it is a regressive manifestation indicating a backward and retarded state of sexual development.* It would also be natural to inquire whether signs of retardation are to be detected also in the *general mental development* of the prostitute.

The Latency Period and Puberty

The next step in the investigation of sexuality is to follow the history of these early infantile components – in other words, to trace the various modifications they undergo. Success in this investigation depends on recognition of a fact round which at one time the most acute controversies raged, viz., that although a number of these early impulses are *auto-erotic*, in the sense that they can be gratified without the interposition of an external sexual *object* (e.g. thumb-sucking or infantile forms of masturbation), the impulses that require an external object are inevitably directed to the parents or other members of the family circle. It is obvious for example, that although a good deal of oral sexuality can be gratified auto-erotically, as in thumb-sucking, the original oral impulses are directed to the mother's breasts. The same is true of infantile genital impulses. They are *directed* towards the parent of the opposite sex. The main difference is that, whereas oral impulses do obtain direct gratification on the external object, the genital impulses are frustrated and repressed. Sometimes the manifestations of this Oedipus situation, as it is called, are quite obvious; but for the most part this infantile sexual situation is, and remains, unconscious. Significantly enough, the Oedipus phase is bisexual, and it is easy to study the infantile homosexual attachments to parents which play such an important part in any later development of manifest homosexuality. As a rule the Oedipus phase reaches its height and disappears at about the age of 5. Space does not permit a complete account of the reasons for its disappearance or disintegration. But, to put it as simply as possible, infantile sexuality is finally shipwrecked on reactions of unconscious anxiety and guilt, in which the policies of the parents (witting or unwitting) play a very considerable part. The result is that the primitive erotic urges of the child towards its parents give place to the so-called *aim-inhibited* impulses of affection. At this stage the *latency* period commences, and continues until puberty, when adult impulses make their appearance. These adult impulses may at first show many infantile or regressive features. Thus, a varying amount of homosexual impulse may make its appearance. But whether this happens or not, the fact is that by puberty the link between sexual impulses and the family has, as a rule, been effectively broken. Sexual impulses are henceforward directed to persons (objects) outside the family. Here again we can make some significant observations concerning the psychology of prostitution. For example, although the prostitute has apparently 'broken away' from the family at an unusually early age, this sometimes ostentatious and rebellious independence is only skin deep. Under the surface there exists a strong 'fixation', as it is called, to the Oedipus phase. Further, the emotions associated with this phase prove to have been markedly *negative* – that is to say, they have been dominated by a number of childish rivalries and hostilities. There exists an acute disappointment with the father, while the relation to the mother is in its own way strongly impregnated with hostility. These facts will be found of some significance when we come to estimate the unconscious homosexual factor in prostitution.

The Dichotomy of Sexuality: 'Sacred' and 'Profane' Love

Perhaps the most important consequence of conflict over infantile sexual urges, certainly one that has a very close bearing on the psychology of the prostitute, is the divorce that takes place between, on the one hand, the physical or sexual (erotic) aspects, and on the other the more idealistic and affectionate (non-erotic) aspects of infantile love. Roughly speaking, this corresponds to the old adult distinction between 'profane' and 'sacred' love, but of course it is an unconscious distinction drawn in early childhood, and therefore gives rise to a more violent and persistent cleavage. Normally, the isolation and mental rejection of the erotic aspects of 'infantile love' encourage what are called the aim-inhibited aspects of family love. But it is essential that, when adult sexuality makes its appearance, this cleavage should be overcome, otherwise the adult will have difficulty in directing his sexual urges and his mental love-feelings towards one and the same object. When, however, the original conflict over infantile love has been excessive, either because the primitive sexual components were too strong, or the associated hatreds and jealousies too violent, or the unconscious conscience too stringent, the cleavage tends to persist in adult life. In this case the adult may love idealized objects, but be incapable of sexual relations with them, or, alternatively, he may be capable of sexual gratification only with 'deteriorated' sexual objects whom he cannot love and, in many instances, despises. It will be seen that these difficulties in the defusion and refusion of erotic and idealized love have a close bearing on the problem of prostitution. Some husbands, it is true, are able to effect an erotic compromise within marriage, as when they persuade their, often inhibited, wives to dress or behave like 'tarts' before intercourse, or, in some instances, to dress in ballet costume and submit to a make-believe rape. But by many people of the highest intellectual and ethical development such compromises cannot be achieved and they may find themselves compulsorily attached to prostitutes, because only with prostitutes are they capable of sexual potency. With their wives they may remain completely impotent. You can see that in such instances *the prostitute satisfies a psychopathological demand*. Indeed, we cannot emphasise too strongly that the problem of prostitution, like practically all sexual problems, is two-sided. You cannot accurately measure any sexual problem unless you take into account the reciprocal relationships existing between the parties to the situation.[1]

Regressive and Defensive Aspects

I have said that this splitting of the early sexual impulses is a normal reaction in childhood. And it is still more or less normal at

[1] [Note 1959] While it is not surprising that the *unconscious services* unconsciously rendered by some types of prostitutes to some young men suffering from the milder types of sexual immaturity or inhibition are not generally recognized, it is indicative of the prejudice surrounding the subject that the *manifest services* rendered by understanding and skilled prostitutes to, for example, some impotent young men are rarely mentioned in the literature. And the same may be said of the ministrations of some cocottes, of some paid mistresses and of a proportion of the demi-mondaines. To be sure, in a large majority of instances of commercialized prostitution, conducted often under the most sordid conditions, the effect is to hamper normal sexual development of the young man by creating aversion, anxiety and guilt, and by debasing the currency of psychic love. But it cannot be denied that in some countries the co-operation of a carefully chosen paid mistress is not disdained by some solicitous mothers. There is equally no doubt that many good marriages have been preserved by middle-aged husbands taking tea with suburban 'widows' with whom they politely discuss interests in whipping little boys, at the conclusion of which exchanges they part with mutual expressions of esteem. It is no service to research into the nature of prostitution to enter into a conspiracy of silence on such matters.

puberty, when adult sexuality activates many of the earlier forgotten or repressed reactions. But we cannot understand the real significance of persisting and pathological cleavages unless we recognize that they are intended to perform an essentially *protective* function, viz., to dissociate sexual desires from the objects (father or mother as the case may be) to which they were first attached. This tendency is sharpened by the jealousy and antagonism aroused by the marital life of the parents. To take the case of the boy: the mother image is split into an idealized and a deteriorated version, into a 'good' and 'bad' mother. The 'bad' image is disapproved of, both consciously and unconsciously: it is the image of the fickle mother who has at least one other lover, to wit, the father. Should brothers and sisters also exist, the tally of rivals is increased. Now although admittedly a large part of the logic is unconscious, children have at times a remarkable capacity to draw logical conclusions – to pursue an inference to its bitter end. True, the child is not familiar with the word 'prostitute', nor with the exact adult connotation of the term, but its emotional conclusion, though unspoken or unconscious, is final enough: *the bad mother image is that of a prostitute.* And so we can see that the man who has compulsive interest in prostitutes is really still fixated to his old infantile profane love. He seeks, without knowing it, to gratify in adult life the tabooed desires of infancy. For her part, the prostitute has similar unconscious aims, but their scope is more ambitious. The client, the 'strange man' who pays for her favours, is the deteriorated image of the father; at the same time, she registers her violently jealous disapproval of her mother's marriage by, as it were, debasing her own feminine currency. No doubt the same factors account for those occasionally recorded cases where the prostitute has open phantasies of being 'the world's greatest courtesan', to say nothing of the fascination exercised by the subject in the minds of many young women who do not, however, become prostitutes. Much more common is the hysterical defence against unconscious prostitute phantasies which takes the form of 'fear of falling' or of 'street anxiety'.

At this point it is desirable to emphasize what, indeed, must have already occurred to you, namely that psychopathological states or, for the matter of that, perfectly normal reactions cannot be attributed to any single factor. All mental constructions are, as the technical phrase goes, *overdetermined*. The state of prostitution is no exception. It is obvious, for instance, that the *number* of sexual 'objects' with whom the prostitute has relations must be of some psychological significance. You might even suspect that the prostitute believes in the adage, 'there is safety in numbers'. In actual fact, sexual promiscuity – which I need hardly remind you is not characteristic solely of prostitutes – is an unconscious protective device. I am not suggesting, of course, that unconscious *displacement from the one to the many* is solely a protective device, or that it applies only to erotic impulses. Displacement is primarily an adaptation mechanism. If we could not transfer our infantile interests to a greater number of extra-familial objects, we would be incapable of normal social feeling. But in compulsive sexual promiscuity, the mechanism can be made to serve the purposes not only of defence, but of repressed impulses. Promiscuity serves to deny that there was a one and only parental object of infantile love. It also represents unconsciously a *search* for the one and only (forbidden) love. An interesting example is afforded in the case of a man whose sexual life consisted exclusively of one ceremony, repeated *ad infinitum*. It was his habit to frequent busy thoroughfares, and to take off his hat to strange women. If they responded, he would walk by their side for about a hundred yards, take off his hat, and abandon them. At this point he would experience a sexual orgasm. Naturally there were a great number of determinants of this behaviour. It is clear, for example, that he combined satisfaction with his success in 'picking up' (or seducing) women with a denial of any actual consummation of his genital wishes. But for the moment I am concerned only to illustrate one of the subsidiary elements in prostitution, namely, displacement of unconscious infantile sexual wishes.

One could go on multiplying the number of factors that influence the selection of prostitution as an occupation or profession. But it is time to consider the results of more direct investigation of prostitutes themselves. In the meantime we may summarize briefly what we have already established. To begin with, it is clear that the problem of prostitution cannot be studied, as it were, in isolation. It is only part of a larger problem, namely, the rôle of sexuality in human affairs. Secondly, the choice of prostitution as a profession is determined by the early history of infantile sexual impulse, and thirdly, it is a problem that cannot be measured without a collateral investigation of the sexual development of the male.

Lastly, there is some evidence that the manifestations of prostitution are more infantile than those observed in normal adult sex life; more closely associated with perverse practices; more isolated from the general stream of adult love feeling; indeed, more isolated from social impulses in general. In a word, *prostitution exhibits regressive characteristics; it represents a primitive phase in sexual development. It is a kind of sexual backwardness.*

INTELLECTUAL AND EMOTIONAL BACKWARDNESS

Here is the appropriate point at which to interpolate the results obtained by making *intelligence tests* of selected groups of prostitutes. I need only remind you that, according to some investigators, almost 86 per cent of prostitutes exhibit some degree of intellectual and emotional backwardness. Allowing an ample margin of error in the selection of cases, and an ample correction for the amount of mental deficiency existing in the community as a whole, it is no coincidence that the degree of mental retardation discovered amongst prostitutes is high. It has to be admitted, of course, that our investigations of the subject are by no means complete,[1] and that the significance and function of what might be called 'normal prostitution' have not yet been accurately assessed. Many more social and anthropological investigations are needed before we can reach final conclusions on the subject. In particular, the rôle of prostitution in primitive religions and primitive societies, and the phenomena of disguised prostitution (the psychology of the 'gold digger' for example) require to be examined. For the matter of that, the correlation between prostitution and marital fidelity

[1] In a paper on 'Juvenile Prostitution' (delivered before the *Scientific Group for the Study of Delinquency Problems* on 19 September, 1956 and published later in the *Brit. J. Delinq.*, 8, 3–12, 1957) Dr. T. C. N. Gibbens stated that of a group of twenty-three juvenile prostitutes (isolated from 400 cases in need of 'care or protection' or 'beyond control') eight were bright and sometimes highly intelligent girls, six were of average intelligence and seven were extremely dull. Although this finding seems to be in marked contrast to the figures sometimes given for confirmed adult prostitutes, it should be remembered that in a considerable number of juvenile prostitutes the condition is a transitory one, particularly where the girl shows no marked psychopathic traits; hence that the 'confirmed' group are likely to show a higher rate of innate or psychopathological defect. It is clear that, as has been suggested above, more extensive study is needed of the standard of intelligence in different age-groups, and psychological types.

deserves some attention. It has often been suggested that prostitution is the price paid for monogamic ideals. Into these matters I have no time to enter. But whatever may be the results of these investigations I think we may assert with some confidence that however common – and in that respect normal – the phenomena of prostitution may be, these manifestations are, nevertheless, *archaic and regressive in character*. Here, then, is a useful argument to be used against the familiar counter of the *laisser faire* school, i.e. that prostitution is a 'necessary evil', a natural manifestation of the old Adam in us. No doubt there is something to be said for the argument: for man and woman share some natural promiscuity with many other animal species. But it is a tendentious argument which overrates the constitutional factor and can be used to retard investigations of those peculiarly human factors which determine the choice of prostitution as a career. In any case the matter does not stop there. For if prostitution is regressive in character, it is likely to conform to the pattern of mental regression in general. It is likely to be activated, in border-line cases, by the *factor of emotional stress*. It is a commonplace of psychopathology that emotional stress is one of the commonest precipitating factors in all mental disorder. And this in turn raises the question: how far are these stresses personal and emotional, and how far are they environmental in nature?

Types of Prostitute

I make no apology for having spent so much of my available space in the study of psychological factors of a general character. It is a well-established fact that the study of childhood mental development throws more direct light on adult mental disorder than does the immediate study of the disease. Nevertheless, in a presentation of this sort, it would be absurd to omit the results of direct study of the prostitute.

The first difficulty we have to face is that, strictly speaking, there is no such thing as a prostitute type. The term, although in common use, has strictly legal connotations. And the law defines its terms in accordance with social standards; it has not so far taken the definitions of individual psychology into account when drawing up the calendar of misdemeanours. This is distinctly unfortunate, since there are at least as many types of prostitution as there are varieties of pilfering – a delinquency, incidentally, that has many close associations with prostitution. It is really absurd to talk at large of remedies for prostitution, without first establishing a reasonably exact classification of prostitutes. For that part, we ought also to have an accurate survey of allied groups, including, for example, 'the enthusiastic amateur', the 'gold digger', or the type of individual who marries for money. And if we go so far we might well consider the significance of the 'dowry' and the 'marriage settlement'. But for the purposes of our present argument, we must confine ourselves to those cases coming within the legal definition. The most cursory study of police court cases (and although these do not by any means include all the recognizable types of prostitution, they at any rate comprise the types that constitute a 'social problem') shows that there are three common groups.

The first consists mostly of street-walkers of the 'drab' type, who in most cases practise prostitution as a life-long profession. They are apathetic and 'hopeless' in attitude, some mentally disordered, others mentally backward; others, again, prone to form associations with criminals. They incline also to excessive use of alcohol. Most of these attribute their choice of profession to emotional disturbances in adolescence. They tend to lapse readily, and only a small proportion become stable.

In marked contrast to the drab type comes the 'young' prostitute – unstable adolescents, often of border-line intelligence, attracted by a 'gay' life; irresponsible, rebellious and defiant, or on occasion indolent and indifferent. Many are over-suggestible, easily influenced by older and more sophisticated 'professionals'. They live from hand to mouth, carelessly, without forethought or even apparent anxiety as to the future. On the other hand, they are more readily amenable to social influences, and, under favourable environmental conditions, often settle down. Between these extremes a great variety of types can be isolated. Prominent amongst these is the 'flourishing' professional, who although known to the police is, by virtue of her business talents, better able to avoid police interference. Flimsy and unstable personalities, they are yet intelligent enough to look after their own interests. But behind their apparent success, they are restless, dissatisfied, and given to excesses of various kinds. Shading off from this group is the type of 'discreet' prostitute, who after a comparatively short period of flamboyance, settles down as a short-term mistress, and often ends as an apparently respectable spinster with conservative domestic interests. And this group, in turn, shades off into smaller and more specialized groups which do not ordinarily come under police scrutiny at all.

In short, it is possible to classify prostitutes in a great number of ways, e.g. according to age, social standing, success, temperament, variety of sexual activity favoured, the amount of publicity involved, the degree and kind of mental abnormality or backwardness present, the extent to which they practise types of delinquent conduct, and, to mention one other significant point, the nature of their after history, i.e. whether they continue as prostitutes until after the climacteric or abandon the career after a varying period.[1] In the absence of detailed psychological investigations of all these types, it is obvious that the psychopathologist must confine himself to a few well-established generalizations. The most convenient test of the validity of these generalizations is that the pathological factors discovered should be present not only in groups of experienced prostitutes, but in what might be called 'larval' groups, i.e. the young groups from which experienced prostitutes are recruited.

The Factor of Unconscious Homosexuality

Amongst experienced types, an extremely common factor is that of *sexual frigidity* – in other words, an absence or marked diminution of either physical or psychical pleasure in the sexual act, and in particular an incapacity to achieve sexual orgasm. But although this factor is highly significant it should be remembered that in one form or another frigidity is common both in neurotic and in apparently normal women. Obviously, then its significance in cases of prostitution depends on its association with other elements. This is true of all mental abnormalities. There is always a *constellation* of causal elements, some of which are plainly manifest, others unconscious. In the case of prostitution, the factors most closely associated with frigidity are those of *unconscious homosexuality* and *unconscious antagonism to the male*. The first of these must be clearly distinguised from manifest homosexuality, which is a systematized adult sexual perversion. The 'unconscious homosexual' may show no signs of conscious homosexual interest.

[1] Dr. Gibbens (loc. cit.) believes that juvenile prostitution is an essentially transitory manifestation

The term implies simply that, during the early formative period of infantile sexuality, the tendency has been to divert sexual impulses from the parent of the opposite sex to the parent of the same sex. It represents, as it were, a sexual policy, often a defensive policy, which, when reinforced by constitutional bisexuality, acts as a constant barrier to normal sexual development. As, however, the whole infantile system is repressed, the only manifest signs present in adult life are either disordered adaptation to heterosexual life or various peculiarities of character and social reaction. Individuals of this type often nourish a good deal of overt or latent hostility to men. This is associated with strong, unconscious jealousy of the male, together with a good deal of unconscious hostility to the client as a substitute father image. It is not difficult to establish that during childhood the father image has been a disappointing one. Hence it is no coincidence that the attitude of many prostitutes to their clients is, in effect, one of depreciation, which frequently ends in some form of injury to (unconsciously, punishment of) the man. For not only does the prostitute seek to exploit men financially, she frequently steals from them and sometimes enters into a conspiracy with her *souteneur* to blackmail them. And of course she may, and frequently does, infect them with venereal disease. As I have pointed out earlier, this attitude of depreciation is either consciously or unconsciously reciprocated by the man. In short, the sexual life of both prostitute and client contains either in manifest or latent form a marked component of sadism. At the same time, it is to be noted that the injurious physical and mental *consequences* of their ways of life are an indication that there is also an unconscious masochistic component to be reckoned with. And this, in turn, suggests that a strong guilt reaction to early sexuality must play a part in the prostitute's make-up. There is, in fact, some evidence that the prostitute's career, so far from indicating strong heterosexual tendencies, is, in a sense, *a denial and denigration of normal sexuality*. And so it is possible to arrive at a somewhat disconcerting conclusion, namely, that in so far as there is a more ostentatious denial of normal sexuality, the prostitute exhibits a kind of primitive, if highly selective, unconscious morality. This may sound absurd, but, of course, similar observations as to the excessive and paradoxical action of a primitive (unconscious) conscience can be made in the case of both neurotic and delinquent persons. In other words the prostitute unconsciously seeks at the same time to block and to punish herself for her original incestuous (infantile) strivings by denying herself normal adult love and marriage.

Juvenile Delinquency and the Larval Prostitute

Turning now to what I have called the 'larval group', viz., cases of precocious prostitution in early adolescence, I should like to remind you again that, strictly speaking, we cannot place the real onset of sexuality at this period. To understand the reactions of this group properly, we would require to investigate more fully the sexual reactions of little girls from 3 to 5 years of age, to say nothing of making a complementary investigation of the reactions of little boys of the same age. Parents recognize this fact when they say on occasion that a small daughter is a 'little tart'. At any rate, we shall be on the safe side if we remember that adolescent girls are not only 'little women' but also 'little children'. In other words, the early phase of puberty is signalized by regressive as well as by progressive tendencies.

The most convenient, as well as the most fruitful, field for investigating early forms of prostitution is certainly that of juvenile delinquency. Here a group of behaviour reactions, e.g. early truancy, wandering, pilfering and the like, are found in close association with precocious acts of sexual seduction and soliciting. Many children and adolescents coming under the legal designation of 'out of control' or 'in need of care or protection' already show sexual tendencies indicating the possibility that they will later become prostitutes. Now the significant point is that, in so far as these types have been analysed, they already show the main unconscious elements that are later on detected in the experienced prostitute. The superficial manifestations may be different, but the unconscious constellation is the same. On the other hand, the *environmental factors* are more easy to elicit and, what is more important, can to some extent be checked by an experienced social worker. It is notorious, of course, that the life histories proffered by experienced prostitutes are extremely unreliable, showing, as they do, a marked degree of fabrication. Amongst the environmental factors in early prostitution, economic motives play a subsidiary rôle. Above all, the significance of *lack of adequate family love* in early and later childhood is unmistakable. To take a case in point, the influence of illegitimacy is not so much that it is associated with economic hardship, but that, compared with other children, the illegitimate child is in the psychological sense extremely insecure. In most cases the amount of family affection displayed is meagre to a degree, if, indeed, there is a real family to provide it. Next in order of prominence comes the factor of *manifest irregularity in the sexual life of the parents.* It is often forgotten that, psychologically speaking, little children have eyes like hawks, and are quick to detect marital differences, estrangements and infidelities, even when the parents are at some pains to hide these emotional breaches in the family. The psychological effect, however, lies not so much in the influence of the parental example, as in the unconscious reactions of hostility provoked by it. The prostitute-to-be is both critical and revengeful about the parents' sexual life. Hence, in the endless and frequently unprofitable series of sexual episodes of which her later life is made up, we can detect an urge to make a mockery of parental love-life. In the same way we can see in the brothel-keeper's mode of existence a sexual mockery of family life. Indeed, I regard it as an essential part of the investigation of tolerated prostitution to have as complete an analysis as possible, not only of the prostitute and her client, but of the brothel-keeper and all her (or his) satellites. Unfortunately, reliable investigations of this sort are not available.

To return to the 'larval' prostitute, this combination of psychological insecurity (insecurity of love), together with an unconscious urge to obtain revenge for neglect, can be borne out by a number of observations. Lack of reliable and friendly instruction about sexuality is a prominent feature, one that indicates how large a rôle lying and deception on the part of the parents play in preparing the ground for sexual aberrations on the part of the children concerned. Moreover, an early history of wandering, truancy and petty pilfering is frequently obtained; and, as has been suggested earlier, in some cases it is clear that the young adolescent is schizoid in type, that is to say presents character reactions of a schizophrenic (psychotic) nature. These conditions can, of course, exist independently of sexual aberration, but it is interesting to note that all of them can be traced to an original insecurity about being adequately loved. It is well known that children who take to compulsive sweet-eating, or who are given to stealing sweets or small sums of money, do so in the main because sweets and money represent to their unconscious minds (*symbolize*, that is to say) the parental love they feel they have been denied, or have had stolen from them by more successful (family) rivals.[1]

The Economic Factor

These facts have a considerable bearing on a controversy, the mere existence of which often puzzles social reformers. In the whole field of delinquency, including sexual misdemeanour, it is too readily taken for granted that economic factors are the prime cause of anti-social conduct; that, for instance, prostitutes are driven to take up their profession by economic hardships. Leaving out of account the fact that although the general subsistence level of most countries is a low one, yet the prostitute rate is also low, there are a number of considerations that cast doubt on this peculiar assumption. I say 'peculiar' because it would be more natural to assume that disordered sexual conduct is primarily due to disorder of the sexual impulses. The evidence for the 'economic' hypothesis is based largely on the stories told by prostitutes of the 'drab' group. As has been mentioned, these are not very trustworthy. Investigation by experienced social workers soon uncovers more emotional factors in the situation. Moreover, the earliest sexual misdemeanours, although not legally chargeable, occur in quite small children who are moved by no grown-up economic considerations. It is true that the adolescent prostitute is frequently attracted by the often illusory prospect of quick gain. But that is rather because of the gay life that can be purchased than because of positive economic hardship. But the most important psychological contribution to this problem is that already indicated above. For not only is money an unconscious

[1] It is interesting to compare the factors described above for cases of both adult and larval prostitution with those observed by Dr. Gibbens (loc. cit.) in cases of juvenile prostitution. Unconscious homosexuality, for example, was a factor amongst those juvenile prostitutes who were mostly normal and stable, whilst in the group of intelligent but unstable girls a large proportion were overtly Lesbian. Other factors which Dr. Gibbens noted are: strong attachment to an inadequate father, complete sexual maladjustment between the parents, almost overt incestuous attachment on the part of the father, hostility and contempt for men or at least inability to feel any real affection for them, jealousy of male siblings, a mercenary and narcissistic temperament, a tendency to fabrication (phantasy elaboration), emotional instability and insecurity, and frequently an undersexed disposition.

symbol (substitute) for love; it can, as the example of the miser shows, arouse quite conscious emotions of love. It is, of course, a debased form of love, and modern society, however little it may know of scientific psychology, has quite spontaneously grasped this distinction. Prostitution is generally regarded as a debased form of love. It is interesting to note, however, that in the deeper layers of the unconscious, money is equated with the excretory products of the body, which small children naturally regard as precious possessions. As I pointed out earlier the infantile forms of love include many components of anal and urethral sexuality; so it is not surprising that the aberrations of adult love include many derivatives from this primitive excretory phase of sexual development. On closer examination, therefore, the fact that the prostitute barters her body for 'filthy lucre' is, psychologically speaking, neither so surprising nor so unnatural as it seems. It is, in fact, one more proof that prostitution is a primitive and regressive manifestation.

To conclude this brief consideration of environmental factors, it would appear that economic motives are only ancillary in nature. The environmental factors that lead to prostitution are essentially psychological, in particular those conditions of upbringing that lower the 'love-security' of the child, and increase its antagonism to normal sexuality. These are more marked where the sexual life of the parents is such as to set up an identification between prostitution and family sexuality. A word of caution is necessary here. These factors would not in themselves prove decisive, were it not for the psychological set-up of the individual prostitute. And this set-up is, in its turn, a product of development. One cannot, of course, exclude what are called constitutional factors – in other words, the inborn temperament of the prostitute. But as psychological research expands, the importance of constitutional factors in all varieties of mental disorder is increasingly curtailed.

Prostitution and Mental Disorder

In this survey stress has been laid mainly on unconscious factors both constitutional and predisposing and on some of the environmental influences that contribute to the selection of prostitution as a career. The survey would not be complete, however, without some reference to the relation between prostitution and manifest forms of mental disorder, in particular to neurosis, to the psychoses (insanities) and to psychopathy. Generally speaking, the neurotic person tends to suffer from inhibition rather than sexual expression. Unconsciously of course the neurosis covers unconscious sexual phantasies of a perverse order. As has been suggested, many cases of street anxiety mask unconscious phantasies of prostitution. But there are occasional cases of anxiety hysteria complicated by transient episodes of a prostitute type. In the psychoses on the other hand, particularly in some forms of schizophrenia, phases of prostitution are not uncommon; and in schizoid characters these phases may become organized in 'confirmed' prostitution. As regards psychopathy (instability in emotional set, impulse, life and character reactions) it is not surprising to find that many psychopaths are prostitutes and that close observation of many apparently 'normal' prostitutes uncovers the existence of a number of psychopathic traits.

These correlations with psychopathic and psychotic (or near-psychotic) disorder are capable of an interesting theoretical extension. In all such cases it is easy to establish that the emotional relations of the psychopath and of the psychotic person with external 'objects' (attachments) are of a tenuous nature and that the structure of the personality is profoundly and pathologically egocentric. This egocentricity (which is technically known as *narcissism*) tends to lead to shallow love-attachments and to relative indifference to the influences of normal love. It is no coincidence then to find that, particularly amongst larval prostitutes, the character structure is flimsy, unstable and egocentric leading to a cultivation of sensual enjoyments which are intended to enhance a weak personality. In other words, excessive narcissism runs like a thread through the whole problem of prostitution. To this, however, the qualification must be added that the factor is not specific, since exaggerated narcissism plays a part also in a great variety of non-sexual disorders or character abnormalities from excessive boastfulness to persecutory insanity.

Tolerated Prostitution

With this brief and inadequate review of the psychopathology of prostitution, my immediate task is at an end. Yet, although the psychopathologist's primary concern is with the causes and processes of disease rather than with its treatment, it would be shirking professional obligations not to indicate what particular therapeutic measures seem most likely to alleviate or eradicate the pathological conditions described. And since this Congress is convened to discuss the question of 'Tolerated Prostitution', we might well begin with that particular issue. From the psychopathologist's point of view, the objection to a policy of tolerated houses is simply that it tolerates the problem as well as the prostitute. *It gives social sanction to a pathological condition.* For whatever views we may hold on the existence of 'normal prostitution' or on its 'necessary evil', we must face the fact that in the majority of instances prostitution is a sign of sexual backwardness commonly associated with a degree of social backwardness. The argument that by sanctioning tolerated houses the incidence of venereal disease is cut down, even if accurate (and other speakers at this Congress will show that this is extremely questionable), is irrelevant. The fact that sanitary services in a tropical war-area may succeed in reducing the incidence of malaria amongst soldiers does not solve the problem of war-making or mitigate the other deplorable consequences that may ensue from it. As for compulsory prostitution, it is enough to say that measures of this sort constitute a betrayal of every principle that makes for stability in human society.

Preventive Measures

But although it is easy enough to arrive at these conclusions, it would be foolish to pretend that purely restrictive and repressive measures, aimed at the abolition of tolerated prostitution, would solve the problem. I do not suppose that any member of this Congress is under any illusions on this point. If we establish that prostitution is a sign of backwardness, it is incumbent on the State to use every device, psychological and sociological, to remedy the defect. No small-scale and haphazard efforts of voluntary societies can hope to deal with defects that develop in society as a whole, and are a reaction to forces inherent in the human race. The problem must be approached from the widest angles. For although individual prostitutes may be stabilized by individual attention, the social phenomenon of prostitution cannot be dealt with merely by paying psychological attention to individual prostitutes. Nothing short of a review of the whole problem of sexual custom, tradition, education and regulation can hope to alter in any permanent way the incidence of prostitution. This is not a matter of speculation. Although statistics of sexual behaviour are, for many obvious reasons, the most unreliable of human data, there is some direct evidence on this point that deserves careful consideration. During the period that has elapsed since the end of the last war[1] we have witnessed a transition in thought, outlook, and to some extent in standards of behaviour regarding relations between the sexes. One need only instance the changing social and economic status of women, the loosening of some of the moral and religious sanctions that previously obtained, the increased efficiency of contraceptive measures, decreased fear of illegitimate births and to some extent a more widespread knowledge of the modern psychological approach to the problems of sexuality. These factors have given rise to a relaxation of the general public attitude to prenuptial and extra-marital sex experience. And there is some reason to believe that this in turn has led to a reduction in the number of confirmed professional prostitutes. However that may be, there is no question that individual and social attitudes to sexual behaviour are profoundly influenced by irrational fears, anxieties and guilts, also that these give rise to superstitious observances of every conceivable variety. Moreover, as I have shown, these reactions are developed in the unconscious as well as in the conscious mind. Hence it is reasonable to suppose that the laws and social codes governing prostitution are to some extent irrational and superstitious. It would be going beyond the scope of this paper to suggest what changes in attitude might be initiated by the State. But obviously these would have to include within their range such problems as the regulation of marriage and divorce. The community, in its turn, might promote changes in the ethics of marriage, e.g. in the degree of social toleration given to the loveless marriage.

But these are wide and controversial issues. In the meantime we need not neglect the more practical steps which could be taken by any enlightened community. These can be classified in accordance with their aim, i.e. whether directed to the individual or to the environment, or again according to the nature of the measure, i.e. whether psychological, sociological, or economic. I am aware that this last sub-division is open to criticism on the ground that economic measures are essentially sociological and that therefore

[1] This refers of course to the First World War (1914–18)

the subdivisions overlap. But I have singled out the economic subgroup partly because the view is widely, but erroneously, held that the main causes of prostitution are economic, and partly for a special psychological reason. No one will attempt to deny that a substantial raising of our present economic standards, together with a substantial improvement in the conditions of labour, and an adequate improvement in recreational resources would serve to eliminate whatever material advantages may attract the commencing prostitute. But it is important to realize that, in the last analysis, economic hardship is a form of *psychological stress*. And mental stress, of whatever kind, is one of the commonest precipitating factors in abnormal conduct. Following this line of thought, it becomes clear that serious attempts should be made, not only to alleviate every variety of psychological stress, but to provide compensatory interests which will tide the individual over periods of psychological hardship.

These measures would not, however, strike to the root of the problem. The behaviour of the adult is determined by patterns laid down in childhood. Hence the solution of the problem of prostitution will depend on the extent to which we can modify those childhood patterns which predispose to the ultimate choice of prostitution as a career. At any rate, we can see to it that the *upbringing of children* is calculated to promote normal sexual adaptation in later life. This alone would involve radical change in our present system of sexual upbringing. It is obviously essential that parents should abandon their 'head in the sand' attitude to, or alternatively their moralistic suppression of, the sexual urges of children. Not only so, the whole system of *sexual education* should be of a liberal nature. And this liberality should begin at home. But before parents can be liberal, they must be honest about their own deficiencies. It is a tragic reflection that much of the abnormal conduct of adults is the price we pay for the warping effect of family upbringing. Granted that in most cases the ultimate determining factors in prostitution are subjective, and therefore not directly amenable to environmental influence, it is still possible that improvement in conditions of upbringing will make all the difference between reasonably normal and definitely abnormal behaviour. Parents and educators alike must grasp the fact that if we deny children the amount of love that is necessary for their normal development and warp their minds with illiberal sexual education, we cannot expect them to love in normal ways when they grow up.

Even so, we must be careful not to exaggerate individual factors such as sexual ignorance. Although it is certainly true that lack of adequate sexual education is an important pre-disposing factor in prostitution, it should be remembered that no child passes through its early development without acquiring much more sexual knowledge than it is given credit for. Although a large part of this knowledge is repressed and disappears from consciousness, it is unconsciously retained and expands in the form of sexual phantasies. These unconscious phantasies, if highly charged, can warp sexual development. In other words, the educational problem is not simply one of supplying accurate information where it is apparently absent but of correcting such distorted phantasies as have unconsciously influenced sexual development in any given case.

Principles of Individual Treatment

As I have suggested before, it does not come within the scope of this paper to describe the methods of *treatment of individual cases* of prostitution. Lest, however, it should be thought that the treatment is confined to social adjustment or readjustment of the prostitute's conditions of life, I would like to refer briefly to the principles of individual treatment. These are governed by the commonsense policy of endeavouring to alleviate those psychological conflicts that were responsible in the first instance for the choice of prostitution as a profession. From this point of view prostitution falls most naturally into the group of sexual aberrations; and experience has shown that these are often amenable to various forms of psychotherapy, from psycho-analysis to suggestion. They are, of course, not so easy to treat as the common neuroses, and one must be prepared for a higher rate of chronicity or recidivism. But the results so far obtained are encouraging, particularly if the case is dealt with in the 'larval' or early stage. Moreover, a good deal of direct prevention could be effected if all the adolescent 'problem' cases were psychologically examined and guided during the difficult phases of puberty. Naturally, all psychological methods are rendered more effective by the employment of trained psychiatric social workers who, acting in co-operation with the psychologist, can do much to secure effective modification of environmental conditions, and so alter the emotional milieu in a way that will render the patient more amenable to psychological techniques of treatment. Already the evidence of child guidance clinics and psychiatric centres goes to show that a great deal can be done for 'problem children'; and the prostitute is pre-eminently a problem child in adolescent or adult disguise. The fact that delinquent behaviour is commonly associated with prostitution is another argument for applying the preventive and therapeutic measures adopted by, amongst other psychiatric clinics, the Institute for the Study and Treatment of Delinquency. Generally speaking the procedures of giving advice and of securing social adjustment are of most service where the individual is passing through unusual stresses or periodic crises in real life. But where there is any evidence of internal mental stress expert psychological techniques of treatment are essential.

Reform of the Law

Finally, we must remember that the definition of prostitution is for all practical purposes a legal one. Hence we must not neglect to consider how far our present legal procedures are responsible for aggravating the very condition they are intended to control. For example, to impose a fine is both irrational and absurd; it encourages the girl to repeat the offence in order to have the wherewithal to pay the fine. To imprison takes away her last chance to find 'respectable' employment later on. In any case, the 'moral' indignation so frequently expressed by magistrates dealing with prostitutes, although strictly speaking no part of their legal prerogative (which is to deal with infringements of law), is a positive encouragement to recidivism. Moralistic fulmination is never a very satisfactory form of therapy. Indeed, the authorities might well consider whether prostitution and other sexual irregularities might not be dealt with solely from the point of view of public decency. Offences against decency, importuning, solicitation and the like could well be the occasion of a summons, not of conviction; and even then only after due cautionings and warnings have been given and ignored. Appearance in court would then be for acting in defiance of the warning.

Lastly it is to be observed that the problem of prostitution affords an unique opportunity to modify and extend the functions of the police force. Up to now the buffer between the convicted offender and the law has been the probation officer combining his authority as a 'supervisor' with his influence as a 'friend'. The cautionings and warnings which it is suggested might constitute a first effort at prevention of prostitution, failing the efficacy of which a first summons could be issued, might well be combined with a degree of 'emergency' social work on the part of women police. Given adequate training in the psychological causes of prostitution (for nothing could be more undesirable than to charter uninstructed social interference), this would provide a kind of 'first-aid' on the part of, say, the women police, which would be of more help to the 'larval' prostitute than a host of disciplinary caveats.[1]

But here again we are confronted with problems far beyond the scope of a paper on psychopathology. And so I would like to end with a cautionary comment on the rôle of experts. The expert witness is, no doubt, useful as an assessor. But his authority runs no further. Like a dictionary or encyclopædia, the psychological expert is very handy to refer to, provided he is put back on the shelf when his purpose has been served. It is no part of a psychologist's duty to grasp at administrative dictatorship. As a private citizen he may think what he likes about subjects like prostitution, but the ultimate responsibility for dealing with this problem lies in the social conscience of the community. It is, I take it, the main function of the International Bureau to see not only that this social conscience is never allowed to sleep but that its energies are directed primarily to the promotion of curative and preventive rather than punitive measures.

[1] [Note 1959] It is typical of the ambivalence of the State to the handling of delinquents (see p. 69) that the Bill dealing with control of street-solicitation at present before Parliament should, on the one hand, aim at applying social services to young prostitutes through a system of police cautions and, on the other, threaten the prostitute with a prison sentence on a third conviction. Interestingly enough the debates on this measure indicate clearly that the animus of many participants is directed not so much at street offences as at the private sexual activities of prostitutes, not to mention the impulses to fornication of those men who are picked up by them. The need for dispassionate research is never so obvious as when a popularly elected assembly engages and becomes entangled in the discussion of sexual mores.

VI. CLINICAL RESEARCH

Part I   Team-Research on Delinquency
Part II Recent Advances in the Psycho-analytical Study of Delinquency
Part III Psycho-Analysis and Criminology: a political survey

SECTION VI

CLINICAL RESEARCH

The development of a multi-disciplined approach to the problems of delinquency has raised in an acute form the necessity of establishing means of communication between the sciences concerned. Up to the present most branches of psychological and sociological science have operated within their own boundaries, each using its own terminology and technique, blandly indifferent to the need for a common pool of concepts. In some cases indeed such disregard was essential to the progress of the science concerned. Psychoanalysis, for example, had perforce to coin terms and formulate theories appropriate to the description of unconscious mental function; and these could not very well find paraphrases in the glossaries of conscious psychology and sociology.

Nevertheless some sort of communication is essential and although in the following essays no attempt is made to provide common definitions of terms, it is hoped that they will promote liaison by concentrating on essential differences *between psychoanalysis and the other disciplines concerned with research on delinquency. The first of the papers was addressed to the* Scientific Group for Discussion of Delinquency Problems, *the second to students attending an* International Training Course; *hence the more general terms in which they are couched. The third is a review of psycho-analytical approaches to delinquency delivered before an* International Congress of Psycho-Analysis *and is naturally expressed in a more technical and indeed more critical vein. While some overlap in material reviewed is inevitable, it is desirable on the one hand to orientate non-analytical workers in the characteristic approaches of psycho-analysis and on the other to indicate to psycho-analysts certain sins of omission and commission in their approach to delinquency.*

PART I
TEAM-RESEARCH ON DELINQUENCY*
[1953]

In the light of developments in criminology during the past twenty-five years, it is almost a truism to say that in no field are team methods of investigation, and incidentally of treatment, more appropriate and more essential. This is well illustrated by the history of the *Institute for the Study and Treatment of Delinquency* and of a number of delinquency research centres at universities, hospitals and elsewhere in this country. Whatever may have been the main aim or direction of research, it has been found necessary to draw upon the resources of a number of cognate sciences. Similar developments have taken place throughout the United States of America. Indeed, no delinquency institute or department can nowadays be regarded as adequate which does not mobilize the services of psychiatrists, psycho-analysts, organic physicians, educational and social psychologists, sociologists, social workers (including, of course, probation officers) and statisticians. Under these circumstances it would seem that the stage is now set for rapid advances in all directions of delinquency research.

Although this is a contingency greatly to be desired, we should not neglect the possibility that extension of team-research involving a variety of scientific disciplines is fraught with the risk of wasting a good deal of energy and ingenuity. For unless the standards of observation employed by all parties to the research are equally foolproof and unless the units of comparison employed are not only selected with the same degree of discrimination but have a corresponding factorial importance or valency, we are just as likely to witness the accumulation of a mass of observations and conclusions of little or no value, and in many cases the formulation of hypotheses fallacious enough or even superficial enough to obstruct or at least retard progress in research. Without some such system of standardization the utmost we could expect would be that the discipline operating with the most dynamic factors would re-discover the already established importance of these factors.

In view of this possibility it is essential that each discipline

* An address delivered before the *Scientific Group for the Discussion of Delinquency Problems* at its third meeting on 10 June, 1953, subsequently published in the *Brit. J. Delinq.*, **4**, 173–88, 1954.

should not only provide serviceable *definitions* of its own concepts, capable of paraphrase in terms of the cognate sciences implicated in any given research, but disclose its code of *interpretations*. For it cannot be emphasized too often that the value of any research lies less in the accumulation of new factual correlations than in the *interpretation* of the correlations. Which is tantamount to saying that unless the various cognate sciences subscribe to common principles of interpretation each particular discipline can only discover in any given research its own preconceptions.

Strictly speaking, therefore, a review of this kind should commence with a history of the *principles* arrived at and *methods* employed by each of the disciplines concerned. This, I fear, would take us too far afield and I must content myself with considering very briefly how far their principles of approach may give rise to differences in definition, in technical method and in the interpretation of whatever correlations are established.

Differences in Approach

To begin with, it is obvious that all methods can be classified in two main groups in accordance with whether or not they take into account *unconscious factors* in mental activity. But this distinction, though radical enough in all conscience, need not unduly hamper the processes of correlation, though, as will be seen later, it does completely alter the processes of interpretation. What does hamper correlation is the fact that the medical or clinical psychologist, and to a certain extent the neuro-psychiatrist, approach their problems with a *radical bias* concerning the dynamic and genetic factors responsible for mental pathology. This raises in an acute form the problem of valency of factors. To the medical psychologist the factor of *mental suffering* (which if he looks deeper can be equated with *mental conflict*) is the governing factor in research; whereas the general psychologist, however much he may take cognisance of conflict factors, is mainly concerned to explain pathological material in functional terms and therefore to apply the same standards and methods as he does in the case of so-called normal products. To the medical psychologist, the normal person is one who does not *suffer* unduly from conflict and is able to tolerate social adaptation. When he comes to study the pathological aspects of delinquency, the medical psychologist is not, however, misled by the fact that the offender shows little conscious conflict regarding the commission of an offence; he continues to look for evidence of mental suffering which might give rise to the social maladaptation including such manifestations of physical and mental disorder as may result from conflict. Naturally if he also believes in the operation of unconscious processes his search for conflict factors will be both wider and deeper.

To jump for a moment to the medical psychologist's valuation of mental tests it will be clear that, starting with these preconceptions, he will assess their utility in accordance with whether or not in arranging the tests first place is given to basic factors such as anxiety, guilt, jealousy, or hostility which induce emotional conflict of an intensity that disturbs normal function. This explains his relative disregard of the results of intelligence tests (though not of performance tests) and his preference for tests which help him to ascertain the emotional set and instinctual balance of the patient.

As for the differences existing between medico-psychological and sociological approaches, it is to be noted that the sociologist, like the general psychologist, is under no obligation to apply psycho-pathological criteria, indeed is free to assume that, for example, delinquent behaviour is nothing more than a willing or deliberate infraction of social codes having no special relevance to the offender's normality or abnormality, except in so far as his behaviour may be in part determined by gross constitutional factors, e.g. mental deficiency. Under these circumstances it is vastly to the sociologist's credit that he should pay as much attention as he sometimes does to pathological factors that lie between the constitutional and the environmental, and are mainly responsible for conflict.

Definitions

Turning from this cursory examination of the principles of approach to review some *practical difficulties and differences*, we may begin with an etiological caption which illustrates the necessity for more precise definitions than at present exist. In recent times the study of delinquency has to some extent become infected with sentimental journalese; the term 'broken home', for example, is now an etiological cliché. To the social psychologist it has come to comprise as many as fifteen different psychological situations, amongst others, death or separation of parents (a period of six months usually qualifying as 'separation', a traumatic standard which incidentally most Anglo-Indian parents, members of the merchant marine and many commercial travellers will resent), divorce, illegitimacy, wartime disruption or absence of both parents on factory work or of the mother on factory work. To this list some psychologists have added conditions such as alcoholism of one or both parents, emotional and social discord within the family and the degree of unwantedness of the child.[1] At this point it is already obvious that the term 'broken home' is generic and can acquire sufficient specificity to throw light on delinquency only by careful isolation of sub-groups, each one of which must be correlated not only with different types of susceptibility but with different types of delinquent conduct, in each case cross-checked by control observations. For if there are as many as fifteen different types of 'broken home' one may assume that there are at least ten *different types of susceptible children and therefore an elaborate series of specific combinations of factors.*[2]

These complications are greatly increased by the psychoanalyst, who, apart from postulating a variety of unconscious factors which might give rise to a broken home in an apparently

[1] Batchelor and Napier, *Brit. J. Delinq.*, **4,** 99–108, 1953.

[2] At first sight this may seem a somewhat arbitrary assumption, yet to those who are accustomed to take unconscious factors into account it is reasonable enough. For if we exclude cases in which the home is broken owing purely to extrinsic factors ('acts of God', wartime emergencies, etc.), the ways in which an adult parent 'breaks' his home are, according to psycho-analysis, determined ultimately by unconscious factors, of a kind which not only have their counterpart in the unconscious mind of the child, but provoke in the child specific unconscious counter-reactions. The most striking case is that where the child himself for reasons of jealousy of parents or siblings, *unconsciously wishes to 'break' the home,* e.g. to separate the parents, to get rid of rival brothers or sisters, or to abandon the home in a search for an 'ideal' home, the last of which unconscious wishes can end in the child 'running away'. When, therefore, one or other parent decides, also for unconscious reasons, to 'break' the home, the child is then specifically susceptible to the break and his traumatic reaction is increased to the extent that he must *repress his own disruption phantasies*. We must of course also allow for the case in which the child has no specific susceptibility but reacts to the *severity* of the trauma, e.g. its suddenness, cumulative effect, setting or immediate emotional intensity. Put in more technical language, the effect of a 'broken home' varies not only in accordance with the quality and degree of the trauma, but in accordance with the type and severity of traumatic response of the receptor and with simultaneously operating (endopsychic) *predisposing* factors.

united family, could maintain with some justice that a family may be 'broken' in respect to one member yet remain 'whole' in respect to another. This can be supported by the contention that the brokenness of a home depends less on the manifest state of disruption of the family than on the state of disruption of the child's ego, a subjective state of susceptibility which varies in accordance with the traumatic emotional factors, both environmental and endopsychic, originally responsible for the weakened ego, e.g. anxiety, guilt, jealousy, hostility, to say nothing of other obvious reactions to neglect or ill-treatment. In short, in some cases the broken home factor should be rated less as an objective (social) phenomenon than as a subjective (individual) state; and could better be described under the caption of 'broken bonds'.[1]

To these arguments the descriptive psychologist or social psychologist might reply, first, that the psycho-analyst rarely defines his data in a form that permits of statistical investigation and, second, that in any case psycho-analytical factors are sufficiently wide in incidence to render them useless for the specific study of delinquency. The first of these criticisms is unfortunately only too well founded, but the second has a boomerang action; for if broken or tenuous bonds can be found not only in anti-social disorders but in neuroses in which anti-social conduct is either at a discount or conspicuously absent, the broken-bond sociology of delinquency is also non-specific.

Factorial Assessments

With these considerations in mind we may proceed to consider the disturbing effect of generic terms when applied in team researches. For example, in their electro-physiological, psychological and sociological study of 100 juvenile delinquents admitted to a classifying school, Sessions Hodge, Walter and Walter [1] based their psycho-social appraisal on an estimate of nineteen characters, each on a three-point scale. The inventory was subdivided into four groups – personal factors, family relations, school relationships and the nature of offence. Taking in the first instance the family relationships group, the following characters were noted: – attitude of the boy to father or father figures, to mother figures and to siblings; father's attitude to boy: mother's

[1] See also R. G. Andry: 'Faulty Paternal and Maternal Child Relationships, Affection and Delinquency', *Brit. J. Delinq.*, 8, 34–48, 1957.

attitude; parental relations; and degree of unsettlement in early life.

For the sake of economy we may confine ourselves to the first of these characters, namely, *attitude to father or father figures*. Now the psycho-analyst, examining this factor not simply for its normal developmental significance but for its etiological importance in a variety of mental disorders including pathological delinquency, would not be satisfied until not only had he checked the conscious attitude (which is a composite end-product) by reference to its unconscious determinants, but, on the strength of this double investigation, had isolated the particular component which specifically related to any mental disorder exhibited by the patient. Dividing infantile development into a few broad phases in which the sexual and aggressive (love and hate) attitudes of the child pass through specific modifications, and in addition checking these phases of attitude to the father by reference to the complementary and interlocking attitudes to the mother or mother substitute, he would find himself with at least six, if not twelve, specific settings accountable, in part be it noted, for, say, an attitude of father negative or hostility.

This, in my opinion, cannot be dismissed as an exercise in ingenuity, it is a clinical necessity. In accordance with the degree to which these specific situations loosened different affective reactions, for example, anxiety, guilt, depression or suspicion, the psycho-analyst would clinically relate each situation to specific forms of disorder. Thus, to take only a few instances, father negative might be a single indication of unconscious infantile sexual anxiety such as is found in hysteria; it might be a cover for an unconscious homosexual fixation to the father associated with manifest homosexual practices; it might be heavily reinforced by a displaced unconscious mother hostility such as is frequently found associated with depressions; or it might be the manifest negative aspect of an ambivalent reaction to the father found in conjunction with persistent pilfering from employers. Incidentally, in none of these instances would the psycho-analyst seek to establish that the *conscious* hostility stood in causal relation to the associated neurosis, psychosis or delinquency: he would, however, maintain that both the conscious hostility to father or father substitutes and the disordered manifestations with which it is associated stem from the same unconscious roots. Not only so, he would maintain that the essence of therapeutic handling of such cases would depend on recognizing those unconscious factors and, by one means or another, reducing, controlling or off-setting their etiological force.

Apart from the necessity to break down generic categories into their most significant constituents, a constant source of difficulty in research lies in the degree of factorial importance to be attached to different elements in a group of characters. For example, in a comprehensive survey of 548 children suffering from conduct and/or neurotic disorders, Warren [2] includes among his *etiological* factors two special groups; viz., factors 'socially ill-suited' to the patient and factors 'emotionally ill-suited' to the patient. Amongst this latter group he rightly gives place to the degrees of anxiety and hostility shown by both parents but includes also maternal or paternal lack, degrees of solicitude or restriction, spoiling, disparity of age between siblings, disturbing personalities in the household, bullying at school, relatively severe educational standards and psychological traumas.[1] His socially ill-suited factors comprise poverty, overcrowding, a bad neighbourhood and bad companions. These various elements are then correlated with the *psychiatric symptoms* found, which are divided into five groups; viz., functional disorders (a most significant group, by the way), emotional attitudes, disturbed relationships, psycho-neurotic symptoms and conduct disorders.

To avoid over-elaboration I would like to indicate briefly what rearrangement of these data would be necessitated by a psycho-analytical approach. To begin with, the psycho-analyst when classifying the data would seek to distinguish between *constitutional, predisposing* and *precipitating factors* leading to the development of symptom-formations or pathological character formations, including pathological delinquency. Evidence for *constitutional factors* he would, in this case, draw chiefly from Warren's psychiatric section, in particular the existence of

[1] Incidentally he does not include, as do Sessions Hodge, Walter and Walter, the attitudes of anxiety or hostility manifested towards the parents by the child; and, of course, unless he had subjected his cases to an analytically directed anamnesis, he could do no more than hazard a guess as to the interaction of the unconscious anxieties and hostilities existing between parents and children.

functional disorders, disturbed emotional attitudes and relationships. The evidence for a *predisposition* to mental disorder of whatever type would be drawn from the same psychiatric sections and correlated with the social and familial influences described in the author's etiological section. The psycho-analyst would, of course, distinguish between *endopsychic* and *environmental* factors in predisposition; in other words he would have to correlate external influences in upbringing with the *susceptibility* both conscious and unconscious of the individual, a search which would throw him back again on a review of constitutional factors. He would certainly arrange both endopsychic and environmental factors in order of *priority* in each case, giving preference in the case of the patient to the factors of anxiety-readiness and especially of guilt-readiness and to the predominance of unconscious mechanisms which would be likely to lead to an externalized (projected) system of discharge as distinct from an endopsychic system; for example, to obsessional pilfering instead of an obsessional neurosis. In the case of environmental factors he would give priority to evidence of parental hostility both unconscious and conscious and second place to parental neglect; all the other factors would be considered together as third-rate influences. On the question of *manifest precipitating factors*, traumatic or otherwise, he would find himself mainly in accord with the findings of the general psychiatrist, the psychologist and the sociologist, although, as we shall see, he would interpret their significance in a different way.

All this, as has been said, would involve a considerable rearrangement of data. To take some isolated items, most of the 'socially ill-suited' factors would have to be transferred to the 'emotionally ill-suited' section. The influence of bad companions would be described as a combined emotional and ego factor and reserved for passive types, evidence for whose existence would be found in the psychiatric rather than the etiological section. Even poverty would be rated as an external emotional stimulus exerting its maximum force on constitutional sensitives with a history of early instinctual frustration. The family history, constitutional factors apart, and the existence of physical disease would be transferred to the predisposition section, and expressed through the 'family-influence' factors and 'traumatic' factors respectively. And, as has been suggested, a large part of the psychiatric findings would be transferred to the etiological section, operating these through the general factor of predisposition.

I hope I have been able to suggest that as a preliminary to team-research not only is it necessary to have standard units of definition and agreed scales of valency of factors but to have some common agreement as to norms of mental development and the particular mechanisms involved in symptom formations whether internally directed as in neuroses or externally directed as in delinquency. Otherwise we are almost bound to end by describing some abnormal formations as causes rather than end-results and some causes as psychiatric disorders, i.e. end-results. In other words we must base our researches on a working theory of mind which can trace both normal and abnormal psychology to common origins and enable us to classify disorders in terms of their developmental significance as well as their dynamic force. In this connection I cannot refrain from saying that some recent attempts to approach the problem of delinquency with a *tabula rasa* in one hand and the styles of a naïve observational system in the other is also naïve in the more popular sense of the term. To look successfully we must know where to look; and it seems a retrogressive step to neglect the existing comprehensive and stimulating body of psychiatric knowledge when approaching what is, in the last resort, a psychiatric problem. In fact the inevitable consequence of a naïve approach is that, however much the author may deck out his conclusions in unfamiliar terminology, they merely confirm what is already common scientific knowledge regarding delinquency.

CLINICAL ASSESSMENTS

To give further point to the necessity for application of clinical principles to the problem of team research, I would refer again to the paper of Sessions Hodge, Walter and Walter. In the 'personal factors' section of their psycho-social appraisal emphasis is laid on the estimation by Rorschach methods of what is called *neuroticism*. Searching for a definition of this term in the published works of its author, Eysenck [3], it would seem that from the point of view of clinical psycho-analysis, the caption is of little clinical value, is nosologically misleading, and, measured by our existing knowledge of mental development, is retrogressive in tendency. Seeking to ascertain some dimensions of personality, and starting, as he was bound to do, with clinical categories, Eysenck, using a variety of tests, discovers a psychic magnitude which is to some extent superordinate to the self (if I may borrow from the terminology of Jung) to which he gives the name of 'neuroticism'. 'Neuroticism', he maintains, is concerned with a normal variant rather than a pathological variant: it is, he holds, similar in concept to the general trait of intelligence and can be explained or described in terms of the conative component of personality, as distinguished from the cognitive component concerned in intelligence, and from the affective component concerned in what Eysenck describes as an introversion series of reactions. Neither neurotics nor, as Eysenck later maintains, psychotics are something *sui generis:* there exists a 'neuroticism' continuum linking 'normals' with neurotics and a 'psychoticism' continuum linking 'normals' with psychotics.

This is the typically flat result of applying descriptive psychology to the subject matter of depth psychology. And, as in the previous instances described, an examination of the various items that characterize 'neuroticism', shows that they constitute a mixture of factors of varying origin, depth and significance. 'Badly organized personality', for example, is an omnibus factor and so are 'dependence', 'narrow interest' and 'absence of group membership'; 'dyspepsia', 'little energy' and 'abnormality before illness' are symptomatic end-results; 'cyclothymia' may be anything from an affective disposition to a psychotic symptom process: 'abnormality in parents' is a hybrid variable, combining as far as the patient is concerned constitutional and environmental factors; whilst 'boarded out' and 'unsatisfactory home' are environmental variables. Taken individually they are each capable of elaborate clinical subdivision and have varying clinical significance.

Even if we waive these clinical objections and avoid nosological controversy by substituting a symbol 'Pl.' for the clinical term, 'neuroticism', it is evident that on the whole the concept retards rather than promotes progress both in theory and in practice. It is true that study of delinquency occurring during the pre-legal age, of delinquency amongst so-called normal adolescents and adults, of undetected delinquency, of delinquency known to the police but not prosecuted and of cases of delinquency 'carried through' seems to suggest a possible continuum of 'delinquentism' reaching from the normal to the patently abnormal. Yet the existence of *characteristic* types of *pathological* delinquency including neurotic, psychotic, psychopathic and what I have described elsewhere as 'functional' delinquency [4], indicates the desirability of avoiding such an unilluminating caption. In the more classical mental disorders it is even more desirable to break down the general concept of a continuum and to revert to the clinical practice of distinguishing and observing the interaction of constitutional, predisposing and precipitating factors giving rise when combined either to latent or to manifest disorders and symptom-formations. Regarded both clinically and etiologically the existence of a 'neuroticism continuum' merely indicates that constitutional and predisposing factors may or may not result in either latent or manifest psycho-neurotic formations.

Prediction Techniques

Having emphasized the necessity that participants in team-research should literally come to terms before embarking on a common project and that they should organize their terms of reference within the framework of a *systematic clinical psychology* and, I would like to add, *clinical sociology*, which take cognisance of *stages* in both *normal* and *abnormal mental development*, it is only fair to add that in one particular branch of delinquency research it is apparently possible to operate with some efficiency using broad and loosely specified terms. I refer of course to work on *prediction*, both preventive and prognostic. It is true that the Gluecks [5] base their predictive scales on as many as 402 distinct factors; yet the three final tables are made up each of five factors which at first sight seems to be non-specific. The 'character structure' scale, for example, comprises: assertiveness, defiance, suspiciousness, destructiveness and emotional lability, and the 'psychiatric' and 'social background' scales are similarly sub-divided, the former being based largely on Rorschach tests and the latter on the degree of affection, discipline and cohesiveness existing in the family. Interestingly enough, all these scales appear to have a common predictive value.

The merit of this prediction system is that it is based throughout on clinical studies of delinquents and that the 'character structure' group consists on the whole of factors of equal valency; indeed it is clear that the character factors chosen, when quantitatively scored, would *tend* to distinguish delinquent from all save psychotic reactions. The psychiatric screen serves to eliminate the psychotic factor and the social background includes at any rate the environmental (precipitating) factors commonly, though by no means exclusively, associated with delinquent reactions. Furthermore, the scale leaves a reasonable margin for error: for it is clear that in psychiatric affairs, a prediction system which cannot be falsified cannot be an accurate prediction system, a seeming paradox to which Peter Scott gives clinical force when he points out, as he frequently does, that hardy psychopaths may, in course of time, spontaneously settle down and without any treatment become law-abiding citizens. I hesitate to put a figure on the margin of *error* necessary for a *good* prognostic test, but, taking into account the spontaneous recovery rates found in non-delinquent disorders, I should imagine it lies between 10 per cent and 30 per cent according to the particular type of delinquency.

Here we have a clue to some of the deficiencies of existing prediction systems. Granted that they have every prospect of telling us with reasonable accuracy whether a given child will become delinquent, they give us only a hint as to whether he will remain a delinquent. Nor so far do they tell us what type of delinquency will be elected. This, I venture to suggest, only a system which takes into account deep dynamic factors and mechanisms, including the influence of symbolism, will be able to do satisfactorily, and with the same degree of accuracy with which a psycho-analyst can predict what form of suicide will be preferred by a given depressive case.

Added to which a flat prediction system cannot be expected to single out with accuracy those types of potential psycho-sexual delinquency where the character scale corresponds more to that of a psycho-neurotic disposition. To do so we would have to draw up a list of prodromata to psycho-sexual disorder, no easy task, except in the case of passive homosexuality. No doubt many of these drawbacks will be overcome in course of time; the system is after all still in its infancy; but to overcome them recourse to specific rather than to general clinical standards will be necessary.

Psychological Tests

Casting a general balance of the *value of tests* in team-research, it may be said that their most outstanding defect is their etiological sterility. Useful in prognosis and although to a lesser extent in diagnosis, when it comes to new etiological investigations they are blunt instruments. Based originally on observational data and working with factors selected on grounds of probable utility or theoretical plausibility, they can assist in correlating the original observations but they cannot do more than confirm or qualify what might have been inferred without test by applying the principles to the data. In other words, tests can break no new etiological ground: they can tell us no more than we already know or perhaps one ought to say no more than, as good clinicians, we ought to have known already. To be sure, they are convenient, and capable of statistical control, and they are at present more standardized than clinical approaches. Hence they provide some check on the slipshodness and lack of unified direction of psychiatric or social observation. It is an open question, however, whether in course of time they will not lead us back to psychiatry, first, because their increasing complexity will call for organization which can be effected only on clinical grounds and, second, because the problems they seek to solve are psychiatric problems. A diagnostic or prognostic short cut cannot be expected to uncover motivation. However fallible our psychiatric systems may be, they cannot be clinically improved from without. Psychiatry must indeed put its own etiological house in order; but it can only do so by establishing a working consensus regarding the theory of mind. It avails little to have a theory of neurosis or of delinquency unless that sectional theory dovetails with a scheme of general mental function which fits the facts of life. Until he can establish this consensus, the psychiatrist will go farther and fare better by examining rather than testing his cases.

Social Factors

Turning now to the *rôle of the social psychologist or sociologist* in team research, a number of important issues seem to me to arise. In the first place sociology is not, or should not be, an exclusively adult study. Secondly, beyond the age at which environmental (mainly familial) factors influence the predisposition to delinquency of infants and minors, the sociological factor is essentially a *precipitating* factor. And precipitating factors must always be read, or rather interpreted, in terms of their emotional significance to the patient. This is most strikingly demonstrated in the case of the psychoses where gross realistic precipitating factors may be absent, yet the patient reacts to minor indications, the shrug of a shoulder, the state of the weather, the time of the day, as if they were major traumata. This of course is due to the operation of what the psycho-analyst calls emotional transferences, i.e. deep emotional patterns of reaction established in infancy and childhood and subsequently displaced along lines of unconscious symbolism to superficial situations. And there is a good deal of evidence that the psychopath reacts in a way similar to that of the psychotic. So clearly the sociologist must be familiar with the endopsychic (symbolic) values which regulate transferences.

Thirdly, the social standards of delinquency are set by society and therefore subject to gross error, due to the operation of a persisting primitive morality or even superstition. The fact, for example, that certain sexual activities, which do not involve either violence or seduction, are rated as 'offences', even if the offender has the highest sense of social responsibility and ethical integrity, indicates that in these instances the search for 'criminological' factors should be directed towards society rather than towards the offender, and that, even if we do find criminological stigmata of a pathological type in the patient under observation, these have no necessary connection with the offence as such. Researches in this direction call for close collaboration between the dynamic or genetic psychologist, the sociologist and the anthropologist. I must add that in this work lawyers and administrators (the law makers, in short) ought also to co-operate; although so far there is little evidence that they are prepared to subject the premisses of criminal law to objective analysis.

In the fourth place, the sociologist, when applying his surveys of predisposing or precipitating factors, must condescend to clinical particulars; *he must invariably check his observations by reference to the type of offence committed*. Even if there were no flaws in our criminal code, delinquency is nevertheless as wide a field as the field of the psychoses or of normal characterology and as much in need of clinical classification. It is only a source of vexation to find that painstaking and sometimes brilliant researches have reference to omnibus groups, e.g. chosen from prison, Borstal or approved school populations or even groups of 'problem' children assembled in homes, hostels or remedial schools, with perhaps only the slenderest indication of the type of offence or offences committed.

Here again the position of the sexual offences is most ambiguous.

Finally, to mention but one point involving not only method but the *training of workers* it has become the habit of psychiatrists, partly for reasons of convenience, to delegate their social or sociological enquiries to a *social worker*. Strictly speaking they should do this work themselves. Fortunately many psychiatric social workers have a psychological flair which, to put it mildly, is not less than that of their psychiatric directors. But we should not gamble on this happy chance. Either the P.S.W. should be trained and graded as a liaison officer between the psychiatrist and the social psychologist and, what is more important, given equal status, or the psychiatrist, adding to his labours, should enter into more direct communication with the sociologist, having first of course learned the language and the scale of values of these environmentalists.

Uses of Psycho-Analysis

Summing up these admittedly tendentious considerations, it would seem that the most practical recommendation the psycho-analyst has to offer those about to embark on team-research is that they should choose their associates carefully; not simply on grounds of professional competence in their own speciality, a qualification the necessity for which goes without saying, but on a community of principles of approach, and as far as possible a community of interest and aim. It is almost a truism that the strength of a team is the strength of its weakest link; or perhaps it would be more accurate to say that in any given investigation the profundity of the conclusions arrived at is in inverse ratio to the scope of the most superficial method employed. On the principle, therefore, that what is sauce for the goose is sauce for the gander, we may consider *whether the average research team can afford to include a psycho-analyst*.

Needless to say there are some obvious objections to the course. Pursuing individual researches in the seclusion of his consulting room; submitting his work to none of the control techniques favoured by natural scientists; profoundly convinced of the dynamic importance of unconscious instincts, affects, ideations, mechanisms and structures in both normal and abnormal behaviour; employing no social worker; having only the most exiguous contact even with organic physicians; using a language of his own and claiming an apparently arbitrary right to interpret his data according to his own ideas, the psycho-analyst would seem to be a thoroughly unsatisfactory and intransigent member of a research team. So much can be freely admitted. The dangers inherent in uncontrolled investigation, especially when conducted by credulous or imaginatively undisciplined observers, are indeed well exemplified in our own time in this country where the established principles and conclusions of psycho-analysis have developed a number of pseudo-mystical accretions which frequently outrage psycho-biological probability.

In spite of these objections which, after all, merely indicate that the psycho-analyst, like the psychiatrist, the psychologist, and the sociologist is under obligation to put his own house in order and to keep it in order, I would maintain that it is essential to include a psycho-analyst in research teams provided his rôle is carefully delimited. It seems to me that his co-operation is invaluable at two points; first, during the preliminary selection of terms of reference; and second, at the end of the research when the various correlations established can be subjected to the indispensable process of interpretation. Having at his disposal a coherent theory of mind, a working classification of mental disorders, a system of dynamic and genetic values and a detailed knowledge of the processes of unconscious displacement, he can help considerably not only to evaluate the relative potency of different varieties of examination and of different factors in examination but to indicate the directions in which research can be most fruitfully pursued.

As far as direct analytical contributions to any given team-research are concerned the psycho-analyst's uses are much more restricted. It is no doubt desirable that, say, out of every 500 cases psychiatrically examined by a team, five at least should be investigated by a full analysis covering a period of two years. But on the whole the clinical uses of the analyst in immediate team research lie in periodic examination of the emergent results, a process, that is, of applying analytic principles of observation and evaluation rather than of direct analysis of cases. Otherwise the psycho-analyst is best left to his own devices.[1]

[1] During the discussion of this paper, Dr. Carroll drew attention to the uses of psycho-analysis in framing the categories for a psychiatric case-history and in drawing up psychiatric questionnaires for use where

I believe, however, that these devices, however scattered their application, are no mean devices. With a minimum amount of direct contact with delinquency, and pursuing his investigations in an almost haphazard way in the fields of neurosis, psychosis, character abnormality and occasionally in the most refractory medium of normality, the psycho-analyst has all the time been contributing to our potential understanding of criminal behaviour. Looking through the various clinical contributions to delinquency research it is somewhat depressing to find how little attention is paid to the importance of guilt-formation, of different forms and directions of hostility and in particular of the relation of hostility to anxiety, of the phenomena of transference, both negative and positive, and their reciprocal relation to the negative and positive counter-transferences of the community, of the operation of displacement, projection and symbolism, of the masochistic tendencies that operate behind the cover of sadistic discharge, and of the mechanisms that interfere with reality-proving and consequently with social adaptation, to mention but a few fundamental factors.

Now whatever may be said against psycho-analytic method it cannot be denied that the psycho-analyst's discoveries in these directions, made, as I have said, in non-delinquent fields, are of vital importance to the study of delinquency. But if we are to make effective use of these discoveries, we must not be too much upset by seeming paradoxes. To take one example: although I do not subscribe to the view that what psycho-analysts call the super-ego exists and operates from shortly after birth, I do believe that by the age of $2-2\frac{1}{2}$ an unconscious system of archaic morality is in comparatively full swing. We must not, therefore, be surprised when the psycho-analyst in expansive, armchair mood, suggests that the immorality of the sexual offender is due sometimes to the

direct case-histories are not feasible. I fully agree that psycho-analytic co-operation is essential in both cases and, instead of implicitly including these activities under the vague heading of 'evaluating the potency of different factors in examination' should have specifically indicated them under preliminary committee work. I doubt, however, whether the other psychiatric members of a team would be prepared to accept psycho-analytical categories in place of their own descriptive case-frames. Nevertheless, the fact remains that the uses of direct case-analysis in a comprehensive team-research cannot for various reasons extend beyond the analysis of 'samples'.

fact that in his infantile years he has been more moral-minded than his then contemporaries; or again, that when the persistent thief forces society to inflict punishment upon him, this is at the same time an indication of lack of conscious moral feeling on the offender's part and of the existence of an older unconscious hyper-morality; by projecting guilt on society and attacking it to the point where it hits back, the offender combines ego-attitudes of revenge with the action of a projected conscience; in other words the intra-punitive mechanisms of the obsessional conscience are replaced by the extra-punitive mechanisms of the delinquent conscience. Incidentally, I view with considerable misgiving the theories advanced in some quarters that delinquent conduct is largely the result of an undeveloped or grossly under-developed super-ego system. It is much more the consequence of a persisting archaic conscience.

Medical Psychology

It is no doubt much to be regretted that the psycho-analyst has contributed so few direct studies of delinquency; and, if time permitted, it would be interesting to consider the reasons for this sparsity of contribution, amongst which incidentally the rigidity of the classical analytical technique and the difficult nature of delinquent transferences would be found to figure prominently. This fact, however, lays all the greater onus on those clinical colleagues who, although not subscribing to Freudian theory, have nevertheless chosen to verse themselves in the direct study of delinquents. I would like therefore to end this review with some words of encouragement to the clinical (medical) psychologist whatever his theoretical credo.

In the first place, even if his concern is with what the psycho-analyst would call (pre-)conscious forces, systems, ideations, emotions, motivations, and moralities, the clinical psychologist can still order his observations, in terms of a working theory of mind. In any case the most effective way to achieve understanding of delinquency is for the clinical observer to soak himself in his material, and to permit his scientific imagination to play on the impressions he has received; for controlled imagination is, when all is said and done, the most potent instrument of research. But although he should have a reasonably systematized set of principles, his clinical contributions need not be too systematic. Actually a great number of research projects in delinquency fail simply because, wittingly or unwittingly, they are too ambitiously conceived. The psychological range of delinquency reaches to the innermost recesses of the mental apparatus and it is futile to expect to discover the 'causes' of delinquency by a tip-and-run survey of 100, or for that matter 1000 cases. On the other hand the happy analysis of an isolated dream fragment in an individual case *may* tell us more about the nature of delinquency than a nation-wide survey conducted by however so brilliant a team.

This brings me to my second point. Psychiatrists are by nature timorous creatures bearing some resemblance, however distant, to poets. Just as the poet lives out some of his conflicts through the medium of his imaginative activities, the psychiatrist lives out some of his conflicts at second-hand through immersing himself in the difficulties of others. But his timidity can sometimes lead him to deny his own vocation as an exploiter of 'rapport' and to dally with the disciplines spread before him by the laboratory worker. Let him not be too intimidated or too easily seduced by the trappings of controlled descriptive science. His main function and virtue lies in creating a psychic situation between himself and his patient which promotes the optimum freedom of mental expression on the part of the latter. Admittedly this imposes certain limitations on his systems of scientific control, but he must respect these limitations: and in fact they are more than offset by the intimate access he gains to human motivation.

I am therefore tempted to add one more to the list of conditions which would promote efficiency in team-research. Important as it is to provide a *lingua franca* by means of which each participant in a research project can translate his operative concepts in terms that can be understood by all the others, it is equally important that all members of the team should clearly understand and respect each other's technical limitations. This applies with particular force to the methods and concepts of psycho-analysis. For unconscious processes are not only more archaic than (pre-) conscious processes but quite different in kind; and therefore call for the application of quite distinct techniques. When the uses of scientific co-operation have been exhausted, the scientific cobbler should return to his last.

REFERENCES

1 SESSIONS HODGE, WALTER and WALTER: 'Juvenile Delinquency: An Electro-physiological, Psychological and Social Study', *Brit. J. Delinq.*, **3**, 155, 1953.
2 WARREN: 'Conduct Disorders in Children, Aged 5–15 Years', *Brit. J. Delinq.*, **1**, 164, 1951.
3 EYSENCK: *Dimensions of Personality*, Routledge & Kegan Paul, 1947; *The Scientific Study of Personality*, Routledge & Kegan Paul, 1952.
4 GLOVER: 'On the Desirability of Isolating a "Functional" (Psychosomatic) Type of Delinquency Disorder', *Brit. J. Delinq.*, **1**, 104, 1950. Reprinted in *On the Early Development of Mind*, Imago Publishing Co., 1956.
5 GLUECK: 'Predicting Juvenile Delinquency', *Brit. J. Delinq.*, **2**, 275, 1952.

PART II
RECENT ADVANCES IN THE PSYCHO-ANALYTICAL STUDY OF DELINQUENCY*

[1954]

It is the custom in most sciences to issue every five years or so a survey of 'recent advances', consisting for the most part of abstracts of papers, setting forth systematically the extensions in theory, practice or methods of research that have taken place in any given field. Useful as this routine procedure is in the natural sciences it cannot be applied with the same degree of success to the relations of psycho-analysis to delinquency. In the first place the number of *direct* psycho-analytical studies of delinquency, meaning thereby by the actual psycho-analysis of delinquents, is relatively small and in any case follows roughly the same course in all cases. And in the second the *indirect* application of psycho-analytic theories and policies in the study and treatment of delinquency is very much in arrears; that is to say, as far as delinquency is concerned a great number of long established psycho-analytical principles have been allowed to lie fallow. The most outstanding example of this neglect is provided by the psycho-analytical concepts of unconscious guilt, sin or need for punishment. These vital aspects of delinquency are usually by-passed by delinquency workers in their haste to find social and individual factors in delinquency of a more 'rational' order. In short it is difficult to avoid the somewhat paradoxical conclusion that *the most rapid advances in the psycho-analytical study of delinquency can be achieved by making good arrears in the application of established psycho-analytical principles to the problem*. All of which is a preamble to the statement that the most important contributions of psycho-analysis to delinquency are indirect. They arise in fact from the application of the *psycho-analytical theory of mind* to delinquency, meaning by this term a group or series of mental disorders, having characteristic anti-social manifestations.

In addition to this it is necessary to recognize the arbitrary limitations imposed on all forms of delinquency research by the

* A lecture delivered at the Fourth International Criminological Course, London, April, 1954.

fact that *delinquency comprises a number of clinical conditions of widely different sort, having sometimes little in common except the fact that some of their behaviouristic manifestations or end-products offend against the law.* This generalization, it should be noted, applies with equal force to conditions of which the *only* symptom is some infraction of the law. According to social estimations, backed by the arbitrary force of public prejudice, one thief is as bad as another. Yet in pathological cases the same type of theft may be classified by the psycho-analyst in different sub-groups correlated in each case with a particular form of occult or manifest mental disorder.

An even better example of the arbitrary force of public prejudice operating through the criminal code is that of sexual offences. Branded as a crime, homosexuality is nevertheless commonly found in persons presenting the highest ethical standards and subscribing to codes of individual and social conduct superior to those followed by the so-called normal person. As far therefore as the social conscience of the 'offender' is concerned burglary and homosexuality are poles apart. Yet judged by the social conscience of the community, burglary when compared with homosexuality is an almost venial offence. It follows that in the case of sexual offences an 'advance' is overdue, not from psycho-analysis or any other form of investigation or treatment, but from the *social conscience of the community*. In an enlightened community homosexuality as such would disappear from the criminal code except in as far as it involved the seduction of minors, offences against public decency, importuning or sexual assault;[1] in other words, the same social controls would apply as already exist in the case of heterosexuality. Not only so, papers on homosexuality would disappear from the agenda of International Criminological Courses such as the present. No doubt psycho-analysts would, in a purely private professional capacity, continue to study homosexuality, and attempt to treat some selected cases at the express request of the patient; but they would be under no necessity to regard the condition either as criminal or as one automatically calling for treatment. In other words *the psycho-analyst's interest in delinquency is secondary to his interest in the conditions of which it is a manifestation.*

[1] [Note 1959] See notes on the *Wolfenden Report* (1957) *on Homosexuality and Prostitution*, pp. 63, 68–9, 394–6.

To take another example, that of the psychopathic character, which, owing to the prominence recently given to cases of criminal psychopathy, tends more and more to be regarded in the popular imagination as a vicious form of crime. Now the psycho-analyst is interested in this condition, or rather, group of conditions, in so far as they represent disorders; (*a*) of the reality ego, both conscious and unconscious; (*b*) of the super-ego (the mainly unconscious conscience of the individual); (*c*) of the instincts (disorders of the sexual and aggressive instincts being common in the group), and (*d*) of the emotions; he is not *primarily* concerned with the fact that some psychopathic characters break the law. In fact the greatest advances in the handling of criminal psychopathy have been made by analysis of psychopaths who do *not* break the law but are nevertheless cases of disordered character-formation. In the psycho-analyst's view it is impossible to understand either criminal or non-criminal psychopathy unless we study the mental processes which lead to the development of the normal ego and super-ego, and thereby shed light on the abnormal ego and super-ego; needless to add this understanding involves extensive acquaintance with the unconscious layers of the mind in which these great mental institutions are rooted.

It follows then that since the psycho-analyst's main interest in delinquency is indirect, his most valuable contributions to research on delinquency are for the most part also indirect. This explains to some extent why so few direct analyses of delinquents have been carried out. It is not of course the only reason; more important factors will be considered when we come to survey the field of treatment, viz. the nature of 'transference', the fact that psycho-analysis depends for its success on its capacity to utilize and in the end dissolve transferences between the patient and the physician, and that in cases of delinquency the transferences are, to begin with at any rate, predominantly of a negative or hostile order.

Despite the scarcity of direct analytic investigations of delinquents it is an interesting and indeed significant fact that the psycho-analyst, throughout his general analytic work with patients suffering from a variety of *non-criminal* mental disorders has unusual opportunities of observing minor and sometimes even major delinquent conduct on their part which is undetected by the police, and therefore does not come the way of the sociologist or even of the non-clinical psychologist. It certainly would be invaluable if analysts as a group were to pool their information on *undetected delinquency*. So far no systematic attempt has been made to do so; but such information as we do possess goes to confirm the suspicion that the so-called normal person has closer affinities with the psychopath than he is willing to admit to himself, much less publicly avow.

Summing up these preliminary impressions we may say that *the uses of psycho-analysis in research far outweigh its uses in pure form as a method of treating delinquency* and that in consequence *its ultimate use will lie more in prevention than in actual direct treatment.* No doubt psycho-analysis has still an important part to play in direct study but so far the amount of work available does not justify including it under the caption of 'advances'. The psycho-analyst in fact is only beginning to experiment in this direction, a state of tutelage he shares with any other worker in delinquency whatever his speciality.

I. Psycho-analytical Research on the Nature of Delinquency

Bearing in mind then that psycho-analytical study of delinquency is, so far, mostly indirect, we may proceed to consider in which directions it has been or can be most usefully applied. And since time does not permit any detailed description of the theory or practice of psycho-analysis we may well begin by singling out the most characteristic features of the psycho-analytical approach.

(1) First in order of importance is the emphasis laid by psycho-analysis on the *unconscious nature of the processes which ultimately determine both normal and abnormal mental activities*. In the welter of modern investigations of delinquency both by psychologists and sociologists, the importance of this factor is pretty generally neglected, a fact which, in my opinion, is chiefly responsible for the uninspiring and unilluminating nature of most non-analytical contributions to the subject. It is or should be axiomatic that when human conduct deviates from the rational, the most illuminating explanations of it must lie in the nature of irrationality; and the nearer we are to the irrational the nearer we are to the unconscious functioning of the mind.

(2) Next in order of importance is the *method of approach to normal mental function*. The psycho-analyst finds it impossible to describe any mental process without following three distinct lines of approach. First he considers the instinctual forces which,

together with the emotional reactions they produce, are responsible for all mental activity; secondly, he isolates the mechanisms (conscious and unconscious) which help to control, distribute or discharge these forces; and thirdly he divides the mental apparatus into a number of institutions which control the mechanisms which in turn control the forces.

(3) Approaching all mental phenomena in this way, the psycho-analyst describes *pathological manifestations* in terms respectively of disordered instincts, uncontrolled mechanisms and diseased structures. Taking the view that delinquency can be and often is a sign of mental disorder he studies the symptoms by this threefold method. His object is not simply to account for the symptoms, but, by study of the symptoms, to establish the diseased process giving rise to them and to detect the deviations from normal function which permit or stimulate the development of the disease.

It will be seen that psycho-analysis is not just a special form of psychotherapy or a method of research; it constitutes a theory of mind; and without a fairly consistent theory of mind that takes cognizance of unconscious processes only a descriptive psychology or sociology of delinquency is possible. To be sure, the general psychologist and sociologist seek to correlate the phenomena of delinquency with the present or past environment, but, as we shall see later, they make no attempt to consider the unconscious significance of mental processes or for that matter the significance to the unconscious mind of environmental processes whether past or present.

To these matters we shall have occasion to return; in the meantime we may formulate a generalization which, as has been hinted before, should regulate all surveys of 'recent advances' in any form of delinquency work. Most research students are concerned with the discovery of something 'new' without pausing to reflect that the 'old' may not yet have been systematically applied; hence *the first concern of the psycho-analyst is that the concepts of psycho-analysis should infiltrate as rapidly as possible all researches on delinquency*. This would in his view constitute a real advance.

Here again it must be admitted that so far the percolation of psycho-analytic ideas to delinquency has been mostly through devious channels, partly through general psychiatry, partly through educational psychology and to a considerable extent through the medium of child-study conducted either by teachers or by the general staff of child guidance clinics. Many of the concepts current in these fields have been taken over from psycho-analysis without any very clear realization of their origin. And in course of absorption many of them have been watered down to suit the needs of a 'conscious' psychology.[1]

Two examples of this watering down process come readily to mind. The first is the general importance now attached to the 'first five years'; and the second the emphasis laid both by psychologists and sociologists on the effects of a 'broken home'. The importance of both of these factors has been emphasized from the earliest beginnings of psycho-analysis; yet the spread of these ideas through psychiatry and general child psychology has converted both of them into psychological clichés which have lost their directive force. The emphasis now generally laid on these factors is limited to the direct interaction of environment (nurture) on the constitutional disposition of the individual child, thereby leaving out of account the most important factor of all, namely, that of *organized unconscious predisposition*, i.e. the endopsychic factors which lie between the constitution of the particular individual and the changing circumstances of his environment.

Apropos the 'first five years', we may add here one more to the features characteristic of psycho-analytic investigation, viz., *the developmental approach to mental disorder*. This is based on the general assumption that there is no adult mental disorder without infantile antecedents. It follows that since infantile mental life passes through a series of normal 'phases', each subject to characteristic infantile disorders, adult disorders can best be classified according to this developmental scale. The method has already been applied systematically in the case of the classical mental disorders, the neuroses, psychoses and transitional states. The so-called 'fixation points' of, e.g. the hysterias, obsessions and the various psychoses have already been established. *Classification in depth* has also been applied, although not with the same degree of accuracy, to the sexual perversions and inhibitions but so far its application to the problems of delinquency has been sporadic and haphazard.

Nevertheless some progress has been made. Most delinquency

[1] An excellent series of psycho-analytical source-books on the subject is *The Psycho-analytic Study of the Child*, Vols. I–XIII, Imago Publishing Co.

clinics have succeeded in distinguishing, or perhaps one should say have been compelled to distinguish, different grades of delinquency ranging in depth from so-called 'psychoneurotic' delinquency[1] through alcoholic delinquency to psychotic delinquency eventually to the delinquency of mental defectives. And it is in the highest degree probable that a detailed classification in depth can be arranged running parallel to that which psychoanalysts have already established in non-criminal mental disorders.[2]

Following this line of approach I have recently suggested that a separate group of delinquencies can be isolated, lying between the mainly 'constitutional' groups and those groups isolated on the strength of their association with neurotic and psychotic *levels* of development. These I have described as 'functional' in type, indicating thereby that the disorder lies not so much in the structure, instincts or mechanisms but in the inadequacy of the mental apparatus to deal with traumatic stimulation (particularly in the direction of frustration or damming-up of impulse).[3] This form of predisposition is perhaps the most obvious example of a direct combination between constitutional and environmental factors and is formed in the period between birth and 3 years. And I believe that a heterogenous assortment of 'outbreaks' of delinquency, the best example of which is the 'pubertal antisocial crisis', can be reduced or traced to this early functional inadequacy.

The possibilities of advances along these lines are endless. Whereas a number of separate groups of delinquency can now be isolated and correlated with different developmental layers and predispositions, there are some which call for special subdivision in developmental terms, in much the same way as the omnibus

---

[1] Some observers object to the use of this caption, holding that neurotic types of delinquency are essentially psychopathic. Yet, to take only one example, in view of the typical obsessional features observed in the so-called kleptomania of persons who otherwise manifest no anti-social conduct or characteristics, it seems desirable to retain the distinction.

[2] See, for example, Glover: 'A Psycho-analytic Approach to the Classification of Mental Disorders', reprinted in *On the Early Development of Mind*, Imago Publishing Co., 1956.

[3] Glover: 'On the Desirability of Isolating a "Functional" (psychosomatic) Type of Delinquency Disorder, reprinted in *On the Early Development of Mind*, Imago Publishing Co., 1956.

group of alcoholisms can be subdivided in terms of developmental depth, e.g. hysterical, compulsive, depressive and paranoid types. The psychopathic group in particular require subdivision in this way. Many of the baffling 'mixtures' of psychopathic symptoms or idiosyncrasies of 'character' can be reduced to order by correlating the main characteristics with different fixation points. For there is no doubt that the fixation points of psychopathy are widely and deeply scattered. It was indeed for this very reason that I referred earlier to the retarding effect on research of what were in their time important advances. It certainly was an advance to split off neurotic, alcoholic, epileptic, psychotic and, recently, functional types of delinquency from the omnibus group of psychopathic characters; and it was equally certainly an advance to exclude the purely sexual disorders and perversions previously labelled 'sexual psychopathy'. But it was a mistake to assume that the residue, constituting the hard core of psychopathy, had in every case the same constitutional, predisposing and precipitating factors. Progress in the understanding of psychopathy can be achieved only by applying atomistic methods to this apparently hard core.

It is time now to consider the different aspects of psycho-analytical work and to enquire not simply whether fresh advances have been made in recent years but also whether existing psycho-analytic knowledge has been adequately applied; and, as before, it will be found convenient to approach the subject by considering, in the following order, the instincts (together with the affects they produce), mental mechanisms and ego-structures and the processes of symptom-formation.

(1) *Instincts*. It is, I imagine, common knowledge that the first great advance made by psycho-analysis lay in the study of the libido, or energy of the *sexual impulses*, the unconscious origins of these impulses, their infantile (polymorphous) manifestations and the great unconscious infantile crisis that arises when the child's genital libido is directed towards family objects (the Oedipus complex). And it is not surprising that many forms of delinquency, some varieties of theft, for example, have been attributed to unconscious displacement of demands on infantile love-objects to other forms of property, also that the aggressive jealousy and revenge reactions of the child can readily be displaced to extra-

familial figures or groups, in the long run to society. Since then many attempts have been made to trace back to early infancy many of the constituents of the three to five year old Oedipus trauma. But the results of these investigations are so far too indefinite and indeed too speculative to be regarded as advances: some of these conceptions have actually proved to be stumbling blocks. Nor, in spite of an increasing number of investigations of sexual perversions and inhibition, can it be said that much has been added to our knowledge of the libido. And as I have already mentioned, classifications in depth of these conditions have not been very clearly established. All this deserves immediate attention.

On the other hand care is now taken to distinguish between, on the one hand, *reactive* sexual disorders, due to frustration of other components of the libido, and, on the other, more specific sexual *organizations*, e.g. between the *function* of exhibitionism and the *structure* of some types of homosexuality, conditions which are a common source of criminal proceedings. And it is now better realized that where an organized type of sexual perversion exists it is impossible to isolate treatment or 'focus' it solely on the sexual symptoms. These must be correlated with the balance of ego and other life activities before any effective leverage can be brought to bear.

But this is to trespass on the subject of treatment. Perhaps of greater significance is the emphasis now laid in all branches of delinquency work on the importance of early love-relations and the fact that interruption of these psychic relations gives rise to what is now almost popularly called 'separation-anxiety'. This is fast becoming as much of a cliché as its congener – the 'broken home'. And, to the extent that it is coming to be regarded as a determining environmental factor in some cases of delinquency, it is losing the significance it acquired when the endopsychic (predisposing) reactions to loss or separation were originally taken into account by psycho-analysts.

And here we may chronicle on one of the few advances to be recorded in this section, viz., the fact that psycho-analysis is making good a deficiency in the earlier range of interest, by *observing* analytically those infants who by reason of their mental immaturity cannot be directly analysed, i.e. up to the age of 3–4 years. This of course is an advance in applied analysis not in psycho-analysis and involves the analyst in the acceptance not only of factorial psychology but of the statistical methods by which the importance of the factors can be accurately assessed. Needless to say, once the factors have been estimated they must be given analytic interpretation. Without interpretation factorial psychology can give us at best no more than a hint of the operation of unconscious factors and in many instances actually obscures the dynamic unconscious situation.

In the case of research on the *aggressive impulses*, which obviously are of prime concern to the student of delinquency, the situation is not very different from that indicated in the case of the sexual instincts. Little more is known of their infantile forerunners than was common analytical knowledge a quarter of a century ago. Here too a percolation of psycho-analytical findings through the fields of psychiatry and child psychology has taken place. And again the result has been the development of clichés, as, for example, the now commonly accepted distinction between *direct* discharge of aggression and the *reactive* aggression, or more specifically hate, developed as a consequence of sudden or cumulative charges of *anxiety*. In both cases it is necessary to distinguish between *functional* reactions and those specific mechanisms that lead to more *permanent modifications* of the ego or super-ego. This is particularly true of the psychopathic case, for although he too suffers from recurring functional crises, he illustrates, more than any other delinquent except perhaps the psychotic offender, the persistence of faulty ego reactions from early childhood. A good example of the detailed mechanisms by which these changes are brought about is afforded by the child's process of 'unconscious identification with the aggressor' on which Anna Freud has recently laid so much stress.

It should be remembered in this connection that the isolation of pure aggressive impulses is a classroom device adopted for convenience in presentation. There is invariably some degree of *overlap or fusion* with libidinal impulse. For this reason it is impossible to disentangle the problems of *unmodified or primary aggression*, which is difficult enough to distinguish from sadism, from the problems of *anxiety, hate and reactive aggression*. Yet the whole future not only of delinquency research but of psycho-analytical research itself depends on being able to trace or reconstruct the inter-relations between excitation, aggression, affect and instinctual discharge.

Here again we may note how the percolation of analytical ideas in non-analytical fields can have a retarding effect on research. Theories of anxiety have been taken over, divested of their unconscious significance and regarded as conscious factors. Secondly, emphasis on the conscious aspects of reactive aggression has obscured both specific unconscious hate factors and the relation of hate to unconscious sadism. Most remarkable of all, the factors of *unconscious guilt*, or as it is more accurately expressed, of the *unconscious need for punishment* is consistently neglected in non-analytical researches. Yet here surely is the key to all problems of delinquency. To be fair to the psycho-analyst, he cannot be held responsible for this neglect or delay in applying cardinal discoveries: for it is no exaggeration to say that, outside theological circles, no one has paid more attention to the problem of sin than the psycho-analyst. Indeed had the concept of sin not existed it would have been necessary for the psycho-analyst to invent it. Theologians, it should be added, have got no closer to the concept of unconscious guilt than is permitted within the connotation of 'original sin', in other words of inheritance.

Neither is it an exaggeration to say that the most important advances in the psycho-analytical approach to delinquency problems lie in the discovery and classification of various forms of unconscious *guilt-avoidance*. The form of avoidance most interesting to delinquency students can be described as the 'reverse action of unconscious conscience'. For whereas, using the mechanism of introjection, the psycho-neurotic deals with his unconscious guilt through mechanisms of self-punishment (the neurosis), the delinquent, using the unconscious mechanism of projection, deals with his guilt by the mechanism of punishing the environment (delinquency). This of course is an old psycho-analytical discovery: one of Freud's earliest communications on the subject of delinquency described the offender whose anti-social conduct is determined by his unconscious guilt feelings. But with the extension of psycho-analytical knowledge of the manic-depressive psychosis in which the alternations of mood and activity can be correlated respectively with fall and rise of unconscious guilt, it is possible to include amongst the more manic types of reaction, many of the outbursts of delinquency which have previously been regarded as characteristic of the paranoid type of psychopathy.

It is only fair to add that, although most students of delinquency neglect these vital considerations, some psycho-analysts have gone to the opposite extreme by postulating organized unconscious guilt too early in development, e.g. during the first two years of life. This could only apply to the delinquencies of some psychotic types, of mental defectives and of a sub-group of psychopaths. Moreover some analysts tend to assume an absence of super-ego or unconscious conscience formation in a large number of delinquents. This is not at all true even of the psychopath who is frequently shocked by the conduct of other psychopaths, not to mention that of quite ordinary persons. In many respects the psychopath has not only a normal conscience but an abnormally acute conscience, albeit somewhat primitive in ideology and action.[1]

These two instances illustrate the dangers of forming too *premature conclusions*. No doubt it is a fault on the venial side; nevertheless it would pay both analysts and non-analysts to adopt a conservative attitude on such moot points, until more direct analytical work is done on the subject. And incidentally it would pay communities which suffer unestimated but certainly enormous losses from the existence of criminality in their midst to spend a few hundreds of thousands on research on this group of problems alone.

(2) *Mental Mechanisms and Ego-Structures*. Turning now from a review of research on the instincts and affects to consider the work done on unconscious mechanisms and on delinquent ego-structures, we find that most of the comments and criticisms applicable to the former field apply in equal measure to the economic and structural aspects of delinquency. These immense fields of study lie practically fallow or even totally neglected. A new tendency is, however, now recognizable in psycho-analytical circles. Although bound to a certain extent by his methods of investigation to an atomistic approach to mental disorder, the psycho-analyst has never neglected the urge to *synthesis* that exists in the mental apparatus. And in fact his description of the

[1] M. Schmideberg: 'Is the Criminal Amoral?' *Brit. J. Delinq.*, **4**, 272–81, 1954.

developmental stages of this apparatus is pre-eminently an essay in synthesis. More recently he has begun to pay attention to the effect of *combinations of primary affects, of mental mechanisms and of ego-institutions* in both normal and abnormal states. The importance of this trend is clear, not only in the case of delinquent activities but in the non-criminal disorders also. The etiological formulæ of psycho-analysis have inevitably proved too generic. Clinical psychology cries out for the isolation of specific combinations of factors characteristic of different clinical conditions; and it is reassuring to think that in course of time these more adequate formulæ will be forthcoming.

(3) *Study of Symptom-Formations.* Progress in the direction of more accurate etiological differentiation will no doubt be accelerated by keeping constantly in mind the main groups of factors which give rise to symptom-formation. I have already indicated the main flaw in much psychological and sociological research on delinquency. This can now be described more precisely. *The psycho-analysis of symptoms depends on the distinction of three main groups of factors; (a) constitutional; (b) predisposing, and (c) precipitating.* Of these the most important, in the analyst's reckoning, is the second or *predisposing group.* It was one of the early contributions of psycho-analysis to clinical problems to point out that the early struggle between constitutional tendencies and the environmental restrictions (frustrations) imposed on the infant plays a decisive part in the formation of predisposition, that in fact an essential part of early mental development is the formation of such predispositions. They can be rather crudely described as unconscious systems of valuation and reaction established as the result of inner stresses and experiences of the outer world under the influence of infantile unconscious ideation and emotional reaction. Of course both psychologists and sociologists (particularly what might be called 'familial' sociologists) are prepared to include constitutional and environmental influences in the formation of infantile patterns but most frequently they ignore the unconscious *endopsychic* reactions and valuations which determine the pre-delinquent and delinquent reactions of the individual. The result is superficial etiologies and superficial descriptive classifications.

Equally important is the misdirection of research effort consequent on taking *precipitating factors* at face value. It is true that already some early preconceptions have been reduced or removed: no reputable sociologist will nowadays maintain that the main factor in delinquency is economic. This change is all to the good, but it does not go far enough. Psycho-analytical investigation of the psychoses has shewn that in these conditions the importance of precipitating factors depends less on the actual strength of immediate frustration than on the unconscious symbolic significance of the frustrating circumstances: in other words, the extent to which they are unconsciously identified with infantile traumata. Psycho-analysts were the first to point out that stealing of food, ornaments, money and other objects by minors was a reaction to an inner apprehension of loss of love on his part. A similar situation is seen in the apparently trivial causes of psychopathic outbursts, e.g. the look on the victim's face, an apparently minor slight or trivial frustration. And there appears to be little doubt that the symbolic significance of the article stolen can have the same degree of significance as the method of suicide preferred by the suicidal depressive. Obviously examination of the nature of particular offences will be greatly facilitated by the application of such methods of appraisal. Even the simple devices of occupational therapy owe some of their virtue to the action of symbolism taking effect along channels of sublimation. So far, however, there has been an astonishing lack of interest in these matters. In the eyes of the law a theft is a theft and it is nothing more; to the psycho-analyst it signalizes the discharge of a long series of inter-related tensions finally directed at a particular type of object in the external world.

II. Treatment of Delinquency

You will have observed that I have devoted the most of my available space to recording the progress or lack of progress made in the study of delinquency. This is in keeping with the facts that in principle at any rate few if any advances have been made in the psycho-therapy of delinquency during the past twenty years and that in practice real advances in the therapeutic field depend on fuller application of already long-established psycho-analytical knowledge. It is true that nowadays we hear of all sorts of treatment going by unfamiliar names and may be led into the misapprehension that these represent new and advanced forms of therapy. Whereas the fact is that in most instances there is little new about the technique apart from its title. *Group therapy*, for example, is enjoying at present an unexampled period of popularity, partly no doubt because it offers a more rapid approach to larger numbers than does individual psycho-therapy. Actually group therapy springs from an early derivative of psycho-analytical therapy (Trigant Burrow). But it is much older than psycho-analysis; it is as old as evangelical systems of common confession (giving testimony), as old as the prayer meeting and the sewing circle, the club or the dames' school playground; it is in fact as old as group formation and owes what efficiency it possesses to the same factors which at the dawn of history led to the formation of primitive groups; for *it depends, as all other forms of psychotherapy depend, on the spontaneous or purposive handling of what are called transferences, and, in the case of psycho-analysis, on their resolution.* You may recall that in Aichhorn's opinion the alpha and omega of delinquency therapy is the handling of the transference. And it can also be said without fear of contradiction that if the therapeutist refused to treat his patients by transference, they would proceed to treat themselves by spontaneous transferences. The delinquent himself does this on occasion, hence many of the so-called spontaneous 'cures'.

The Factor of Transference. To avoid confusion we may remind ourselves here that transference is a form of unconscious displacement whereby the dominant infantile attitudes to important family figures are repeated in type and emotional reaction in the present day – in the case of psychotherapy having their focus on the person and attributes of the psycho-therapeutist; also that they can be subdivided into positive and negative types corresponding to mainly friendly and mainly hostile attitudes. In many cases the two attitudes are merged in roughly equal proportions giving rise to ambivalent transferences.

You may recall that when discussing the sparsity of direct analyses of delinquent cases, I pointed out that this was due to the fact that classical psycho-analysis could be successful only when the patient was sufficiently 'accessible'. And since accessibility, as is most clearly seen from its deficiency in the case of the psychoses, represents the capacity of the individual to form object attachments it follows that transference-capacity is one of the most accurate measures of it. Now if the psycho-analyst were to apply strictly the standards of accessibility he adopts in non-criminal cases of mental disorder he would be bound or at any rate inclined to reject all but a small proportion of delinquency cases on the grounds that the delinquent usually commences treatment in a state of negative or at least ambivalent transference. This, as experiment has shewn, would be an unduly pessimistic conclusion. It does not apply in the case of psycho-neurotic delinquency and in pubertal anti-social crises; and in any case, even in the non-delinquent psycho-neuroses (the most 'accessible' of all disorders) success turns not simply on the exploitation of the positive transference but the uncovering and liquidation of negative transferences.[1]

Already we can formulate the general conclusion that the elaborateness of a therapeutic technique is less important than the complications of the transference system existing in the individual offender. And with this criterion in reserve we can proceed to correlate different types of purposive delinquency therapy. These can be conveniently divided into institutional and ambulant types.

Listening the other day to one of your lectures on *penal institutions* I was encouraged to hear the speaker refer to the influence on the prisoner of the fact that in certain disciplinary respects the prison performs some of the functions of a home from home, the idea being of course that prison life repeats some of the situations of childhood. This merely reinforces the validity of the view that the prison regulations and conditions as such represent a form of transference therapy. The important question is the degree to which prison routine evokes positive or negative transferences. In the unreformed prisons of past times there was no doubt as to the answer; on balance the penal method was one of negative transference therapy. *Prison reform has in fact consisted in so arranging the system of contacts that some possibility exists of evoking the mostly concealed positive transferences of the inmates.*

At this point it is necessary to recall that the transferences of the patient are paralleled or offset by the counter-transferences of the therapeutist. These too can be divided into positive and negative varieties. By this rating the old punishment systems could be

---

[1] Incidentally this question of transference has considerable bearing on the desirability of making 'treatment' a *compulsory* condition of probation. In private practice compulsory treatment except in the case of minors usually fails.

equally well described as negative counter-transference therapies. For that matter the spontaneous reactions to delinquents of the community at large can be described as counter-transference-therapy: for the most part opprobrium is a form of negative counter-transference by means of which society seeks to counter the negative transferences expressed in the social offences of the delinquent. For many reasons belief in the virtues of negative counter-transference dies hard, leading, as it does, to neglect of the economic principle that the ego cannot grow or adjust so long as it is entangled in negative transferences derived from past experiences.

When we compare institutional methods of treatment with those employed at modern delinquency clinics or psychiatric centres (*ambulant treatment*), it will be apparent that whatever the methods employed they depend also on transference factors with this essential difference that no attempt is made to employ the penal sanctions, compulsions or restrictions that prevail in the institution whether it be a prison, an approved school or a Borstal institution; in other words the clinic openly eschews the methods of negative counter-transference therapy. It is then no exaggeration to say that everything that happens to a delinquent from the arrest or summons to the carrying out of sentence constitutes 'treatment' and that its results depend on the accurate recognition of the offender's transferences and their manipulation either in the direction of increasing the positive reactions or the liquidation of both positive and negative infantility. Of these the liquidation of infantile transferences is in the long run the most satisfactory device in that it permits the offender to make a re-adaptation to the regulations of society unhampered by past experiences. But it must be admitted that in the case of many delinquents this resolution of infantile transference is much harder to achieve than it is in disorders such as the psycho-neuroses.

At any rate I hope it will be clear that at present the greatest advance that can be made in the treatment of delinquents is so to train the personnel of the institution or clinic that they can recognize and regulate the effects of the offenders' transferences and of the counter-transferences they themselves produce in return. It is a commonplace of psycho-analysis that the best laid plans of the psycho-therapeutist can be frustrated by the negative counter-transferences exhibited, for example, by the patient's family and friends. *Mutatis mutandis* the same can be said of the treatment of delinquents of whatever variety. It is chastening to reflect how often the well-meant endeavours of prison psychiatrists are jeopardized by the negative counter-transferences to the prisoner of non-psychiatric personnel, a state of affairs which is unlikely to be remedied until the governors themselves, to say nothing of the general lay staff, are, as they should be, trained in at least the rudiments of clinical psychology.

Considerations of time preclude any close examination of the different varieties of treatment, under whatever names these may pass. Nor do I think that this is strictly speaking necessary on this occasion – for the main point I have to make is that *we cannot expect true advances in treatment, until we are in a position to make accurate diagnoses and modify our treatment accordingly*. This in turn will depend mainly on the work on predisposition I have indicated under the heading of research.

For the same reason I have not considered it necessary to enter into the various forms of applied psycho-analytical research, e.g. the advances that can be made by securing effective liaison between psycho-analysis and other disciplines. This would involve a too lengthy disquisition on the part that is beginning to be played by psycho-analysts in formulating personality tests, preparing social questionnaires and research projects. In any case there is so far little to report on these aspects of the problem except perhaps in the case of analytically oriented child observation which is steadily increasing and adds to the impetus of delinquency research or therapy; provided always the results are subjected to the process of interpretation.

Returning, in conclusion, to the main thesis of this paper, namely, that the main contributions of psycho-analysis to delinquency work lies in the application of psycho-analytical theories of mind in the fields of diagnosis and prevention and of such practical details as can be incorporated in the handling of delinquents, I should like to refer again to the question of the accessibility of the delinquent to analysis and to the fact that few direct analyses of delinquents have been undertaken. I would not like these views to be taken simply to imply a natural limitation to psycho-analytic work on delinquency. Naturally most psycho-therapeutists and for the matter of that most penal administrators have a preference for measures that promise success in the form of social rehabilitation. To make this also a guiding aim of research policy would, however, be both socially and scientifically, a counsel of despair. Despite the economic advantages of case-selection, it is still essential that *a psycho-analytic approach should be made whenever possible to advanced types of recidivism* – to the so-called Dartmoor type. Schizophrenia is notoriously difficult to heal by psychoanalysis yet psycho-analytical study of this state has added greatly to our knowledge not only of the psychoses but of the reactions of children, normal persons and of the less severe mental disorders. The same applies, I am convinced, to the study of delinquency. Expressing this in terms of advances in study and treatment, I would make bold to say that some of the most important advances in diagnosis and treatment are effected by study of our failures. When all is said, however, it remains true that psycho-analysis will tell us even more about delinquency by the study of non-delinquents, by the observation, that is, of mental activity in all its aspects, and in particular of the unconscious mechanisms that are responsible for character formation whether normal or abnormal.

PART III

PSYCHO-ANALYSIS AND CRIMINOLOGY: A POLITICAL SURVEY*

[1955]

In many branches of the International Psycho-Analytical Association, and certainly in the British Society up to the end of the Second World War, a policy of rigid seclusion and isolationism *vis-à-vis* other branches of psychology and sociology was pursued with not a little esoteric zest. To be sure, psycho-analysts had always been ready to invade other territories with or without sanction, but they had never been disposed to encourage reciprocity in this respect. In any case, these were mainly armchair invasions. With the exception of some scattered essays in psycho-analytical field-anthropology, they did not involve any special knowledge of the data and technical methods of the cognate sciences concerned. They were in fact mainly forays in search of evidence confirmatory of psycho-analytic conclusions.

This isolation has been dictated in the main by the fear that too close intercommunication with other more superficial and less dynamic disciplines would lead to a watering down of psycho-analytical principles and a bowdlerization of psycho-analytical conclusions – a fear which, though no doubt defensive in origin, was not altogether unjustified. For, after twenty-five years' experience of multi-disciplined research, it is still my opinion that when psycho-analysis enters into co-operation with other sciences for purposes of research, it ends by scaling down its standards to meet the necessities of the most superficial discipline represented in the team.

This self-protective attitude does not, however, account for the marked abstention of psycho-analysts from work in the criminological field. It is after all only in the past few years that criminology has had any claim to be called a science; even so it has as yet no coherent, integrated theory and such technical methods as it has

---

* An abbreviated version of this paper was given at the 19th International Psycho-Analytical Congress, Geneva, 24–28 July, 1955; it was first published in the *Int. J. Psycho-Anal.*, 37, 311–7, 1956.

pursued have never constituted a threat to psycho-analysis, although they have thrown into relief some of the limitations of pure psycho-analysis as a psycho-therapeutic system. I need hardly quote here the thoroughly deserved strictures passed by the ortho-psychiatrist and criminologist Ben Karpman [1] on the absence of *organized* work on criminology on the part of psycho-analysts, a criticism which has been very temperately expressed by Carroll [2] when he describes many psycho-analytical case studies of delinquency as 'partial reports of an intriguing case encountered in the course of a preoccupying practice'. From my own editorial experience I would have said that in Britain for one clinical paper offered on delinquency there are at least twenty written by social, educational and general psychologists; and, at that, the clinical paper is usually the work of a non-analytical psychiatrist, using frequently psycho-analytical concepts of the most dilute variety. The truth is that psycho-analysis has acquired much more prestige in criminology than is justified by the amount of actual work it has done in the field. Apart from a few pioneering studies and some fragmentary records mostly of non-criminal cases its influence is largely *indirect*, through the percolation to the field of delinquency of some metapsychological generalizations on infantile development, unconscious mechanisms and institutions, and unconsciously motivated behaviour.

With this preamble I should like to divide the present brief survey into two parts, the first dealing with psycho-analytical contributions to criminology and the second with the relations to psycho-analysis of other sciences concerned with delinquency.

i. CLINICAL ASPECTS

First of all regarding *clinical material:* it should be recognized that from early adolescence onwards criminality is for all practical purposes a closed field access to which can be obtained only by grace and favour of the penal administration. Psycho-analysts rarely see or study at first hand 'real criminals' or recidivists or, for that matter, approved school and Borstal cases; yet it is as important that they should have first-hand institutional experience up to and including Dartmoor and Broadmoor types, as that psycho-analytical psychiatrists should spend some time on the staff of mental hospitals. To be sure they can attend general psychiatric centres and see there a few selected cases of delinquency; and, of course, by taking posts in child guidance clinics they can get excellent experience in the study of criminal predisposition and less satisfactory experience in juvenile delinquency; for under existing laws many so-called juvenile delinquents do not belong strictly to a criminal group. This is best exemplified by that group of children known to the juvenile courts as 'in need of care or protection', which includes a number of cases of 'pre-delinquency' but is otherwise mainly non-delinquent. The category is in fact more suitable as a child-guidance label than as designating a penal group.

Next as to *discrimination and selection of cases*. The mere fact that such analytical papers as are written usually make use of general captions, 'juvenile delinquency' or 'crime', shows how little discrimination is exercised in the clinical approach to these omnibus, descriptive, and socially defined groups. This is borne out by the fact that psycho-analysts when writing of crime do not seem to have made up their minds whether they are dealing with pathological crime, with crime that is associated with psychopathological manifestations, or with the behaviour of comparatively normal persons with a low threshold to stress and an equally low threshold to temptation. Sometimes, as in the case of sexual offences, they seem to recognize pathological groups: in other instances they appear to apply their views to criminal conduct as a whole without any discrimination of pathological factors and applying only classical psycho-analytical etiologies.

Classification

It is due primarily to this undefined approach that psycho-analytical *classifications* of delinquent types are so inadequate and so confusing, and that as a rule it is impossible to extract from analytical papers any specific series of etiologies appropriate to different types of crime, any satisfactory clinical gradings or prognostic groupings, and of course any reliable statistics of results of treatment applicable to the numerous sub-groups into which delinquency states are divisible. There is, in fact, a remarkable contrast between the clinical groupings followed, for example, at the Portman Clinic in London, a clinic with an eclectic staff (which now, I am glad to say, includes a small number of psycho-analysts), and the metapsychological categories on which most of the admittedly rudimentary psycho-analytical classifications have been based and which on the whole do more to give rise to clinical confusion than to promote understanding. An exception comes from the juvenile field where Bowlby [3] has applied to one particular form of crime, viz., juvenile theft, mainly psychopathological criteria, which, however, overlap with descriptive emotional standards and merge too closely with normal factors. This overlapping of delinquent and normal types must persist until we are able to apply tests that isolate the pre-delinquent from the pathological delinquent and both from the facultative delinquent, who is under unstressful circumstances law-abiding.

The most striking evidence of confusion in classification is to be found in analytical approaches to the concept of *psychopathy*. Sometimes analysts seem to equate criminality with psychopathy, a tendency which, incidentally, ignores the existence of non-delinquent psychopathy. But even when they do not, there is no attempt to distinguish characteristic sub-groups of psychopathy. Admittedly the term itself is not an illuminating one, although the condition was beautifully described by Prichard over 100 years ago, but in the absence of more precise structural and dynamic gradings it has its practical uses and remains a standing reproach to psycho-analysis, which in my opinion is alone able to provide the necessary etiological and characterological standards, but so far has not done so.

The bearing of all this is I think obvious. However much confusion may have existed during the early days of psycho-analysis regarding the clinical range of the psycho-neuroses, subsequent investigations and etiologies were concerned with *distinct psychoneurotic entities*. In other words the clinical focus of investigation was established and sub-groups were accurately distinguished. To that extent the number of *clinical variables* in the research situation was reduced. In the psycho-analytic approach to delinquency the situation is quite otherwise. The number of clinical variables is unlimited. Etiological generalizations are advanced without any specific clinical typing. Even if we agree that the psycho-analytical method itself does *not* vary – a proposition that does not accord very well with the facts – the number of etiological and clinical variables is such as to render it impossible to arrive at any statistically significant psycho-analytical conclusions regarding delinquency and its sub-groups.

Etiology

The number of *etiological variables* is increased by the fact that acute differences of opinion on etiology exist within psycho-analysis itself. But even if no such differences of theoretical opinion existed, it would have to be admitted that so far *psycho-analytic etiologies display two antithetical tendencies;* first, to apply the same unconscious formula in all cases, and, second, to vary widely the emphasis laid on etiological factors according to the theoretical predilections of the observer or the type of case he observes. Added to which confusion arises from lack of adequate distinction between unconscious mechanisms and pathological formations which latter present *inter alia* a defensive exaggeration of unconscious mechanisms. This is best illustrated in the non-delinquent field by the confusion of manic or paranoid types of *character reaction* which may exist in otherwise normal persons, with manic or paranoid *symptom constructions* in which introjection and projection processes respectively are pathologically exaggerated. Similarly in the case of delinquency; psycho-analytical observers are inclined to apply the same standards to adolescent cases of compulsive theft, to pubertal crises of stealing, to the obsessive stealing of children in the latency period and to the sporadic stealing of younger children who in fact are not particularly abnormal.

In this connection, it is important to record a recent tendency which threatens to undermine one of the established findings of psycho-analysis. The outstanding etiological merit of psycho-analysis lies in the distinction of early *unconscious predisposing factors* (so-called endopsychic factors) from *constitutional* and *precipitating* factors in symptom-formation. With the development of the child guidance movement and the infiltration of psycho-analysis by child psychiatry, we find that for all practical purposes the sociologist with his environmental and descriptive measures has invaded the field of familial development. To be sure he may call himself a child ortho-psychiatrist or sociometrist or even a child analyst, but his values remain superficial, and have given rise to a number of *etiological clichés*. To the journalistic concept of the 'broken home' we have now added the traumatic concept of 'separation anxiety'. It requires no great mental effort to assume that traumatic separation in early infantile years must have a traumatic effect; but to convert this into a *direct* determining environmental factor in delinquency is to neglect the central proposition of psycho-analysis that these predisposing elements acquire their pathological force and form in accordance with the effect of their passage through the varying phases of the unconscious Oedipus situation.

Moreover if pathological delinquency is to be regarded as in the main an *object-relation disorder*, a view for which there is much to be said, we must really distinguish between transient crises of disorder due mainly to *functional stress* [4], and *symptomatic* reactions to Oedipal *conflict*. Here again many psycho-analytical observers fail to distinguish delinquencies due to pubertal stress from those which are due to Oedipus conflict and which develop an organized symptomatic form that tends to persist well into the twenties. To be sure, unconscious conflict exists in all cases, delinquent and non-delinquent, but it does not in all cases give rise to a defensive *symptom construction*. Our new psycho-analytical, familial sociologists must recapture the original psycho-analytical significance of two concepts, (*a*) unconscious conflict, and (*b*) unconscious predisposition to symptom-formation, and they must be ready to distinguish between the effects of these two distinct factors with or without the additional precipitating factor of stress. Otherwise they will remain nothing more or less than environmentalists or peripheralists, certainly not psychologists of the unconscious.

Admitted that it is easy to err in the opposite direction and, for example, by the use of generic terms such as 'super-ego' to arrive at etiological generalizations regarding the presence or absence of super-ego formation in delinquency, which if valid at all (for the view that in certain cases no super-ego development at all occurs is extremely questionable), apply only to certain aspects, facets or phases of super-ego formation. Confusing as this tendency is, it becomes a positive obstruction to clear thinking when, as is often the case, these undifferentiated generalizations are made the basis of classifications that fall apart when applied to the clinical complications and variety of end-products found in delinquency states.

The position is best illustrated by Friedlander's essay on classification, an attempt which, incidentally, had the considerable advantage of being based on extensive first-hand observation and treatment of delinquent children [5]. For all practical purposes

Friedlander's tripartite classification can be reduced to one omnibus group of *anti-social characters;* her second and third groups, viz., ego-disturbances of organic origin (particularly mental defect) and of psychotic origin respectively, cover only a small proportion of the offenders sent by courts to delinquency clinics. Her further analysis of the anti-social group resolves itself into an estimation of 'the relative strength of the three domains of the mind, the Id, the ego and the super-ego'; briefly, strong unmodified instinctual urges, a weak ego and lack of independence of the super-ego. Subdivisions of this omnibus group are then effected in accordance with the degree to which (*a*) environmental stress, (*b*) neurotic conflict, and (*c*) 'acting-out' of neurotic phantasy combine with varying degrees of anti-social character formation to form distinct delinquent groups.

Now it can be argued that each of these three secondary factors also owes its importance to the 'relative strength of the three domains of the mind', for even in the case of environmental stress, the effect of psychic trauma depends on the specific sensitiveness of the *endopsychic* receptors. From this point of view the classification is based on metapsychological categories that are not specific to delinquency and does not correlate etiology with specific groups of end-products (delinquent behaviour). Even so it may be vitiated at any moment should Parliament decide to strike sexual perversions from the criminal calendar, saving always where they contravene laws governing public indecency, seduction, or violence. In any case, and as the study of non-delinquent mental disorders clearly shows, it is essential to regulate the classification of disorders or groups of disorders in the first instance by reference to their clinical manifestations or syndromes. The rôle of unconscious etiology in classification is mainly to correlate manifestations which, though differing in their clinical form, yet belong to the same level of psycho-pathological development (as, for example, in the case of anxiety hysteria and conversion hysteria). Friedlander would in fact have fared better had she been content to make her main category, viz., anti-social characters, a separate *sub*-group and have proceeded to subdivide this further into special varieties of character disorder having a specific relation to specific varieties of offence, as, for example, certain psychotic characters, psychopathic characters, and even some neurotic characters (the hysterical character, for example). This would have left her free to elaborate other groups of delinquency having *specific symptom-formations* with or without a special anti-social *character;* for example, the 'pre-psychoses' or incipient psychoses, the first manifestation of which is sometimes a delinquent episode. Psycho-analysis has unique qualifications to produce such working classifications, although, as I have said, it has not yet done so, largely because it has not yet studied the field closely enough.

CRIME, NEUROSES AND PSYCHOSES

Time permits only the barest mention of other problems in the relation of psycho-analysis to delinquency, in particular the tendency to apply standards derived from analysis of the psycho-neuroses to a variety of delinquent states, and thereby to establish an arbitrary and restricted correlation between the pure neuroses and the delinquencies. That there is a general antithetical relation between the psycho-neuroses and delinquent states is true enough; just as there is a general antithetical relationship between the psycho-neuroses and the perversions (which, it must be repeated, are only criminal offences by courtesy of the prejudices and moral codes of the community at large). But this does not mean that the sole etiological dilemma of criminology is to explain why some persons in a state of conflict take to crime and others to neurosis. Such a view would contract and restrict the etiological problem in a totally unjustified way. We now have reason to know that Freud's dictum regarding the perversions, viz., that they represent the obverse or 'negative' of the neuroses, requires amplification. Some primitive perversions are the obverse of a psychotic symptom-construction [6] and others belong to the category of psychopathic manifestations. The same may be said regarding pathological offences. Some primitive forms of pathological crime, some murders, for example, are not merely *symptoms* of a psychosis but *symptom-equivalents* of a psychosis, and in all probability spare the individual the psychic effort necessary to produce a clinical psychosis. There is every reason to believe that the calendar of offences could be arranged and classified in an ascending (or descending) series in accordance with the degree of equivalence they manifest to a developmental series of clinical symptom-formations ranging from the psychoses and psychotic characters through the addictions and psycho-neuroses to merge finally with the simpler forms of sexual and social inhibition. In any case the concept of a 'pure psycho-neurotic delinquency' has always seemed an etiological contradiction in terms. That some delinquencies exhibit pathological mechanisms which are also to be found in certain psycho-neuroses is beyond dispute, as witness the obsessional features of kleptomania; that other forms may run in association with neurotic symptom-formations is also evident, particularly in the case of juvenile delinquency. To this extent the grouping is heuristically justified. But it would be advantageous to review the group of 'psycho-neurotic delinquencies' closely and to place in a separate category those delinquent pseudo-neuroses which are essentially ego disorders having a neurotic equivalence, meaning by equivalence the existence of *similar defence mechanisms* and an etiology stemming from the *same development level* as that of the neuroses. By confusing certain delinquent states with the psycho-neuroses proper the psycho-analyst is coming closer than he suspects to Eysenck's [7] concept of *neuroticism*, which is a purely descriptive, non-dynamic category and overrides the psycho-analytical concept of a special and qualitatively distinct form of *symptom-formation*.

Psycho-Analytic Therapy

Turning now to the question of *treatment*, without some reference to which no survey of the relation of pure psycho-analysis to criminology would be complete, it must be remembered that by pure psycho-analysis is meant the classical Freudian technique built up on experience of the analysis of the psycho-neuroses and etiologically equivalent disorders, e.g. some sexual inhibitions. In the first place the general conclusion may be stated that if psycho-analysis were to be applied *secundum artem* to delinquency only a few selected cases would ultimately qualify for inclusion in the category of psycho-analytical treatment. No doubt psycho-analytical *principles* are frequently applied in general psychotherapy, but that does not necessarily constitute a psycho-analysis, nor should it be described as such. I have rarely come across true completed psycho-analyses in criminology. It is true that in some cases of delinquency and pre-delinquency, occurring in early childhood and throughout the latency period, something approximating to a classical child analysis can occasionally be observed. But whether it is complete or not is just as open to question as it is in the case of analysis of the non-delinquent disorders of childhood. As I have maintained on other occasions [8], the status of child-analysis, even when carried out according to strictly Freudian principles (and this nowadays is an increasingly rare event), is by no means firmly established. More often than not the analysis is discontinued rather than completed in the sense of analysing out or resolving the transference.

However this may be, there is no question that in the more serious cases of delinquency occurring after the latency period, the peculiar nature of the transference and the conditions under which the analysis must be carried out with true criminal psychopaths, organized criminals, recidivists, and institutionalized criminals necessitate modifications in the classical Freudian technique which most certainly prejudice the 'pure' analytic status of the treatment. This fact has one important consequence, viz., that as analysis is rarely brought to completion in cases of delinquency, psycho-analytic *researches* on delinquency are rarely completed, or indeed very illuminating, certainly as regards the pathological process.

ii. PSYCHO-ANALYSIS AND COGNATE SCIENCES

Considering now the second part of this survey, viz., the relation of psycho-analysis to those other branches of psychological and sociological science which also concern themselves with delinquency, it is convenient to begin by considering its relation to ortho-psychiatry. Psycho-analysis, through its observational studies of infants and children, has in recent years become more ortho-psychiatric in tendency. And up to a point this is a desirable turn of events, for it helps to underline the fact that as far as the plausibility of reconstructions of the first few years of mental development are concerned, the evidence is based on interpretations of *observations* rather than on direct analysis. But as I have already suggested it has also led to over-emphasis of environmental and, in the familial sense, sociological factors in the assessment of causation. Increasingly, clinical records of juvenile delinquents, even those published by psycho-analysts, concern themselves with environmental and mostly traumatic factors in the early familial setting. This means of course that the endopsychic factor is being to some extent overlaid by the precipitating environmental factor in predisposition. This change in orientation has important methodological consequences, including the introduction of *factorial psychology* and *statistical techniques*. And, since factorial psychology can thrive only on narrowly definable descriptive standards, it leads to a very considerable extent to the elimination of *interpretation*, a method which, however open to error, is and will remain the indispensable instrument of psycho-analytical research.

General Psychology

More interesting, however, is the relation of psycho-analysis to *general psychology*. In this connection there are two aspects of importance, one to methodology and the other to the theory of mind. To take the theoretical issue first: although few general psychologists have anything worth calling a theory of mind, there are signs that they are now endeavouring to rise to the belated occasion. A recent and in its way extremely ambitious attempt in this direction can be attributed to the Maudsley School in London. And although in effect it is based on a hotch-potch of Pavlovian neuro-psychiatric *conditioning*, of a *factorial examination of descriptive criteria* (which is responsible for the bastard concept of the continuum, a Kretschmerian product that runs counter to all metapsychology and dynamic psycho-pathology) together with a sprinkling of *psychiatric concepts mostly of a Jungian type*, there is no doubt that it is taking shape and may well set back a good deal the spread of psycho-analytical principles in psychiatric circles.

Interestingly enough, and perhaps unfortunately, the descriptive phenomenology of delinquency lends itself more readily to the concept of the continuum from normal to abnormal than the clinical syndromes of the psycho-neuroses lend themselves to the concept of a continuum between normal and psycho-neurotic persons, or the clinical syndromes of the psychoses lend themselves to the concept of a 'psychoticism' continuum. The concept of neuroticism wrecks itself on the conversion hysterias, to say nothing of anxiety neuroses and the neurasthenias; the concept of psychoticism is stultified by the existence of the pure hypochondrias. But if we are content with purely descriptive standards, the existence of undetected delinquency amongst the normal population, of delinquency cases not 'carried through' by the police (i.e. cases in which owing to lack of convincing evidence no prosecution is initiated), of 'normal' crime and of convicted cases of delinquency associated with various disordered states (pseudo-neuroses, psychopathic states, alcoholism and the psychoses) would seem to suggest the existence of a 'delinquency continuum' from the normal to the abnormal. If, however, such descriptive standards were accepted, we would have to jettison the qualitative concept of unconscious symptom-formation, with the sole and meagre consolation that a delinquency continuum would invalidate the concept of neuroticism and psychoticism, unless of course delinquency manifestations were recognized as a unit common to both series. All of which merely points the necessity of establishing an accurate classification and specific etiology of the various pathological delinquencies, a necessity which has been stressed in the first part of this survey.

Personality Tests

It is in this connection that the issue of *methodology* becomes most acute, centring as it does round the uses of various *personality and other tests*. To be sure the factorial psychologist does not think very highly of those personality tests which are favoured by clinical psychologists and which depend to a greater or lesser degree on interpretation; and he endeavours to clip their wings to a more foolproof statistical pattern. But the vulnerability of the clinical personality test depends for the most part on the fact that the psycho-analyst has so far failed to contribute adequately to *test* and *questionnaire methods* of psychological approach. For it will scarcely be disputed that the soundness of a test depends less on the range and controllability of examination than on the soundness of the basic criteria employed in formulating it. It is of course somewhat mortifying to the psycho-analyst with his haystack of unconscious mechanisms and motivations to find that the usefulness of some tests is in direct ratio to the descriptive and general value of the items used in scoring. That is certainly true of some *prediction tests* which, following the work of the Gluecks [9], have come to stay in the field of delinquency. The Glueck prediction scales are based on as many as 402 distinct factors which are reduced to three sets, each comprising five elements. The 'character structure' group includes: assertiveness, defence, suspiciousness, destructiveness, and emotional lability; the 'psychiatric' scale comprises: adventurousness, extraversion in action, suggestibility, stubbornness, and emotional instability; the third or 'social background' group is based mainly on the degree of affection, discipline, and cohesiveness existing in the family. Taken separately none of these factors is a specific indicator of future delinquency; yet it is clear that, for example, the character set, when quantitatively scored, would *tend* to distinguish delinquent from all save psychotic reactions. The neurotic person though often emotionally labile is not as a rule assertive, defiant, or destructive, and his occasional suspiciousness is more an anxiety defence against object-contact than an indication of aggressiveness towards objects. So that fundamentally the Glueck system, although apparently and essentially descriptive, can in the long run be correlated with etiological formulæ. From the psycho-analytical point of view, however, its main deficiency is a negative one, viz., that it indicates neither the main clinical group in which a prospective delinquent will ultimately fall, nor the specific etiological factor determining each end-product.

Here is surely a task for psycho-analysis, provided always a hierarchy of statistically and clinically definable unconscious factors can be established. But the issue goes further. Comparison of non-analytical psychiatric examinations with test techniques seems to indicate that on the whole the test examinations, within their own limitations, are less subject to variation than the clinical assessments [10]. The question obviously arises: would a psychoanalytically conducted examination prove more reliable? So far little or no work has been done on these lines; but it is encouraging to find that in Britain the ball has been set rolling by Augusta Bonnard [11] who has produced and applied a series of clinical prognostic questionnaires based on psycho-analytical concepts which have prediction value for delinquency; while Grygier [12], Krout and Tabin [13] have attempted to leaven the more academic personality tests with units of a psycho-analytic type. It is important that progress should be made along these psychoanalytical lines, for as I have pointed out delinquency is a study imposed on the mental specialist by society: it will not dance attendance on psycho-analysis. Mohammed must go to the mountain.

Two political conclusions can be drawn from this survey: the first is that, although his interest in delinquency is secondary to his interest in the conditions of which it is a manifestation, the psycho-analyst must nevertheless condescend to examine at first hand the different states which are subsumed under the heading of crime. The second is that the uses of psycho-analysis in research and in methods of prevention far outweigh its uses in pure form as a method of treating pathological delinquency.

REFERENCES

1. KARPMAN, B.: *Proceedings of the Second Congress, International Association of Criminology* (Paris, Presses Universitaires de France, 1950, p. 73).
2. CARROLL, D.: *Proceedings of the Second Congress, International Association of Criminology* (Paris, Presses Universitaires de France, 1950, p. 73).
3. BOWLBY, J.: 'Forty-four Juvenile Thieves', *Int. J. Psycho-Anal.*, 1944, **25** (London, Baillière, Tindall and Cox, 1946.) 'Some Pathological Processes Engendering Early Mother-Child Separation', *Problems of Infancy and Childhood* (New York, Josiah Macy, 1954).
4. GLOVER, E.: 'On the Desirability of Isolating a "Functional" (Psycho-somatic) Group of Delinquent Disorders', *Brit. J. Delinq.*, 1950, **1**, 104, reprinted in *On the Early Development of Mind*, Imago Publishing Co., 1956.
5. FRIEDLANDER, K.: *The Psycho-analytical Approach to Juvenile Delinquency* (London, Kegan Paul, 1947).
6. GLOVER, E.: 'The Relation of Perversion-Formation to the Development of Reality-Sense', *Int. J. Psycho-Anal.*, 1933, **14**, 486, reprinted in *On the Early Development of Mind*, Imago Publishing Co., 1956.
7. EYSENCK, H. J.: *Dimensions of Personality* (London, Routledge, 1947); *The Scientific Study of Personality* (London, Routledge, 1952).
8. GLOVER, E.: 'The Indications for Psycho-Analysis', *J. Ment. Sci.*, 1954, **100**, No. 419, reprinted in *On the Early Development of Mind*, Imago Publishing Co., 1956.
9. GLUECK, E. T.: 'Predicting Juvenile Delinquency', *Brit. J. Delinq.*, 1952, **2**, 4.
10. THOMPSON, R. E.: 'A Validation of Glueck Social Prediction Scale for Proneness to Delinquency', *Brit. J. Delinq.*, 1953, **3**, 4.
11. BONNARD, A.: 'Clinical Standards of Prognosis in Delinquency', *Proceedings of the Third Congress of the International Criminological Association*, 1955.
12. GRYGIER, T. R.: 'Infantile Complexes, their Measurement and Significance for Social Psychology', *Bulletin of the British Psychological Society*, 1955, **26**, 56.
13. KROUT, M. E., and KROUT-TABIN, J. C.: 'Measuring Personality in Developmental Terms: the Personal Preference Scale', *Genetic Psychology Monographs*, 1954, **50**, 289.

VII. SOCIO-LEGAL

Part I   The Concept of 'Recidivism'
Part II   The M'Naghten Rules
Part III   The Prevention of Pathological Crime
Part IV   Psychiatric Aspects of Capital Punishment

SECTION VII

SOCIO-LEGAL

PART I

THE CONCEPT OF 'RECIDIVISM'*

[1955]

The study of recidivism, and of the methods of prediction which serve the preliminary purposes of this study, is unquestionably of great importance to criminology, may indeed prove to be of incalculable value in the field of prevention. For if methods of prediction can be as freely applied in the search for 'pre-delinquents' (under which caption we may also include 'larval', 'potential', 'occult', 'latent' or 'predisposed' cases) as apparently they can be in estimating the future conduct of proven delinquents, there is no reason why preventive effort should not be applied where it is most needed and has most chance of success, namely, during that period in the development of children when they become predisposed to crime. At the very least such a course would check some of the improvident expenditure of time, money and energy on undirected or misdirected efforts at prevention which, more often than not, are based on simple preconceptions or even guesses at the probable causes of crime. Research on the subject would at any rate pay for itself.

Now if our interest in recidivism were confined to its descriptive and social aspects there would be no great need to examine the concept too closely. We could accept it as a penological term of limited sociological utility, intended to suggest that some criminal tendencies are more obstinate than others or, more dispassionately perhaps, that some cases continue to offend in spite of the threats or interventions of the law. As soon, however, as predictive methods are exploited to govern *disposal* of potential recidivists we are under

---

* First published in the *Brit. J. Delinq.*, 6, 116–25, 1955, under the title 'Prognosis or Prediction ? a Psychiatric Examination of the Concept of "Recidivism" '.

obligation to scrutinize closely the exact connotation of the term. And this in turn involves examination of the criteria adopted respectively by psychiatrists, psychologists, sociologists and penologists, not to mention the standpoint of the statistician. The slightest consideration of the subject will show that, although representatives of these different disciplines may combine their energies and merge their principles on a number of criminological occasions, either diagnostic, therapeutic or preventative, the use of the term 'recidivism' is calculated to bring out essential differences in approach which have become somewhat obscured by the recent expansion of multi-disciplined (team) research.

This is by no means a regrettable contingency; for it serves no useful purpose to gloss over the fact that in certain respects the approaches of, for example, the psychiatrist and the penologist are poles apart. Granted that in some instances they may render common service to the needs of the community for protection or of the individual offender for rehabilitation, yet on such matters as punishment or deterrence differences are bound to arise between them. Indeed, before considering the purely psychiatric aspects of recidivism, it is well to be clear as to the differences between the approach on the one hand of the forensic sociologist, social psychologist and psychologist and on the other of the forensic psychiatrist, also to ascertain what their respective positions are in relation to penology.

In the first place, *the psychiatrist, as psychiatrist, is bound by the professional traditions of his speciality to confine his activities to the cure or amelioration of disordered mental states*. True, there are some few psychiatrists who are prepared to maintain the virtues in some criminal cases of punishment, more rarely of corporal punishment. When they do so, however, they are overstepping their professional boundaries, and in any case their utterances, unless based on convincing researches, have no more validity than the opinions of the penologist or, for the matter of that, of the common citizen. Obviously, therefore, the first step in examining the concept of recidivism is to discover whether it is adapted to the diagnostic, prognostic and therapeutic usages of psychiatry or whether it is fundamentally a penological concept having a moral cast and an implicit social bias.

If we are to judge from court practice in this country it is not hard to establish the implicit moral connotation and social bias of the term. In the eyes of the law the recidivist is regarded as in some degree a 'hardened' criminal on the way to becoming an 'incorrigible rogue', who cannot be spared the more severe penal and deterrent disciplines at the disposal of the court. Psychiatrists who take up work at delinquency clinics are soon made aware of this fact. Cases which have been put on probation on condition of psychiatric treatment but which, owing to the compulsive or otherwise disordered nature of their anti-social symptoms, are likely to repeat the offence, either in the early stages of treatment or during any intercurrent emotional crisis, are liable on their reappearance in court to be denied further opportunity of ambulant treatment and despatched forthwith to institutions which, however labelled and however staffed, are essentially penal institutions. And one more 'failure' is recorded in that particular court to the discredit of forensic psychiatry. Yet, if we assume for the purposes of argument that the case has been well selected by the psychiatrist in the first instance, this increase in sentence merely substitutes retributive punishment for incomplete treatment.

To be sure, the tendency to get angry with refractory cases and to react to them as if they were wicked is not confined to the judiciary. It is not unknown in the fields of organic or psychological medicine. But as a rule the organic physician and the psychiatrist would, if pressed, admit that these reactions are subjective and retributive. As far as is humanly possible they try to control or eliminate them; and in any case they do not seek to justify them on the grounds of social expediency. No such restraint need be recognized or exercised by the penologist who, without self-questioning, can plead social expediency in extenuation of his appeal to punishment and discipline.

This professional bias on the part of the psychiatrist permits a ready distinction between his approach to delinquency and that of his co-workers, the social psychologist, the sociologist and the general psychologist. For we need not on this occasion concern ourselves too much with the position of the statistician, who is simply a maid of all work applying his mathematical techniques and statistical controls without any obligation whatsoever to consider the individual or social issues which underlie the data he examines.

To begin with the social psychologist: it is clear that he has a much broader and of necessity more courageous approach to the problem of crime than has the pure psychiatrist. This is no doubt due in part to his lack of intimate contact with the individual offender, to say nothing of his lack of equipment with which to approach him. But in the main it is due to the fact that it is not incumbent on the social psychologist to accept the professional standards, aims and ethics of the psychiatrist. When he approaches the subject of crime he is compelled to approach it as a whole. He need not, indeed cannot, take refuge, as the psychiatrist usually does, behind the unchallengeable position that breaches of the law due to mental or physical disorder should be treated rather than punished. When he makes suggestions regarding the causes of crime or the classification and disposal of criminal offenders, these must be such as apply to the criminal population as a whole. No doubt if the social psychologist were in the habit of giving evidence in court he would find even more difficulty than does the psychiatrist in influencing the bench. Fortunately for him, he is not called upon to do so and exercises his influence on penal practice largely through the prestige he has gained in administrative circles. As far as punishment and deterrence are concerned, his views, unless based on controlled investigation, have no more prescriptive authority than those of the man in the street. Nevertheless, not being bound by medical ethics, he is free to support penal measures on the score of social necessity.

The sociologist, by virtue of his training, technique and angle of approach, has even less contact with the pathological aspects of individual crime, and his conclusions, like those of the social psychologist, are consequently applicable to crime in general. A student of community or group life, such ameliorative urges as he may possess are motivated primarily by concern for the stability of the group. He, too, is free to support penological measures on the score of social necessity. That in many cases he refrains from so doing is in fact a tribute to his common humanity rather than to his scientific predilections.

The general psychologist is in slightly different case. He does possess techniques of approach to individual crime (mostly, it is true, of a descriptive, characterological type), and in recent years has been increasingly ready to use them in the interests of the individual offender. On the other hand, he has not the overriding interest in and understanding of *pathology* which governs the approach of the psychiatrist. As a general psychologist, he is under no obligation to distinguish 'pathological offenders' from types in which no gross abnormality can be detected. When he does so, as in the application of various personality tests, he is simply acting, whether he knows it or not, as a lay psychiatric assistant. Otherwise his approach is of necessity a general one, without discrimination of disorder, and his conclusions and recommendations, like those of the sociologist and social psychologist, must be applicable to the criminal population as a whole, that is to say, without benefit of psychiatry. He too is free to support the use of penal measures although in fact, like the forensic sociologist and social psychologist, he seldom does so.

It is essential to emphasize this freedom of the social psychiatrist, sociologist and general psychologist from professional restrictions, because it accounts for the fact that the term 'recidivism' is less obnoxious to them than it is to the dynamic psychiatrist, whose approach to delinquency is governed throughout by concepts of disordered or pathological function, and whose primary interest is in the cure of the pathological offender. It accounts also for the fact that their standing with administrative authorities is higher than that of the psychiatrist. It is indeed more than probable that in the long run the sociologist and social psychologist will do more than the psychiatrist to bring about enlightened measures of disposal applicable to the criminal population as a whole.

Turning now to the history of forensic psychiatry, we find what at first sight appears to be a confusing course of events. For it would appear that, prison medical officers apart, the pioneers in forensic psychiatry were more concerned with the motivation of crime as a whole than with the purely pathological type of persistent offender. This was due in part to the influence of psycho-analytical thinking. During the past thirty years or so psychiatrists have been more influenced by psycho-analytical concepts and principles than most of them would be prepared to admit. And psycho-analytical views on crime were not based on first-hand studies of criminals but were formed at second-hand by sporadic study of such criminal tendencies as might be observed during the analysis of non-criminal disorders. Moreover, psycho-analysts, being specially interested in the influence of unconscious mental mechanisms on human behaviour, tended, and still tend, to apply their principles to *any* form of persistent criminal behaviour, not just to those cases where manifest mental or physical disorder can be established. This explains why court reports presented by psycho-analysts tend to be discounted by magistrates, who are neither persuaded of the existence of unconscious mechanisms nor prepared to accept them as extenuating factors in all and sundry cases of criminal conduct.

Despite this indirect psycho-analytical influence, and no doubt goaded also by long and bitter experience as an expert witness, *the forensic psychiatrist has tended in recent years to confine his diagnostic and therapeutic energies to cases where definite evidence of the existence of pathological factors in criminal conduct can be established.* He has in fact, and in the face of strong opposition, worked to amplify the doctrine regarding criminal responsibility which exists in larval form in the M'Naghten Rules, and to extend its reference from cases of murder to all pathological crime. In this respect his position is unchallengeable and there can be no doubt that in this particular field his authority and influence will increase, except possibly in the case of psychopathy. In the meantime it is sufficient to note that the majority of forensic psychiatrists are reluctant to advocate the application of their findings to anything outside 'pathological crime'. Within that strictly limited field they are concerned with the diagnosis and prognosis of disorders which, although as yet not too well defined, have this in common: that they give rise to anti-social conduct. These conditions forensic psychiatrists propose and, given the opportunity, attempt to treat to the best of their ability.

All of which leads to the main point of this argument, namely, that *to the forensic psychiatrist the term 'recidivism' and, to the extent that prediction is concerned with the forecasting of recidivism, the term 'prediction' are, with one possible exception, redundant, misleading and tendentious.*

To start with the exception: the psychiatrist might be prepared to accept the term 'recidivism' as a description of pathological cases in which the disorder is *episodic, intermittent* or *relapsing* in nature, in the same way as he accepts the cycles and intermissions of manic-depressive insanity or the repetitions of obsessional neurosis. Even so he is chary of making clinical use of a term which has so many social and moral connotations and which tends in court practice to bring about the abrogation of what he considers to be the treatment of election, namely, psychiatric treatment of one form or another.

Excluding for the moment the consideration of such episodic cases, the situation can be simply stated as follows. There is no more reason to describe the persistence of symptoms of pathological delinquency as recidivism than to say that tubercular symptoms which persist beyond the average time range or in spite of various measures of treatment are signs of recidivism. It would be equally absurd to describe the victim of a skin disease as a recidivist because his rash continued after tentative steps had been taken to control it. If the diagnosis has been accurate enough and a careful prognosis arrived at, the physician should be in a position to indicate with rough accuracy what the duration of the disorder will be, e.g. whether it will heal spontaneously or by first intention, whether it will require treatment, how long that treatment should last and whether it will end in cure, or some degree of improvement, or leave the patient *in status quo*. *He has no need of a special term to describe chronic or terminal phases.* If on the other hand the case is likely to be intermittent or episodic, he should again be in a position to say so; indeed, in such instances it is incumbent on him to warn both the patient and those responsible for him of the intermittent nature of the disorder and to insist that the proper treatment should be continued in spite of or even precisely because of what might appear to be 'relapses'.

To be sure, he recognizes the right of the community to be protected against the depredations of the intermittent or chronic delinquent, but he is entitled to claim that the alleged 'relapsing' case should not be *punished* for his pathological relapses and that the degree of supervision necessitated by considerations of social safety should not exceed that necessary to secure social safety and should permit the continuance of full measures of treatment. In place of the term 'prediction' he would therefore substitute the clinical concept of 'prognosis'.

To the argument that there is no essential difference between prognosis and prediction it can only be replied that the *essential purpose of prognosis is to guide the course of treatment from the outset*. And it would be against all medical ethics to allow treatment to be suspended because of the prospect of failure. It cannot be said that the sole object of predictive techniques in criminological work is the regulation of treatment. The object of predictive techniques varies with the standpoint of those who have recourse to them. In the case of the statistician no discernible object save that of satisfying curiosity need exist. And at this stage of affairs it would scarcely be fair to expect the penologist to forego any penological advantages that might be secured by the use of prediction techniques.

But, even if we were to waive all terminological considerations, the fact that predictive methods are most commonly employed to estimate the chances of 'recidivism' is liable to give rise to all sorts of misconceptions and tendentious conclusions and to strengthen many existing preconceptions regarding the disposal of offenders. For example, it seems to be generally assumed by the penologist, the judiciary and the public that because an offender has been given a prison sentence, or for the matter of that a suspended sentence (for a suspended sentence is none the less a form of penological influence or, in simpler terms, a threat), he really should not commit the same or any other crime again. In the same way it is generally assumed by courts that, if an offender repeats his offence during treatment, either the treatment has failed or the case is a hardened one. Neither of these propositions will bear close examination. To the contrary, the forensic psychiatrist maintains that in case of 'pathological crime' recidivism is not to be regarded simply as a special manifestation indicative of the failure of remedial, preventive or punitive measures nor simply as an after-history caption, but as *an intrinsic part or natural phase of the disease*. Even so, it is useless to talk of recidivism in cases of pathological crime until all avenues of remedial approach have been fully explored. In any case, it would be more appropriate to use the simple clinical term 'chronic' than to burke conclusions and beg unanswered questions by describing the offender as a recidivist.

To all this the sociologist may well reply that the use of the term cannot be fully argued on the case of pathological crime alone, that pathological criminals represent only a small proportion of the criminal population, and that therefore recidivism remains a pressing problem which cannot be ignored either scientifically or penologically. And the psychiatrist may be compelled to admit, ruefully enough, that the first and last of these contentions are certainly true. But he objects to the second generalization. He can point out what is equally undeniable, that the proper examination of recidivist cases is only in its infancy and that the *statistical boundaries of pathological crime have never been established.* It is true the forensic psychiatrist working at a delinquency clinic deals with a relatively small number of selected cases, and these mostly of a 'favourable' nature. In fact, he only touches a favoured fringe of the subject. On the other hand, such systematic work as has been done on *unselected* groups of recidivists indicates that a very considerable number of them suffer either from pathological stigmata or have acquired these stigmata through penological mishandling. Until proper measures of investigation and disposal have been applied to unselected recidivists and the boundaries of pathological delinquency clearly established it is really absurd to draw hard and fast conclusions on the subject.

Moreover, the forensic psychiatrist maintains that it is in the tradition of both psychological and organic medicine to treat the problem of chronicity as a challenge to the resources of diagnosis and treatment, not as an excuse for defeatism or an incentive to the use of penal measures. Cases of so-called 'chronic lunacy' which were once allowed to languish untreated in mental institutions are now given at least the opportunity of reacting favourably to modern methods of physiological therapy. And in an encouraging number of cases a favourable response ensues, proving thereby that *what at one time appeared to be the 'hopelessness' of the chronic case was actually a measure of the inadequacy of treatment or, what comes to the same thing, the lack of knowledge of the psychiatrist.* From the point of view of research and, in the long run, from the point of view of treatment it is essential to deal with impartial concern with every variety of disorder, acute, sub-acute or chronic, short or long lived, intermittent or continuous, favourable or unfavourable in prognosis, refractory or amenable to treatment; not just to separate the sheep from the goats on grounds of public safety.

Needless to add, the isolation of recidivists in whom pathological factors can be established would not limit the scope of psychiatric approach to the problem of recidivism. Even in cases where no clinical abnormalities can be detected the factor of mental stress is often decisive, and no one is in a better position than the psychiatrist to estimate the importance of this precipitating factor. Without wandering too far from the subject, it may be said that the phrase 'extenuating circumstance' is, like the term 'recidivism', a popular caption which can be better understood by translation into dispassionate terminology and measured in terms of resistance to stress.

Having advanced the psychiatric case for abolition of the term 'recidivism', certainly in cases of 'pathological crime' and possibly in all cases of persistent criminal conduct, it is only fair to add that if this course were followed the responsibilities of the psychiatrist, to say nothing of his sociological co-workers, would be greatly increased thereby. Forensic psychiatry being a comparatively new field of endeavour, it is not surprising that psychiatric classifications of delinquency disorder are woefully inadequate and that they frequently conflict with one another. Nevertheless, the principles on which classifications can be effected are already clear enough and, if carefully applied, would render superfluous the use of such indiscriminate terms as recidivism in pathological cases. Even if recidivism were synonymous with relapse it would be no more justifiable to apply the term without discrimination than to maintain that all cases of intermittent organic disorder were of the same nature. A recidivist category is essentially a symptomatic grouping, and symptomatic criteria are ill adapted to the purposes of classification. They create more confusion than they eliminate.

Even so, our existing systems of psychiatric diagnosis would go far to reduce the omnibus group of recidivists to some order. If recidivists were examined with the same comprehensive care as is shown in any reputable delinquency clinic, the pathological types would fall easily into well-recognized groups. And each of these could be sub-divided into sub-groups having prognostic standards of their own. To take, for example, the group of so-called 'neurotic' delinquents, it is obvious that the obsessional type is certain to be more chronic than the hysterical type, which tends to be more intermittent and responsive to stress. Even without subdivision (desirable as that is) the psychopathic group could be recognized as in the main 'chronic'. And the same applies to certain forms of sexual offence, e.g. exhibitionism. If in addition some care were taken to estimate respectively the constitutional, developmental and precipitating factors operative in each case, it would not be hard to distinguish those cases which are by their nature chronic from intermittent cases and from cases which are 'recidivist' solely through lack of adequate treatment or through penal mishandling. Needless to add, the therapeutic responsibilities of the psychiatrist would also be greatly increased by psychiatric sifting of the unselected recidivist group; always assuming that the law allowed him the facilities necessary to carry out appropriate treatment of pathological types. The challenge of the refractory case is one that no self-respecting therapeutist would seek to avoid.

One further consideration. Recidivism, however defined or approached, is not a static problem. Admittedly, in the absence of suitable methods of mass prediction cross-checked by the examination of control groups, it is impossible to do more than hazard a guess as to its course in the next few generations. But it is not unreasonable to suppose that with the isolation and appropriate treatment of the pathological group the figures will dwindle considerably. The residual problem of the non-pathological recidivist must, however, be approached with expectant reserve. It is true that recidivism is to some extent a legacy from the inadequate penologies of the past. And to that extent the application of more sensible penal systems will no doubt assist materially in the reduction of persistent crime, whether pathological or not. But we cannot expect it to solve the problem. Observers differ as to where the hard core of recidivism really lies, whether it is to be found in what the psychiatrist regards as the pathological group or in the non-pathological group. In view of the fact that the successful (undetected) recidivist merges with the law-abiding and apparently 'normal' population it seems safer to assume that the second of these views is the more accurate. And this bodes ill for the reduction of non-pathological recidivism, unless of course effective methods of prevention can be applied at the pre-delinquent stage.

On the other hand, we may look forward to a reduction in the upper age limit of recidivism. It was one of Freud's greatest services to psychiatry that he established the relation between adult neuroses and child neuroses: 'No adult neurosis without a child neurosis'; and the same correlation has now been established for other disorders, not excluding pathological delinquency. In a sense, therefore, the young adolescent offender can be regarded as already a recidivist, a recidivist to the anti-social mechanisms of his early childhood. It is one of the objections to the use of flat descriptive terms such as recidivism, *l'état dangereux* and the like that they tend to obscure this vital correlation. We have not yet established firmly the dynamic and structural distinctions between the early case, the gradually organizing adolescent case and the adult 'hardened' case. Biased by our need for social safety, we tend to concentrate our attention on the adult type of recidivist and consequently to react to him with a more rigid and disapproving discipline than in the case of young repeaters. With a more elastic attitude and more appropriate measures of prevention and treatment there seems to be no reason why the ceiling of genuine recidivism should not in the long run be reduced to the twenty-five-year mark. But this will involve paying much more attention to the under-seven-year olds, a field which has the advantage of being free from the interference of the penologist, and one where the psychiatrist, the psychologist, the social psychologist and the sociologist can really meet on common ground. It is in this direction that the predictionist should persistently turn his attention with perhaps a greater appreciation than he has at present of the uses, aims and psychiatric traditions of prognosis.

PART II

NOTES ON THE M'NAGHTEN RULES*

[1951]

'... *to establish a defence on the ground of insanity, it must be clearly proved that at the time of committing the act, the accused was labouring under such a defect of reason, from disease of the mind, as not to know the nature and quality of the act he was doing; or, if he did know it, that he did not know he was doing what is wrong*'.

(1) The M'Naghten Rules, however limited their scope, recognize the *principle* that the state of mind of a convicted criminal offender should be taken into account before determining his disposal.

(2) They are limited in scope to the extent that they are concerned with defence on the ground of 'insanity' and only with such cases of 'insanity' as conform to a legal and therefore in the last resort a social definition of irresponsibility.

(3) This socio-legal limitation of the applicability of the M'Naghten Rules conflicts with modern *scientific* concepts of pathological crime, meaning by pathological crime the commission of offences attributable to mental or physical disorder or both.

(4) Criminal responsibility is at present assessed by *social standards* of individual behaviour, in particular the assumption that unless an offender is manifestly insane ('it must be *clearly* proved') he is a normal person responsible for his actions.

(5) Even this limited social recognition of criminal irresponsibility is due, not to a general appreciation of the manifestly abnormal nature of certain crimes and not solely to a general concern with the justification of punishment, but mainly, as in the case of capital offences, to the *nature of the punishments* legally inflicted, e.g. capital punishment.

(6) Existing methods of disposal of criminals also constitute a social issue: they are determined by a consensus of *social opinion*.

* First published in *Brit. J. Delinq.*, 1, 276–82, 1951.

(7) Criminal responsibility and the disposal of convicted criminals, although to this limited extent correlated in law, are nevertheless problems of an entirely distinct nature. The former is concerned with the *diagnosis* of the state of mind or body of offenders; the latter with their *treatment*.

(8) The diagnosis of states of mind or body requires a prolonged technical (scientific) training and can be assessed with accuracy only when an expert examination is made of the constitutional, individual and social factors that determine either normal or different varieties and degrees of abnormal behaviour.

(9) The treatment of abnormal states of mind or body likewise calls for expert knowledge.

(10) Although the M'Naghten Rules were originally formulated to meet the special case of responsibility for murder (the penalty for which in this country is death) the issue of criminal responsibility cannot be met by the abolition or further restriction of the death penalty or of any other special form of punishment for any special crime.

(11) The issue of criminal responsibility calls for a *system of judicial rules* applicable to *any* crime.

(12) Despite their limited scope the M'Naghten Rules are expressed with a brevity that is inconsistent with the complication and importance of the problems to which they refer. Policies that should be extended in a judicial code are compressed into a legal formula.

(13) Rules governing criminal responsibility in democratic countries can be formulated in terms of (*a*) a consensus of *social opinion* as given expression by the legislature; (*b*) a consensus of *scientific opinion* regarding the behaviour of individuals; or (*c*) a combination of (*a*) and (*b*).

(14) Scientific views regarding individual behaviour involve (*a*) a distinction between normal and abnormal behaviour and (*b*) in the case of criminal behaviour, a further distinction between crime occurring in 'normal' persons (i.e. persons in whom no abnormality can be detected) and pathological crime due to mental or physical disorder.

(15) Behaviour can (and should) be assessed scientifically, viz., in accordance with the main factors or faculties governing it.

(16) The main factors or faculties governing behaviour are, in order of priority or urgency:

(a) The nature of the instincts.
(b) The nature of the emotions.
(c) The nature of the moral faculties.
(d) The reality (social) sense.
(e) Reasoning capacity.
(f) The degree of intelligence.

(17) The effect of physical health and of environmental conditions (social circumstances) on behaviour is measured by the degree to which they modify any or all of the priority factors or faculties enumerated above.

(18) Where disease of the instincts or the emotions, the moral faculties, social sense, reason or intelligence exists and can be established *as the cause of any given criminal offence*, the individual in question cannot be regarded as normally responsible.

(19) Whereas the degree of responsibility in normal persons varies widely and is difficult to estimate, the degree or severity of disease or disorder giving rise to states of criminal irresponsibility, although varying from one pathological group to another, can be estimated with relative accuracy.

(20) For this reason the authority of a social consensus of opinion regarding criminal responsibility and disposal should be limited to cases where no abnormality can be established: the authority of a scientific consensus should, for the time being, be limited to cases where disease or disorder can be established (see Appendix).

(21) The existing M'Naghten Rules take cognizance only of a restricted number of the factors or faculties that determine criminal irresponsibility.

(a) *'Defect of reason'*. The *fifth* factor in the priority series given above is placed *first* in the M'Naghten Rules. In this connection no specific mention is made of defects of intelligence.
(b) *'Disease of the mind'* is placed *second* and is a non-specific category and therefore a source of confusion.
(c) *'To know the nature and quality of the act'*, the *third* factor in the M'Naghten series, refers presumably to the offender's 'reality sense', both individual and social. Here again no specific reference is made to the factor of intelligence.
(d) *'That he did not know what he was doing wrong'* implies a

disorder or absence of the moral faculties. It is placed *last* in the M'Naghten series.[1]

(22) *No* specific mention is made in the M'Naghten Rules of disorders of the instincts or of the emotions, or of the intelligence.

(23) The M'Naghten Rules do not distinguish between chronic disorders affecting criminal responsibility and acute conditions such as might give rise to criminal behaviour in persons apparently normal in other respects and at other times. Phases of acute alcoholic intoxication or of morbid jealousy may, for example, be due to underlying disease of the mind in persons apparently normal in other respects and at other times, and may give rise to defects of reason, reality sense and the moral faculties.

(24) By limiting their applicability to the state of mind of the offender 'at the time of committing the act' the M'Naghten Rules prevent cognizance being taken of anything but manifest and gross abnormality, and thereby ignore those phases of onset of disease of which criminal behaviour may be the only sign; e.g. a schizophrenic case might be apparently normal at the time of the commission of the act, yet develop a manifest acute schizophrenic attack within a few weeks, in which case there is strong presumptive evidence that his criminal conduct was a sign of the oncoming mental breakdown.

(25) The M'Naghten Rules not only recognize the *principle* of criminal irresponsibility but implicitly recognize the *authority* of the psychiatrist to diagnose it, and to give evidence as an expert witness bearing on the disposal of the criminal. ('It must be clearly proved.')

(26) Since, however, the status of the psychiatrist is not defined in the Rules and since the empirical psychiatry tacitly recognized in the Rules was the psychiatry of a hundred years ago, and, further, since the social consensus of opinion on the justification and nature of punishment has altered in a hundred years, *the conclusion is inescapable that the M'Naghten Rules require both revision and extension.*

(27) A revised set of rules should be expressed in terms which can be understood by the community at large, by judicial authorities and by criminals.

[1] See also Morris, *Modern Law Rev.*, Oct. 1953, and Hall Williams, *Brit. J. Delinq.*, 5, 72–4, 1954.

(28) Such technical expressions as are unavoidable should be precisely defined in an appendix to the rules.

(29) The revised rules should include a preamble indicating and defining clearly not only standards of responsibility but standards of irresponsibility.

(30) They should also indicate, in general, the standards applicable respectively to 'normal' persons and to persons suffering from diseased or defective processes.

(31) They should further indicate clearly to what extent these standards are based respectively on a social consensus and on a scientific consensus of opinion.

(32) They should *specify in particular* those recognized forms of disease or defect either mental or physical in which criminal responsibility cannot be established; as, for example:

(a) *Diseases of the instincts:* Sadistic and other perversions: regressive diseases or disorders such as occur at adolescence or the climacteric (change of life).
(b) *Diseases of the emotions:* Manic-depressive insanity.
(c) *Diseases of the moral faculty:* Psychopathy and psychotic character.
(d) *Diseases of the reality and social sense:* Paranoia, schizophrenia.
(e) *Diseases of the reasoning capacity:* The psychoses, psychopathies and certain compulsive or impulsive forms of neurotic disorder.
(f) *Diseases or defects of the intelligence:* Mental deficiency.
(g) *Organic diseases involving mental defect or disorder:* Epilepsy, encephalitis, general paralysis, psychoses of organic origin.
(h) *Diseases presenting any combination of the above features:* Traumatic neuroses and psychoses, drug and alcohol addictions.

(33) The new rules should contain a clause providing that in *all* cases of proven murder the offender *must* be adequately examined and observed by an official specialist panel before sentence, and also, on request being made by the legal representatives of the accused, by an independent panel.

(34) They should contain a further clause sanctioning re-examination by official and independent panels on appeal *after* sentence; also a second re-examination by specialist officers

appointed by the Home Secretary between any rejection of appeal and the execution of sentence. In the latter event at least one of the specialists appointed by the Home Secretary should be of independent status, i.e. not an officer of the Crown, police or prison official.

(35) The new rules should define precisely and in accordance with medical standards the status of a psychiatrist *and should insist that all psychiatrists on the Appeal Panel should have special experience in the diagnosis and treatment of delinquency.*

(36) *The new rules should contain a clause whereby they can be invoked also in crimes of a degree lesser than that of murder.*

(37) The view that the M'Naghten Rules could be suitably extended by recognizing 'degrees of responsibility' may appeal to the social sense and sense of equity of the community; it may indeed be desirable in the case of 'normal' persons committing criminal offences (as where 'extenuating circumstances' are taken into account); but it cannot be logically applied to *pathological* offenders and therefore does not satisfy scientific requirements.

(38) Where any given crime can be traced to disease or disorder of the mind or body, the subject is criminally irresponsible however normal he may appear *in other respects and at other times*.

(39) In so far as any individual is normally responsible, his conduct is as a rule non-criminal, or if criminal cannot be attributed to any specific disorder.

(40) A psychiatrist can, however, establish *degrees of disorder* in cases of pathological crime; he might also be able to establish in certain cases of mental disorder that the crime was nevertheless *not* due to the disordered action of the mind; but where the crime is due to mental or physical disorder he cannot establish *degrees of responsibility*.

(41) By establishing *degrees of disorder* in pathological crime (i.e. by making an accurate diagnosis) the psychiatrist can assist the Court in the matter of scientific disposal; e.g., whether institutional care or out-patient treatment is necessary.

(42) The M'Naghten Rules should therefore include a clause calling for a report not only on the nature of the disorder responsible for any pathological crime but the form of disposal that would be suitable to the needs of the case and at the same time have due regard to the need for public safety.

(43) Although criminal responsibility and capital punishment are distinct problems, the fact that persons convicted of murder

may be executed introduces an element of confusion; rules regarding criminal responsibility are in some cases specially framed because of the existence of capital punishment.

(44) The confusion indicated is due to two sets of factors, one emotional and ethical and the other scientific.

(45) Strong emotional and ethical prejudices exist both in favour of and against the practice of execution for murder.

(46) Owing to the absence of adequate research only provisional scientific opinions can be offered regarding either problem.

(47) The issue of capital punishment is therefore in the first instance an ethical issue; namely, is it a good or an evil practice.

(48) Scientific arguments in favour of and/or against capital punishment do not modify this primary ethical issue; they are relevant only to the possibility of *justifying, extenuating or condemning* capital punishment irrespective of whether it is a good or an evil practice.

(49) There is strong presumptive evidence that capital punishment is a superstitious, animistic practice derived from the ancient *lex talionis* and other and more primitive social habits.

(50) There is no reliable scientific evidence that capital punishment for the act of murder has a general deterrent effect.

(51) There is evidence that it has no specific deterrent effect on pathological criminals.

(52) There is no evidence that it is essential in the interests of social security; and there is evidence that some humane and more effective measures of security could be taken.

(53) There is so far, therefore, no reliable scientific evidence to justify or extenuate the practice.

(54) Both ethically and scientifically regarded there can be no justification or extenuation of the practice of executing persons who are either mentally disordered or otherwise not responsible for their criminal acts.

(55) If murder be an evil practice, the habit of judicial execution cannot be exempt from ethical condemnation. The authority of the group over the individual, and in particular the exercise by the group of the *vitæ necisque potestas*, has no inherently virtuous sanction.

Appendix

Future Extensions of the M'Naghten Rules

It has been laid down (para. 19) that the degree of responsibility in normal persons is difficult to determine and (para. 20) that the authority of a scientific consensus of opinion should be limited *for the time being* to cases of pathological crime, i.e. where disease or disorder can be established as the cause of the act. Nevertheless (para. 37) it is noted that already the disposal of 'normal' criminals may be modified because of 'extenuating circumstances'. This being the case, it is clear that, as knowledge regarding the behaviour of 'normal' persons increases, some attempt will have to be made to reduce 'extenuating circumstances' to scientific order, i.e. to express them in terms of *endurable or unendurable stress of mind*. When that stage has been reached it will be desirable to extend still further the M'Naghten Rules. In the meantime, it is undesirable to confuse the issue of pathological crime by extending the same rules to non-pathological crime. It is due to the confusion of these issues and the consequent belief that extended M'Naghten Rules would give legal cover to the actions of 'ill-doers' that so much opposition exists to revising and extending the Rules.

PART III

THE PREVENTION OF PATHOLOGICAL CRIME

[1950-59]

The views presented in the foregoing essays have a direct bearing on the problem of prevention. For if, as has repeatedly been affirmed, pathological delinquency can be traced respectively to constitutional predisposing and precipitating causes, it follows that measures of prevention must be directed to the second and third of these factors. Except in the case of certain curable deficiencies and handicaps the constitution*al factor is refractory to direct influence.*

From the point of view of practical measures of prevention the factors of precipitating stress *are of so varied a nature that with the exception of certain well recognized and defined stresses the psychological effects of which can be exactly determined and where possible eliminated, they do not lend themselves to a general preventive scheme. And in any case the removal of immediate stress provides no guarantee of resolution of developmental predisposing factors though when combined with positive measures of support, it may sometimes succeed in redressing the balance of an unsatisfactory developmental phase.*

To establish an effective preventive system we must therefore be able to recognize a pre-delinquent phase *in the history of delinquent disorder. The scheme outlined below is intended to call attention to the possibility of sifting the school population in order to recognize at the earliest possible moment and to treat children who by reason of predisposition are likely to become delinquent. It was presented (June 5, 1950) as a supplementary memorandum to the Royal Commission on Capital Punishment to which the writer had already presented on behalf of the I.S.T.D. a general memorandum which he later supported by oral evidence.*[1] *In this general memorandum the passages relevant to prevention were as follows:*
(*1*) '*Many crimes of violence are the result of pathological conditions which, although not recognized under the M'Naghten Rules, are nevertheless characteristic forms of mental disorder capable of great improvement, sometimes of cure, by scientific processes of*

[1] *Memorandum and Minutes of Evidence,* No. 21, May 4, 1950. H.M.S.O.

treatment. This applies particularly in the clinical group described as the psychopathic states in which crimes of violence, both sexual and non-sexual, are a common feature.' (2) 'It is a general rule that in cases of pathological outbursts of violence it can be established that disordered acts of the same kind have occurred in early childhood.' (3) 'If sufficient trouble were taken, pathological cases liable to commit murder could be detected during early childhood; in other words pathological murder is potentially preventable, or, at least, the tendency can be detected at a time when measures of prevention can be taken.' It was also suggested that the early diagnosis and treatment of potential murderers could be dealt with by an adequate service of child psychiatry. (4) 'This would strike seriously to the root of the problem of murder and its prevention' (oral evidence, p. 501). It was further pointed out that 'whereas in most pathological cases of criminality the threat of punishment is not deterrent and in some cases acts as an additional incentive to criminal conduct, the pathological group to which some murderers belong can be dealt with by suitable treatment along medico-psychological and social lines. In particular it had been shown by the I.S.T.D. that the psychopathic group, often regarded as intractable, is almost as amenable to treatment, if taken young enough and if the treatment is continued long enough, as the so-called "neurotic types" of delinquency'.

As has been noted the 'screening project' put before the Commission was of necessity concerned with capital crimes of violence. This does not militate against its application to pathological crimes in general, for even in non-indictable offences a predisposition to delinquency can often be discovered during childhood. The following screening project was first published in the British Journal of Delinquency (**2**, *147, 1951*). It is reproduced here with one additional paragraph referring to the uses of methods of delinquency prediction.

A Method of Prevention of Pathological Crimes of Violence

In his *Memorandum to the Royal Commission on Capital Punishment* the writer suggested that since in the great majority of observed cases of pathological crimes of violence, some indication of the pathological tendency has been found to exist since childhood, it would be possible to 'screen' the child population of

Britain in order to detect such cases at an early stage and to keep under medico-psychological supervision and/or treatment all children or youths who show abnormal tendencies to violent conduct. On the question being raised whether this would not involve a costly and extensive investigation which might not be justified by results, the writer pointed out that a skeletal psychiatric organization already existed and would in the ordinary course of events be expanded, which with a little adaptation and expansion would serve the purpose of a preventive screening system.

The main outline of the preventive scheme is as follows:

(1) Assuming that the Royal Commission thought fit to recommend to the appropriate authority, e.g. the Home Office, that the preventive scheme be initiated, it would be necessary for that authority to secure a Cabinet directive to the Ministry of Health and the Ministry of Education.

(2) As far as the Ministry of Education is concerned, the aim would be to screen the existing school populations. There are two methods of approach to this problem. Each school child at present has a statutory examination three times during his school career. Attention is paid to physical difficulties but some school medical officers with psychiatric knowledge are able to detect early behaviour and emotional problems. Recent legislation also permits the educational authorities to give complete vocational guidance to children leaving school and several authorities already do so; the best example being that of Warrington, Lancs.[1] These vocational examinations involve the use of mental tests and provide an additional check on the mental stability of children already examined.

The second approach involves the co-operation of teaching staffs. Teachers of experience can readily recognize behaviour problems, and the potentially anti-social and violent child is one of the most easily detected educational problems. They should be instructed to report such cases to the headmaster, who in his turn would refer them to the school medical officer.

What is urgently necessary is an expansion of the psychiatric side of school examination, and this will certainly take place irrespective of any special aim such as is indicated here.

(3) In the absence of extended psychiatric facilities in the school

[1] Acknowledgement is made to Dr. Alfred Torrie of the National Association for Mental Health for information on existing facilities.

medical service, both school medical officers and teachers can make use of the existing child guidance centres where skilled psychiatric examination is available.[1] All 'suspect' cases could be recommended for preliminary examination by projective tests (e.g. the Rorschach Test) or brief psychiatric examination, and such cases as appeared to require it could then be given detailed medico-psychological examination. If any doubt remained after such detailed examination, it would be desirable to apply some of the recognized prediction tests by which there is a reasonable chance of determining whether the child is likely to become delinquent. Although so far it is not possible to predict exactly the form of delinquency it will take, a fair estimate as to whether crimes of violence were likely to occur could be arrived at a final case-conference which the various diagnosticians and observers would attend. By grading the examinations in the way suggested 'from superficial to deep' it would be possible to reserve the main diagnostic resources for really important cases and so prevent overcrowding of diagnostic centres.

(4) The next step would involve organizing a form of 'notification' similar to that already existing in the case of certain infectious diseases. Potential violent offenders would be notified to the local health office, whose duty it would be to see that records were kept of various examinations, that treatment had been carried out and that proper after-histories were kept.

(5) Measures of observation, advice to parents, re-education and where possible individual psychological treatment would be the concern of the local child guidance centre or nearest hospital psychiatric centre or, where existing, delinquency clinic. Observation would be continued until the end of the school period when a final review would be made and such cases as still required attention passed to the appropriate adolescent or adult psychiatric centre. Already some of these measures are in existence. The Bristol child guidance clinic, for example, sees all young offenders, and other child guidance clinics see from 3 to 5 per cent at least of such cases.

(6) In addition to these general measures, special attention would be paid to the screening of *remand home populations*, *approved schools* and *Borstal institutions*. Already twelve remand

[1] There are at present about 700 such clinics in England and Wales alone.

homes have a regular service of psychiatric consultation. About six to seven approved schools have regular psychiatric help, and one Borstal at least has a resident psychiatrist on the staff. All of these places could, with skilled help, detect a potentially violent psychopath. All that is necessary therefore is to increase the psychiatric facilities at such points or to make use of other local psychiatric facilities.

(7) A logical and essential extension of the screening system would be the examination of all *cases convicted of violence*, whatever the sentence or order of the court. It is important to deal with this aspect of the problem because in the experience of the I.S.T.D. (Portman Clinic), cases of this sort are too rarely sent for examination, being dealt with summarily by sentences of fine or imprisonment. Because of this practice violent offenders escape examination and, from the preventive point of view, are lost sight of.

(8) By such means it would be possible in course of time to screen, isolate and treat a large proportion of potentially violent criminals, and a fair proportion of actually violent offenders. Even if no addition were made to existing psychiatric services, it would be possible to do extremely valuable work in this direction.

(9) The clinical material so collected would be put at the disposal of research teams and thereby an invaluable *long-term research* into the problem of criminal violence set on foot.

[Note 1959] Although this project was first advanced in 1950 it is only within recent months that any official notice has been taken of the necessity to establish some liaison between the Home Office, the Ministry of Health and the Ministry of Education. But effective liaison cannot be established unless in each of the Ministries concerned a special department is set up to deal with problems of pre-delinquency. Although it seems likely that something will be done to recognize children prone to violence, it need scarcely be repeated that a proper screening project would be on the outlook for any type of potential (pathological) delinquency. Not only so, one of the advantages of such a project would be to break down the at present somewhat artificial barrier or no man's land existing between 'pathological' delinquency and so-called 'responsible' delinquency.

Arguments of lack of sufficient economic and professional resources have already been advanced but need not obstruct the development of a new system. There is indeed a shortage of the various facilities referred to in the project, and, for the scheme to be effective, an interlocking administrative system is certainly called for. But these difficulties are there to be overcome. In the meantime a beginning could be made in the scientific application of preventive measures.

PART IV

PSYCHIATRIC ASPECTS OF CAPITAL
PUNISHMENT*

[1954]

Although it is natural for the psychiatrist, reading through the Report of the Royal Commission on certain aspects of Capital Punishment, to devote most of his attention to the chapters on insanity and criminal responsibility, it can be said at once that every section, almost every page of this blue book, raises issues that are the proper professional concern of the psychologist, the sociologist and the psychiatrist. Indeed, the first few paragraphs of preamble and introduction present the reader with an intriguing psychological puzzle: viz., why, having elected to submit the question of capital punishment to the attention of a Royal Commission, the Prime Minister of the period, Mr. Attlee, should have decided to hamstring the work of the Commission by excluding from the terms of reference the pressing question of abolition. The Commission was in effect compelled to proceed on an unproven assumption, that capital punishment is efficacious as a deterrent and to consider how it might be limited 'without', as the introduction dryly remarks, 'impairing the efficacy attributed to it'. For 500 pages we are permitted to follow the Commission's attempt to apply the processes of reason to a subject so macabre that it has defied those very processes for centuries. And for all its painstaking efforts to be impartial it is clear that from its first session the Commission was oppressed by the very problem specifically excluded from the terms of reference.

In its own innocent way the Commission registers a protest against having its hands tied behind its back; for, at the end of the first chapter, a brief subsection is introduced dealing with the question of deterrence, of which the most important paragraph

* This article first appeared in the 'Symposium on the Report of the Royal Commission on Capital Punishment', *Brit. J. Delinq.*, 4, 162–8, 1954; it was reprinted with some additional footnotes in the *Modern Law Review*, July, 1954.

(64) is that wherein the Commission agrees with Professor Thorsten Sellin who, discussing the homicide rates in the U.S.A., informed the Commission that 'Whether the death penalty is used or not or whether executions are frequent or not, both death penalty States and abolition States show rates which suggest that these rates are conditioned by other factors than the death penalty'. Having entered this quiet protest, without apparently being aware that it has thereby blown its terms of reference sky-high, the Commission then proceeds to its imposed task of finding ways and means of reducing the execution rate without, however, making it so small in proportion to the number of murder convictions that the argument for deterrence would become manifestly absurd to its most convinced proponent.

It is impossible to read this early subsection without reflecting on the methods employed by Royal Commissions to test the scientific validity of 'expert evidence'. For a Royal Commission is after all a kind of special jury empanelled to listen to the evidence of individuals who vary widely in scientific training and in experience of the problem under investigation. For instance, the Commission felt it 'could not treat lightly the considered and unanimous views' in favour of the deterrent effect of execution expressed by representatives of the police and prison services, supported as they were by some of the most distinguished judicial witnesses, including the Lord Chief Justice. Why ever not ? The issue was one of deterrence, not of familiarity with prison or court manners; and to speak with authority on deterrence requires extensive acquaintance with psychological norms, *with the effectiveness of distant anxiety as an inhibiting force*, with the after-history of every variety of behaviouristic disorder, to say nothing of an expert knowledge of statistics and of statistical method. Did the police or even the judicial witnesses possess these qualifications ? If not, then their evidence was, to say the least of it, merely hearsay.[1]

---

[1] The fact that the most weighty evidence against the deterrent effect of the death penalty was drawn from sociological sources calls for some comment. Owing to their almost exclusive concern with the diagnosis and treatment of 'pathological' crime, psychiatrists have paid very little attention to the fallacies of penal 'deterrence', and have left this field of general investigation to the sociologist and penal reformer. Yet the mere fact that, in spite of repeated demolition by penal reformers of the stock arguments in favour of corporal punishment, advocates of physical

A similar problem arises even in the case of psychiatric witnesses. Having listened to the evidence of numerous experts on the subject of psychopathy,[1] the Commission ventured on a num-

retribution continue to repeat their unsubstantiated and therefore prejudiced assertions, surely requires psychiatric explanation. This can only be achieved by examining the unconscious roots of the urge to punish, an explanation which leads directly to the close connection between punishment and man's unconscious sadistic urges, not to mention his unconscious guilts. Some even of the details of execution ceremonies are derived by anthropologists from earlier superstitious observances, e.g., the medieval belief that blindfolding the condemned protects the executioner from the evil eye. Far-fetched as the recommendation may appear, there is some justification for including anthropological evidence when dealing with such an atavistic ritual as capital punishment. (See in this connection 'The Psycho-Pathology of Flogging' by Edward Glover, Howard League for Penal Reform, London, 1937).

[1] It is not generally known that the term psychopathy, now widely accepted by psychiatrists, refers to a group of disorders which has been recognized for over 100 years, from the time in fact when Prichard first described *moral insanity* or *imbecility*. The symptoms of the conditions include disorders of ego-structure (commonly described as character-disorders), instability and lack of restraint of emotional discharge, an incapacity to control behaviour detrimental to the community or to the subject himself, disregard of social consequences of behaviour, a striking absence of conscious remorse or conscience and as a rule a number of psycho-sexual peculiarities or perversions. These various disorders have usually manifested themselves without interruption since childhood. The seriousness of the condition can be suggested by saying that it is graver than a neurosis and not so grave as a psychosis (insanity). The reason that psychopathy is not generally recognized is that even advanced psychopaths are sometimes able to maintain an apparently normal façade and are often regarded as normal persons not only by those who come in superficial contact with them but by most judicial authorities who see them in the dock. Extensive team researches on the subject, made in this and other countries, and the use of an increasingly refined system of tests (electro-physiological, psychological and psychiatric), now enable a diagnosis to be made with reasonable certainty, and what is more important, have provided the basis of predictive examinations. In other words it is possible to set on foot a system of preventive examination by which the potential criminal psychopath can be detected and notified during an early (school) age. These facts were brought to the attention of the Royal Commission by the present writer, giving evidence on behalf of the Institute for the Study and Treatment of Delinquency, but were apparently disregarded. At any rate no mention was made of them in the Commission's Report (see Glover & Grygier, *Brit. J. Delinq.*, **2**, 144–9, 1951: also Glover 'On Psychopathy', *Proc. R. Soc. Med.* Section of Psychiatry, 1954). [See also pp. 347–51 this Section.]

ber of conclusions of which I shall instance only two. In paragraph 397 it is laid down that 'to say of a criminal that he is a psychopath is therefore to say something positive about him which could not automatically be assumed from his behaviour'. This comes apropos of the alleged difficulty of distinguishing psychopaths from thugs, and carries with it the assumption that the psychopath does not suffer from a *disease* of the mind. But the same could be said of many persons suffering from paranoia or even from psycho-neuroses, who effectively conceal their disorder from the public gaze, yet are by professional agreement held to be suffering from diseases of the mind. Moreover, in paragraph 401 it is maintained that 'there is no qualitative distinction but only a quantitative one, between the average normal individual and the psychopath'. This in the face of evidence by Hill, Stafford-Clark, Taylor and Henderson (itself extensively quoted in the Report) to the opposite effect. Who is to decide this matter? Who is to give weight to the evidence? Certainly not a lay commission[1] which with the best will in the world can only record differences by a method of nose-counting without being able to assess the qualifications of titular experts to speak with real authority.

The assessment of expert evidence on psychopathy is the more important in that the conflict between the law and psychological medicine on the matter of criminal responsibility turns precisely on the capacity of the psychiatrist to distinguish delinquent psychopathy from non-pathological criminality. Except in the case of latent insanity and intermittent insanity (psychotic episodes) there is rarely any great difficulty in recognizing those cases of insanity for the benefit of which the M'Naghten Rules were originally devised. And a flat ruling that cases where a state of psychosis existed shortly before, during, or shortly after the commission of the offence should not be held as 'responsible' would meet the professional requirements of doctors and at the same time satisfy the public conscience. A flat ruling is clearly called for also in the case of mental deficiency. What appears to perturb the legal mind and arouse the moral indignation of many members of the community is the possibility that a thug should 'get off' the death penalty on a mistaken diagnosis of mental abnormality, an attitude

---

[1] The Commission included, it is true, one neuro-psychiatrist but cannot on that account be rated as a scientific body entitled to make authoritative pronouncements on psychopathy.

incidentally which indicates that retribution rather than deterrence is still the mainspring of capital punishment, that, in fact, the writ of the *lex talionis* still runs in this country. Ever since the M'Naghten Rules were promulgated the main concern of the law has been not that they should be applied in cases of insanity, but lest they should be extended beyond the field of insanity. All this was complicated and indeed camouflaged by the fact that, owing to their being worded in the days of a 'rational' psychiatry devoid of any understanding of emotional disorder, the rules opened the door to endless and fruitless discussions and interpretations of matters that are clearly outside the scope of rational psychology.[1]

Nevertheless the M'Naghten Rules did establish a precedent, the logical extension of which is to consider which disorders apart from insanity should absolve a murderer of criminal responsibility. In countries like Scotland where the concept of 'diminished responsibility'[2] is recognized in law, this logical requirement is met to some extent, although, it is interesting to note, not in the case of the psychopath. And in fact, the present Commission considers that the Secretary of State should 'give rather greater weight to psychopathic personality *as a ground for reprieve*' (reviewer's italics), implying thereby that psychopathy should be considered as an 'extenuating circumstance' rather than a reason for waiving criminal responsibility.

Admittedly the Commission was handicapped in giving any dependable rulings on these matters by three factors: (1) that it was not qualified to give an authoritative opinion; (2) that the psychiatric evidence was not unanimous; (3) that, if the M'Naghten Rules were to be modified, such modifications would have to be

[1] For a detailed analysis and discussion of the M'Naghten Rules see Glover, 'Notes on the M'Naghten Rules,' *Brit. J. Delinq.*, 1, 1951 (see Section VII, Part II, this volume).

[2] The concept of 'diminished responsibility' although opening the door to a more scientific approach to the problem of criminal responsibility is itself based on the same misconception that leads the man in the street to regard the psychopath as a normal person. Because the psychopath appears to be more normal than the insane person, his abnormal conduct when manifested is regarded as 'normal abnormality' (plain bad conduct). Where criminal conduct is a direct manifestation of mental or physical disorder and is beyond voluntary control or where it can be causally traced to mental or physical disorder beyond control, the offender is criminally irresponsible however normal he may appear to behave at other times or places, or, for that matter, at the time of the offence.

expressed in general legal rather than in psychiatric terms; but it would have lent greater force to its two recommendations regarding the Rules if the Commission had added a third, viz., that a technical commission should be appointed forthwith to consider the more specific formulation of psychiatric categories or clinical entities which would automatically exclude the capital penalty or prevent its operation. For there is no question that at present psychiatric knowledge is far in advance of both legal and public opinion on the matter of criminal responsibility, as indeed the present Report clearly shows.

The inevitable consequence of working against these handicaps is a hedging of recommendations. On the one hand, it is suggested that if the Rules are to be maintained the addition put forward by the British Medical Association should be accepted, viz., 'that [the accused] was incapable of preventing himself from committing it [the act]'; on the other hand, the Commission suggests the abolition of the Rules leaving to the jury the task of determining on medical evidence the degree of responsibility. As, however, it is elsewhere recommended by the Commission that the jury should also determine the force of 'extenuating circumstances' (not due to mental disease) justifying a reduced sentence or alternatively a reprieve, it will be seen that the second recommendation is wider than it appears. *For what the jury generally regards as extenuating circumstances can be translated in psychiatric language as the amount of mental stress which would loosen an uncontrollable impulse in an otherwise reasonable person.* Extenuating circumstances in fact can be classified under the heading of 'traumatic states of excitation' with or without a prolonged history of otherwise normal conduct, and there is therefore every reason that some future psychiatric commission should attempt to bring order into what must otherwise be a group of 'emotional variables' to be assessed according to the variable emotions of different juries. Hence, quite apart from the possibility that a legal battle may arise over the delegation of these responsibilities to a jury, we may for the moment be thankful for the small mercies contained in the Commission's first suggestion, namely, to extend the existing rules. No doubt in this extended form they would still give rise to endless confusion and debate, but at least they would permit cases of homicidal and sexual psychopathy to be considered on their psychiatric merits as cases of grave mental disorder, the main feature of which is precisely criminal irresponsibility. The truth of the matter is that punishment by execution and the responsibility of criminals are two entirely different problems, the former being a problem in social ethics, the latter an individual psychiatric problem. When brought in penal juxtaposition the issue of deterrence becomes a red herring diverting attention from the ultimate necessity of establishing precise psychiatric scales or responsibility for *all* crimes, not just the crime of murder.

There is almost no end to the inherent inconsistencies that can be brought to light by a psychiatric analysis of this Report, or perhaps one ought to say of the issue of capital punishment. The Commission's majority recommendation (six to five) that the statutory age-limit should be raised from 18 to 21, for instance, was based on the view that normal persons under this latter age are liable to instability in mental and emotional development and therefore presumably unable to stand unusual stresses. If instability of *normal* young persons is to be regarded as an adequate reason for waiving the death penalty, as most psychiatrists would agree, why should it not be so regarded in the case of *abnormal* persons of any age? e.g. psychopaths whose emotional and mental development is immensely more unstable than that of normal persons of 18 to 21 and who, as can be shown by both physiological and psychological tests, have a 'stress-level' corresponding to that of children under 14 years. It is only burking this issue of responsibility to say (paragraph 200) that 'these disordered cases should be considered by the Minister responsible for advising a *reprieve*'.

Take again the conclusion that there are '*no rational grounds* on which women could be relieved of the liability to suffer the death penalty *while it still applies to men*' (reviewer's italics). The Report does not conceal its view that opposition to the execution of women is likely to be based on emotional (which is, of course, a euphemism for sexual) prejudice. But, as is clearly indicated by the figures for reprieve (of 135 women condemned to death in England and Scotland from 1900 to 1949, *only thirteen, one in ten, were executed*, i.e. 90 per cent of the sentences were commuted or respited), the argument for the deterrent effect of execution in the case of women is reduced to absurdity; and if the factor of deterrence is one of the main justifications of capital punishment, then to say that there is no rational argument for not executing women is itself irrational, or, not to put too fine a point on it, itself a sign of sexual prejudice, a fact which is in any case implicit in the wording of the Commission's conclusion, viz., 'while it still applies to men'. And it is no use sidetracking the argument, as the Commission does, by eliminating the figures for women in coming to conclusions about deterrence. Nor does it improve matters to argue (as in paragraph 186) that amongst the women executed are those who have committed 'cold-blooded and atrocious' murders, such as baby farming and slow poisoning. If the 'heinous nature' of the offence is to be taken cognizance of, either in confirming or in commuting the death penalty, then the Commission's laboriously constructed argument in favour of the conclusion that 'it is impracticable to find a satisfactory method of limiting the scope of capital punishment by dividing murder into degrees' falls to the ground. For if it is practicable for a responsible Minister to recommend reprieves in terms of the degree of heinousness, it should be no more difficult for a Royal Commission to distinguish degrees of murder in the same terms.[1]

Summing up, two conclusions are irresistible. Brilliantly written and marshalled with skill, judgment and a patent regard for reason, the argument of the Report demonstrates how impossible it is to be reasonable about an emotional issue without full knowledge of unconscious sources of bias. The second conclusion is essentially a practical one, for never in the history of penological literature has such a devastating indictment of capital punishment been set before the public that is ultimately responsible for its maintenance.

[1] Incidentally the Commission admits that 'the system [of establishing degrees of murder] as now operated [in the United States] undoubtedly does much to limit the scope of capital punishment'; and since limitation of this penalty was one of the avowed aims of the Commission, it does not seem that the formidable array of legalistic arguments led by the Commission against establishing the practice in this country justifies the view that this line of approach to limitation is 'chimerical'. If, as the Commission states (para. 53), 'the law cannot ignore the public demand for retribution which heinous crimes undoubtedly provoke' it is also incumbent on the law to give statutory force to this popular discrimination of degrees, not just leave it to juries or to Home Secretaries to act as keepers of the social conscience. This would involve a psychiatric investigation of murderers as well as of the act of murder, *a contingency which curiously enough never seems to have occurred to the Commission,* whose brief and inadequate researches on the subject are confined to elementary classification of the act

VIII. *OBITER SCRIPTA*

I   Delinquency: a Special Study
II   Normal and Abnormal Behaviour
III   Social Psychiatry and the Law
IV   Juvenile Delinquency Acts
V   Narcosis and Court Reports
VI   The Ambulant Clinic
VII   Institutional Treatment
VIII   Social Defence or Social Aggression?
IX   Crime or Perversion?
X   Research in Delinquency
XI   Co-ordination of Research
XII   Study of Advanced Cases
XIII   Classification
XIV   Definition and Classification
XV   Psychopathy
XVI   Psychopathy: Classification and Treatment
XVII   Depression and Crime
XVIII   Bed-wetting and Delinquency
XIX   Sexual Offences
XX   Homosexuality
XXI   The Roots of Homosexuality
XXII   The Castration of Sexual Offenders
XXIII   The Government and the Wolfenden Report on Homosexuality and Prostitution
XXIV   Capital Punishment

SECTION VIII
OBITER SCRIPTA
[1950-59]

When the British Journal of Delinquency *was founded in 1950 an Editorial Section was developed with the object, inter alia, of correlating the original papers published in each number with current trends of research both clinical and sociological. This work of correlation and evaluation was shared between the co-Editors, Dr. Hermann Mannheim, Dr. Emanuel Miller and the present writer. The following excerpts consist of some psychoanalytical glosses contributed by the author. Item XXII, on the practice of castrating sexual offenders that is followed in some Continental countries, was published as a matter of public concern in the correspondence columns of the* Journal.

I. DELINQUENCY: A SPECIAL STUDY*

If we accept as a working definition of delinquency that it is the co-efficient of friction between the individual and his environment, or between man and society (as represented by the law), or again between primitive (infantile) systems of adaptation to life and a more or less adult acceptance of convenient and desirable social regulations, it follows that the methods adopted in the study of delinquency cannot be the exclusive preserve of any one branch of science. The very fact, however, that it involves the application of a variety of scientific disciplines entitles it to be regarded in the strict sense of the term as a 'speciality' in its own right.[1]

II. NORMAL AND ABNORMAL BEHAVIOUR†

The invasion of the social sciences by the psychiatrist raises some professional problems that are not easy to solve. In particular

* *Brit. J. Delinq.*, 1, 3, 1950.
[1] It is absurd to think that a general training in psychiatry or sociology or social psychology entitles anyone to speak with authority on a complex problem that calls not only for extensive first hand experience of the nature of criminals but for a working acquaintance with a great variety of techniques of investigation and treatment.
† *Brit. J. Delinq.*, 6, 4, 1955.

the distinction between normal and disordered behaviour has lost some of its former sharpness. In the case of delinquency work, this is well illustrated in the concepts of 'psychopathy' and of 'sexual disorder', or 'sexual psychopathy', on the strength of which the psychiatrist frequently claims prior authority in the disposal of accused persons suffering from these conditions. But whereas the clinician has encountered comparatively little organized opposition and has acquired a sometimes pontifical authority in such fields as industrial efficiency, marital compatibility, educational and personnel selection, to say nothing of the upbringing of children, in the case of his criminological enterprises he has had to face the superior authority of legal and penal codes. There are natural limits to the validity of 'pathological' criteria in the diagnosis and treatment of criminal offenders. Needless to say, the issue turns ultimately on the importance of unconscious factors in criminal conduct, and on the psychiatrist's capacity to distinguish a preponderance of 'pathogenic' factors in any given case. There is, in fact, no answer to this problem save further research, during the carrying-out of which, however, the officers of the law, having maintained their primary aim of promoting public safety, might well preserve an open mind regarding the ultimate nature of responsibility. For if the standards of abnormality are difficult to establish, it follows that, except in the narrow statistical sense, the standards of normality are equally obscure. Whatever may be the outcome of attempts to delimit the frontiers of normality, it is at any rate an intriguing and possibly a reassuring thought that in the silent and often unrecognized struggle for authority between the man in the street and the psychiatrist, the law has so far supported the rights of the individual by maintaining in effect that the common citizen must be allowed the privilege of breaking the law without benefit or redress of psychiatry.

III. SOCIAL PSYCHIATRY AND THE LAW*

It is too frequently assumed that progress in modern criminology can best be measured by the advances made in the fields of psychology, psychiatry, sociology and penal administration. This would leave out of account one of the most practical standards, namely, the state of diplomatic relations existing between social psychiatry and the law. Unless a reasonable degree of harmony and mutual

* Brit. J. Delinq., 4, 79–80, 1953.

understanding prevails between those who administer the law and those whose duty it is to study the disordered mentality and disrupted social background of some offenders, there is little prospect that scientific advances in criminology will be adequately reflected in our judicial systems. In the past the relations between psychiatry and the law were, to say the least of it, clouded by an atmosphere of mutual distrust, which indeed has not yet been fully dissipated. Chief amongst the sources of this distrust came the uneasy feeling in legal circles that the psychiatrist's interest in his patient might lead him to ignore the question of criminal responsibility, that in short, the psychiatrist was either a crank or a sentimentalist or both. The psychiatrist, on the other hand, tended to feel that his professional efforts were obstructed by a conservative reaction on the part of the bench, an attitude which, in the case of psychological diagnosis, seemed at times to border on hostility if not open derision.

One of the simplest methods of estimating progress in this particular direction is to study the present form of psychiatric court reports and to observe the varying reaction of the bench to these documents. It may be observed that the onus of producing a report which is at the same time accurate, helpful and comprehensible, lies at present a little too heavily on the shoulders of the psychiatric specialist. As Dr. Scott points out,[1] the psychiatrist, in his anxiety to produce a document that can be understood by the intelligent layman, can very easily be led into over-simplification and thereby leave the door open to misunderstanding. The ultimate issue is therefore not whether psychiatrists can write reports, but whether magistrates can be trained to read them.

It would, of course, be unreasonable to expect that magistrates should undergo a full training in modern psychiatry; but it is not unreasonable that they should supplement the intelligent layman's somewhat garbled and exiguous knowledge of psychology with at least the same degree of orientation which is now generally demanded of probation officers and other social workers in delinquency. At the very least, he should know enough to be able to protect the offender from the more exaggerated forms of psychiatric bias, should these present themselves in the report. It is not enough to depend on robust commonsense, invaluable as

[1] Peter D. Scott: 'Psychiatric Reports for Magistrates' Courts', *Brit. J. Delinq.*, 4, 82–98, 1953.

this natural form of judgment undoubtedly is. Psychiatrists are too readily accused of a lack of this commodity when, in many instances, the apparent incongruities of the report merely reflect the peculiarities of the offender. The most obvious feature of delinquent conduct, although one which is frequently regarded as a sign of perversity rather than of disorder, is precisely its lack of common sense. Already the intelligent layman is willing to concede that the delusions of the insane are due not to lack of common sense but to a defect in the mental faculty which goes by the name of 'reality testing'. What magistrates must be led to realize is that behind the mask of apparent perversity, the psychopath, for example, suffers from an inhibited or distorted development of his reality sense. Our relatively greater understanding of juvenile delinquency is due not simply to our appreciation of the tender age of the offender but to the fact that we do not expect the child to exhibit the same sense of reality and value as the grown-up.

IV. JUVENILE DELINQUENCY ACTS*

Enlightened as were the aims of this legislation, there is no doubt that the Acts can be used to invoke, if not the majesty, at least the machinery of the law, not only for peccadilloes, but for minor delinquencies that might be dealt with more appropriately by familial, educational and other institutions.

V. NARCOSIS AND COURT REPORTS†

It is pertinent in this connection to recall the crisis which confronted Freud during his researches on the unconscious factors in hysteria and other psycho-neuroses. In the course of his earlier investigations of these conditions Freud had discovered apparently convincing evidence of the existence of sexual traumata occurring during childhood, e.g. parental seduction. These had, it seemed, been repressed but had subsequently led to the formation of neurotic symptoms. Further investigation showed, however, that, although some of these alleged experiences had actually taken place, the occurrence of others could not be substantiated. Nothing daunted by this discovery, Freud continued his investigations and arrived at the conclusion that, other conditions for the

* *Brit. J. Delinq.*, 1, 81, 1950.
† *Brit. J. Delinq.*, 2, 3–4, 1951.

formation of symptoms being operative, *unconscious phantasies* could, by producing traumatic conflict, lead to the formation of symptoms. This is a conclusion which has been amply confirmed by evidence obtained from the study of a variety of mental disorders, to say nothing of the dream life of normal persons; it might indeed have been inferred from the phenomenon of false confession, where individuals often of a neurotic type confess to crimes they have never committed. Apart therefore from any issue of professional or social ethics, the plain fact is that, regarded as evidence, data obtained under narcosis are extremely unreliable and can never be made the basis of reality estimations. They are just as inadmissable in court as 'what the soldier said' or any other form of hearsay evidence, to which in fact they have a close affinity.

But the fact that the method is subject to gross error does not dispose of the matter. It raises in an acute form the issue of *professional secrecy*. At present the medical expert subpœnaed to give evidence can formally refuse to break his professional oath but when, on the direction of the judge, his objection has been over-ruled, he is under obligation to communicate information acquired under professional seal. The situation of the psychiatrist employing narcosis, or hypnosis or analytical techniques during either consultation or treatment, differs not only in degree but in kind. He may be in a position to communicate to the court information of which the patient himself may have been unaware at the time of the examination or which, had he been aware of it, he would certainly not have communicated save under conditions of *absolute discretion*.

This is an issue which must sooner or later be openly deliberated by legal authorities acting in conjunction with the ethical committees of various medical organizations. Indeed the whole code of medical discretion requires re-examination in the light of changing professional conditions. Particularly in the case of the psychiatric examination of accused persons the position of the mental specialist is becoming extremely ambiguous. As State medicine develops there are bound to be an increasing number of occasions when the physician has to decide whether his operative allegiances are to the community or to the individual. The privacy of medical records is a case in point. A dozen and one medical organizations both military and civil now keep the most elaborate records regarding the personal health and private affairs of those who come under their supervision. Most ambiguous of all is the position of those medical specialists attached to various types of penal institution who, as servants of the law, may be called on to bear witness as to psychiatric fact before as well as after the verdict on an accused person.

It is sometimes argued that if the individual offender may invoke specialized psychiatric help in order to mitigate sentence, the State is likewise entitled to exploit the resources of psychiatry to establish the guilt of an accused person, in the same way as it now exploits the most refined chemical tests in order to convict a poisoner. But apart from the fact that in the former case the psychiatrist is concerned to establish, not the prisoner's guilt but the state of mind of the guilty prisoner, the right of the State to use as evidence data acquired from prisoners who have first been rendered totally unconscious and then roused to a state of partial consciousness in order to answer questions is challenged by the counter-assumption of the law that an accused person is entitled to defend himself against any charge on the understanding, of course, that if he lies he may have to stand the additional charge of perjury. The argument in favour of accepting evidence from a narcotic seance might equally be advanced in favour of using either physical or mental torture to obtain evidence against the tortured. As has been pointed out, the ethical sense of civilized communities, which is at the same time the soundest basis of the law and the most effective protection against its abuse, has laid it down that accused persons must not be intimidated or subjected to duress in order to obtain evidence of their guilt; and no plea of scientific method can be allowed to obscure the fact that obtaining evidence by the induction of narcosis is in principle no different from the application of the 'third degree' or of any other forms of duress, not excluding the trial by ordeal. The psychiatrist as citizen is subject to the laws of the land; as a mental specialist he is subject to codes of professional ethics; as an expert witness he is subject to the laws of evidence; it is no part of his duty either to give scientific cover to the methods of the Star Chamber or to act as a common diviner.

VI. THE AMBULANT CLINIC*

The modern tendency to diagnose and treat cases of delinquency at special out-patient clinics or at psychiatric and child guidance centres, although entirely appropriate and indeed deserving of wide and rapid expansion, is, from the psychiatrist's point of view, subject to some disadvantages, chief of them being that, under out-patient or 'ambulant' conditions, psychiatric interest is inevitably circumscribed. The existing system of referral of cases by courts and other social agencies tends to focus his attention mainly on the delinquencies, most frequently of juveniles and young persons, who are either first offenders or, if not, whose anti-social conduct seems likely to be amenable to medico-psychological treatment. A certain number of 'self-referred' cases or of uncharged persons presenting 'behaviour problems' come his way; but on the whole his case material is a selected sample, consisting mainly of 'pathological' delinquents. He rarely sees the so-called 'normal' delinquent and, with the exception of occasional cases of exhibitionism, and of cases relapsing after treatment, he has little or no contact with the chronic recidivist. Hardened criminals of the so-called 'Dartmoor type' he very rarely encounters.

Although this may seem to be merely a roundabout way of stating the obvious, namely, that out-patient psychiatrists have little experience of 'institutional' types, there are certain important consequences of this state of affairs. In the first place the clinic psychiatrist, whatever his private convictions on the subject, is chary of applying to *criminal conduct in general* the conclusions regarding the causes and mechanisms of crime he arrives at from observation of 'ambulant' *pathological* types. This task he leaves either to the prison or other institutional psychiatrist or to the sociologist. By so doing he escapes, though not of course entirely, the popular criticism that he is a sentimentalist seeking to whitewash or condone anti-social conduct.

The sociologist on the other hand is compelled, by reason both of his method and of the data to which he has access, to seek for causes and mechanisms of criminal conduct amongst apparently normal or at any rate 'criminally responsible' groups. To be sure, these larger groups include also recorded cases of 'pathological'

* *Brit. J. Delinq.*, 4, 223–4, 1954.

crime. Nevertheless the conditions of his work compel the sociologist to concentrate on causal factors that are common to the general population, and to estimate the significance of 'remedial measures' in terms of 'normal' rather than of 'abnormal' psychology.

These reflections are stimulated by Melitta Schmideberg's paper.[1] Drawing her observations mainly from the study of hardened criminals, she examines the common belief that the criminal at large is amoral, and confirms the conclusion, already held by many psycho-analysts, that not only does he share many of the moral values of the normal person, but that his absence of moral feeling in the matter of his delinquent activities is a clinical phenomenon, the result of a number of unconscious mechanisms used to protect himself from the action of a more primitive but unconscious form of conscience. These are matters which call urgently for extensive investigations conducted by teams of individual and social psychologists. It is indeed remarkable how little attention is paid in otherwise ambitious researches to the simple fact that the key problem in all delinquency work can be none other than the problem of guilt.

VII. INSTITUTIONAL TREATMENT*

In his preamble to a study of indications for residential treatment of the delinquent child, Dr. Maclay[2] is careful to remind us that the treatment of delinquency is not purely a medical problem, but always a social and finally a legal one. And, as he points out later, the court when considering psychiatric recommendations must also have regard to the claims of society for protection. The importance of this particular social factor can be gathered from the circumstance that the rates of institutionalization are highest in cases of violence and wounding, gang-stealing, recidivism and 'unsatisfactory associations'. Even so, the category of unsatisfactory relationships combines a psychiatric standard, namely, difficulties in making contacts, with a social standard, namely, bad companionship.

[1] M. Schmideberg: 'Is the Criminal Amoral?' *Brit. J. Delinq.*, 4, 272–81, 1954.

* *Brit. J. Delinq.*, 7, 2–3, 1956.

[2] D. T. Maclay: 'Indications for Residential Treatment of the Delinquent Child', *Brit. J Delinq.*, 7, 27–43, 1956

A number of clinical and social problems arise from this confusion. With the query: how often are magistrates influenced by psychiatric recommendations, runs the companion problem: how often are psychiatrists influenced in their recommendations by social valuations or penal prejudices? To what extent is the psychiatrist's therapeutic recommendation of compulsory residence governed by his knowledge of the therapeutic facilities available at any given institution? Because unless he is satisfied that those facilities are adequate, his psychiatric recommendation is little more than a penal gesture.

Dr. Maclay adds point to this issue when he remarks that there is no means of knowing in the case of those sent to institutions what would have been the outcome had they been allowed to remain at home. From the experimental point of view there is only one answer to this question, namely, to have the courage to experiment. We have not yet ascertained the limits or limitations of ambulant treatment. All we know is that it is possible and can be successful in a large proportion of juvenile delinquents, to say nothing of adult types. The aim of psychiatry, society and the law should be to increase that proportion without being intimidated by possibilities of failure.

VIII. SOCIAL DEFENCE OR SOCIAL AGGRESSION?*

The paramount necessity of a multi-disciplined approach to crime cannot be met by concentrating solely on the now widely accepted forms of scientific discipline. Psychology, psychiatry, or even sociology cannot have the last word in the disposal of offenders, but must always stand corrected by the social needs not to mention the prejudices of the community at large. It is essential therefore that those social groups which guide, if they do not always control, the penal, ethical and self-preservative urges of society, having searched their own hearts for subjective error, should deliver themselves of their criminological philosophy. For if the sentences of the court must satisfy to some extent the public sense of justice and the spontaneous doctrine of retribution, and if the practical application of scientific principles in the disposal of offenders may clash with the principle of the liberty of the subject, we are faced with the not easily soluble problem of steering between social defence and social aggression, a peculiarly totalitarian dilemma.

* Brit. J. Delinq., 5, 97, 1954.

Indeed, should the amount of personal interference effected in the name of rehabilitation[1] continue to increase at the present rate, the time may well come when the most ardent supporters of 'purging an offence through punishment' may be found amidst the ranks of hardened criminals themselves.

IX. CRIME OR PERVERSION?[*]

The suggestion made by Dr. Schmideberg[2] that delinquent acts are in the nature of perversions serves to remind us that the essential rôle of psycho-analysis in the investigation of delinquency or, for the matter of that, of any mental abnormality lies in assessing the importance of unconscious (endo-psychic) factors. The recent tendency of some psycho-analysts and of most medical psychologists to be content with emphasizing the importance of environmental factors during early child life (witness the stress laid by many writers on the etiological importance of the 'broken home' or 'separation anxiety') has obscured the importance of the psycho-analytical approach to delinquency. The emphasis these writers lay on infantile or child environment is largely an extension of sociological methods from the adult to the infantile (familial) sphere. Regarded psycho-analytically the 'broken home' is no more than a precipitating factor. What form of behaviour it will precipitate depends ultimately on unconscious predisposing factors, amongst which the influence of unconscious symbolism is in many cases paramount. This is very clear in the case of fetichism and of course it is a long time since psycho-analysts pointed out the importance of sexual symbolism in determining the choice of objects stolen by compulsive pilferers. The factor of symbolism is also decisive in many cases of arson, strap and pigtail cutting, cushion slashing and the like. To be sure, it is necessary to correct possible exaggerations of this particular element in motivation by assessing the relative importance in any given act of other factors, conscious or unconscious. Neglect of this precaution was no doubt responsible in part for the scepticism with which psycho-analytical

---

[1] Consider for example the significance of 'preventive detention', and the view held by some psychiatrists that 'indeterminate sentences' are justified by the need for sufficiently lengthy treatment.

[*] *Brit. J. Delinq.*, 7, 1–2, 1956.

[2] M. Schmideberg: 'Delinquent Acts as Perversions and Fetiches', *Brit. J. Delinq.*, 7, 44–9, 1956.

interpretations of criminal motivation have been met. On the other hand it serves no useful purpose to discount analytical interpretations by laying undue stress on the (seemingly more natural) influence of infantile environment.

X. RESEARCH IN DELINQUENCY*

Regarding the selection of subjects, it can be taken as axiomatic that, although there is ample room for investigation in every branch of delinquency work, the most rapid progress and the greatest economy of effort can be secured by concentrating attention in the first instance on key problems. In the field of delinquent psychology, for example, progress is constantly hampered by the lack of precise information on such subjects as the mental structure of the psychopath, the developmental relation between moral sense and reality sense, the individual function or value of criminal behaviour or the nature of therapeutic processes in delinquency. Every department of criminological investigation can produce its quota of riddles, the essential point of which lies not so much in the peculiarity of the subject matter as in the absence of a suitable etiological formulation of it. So far as selection of subject is concerned, effective research depends to a considerable extent not only in knowing where to look for what one hopes to find, but in treating gaps in information as sources of actual rather than merely potential knowledge. Precisely delimited ignorance, in other words, is an obversive or rather a negative form of knowledge. Allowing a generous margin for subjective error, the accurately posed question contains its own answer.

Concerning methodology there is, it would seem, a general consensus of opinion between psychologists and sociologists. Stung no doubt by the persistent criticisms of the natural scientist who tends to view their methods of investigation with some suspicion, the general psychologist and sociologist take a special pride in following those standard scientific disciplines which are intended to eliminate subjective error and bias. This is all to the good. But to confine research within these rigid boundaries is to court stalemate. The most austere statistical control, for example, cannot redress the debit balance of a badly chosen subject, superficial examination or a prejudiced approach. It is as true of re-

* *Brit. J. Delinq.*, 1, 157–9, 1951.

search as of other activities of life that one cannot make a silk purse out of a sow's ear.

In any case, too exclusive insistence on the discipline of the control group' has the disadvantage of ruling out one of the potentially most valuable instruments of investigation, viz. the exercise of trained imagination, or more precisely, the interpretation by individual investigators of isolated data. Anathema to the natural scientist as interpretative methods of investigation may be, they are nevertheless essential to the progress of any dynamic psychology which concerns itself with unconscious factors. In a comparatively fallow field such as the psychology of delinquency it seems likely that for some time to come increase in understanding will depend at least as much on the interpretation of unconscious factors as on the formal analysis of descriptive data.

All this has an important bearing on the classification of research personnel. Clinical workers in the field of delinquency suffer from an increasing sense of frustration in that their varied practical experience is not adequately exploited in the more organized projects of research sponsored by trained investigators. It is a matter of some urgency that this sense of frustration should be relieved. To the practical worker, nothing is more depressing than to see the material he has accumulated during years of laborious effort go to waste for lack of proper screening. On the other hand, nothing is more depressing to the research student than the sight of cartloads of case-records which, because of incomplete and indiscriminate case-taking, are valueless for research. Granted that special researches call in most instances for special case-records; granted further that only a small proportion of day-to-day workers in applied psychology or sociology are of the stuff of which investigators are made; and, still further, that the born research worker, whether descriptive or interpretative, must also be made by intensive training in his particular technique, it does not seem impossible to devise some means whereby better use can be made of the innumerable and valuable observations made by field workers who, whether or not they are gifted in drawing conclusions, stand in the most immediate contact with case-material.

A first step in this direction is obviously the development of case-frames which can serve the practical purposes of the clinical worker and at the same time satisfy the requirements of the research student. The systematization and publicizing of research problems would also promote economy of effort. But even more important than these is the recognition by the humblest clinical worker of the essential part he can play in promoting research. If he can interpret as well as make observations so much the better. But if he cannot, and in many instances he has neither the time, nor the necessary flair, nor even the urge to do so, he can at least put his data at the disposal of those who can.

To make such a system effective two conditions must be fulfilled. In the first place, a 'screening' organization of trained research workers must be built up in order to sift, elaborate and interpret data that have not been worked over. This in turn calls for generous subsidies by interested bodies both public and private. The preliminary surveys and pilot-researches necessary to establish the frames of reference of any given project may cost up to £1,000. Indeed, it is high time that a psychological and sociological counterpart of the Medical Research Council were organized and provided with funds adequate to deal with the extensive arrears of research in these subjects. And in the second place, there is urgent need for propaganda amongst field workers to convince them that they can play a fruitful part in research. Clinical workers are notoriously hard to persuade in this matter. Devoted to the practical aspects of their work, and often with a positive distaste for theoretical exploitation of it, they rarely respond to appeals for scientific contributions, however small. Needless to say, it is not the size of the contribution that matters. The simple record of a dream, brief observations of unusual clinical data might well provide the missing link in a chain of evidence or even the first stepping stone to some revolutionary discovery. Like the soldier who carries a field-marshal's baton in his knapsack, the field worker who trains himself for the purpose may acquire more than passing fame as a pioneer of research.

XI. CO-ORDINATION OF RESEARCH*

To co-ordinate policies successfully it is necessary to have some fundamental principles to co-ordinate. The chief obstacles to an effective policy of prevention and treatment of crime are the absence of adequate information regarding its effective causes and absence of national organizations capable of undertaking the

* *Brit. J. Delinq.*, 5, 98, 1954.

training of workers who engage in criminological research or staff the institutions or clinics, open and closed, devoted to the disposal (treatment) of criminals. The most perfect international organizations cannot conceal either the poverty of research activities or the scarcity of workers capable of carrying them out; though they may well serve to indicate the directions in which research is most urgently required.

It is also clear from references to the 'ever-narrowing limitations of the United Nations Budget' that little practical help in this direction can be expected from international sources and that, if criminology is to advance, some central body must be organized in each country having functions similar to those exercised in organic medicine by medical research councils.

That a central organization for the co-ordination of training schemes is also essential to the progress of criminology can scarcely be disputed, although the tradition that any scientific worker who cares to apply his particular methods to the study of delinquency is *ipso facto* a trained delinquency worker, dies hard. Important as it is to cultivate team work in the investigation of criminal behaviour, it is even more essential that every research worker should have a lengthy and close acquaintance with the clinical aspects of delinquency. Here again, it is essential to create a central organization having powers to organize official training courses in criminology and to grant a special diploma such as is required of specialists in most scientific disciplines. Although these are clearly matters for internal organization on a national basis, the U.N. Section of Social Defence could add greatly to the force of its international propaganda by drawing the attention of the governments concerned to the urgent necessity of setting their houses in order in these respects. The ultimate reward in the shape of fruitful researches and well-directed policies would more than repay the arduous effort required.

XII. STUDY OF ADVANCED CASES*

It is just as essential to the progress of criminology that the chronic or incurable case, sometimes called the Dartmoor type, should be carefully investigated as it is essential to psychiatric progress that investigations of the 'larval' or 'pre-psychotic' case should be correlated with studies of advanced schizophrenia.

* *Brit. J. Delinq.*, I, 4, 1950.

XIII. CLASSIFICATION*

Neither psychiatric, nor sociological, nor again legal standards provide of themselves a satisfactory basis for classification. Nor can satisfactory criteria be arrived at by determining the highest common factor of psychiatric, sociological and juridical agreement regarding the nature of delinquency. Following different approaches, frequently using different definitions and in the main serving different purposes, these applied sciences are bound to collide at some point of their approach to the problem. For this reason alone the search for a diagnostic and prognostic 'index' is bound to end in some disappointment to all concerned. The law, for example, for reasons either of social or of moral expediency, chooses to regard certain forms of sexual conduct as social delinquencies rather than sexual disorders. Yet, as Dr. Roper rightly points out,[1] the homosexual offenders coming under his observation were in other respects law-abiding, well-behaved and worthy citizens, who, he might well have added, attain and often promote a high level of cultural achievement. Clearly then the inclusion of this group in any study of a 'delinquent' population is bound to broaden greatly the margin of error incident to such investigations, if indeed it does not reduce 'delinquent typology' to nonsense. Nor will the working distinction of 'pathological'[2] from 'non-pathological' delinquency eliminate this error ...

... the term 'recidivism', although generally used to denote a category of delinquent behaviour, is, psychiatrically regarded, a misnomer, certainly in cases of crime that are manifestly of pathological origin. Translated into psychiatric terms, recidivism refers only to the *duration* of any disease of which delinquent behaviour is a symptom. It means merely that in its later stages the course of the disease tends to be intermittent. To be sure, the treatment meted out to the delinquent may promote or aggravate recidivism; or again it may reduce recidivism. But these facts can be better appreciated if we say quite simply that treatment may

---

* *Brit. J. Delinq.*, 1, 239–40, 1951.
[1] Roper: 'A Comparative Survey of the Wakefield Prison Population in 1948', *Brit. J. Delinq.*, **1**, 15–28, 1950.
[2] The term 'pathological delinquency' implies that the offence in question is either one of the symptoms of a current mental or physical disorder or itself constitutes the sole symptom thereof.

prolong or shorten the disease. To regard recidivism as if it were a particular form of social perversity noted in certain delinquent types may be socially expedient, but it offends every canon of psychiatric diagnosis.

Happily these difficulties in definition and classification are not entirely insurmountable. We can always follow the example of those clinical observers who, in forming a diagnosis, take into account constitutional, predisposing, and precipitating causes, including both individual and environmental (social) factors. In other words, the most reliable variety of classification is an etiological one. Even so, the most painstaking diagnosis should be constantly checked by an assessment of the soundness of socio-legal standards. In organic medicine the diagnostic methods may be fallible but at least there is no uncertainty regarding the *existence* of disease. Not so in social psychiatry. Along with the uncertainties of sociological and psychological diagnosis must be reckoned the variability of social *mores*, and the emotional nature of social prejudices. A good classification must make due correction for the errors of social assessment, reprobation or expediency.

XIV. DEFINITION AND CLASSIFICATION*

Needless to say, accurate translations and polyglot glossaries are no mere domestic ancillaries to scientific research. They subserve also the purposes of definition. And accurate definition is the most urgent of all criminological needs, albeit one that cannot be met by the unilateral activities of an exclusively criminological organization. Only by the most painstaking collaboration between experts in the fields of psychiatry, psychology, sociology and anthropology can we hope to achieve adequate definition of the common terms (or of their equivalents) so necessary to a multi-lateral criminological approach. Even when it is impossible to find suitable equivalents, to give, for example, a sociological paraphrase of a psychological expression, at least the exact connotation of the original term should be clearly set out; so that when a sociologist wishes to talk in the language of individual psychology, as he very well may, indeed sometimes must, he can do so without fear of contradiction. And no doubt clinical psychologists would be glad to be apprised of the exact socio-legal equivalents of such technical terms as the 'precipitating factor' in mental dis-

* Brit. J. Delinq., 2, 194–5, 1952.

order; in return for which service they might well be prepared to produce a classification of 'extenuating circumstances' based on psycho-dynamic factors, e.g. mental stress.

To illustrate the urgent necessity of accurate definition, we need only consider the psychiatric aspects of the 'law of the constancy of crime'. The day is now past when we can be content, as was Henry Thomas Buckle, to see in Quetelet's 'law', an additional proof that murder or suicide or any other felony 'is merely the product of the general conditions of society, and that the individual felon only carries into effect what is a necessary consequence of preceding circumstances'. 'In a given state of society,' wrote Buckle about 1857, 'a certain number of persons must put an end to their own life. This is the general law; and the special question as to who shall commit the crime depends on special laws; which, however, in their total action must obey the large social law to which they are all subordinate.'

Now it is precisely towards those 'special laws', and not to any 'large social law', which is after all only a statistically based generalization of any constancy of relationship between phenomena, that the dynamic psychologist directs his special attention. Moreover, should he be convinced of the operation of unconscious mental mechanisms, his immediate concern will be to establish, in, for example, the case of suicide, 'unconscious constants' of depressive reaction which, acting in conjunction with other more variable and often developmental factors, give rise to the risk of suicide in certain groups, not in society as a whole. His next concern will be to establish what proportion of the population suffers from pathological depression, what proportion harbours larval depression and what proportion is, *ceteris paribus*, non-depressive. And he is prepared to follow the same approach in the case of other psycho-social constants, whether they be psychotic, psychoneurotic or delinquent, provided they constitute a specific group of disordered mental functions.

Here he will encounter peculiar obstacles. Although it is not difficult to diagnose and isolate 'pathological' groups, and thereby to measure the constancy of unconscious mechanisms in these groups, no satisfactory method has so far been established to measure accurately the size of 'larval groups'. Methods of psychiatric diagnosis vary widely not only in practice but in principle. Moreover, should the psychiatrist have the temerity to attempt to establish constants common to antithetical types; for example, to correlate 'compulsive crimes' with 'compulsive (obsessional) psycho-neuroses', his margin of error will promptly increase tenfold. For he will find that there is no precise definition either of a 'neurosis' or for the matter of that of 'crime'. He will find that whereas many writers fail to distinguish between a 'neurosis' and a 'neurotic character', others write of a vague entity which they label 'neuroticism', a clinical concept that is neither fish, flesh, nor good red herring. Failing a solution of these problems in definition, the student will in all probability content himself by searching for constants within the terms of his own definition and within the limits of his personal observation. More than any other circumstance this retreat is responsible for most of the lacunæ existing in any individual psychology, and for the too-wide gulf that lies between individual psychology and sociology. The task of theoreticians on both sides is to bridge this gulf with serviceable definitions.

XV. PSYCHOPATHY*

Fifty years of sporadic investigation of this subject have resulted in little more than a profusion of contending generalizations; in fact, our understanding of psychopathy is still rudimentary and our researches wretchedly inadequate. We are equally well aware that, following the popular clamour for effective measures of crime prevention, the existing facilities and shibboleths of psychiatry and of social psychology will tend to be applied to the problem somewhat hastily and without due regard to their suitability. Inevitably therefore the poverty of our etiological formulations will continue to be cloaked to some extent in technicalities which do little more than express the theoretical preconceptions of their sponsors. For it must be admitted that the current wave of psychological and sociological interest in delinquency has created a false impression, amongst technical workers as well as the lay public, that we already know all that is to be known about the causes of crime.

One indisputable gain accruing from recent investigations can, however, be recorded. It is no longer possible to maintain without fear of brisk contradiction that the concept of psychopathy is a psychiatric fiction covering inadequacies in clinical classification.

* Brit. J. Delinq , 2, 77–8, 1951.

However slight the descriptive value of the caption may be, psychopathy has now emerged as the most important of the great transitional groups of mental disorder: meaning by transitional that the group occupies a fixed intermediate position in a hierarchy of developmental disorders, combining some of the characteristics of the more familiar psycho-pathological states (psycho-neurotic, psycho-sexual, psychotic and characterological) in a framework which is often difficult to distinguish from that of the so-called normal individual, or, at any rate, from that which passed as normal among our more immediate ancestors.

Equally inevitable is the necessity to direct our researches in the first instance towards those root problems which give rise to acute differences of scientific opinion. For no sooner do we suggest that the psychopathy of one age or generation may have been the 'normal' reaction of an earlier stage of racial development than we stir up the long-standing controversy between the 'constitutionalists' and the 'environmentalists'; between those who regard mental disorders as being determined in the main by factors of inheritance and those who are convinced that they are due in the main to the process of upbringing. And not only a controversy between these 'central' and 'peripheral' schools respectively, but an internecine war in the constitutional camp. For the central school is clearly divided into those who, pessimistically enough, attach most weight to inheritance and those who believe that during early childhood specifically endopsychic factors combine with specific constitutional and environmental factors to bring about a *specific predisposition* to psychopathy. Here we have one of the key problems in research, failing a solution to which the conclusions arrived at by more circumscribed and fragile researches must remain for the time being in the air.

XVI. PSYCHOPATHY: CLASSIFICATION AND TREATMENT*

Sir David Henderson's formulation[1] of a simple tripartite classification of psychopathy does not absolve clinicians from the task of producing more elaborate etiological formulations which must of course be as specific as the clinical sub-groups they are

* *Brit. J. Delinq.*, **6**, 1, 2, 4, 1955.
[1] Sir D. Henderson: 'Psychopathic States', *Brit. J. Delinq.*, **2**, 84–7, 1951.

intended to explain. The real difficulty with which the clinician is faced is lack of understanding of the process of 'normal' character formation. It is at least as difficult to distinguish a psychopath from a 'normal' person as it is to differentiate him from a schizoid character. Psychopathy in fact provides an exception to the general psycho-analytical proposition that one learns of the normal through study of the abnormal: to understand the psychopath one must grasp the larval abnormality of the normal.

As Sir David Henderson points out, the psychopath who finds his way into an adult court is already in a state of malignant organization, and the fact that such cases are notoriously refractory to therapeutic measures is no more surprising than the fact that advanced cases of phthisis have a poor prognosis. We now know that the 'early' case of consumption has a good prognosis; and there is no reason why the early case of psychopathy should not respond if taken before the therapeutic ebb. Work at the Portman Clinic (I.S.T.D.) suggests that, given appropriate handling, the prognosis of early psychopathic cases is not less favourable than that of neurotic delinquency.[1] In the meantime it is encouraging to have even the qualified support of so eminent an authority as Sir David Henderson. One thing is certain about the treatment of psychopathy: it should never be undertaken by those who cannot endure disappointment, and who, by the same token, have failed to recognize that the unconsciously revengeful compulsion to disappoint is a characteristic feature of psychopathy, not an aspersion on the psychiatric authority of the therapeutist.

XVII. DEPRESSION AND CRIME*

Dr. Woddis's paper on 'Depression and Crime'[2] raises issues that strike to the very roots of clinical criminology. For not only do his observations indicate the relation existing between on the one hand some states of depression and on the other anti-social conduct of various types, and thereby extend considerably the range of 'pathological crime', but they underline the necessity of establishing closer correlation between disorders leading to

[1] See Grygier and Glover: 'Preliminary Notes on the Application of Individual Methods of Research to the Problem of Psychopathy', *Brit. J. Delinq.*, 2, 144–5, 1951.

* *Brit. J. Delinq.*, 8, 81–2, 1957

[2] Woddis: 'Depression and Crime', *Brit. J. Delinq.*, 8, 1957.

criminal conduct and those classical disorders which have hitherto been the main concern of the psychiatrist and in which, with some exceptions the injuries caused by the disease are confined to the individual himself and to his immediate entourage. This represents a significant swing of the pendulum in forensic psychiatry. Originally at pains to establish the pathological nature of some forms of crime and to *contrast* these with, for example, the psycho-neuroses in which anti-social conduct is, as a rule, significantly inhibited, forensic psychiatrists must now retrace their steps and discover what manifestations or roots they have in common. Or perhaps it would be better to say that just as it is important to uncover the anti-social impulses that are unconsciously held in suspense by neurotic and some psychotic mechanisms or constructions so it is essential to establish what part these mechanisms and constructions unconsciously play in the *sequence* leading to anti-social abreaction.

Interestingly enough, psychiatrists are faced with a similar problem in the field of the psychoses. Clinically the alternating phases of mania and melancholia in the manic-depressive sequence stand in marked behaviouristic contrast; yet there is no doubt that during the manic phase and despite the happy or even frenzied externally directed activity of the maniac, at least an undercurrent of depression can be detected. Even here there are contradictions; for, as Dr. Woddis points out, criminal violence is less frequent in mania than in depression.

Yet another problem arises from consideration of Dr. Woddis's paper. Most observers emphasize the absence of normal conscience reactions in cases of psychopathy; and it has become a habit amongst the analytically minded to attribute this either to lack of development of the unconscious conscience (super-ego) or, at most, to stunting of its development. If, however, it is possible to establish either manifest or occult depressive features operating *before* the periodic outbreaks of anti-social conduct in psychopaths, it is clear that we must think in terms of warping or hypertrophy rather than of stunting of unconscious conscience, a warping which is countered by projective methods rather than by further introversion. Schmideberg maintains[1] that the criminal psychopath shows many signs of normal super-ego activity; and it is certainly true that in such psychopaths as do *not* manifest anti-

[1] 'Is the Criminal Amoral?'. *Brit. J. Delinq.*, **4**, 272–81, 1954.

social tendencies, depressive and self-injuring mechanisms are a common feature. There is therefore good reason to consider whether some psychopaths by their criminal abreactions save themselves a major psychotic depression or for that matter an attack of schizophrenia. Both schizophrenia and psychopathy have multiple fixation points, and indeed, descriptively speaking, the term 'split mind' is much more applicable to the psychopath than to the schizophrenic. However that may be, it is encouraging to realize that the dynamic approach to the individual aspects of crime is very far from being exhausted.

XVIII. BED-WETTING AND DELINQUENCY*

A recent paper on the incidence of chronic bed-wetting in cases of delinquency[1] is of more than diagnostic interest; it raises a number of important issues regarding not only research methods in delinquency but the existing state of psychiatric classifications. In recent years, and especially since the investigation of wartime 'evacuation-neuroses', it has been the habit of many child psychiatrists to regard bed-wetting as an anxiety manifestation of the 'separation' type and to rate it at the same etiological level as a child-neurosis. Some indeed describe it quite simply as a *symptom* of child neurosis. These were never very satisfactory assessments of a functional disturbance such as bed-wetting, which, in the first instance at any rate, is regarded by most parents, not without some justice, as an anti-social (domestic) habit; and the discovery that it is a common accompaniment of delinquent states makes an exclusively 'neurotic' rating more than dubious. To be sure, the clinical classification of pathological delinquencies has led to the isolation of a special group of 'psycho-neurotic' types in which the delinquent behaviour has, for example, followed an obsessional pattern (as in kleptomania). But this does not alter the fact that the vast majority of persons suffering from a psycho-neurosis are more law-abiding than the so-called 'normal' person. The apparent contradiction can to some extent be resolved by regarding bed-wetting as a functional disturbance which may exist in an isolated form or accompany any of the various psychiatric disturbances to which children are subject (psycho-neuroses, pre-psychotic

* Brit. J. Delinq., 3, 83–4, 1952.
[1] Joseph J. Michaels and Arthur Steinberg: 'Persistent Enuresis and Juvenile Delinquency', Brit. J. Delinq., 3, 114–23, 1952.

states or perversions of instinct). Such a view would lend support to the theory advanced[1] that some forms of delinquent conduct can be regarded as 'psycho-somatic equivalents' due to disturbance in the balance of excitation and discharge within the mental apparatus. However that may be, it is clear that before the position of the various delinquent states can be accurately determined the classifications of child-psychiatry must be carefully revised and extended. It is also clear that the study of pathological delinquency promises to render at least as important services to psychiatry as psychiatry has so far rendered the study of delinquency. The delinquent psychopath is in fact the missing link between abnormal and normal psychology.

The paper of Michaels and Steinberg also raises in an acute form the problem of research methods. In recent years the method of team observation controlled by careful statistical techniques has been taken over from sociology and applied widely in the psychological field. And although the strength of team-research may be said to be the strength of its weakest link, there is no doubt that despite this limitation the method can be both appropriate and fruitful. With one reservation however: that it should not lead to neglect of uncontrolled and isolated observations, whether clinical or analytical. Michaels' original observation regarding bed-wetting was of the latter order; and despite the fact that it is now possible to follow this up with the help of team-research and statistical control it should not be forgotten that without the original clinical observation there would be nothing to investigate. Until comparatively recently the word 'bed-wetting' could not be found in the standard psychiatric case-history forms. It should not therefore be thought that the day of the isolated individual observation is over. A great deal of modern psychiatry owes its existence to the individual discoveries of Freud; yet to this day these have not been subjected to adequate statistical control, least of all by psycho-analysts. Perhaps the day of analytical statistics is at hand; but whether or not, the spearheads of research are still to a large degree forged from individual operations. Neglect of this fact taken in conjunction with the absence of

[1] Glover: 'On the Desirability of Isolating a "Functional" (Psycho-Somatic) Group of Delinquent Disorders', *Brit. J. Delinq.*, **1**, 1950, reprinted in *On the Early Development of Mind*, Imago Publishing Co., 1956.

adequate psychiatric and social classifications of data is responsible for much waste of research energy. For unless team research operates with new and fruitful clinical concepts it can do little more than corroborate what we already know; and unless the data of psychiatry and of social observation are more thoroughly examined, classified and correlated, we are unlikely to arrive at new and fruitful clinical concepts. It should not be forgotten that although the study of delinquent states is as yet in its infancy, so too is the study of child-psychiatry and of social psychology. In short, successful research depends not only on the selection of a subject and of a suitably trained team but on periodic sharpening of the instruments of investigation.

XIX. SEXUAL OFFENCES*

Among the many problems that confront the criminologist perhaps the most urgent is that of the sexual offender. From almost any point of view, the subject is beset with confusion, which is further confounded by the deep moral prejudice aroused in otherwise reasonable people by any consideration of sexual matters. Difficult as it is to persuade those concerned with the making and administration of the law that some common forms of anti-social behaviour may be signs of mental disorder, it is still more difficult to convince them that sexual offences are not just signs of moral depravity. Even amongst trained criminologists a remarkable diversity of opinion exists regarding the nature of sexual offences; and this inevitably is reflected in their scientific work. Perhaps the best example is afforded by investigations of so-called 'criminal types', and of the response of the latter to various forms of disposal. Since sexual offences bulk largely in the criminal calendar, it seems reasonable enough to include a quota of sexual offenders in any case-sample examined whether of probationers or of prisoners. On the other hand to include amongst 'criminal types' cases of homosexuality whose cultural, ethical and social standards are often well above those of the average law-abiding citizen is to reduce criminal typology to nonsense.

Some of these difficulties will no doubt be overcome when statisticians take into account the variety of offence committed, a precaution which has been somewhat conspicuously neglected by many reputable observers, psychiatrists and sociologists alike.

* Brit. J. Delinq., 3, 2-4, 1952.

But this alone will not solve the problem of research. It is essential to distinguish not only between different types of offence, but also between different varieties of the same offence. In this respect the socio-legal diagnosis (or charge) on which criminal records are based, is singularly uninformative. While the technique of theft, for example, may justify the inclusion of all cases of theft in one large group, such mass-procedure ignores the fact that stealing may have an entirely different significance in psychopathic, psychotic, psycho-neurotic and other types of disorder, not excluding pubertal stress.

Research on these matters calls for further effort on the part of the individual psychologist or psychiatrist. Grateful as we must always be to those pioneers in sexology who first uncovered the tap-roots of sexual disorder, we must nevertheless insist that their successors should provide more detailed studies not only of the main groups of sexual offence but of the characteristic variations existing within any one group. A case in point is raised in Dr. Maclay's paper.[1] It is customary to regard exhibitionism either as an independent form of sexual aberration, or, since the work of the psycho-analysts, as being at the same time a remainder and surrogate of a polymorphous infantile sexuality. Dr. Maclay enters a modest plea for the recognition of a number of sub-groups of exhibitionism, one of which he describes as a simple retardation of the normal adult heterosexual impulse.

Now although the psycho-analyst maintains that most sexual aberrations are defensive regressions from adult sexuality, he is bound to admit that the depth of the regression varies in accordance with the level of development at which the child first experienced, even if only unconsciously, the anxieties of genital sexuality. And in fact, just as we may arrange the classical mental disorders in a developmental series, e.g. psychoses, neuroses, inhibitions, etc., so the sexual perversions can be arranged in accordance with their depth. Active homosexuality, for example, is by far the most advanced and organized of the sexual aberrations. Exhibitionism on the other hand may draw force from any of the early stages of development, and for this very reason it is essential to establish different grades and conditions of the disorder. Mild forms of exhibitionism are probably of the same developmental level as

[1] David T. Maclay: 'The Diagnosis and Treatment of Compensatory Types of Indecent Exposure', *Brit. J. Delinq.*, 3, 34–45, 1952.

mild hysterias or mild impotence; whereas the exhibitionism of the psychopath is of a deeper and more intractable nature, or, to use the technical term, is more narcissistic.

All this has a very obvious bearing not only on the individual treatment of exhibitionism but on the socio-legal aspects of the problem. Even if we exclude the possibility that, except in the case of exposure before minors, society adopts an unnecessarily prudish reaction to the offence, and thereby in many cases incites the exhibitionist to activity, it is essential that the disposal of the convicted offender should in every case begin with a psychiatric approach. Society is entitled to lay down laws of common decency and to mark its disapproval of infringement of these laws; it must recognize, however, that penal methods are not an appropriate first resource either in the treatment or in the prevention of sexual disorder.

But in the last resort and after the psychologist, the sociologist and the forensic expert have all had their say, it is to the anthropologist that we must turn in the handling of sexual problems. Not only can he trace the history of sexual prejudice to its beginnings in the earliest known periods of human development, but, from his study of the sexual controls and methods of sexual upbringing practised in uncontaminated primitive cultures, he can indicate in which respects modern societies seem to have gone astray in their attempts to control the sexual instincts. No doubt much anthropological investigation is undisciplined and often speculative; yet it seems clear from observation of primitive sexual mores that the massive control of infantile sexuality generally applied in sophisticated cultures was a step in the wrong direction. Confirmation of this assumption is not hard to obtain from the records of child guidance clinics in modern cities. It remains to be seen whether our publicists will have the moral courage to draw and give effect to the logical conclusion.

XX. HOMOSEXUALITY*

Recently in this country a wave of popular interest in 'homosexuality' and 'bisexuality', swollen no doubt by reports of 'sensational' cases, has reached the point at which ordinarily it would be liable to spend itself in hasty and prejudiced action. Fortunately this more sensational approach, which already has

* *Brit. J. Delinq.*, 5, 2–3, 1954.

produced in homosexual groups the feeling that they are about to witness and suffer from an outbreak of 'witch-hunting', has been offset by the genuine concern freely expressed in Press and Parliament that these root problems, which lie so close to the foundations of human society, should be re-considered and dealt with in a manner consonant with their gravity, that is to say with dispassionate understanding and compassionate laws. The appointment of a special Departmental Committee on Homosexuality and Prostitution provides yet another occasion for the mobilization of enlightened opinion, an aim which, however, cannot very well be realized unless each of the sciences whose fields of observation and methods of examination bring them in close and objective contact with these problems is ready to publicize its own conclusions and attitudes regarding the subject.

But, although we may look forward in a fairly sanguine mood to the deliberations of the Home Office Committee, we must restrain any undue optimism regarding extensive changes in the laws defining sexual offences that may result from these deliberations. To turn for a moment to a recent Norwegian survey:[1] it is a chastening thought that a country where social opinion is enlightened enough to be prepared to cease penalizing homosexuality as such is nevertheless prepared to sanction castration as a remedy for some sexual offences.[2] True, in Norway this talion penalty is facultative in the sense that the offender must give his 'consent' to the operation; but since a 'certain amount of social pressure' is exercised on the inmate by telling him that he will not be released unless he is willing to be castrated, it seems that on occasion a penological factor is brought to bear on what might otherwise be regarded as an experiment in therapy. However that may be, it is clear that we cannot hope fully to understand the regulations governing sexual offences until we investigate the deep and mostly unconscious forces that govern public opinion in this matter.

XXI. THE ROOTS OF HOMOSEXUALITY*

But when all is said clinical records provide little more than skeletal surveys of a subject or problem that is immensely more

[1] Andenaes, Halvorsen and Kjolstad, *Brit. J. Delinq.*, 5, 29–33, 1954.

[2] A similar barbaric practice is carried out in special institutions in Denmark (e.g. in Herstedvester) and is justified on the thinnest of rationalizations (see this Section, XXII).

* *Brit. J. Delinq.*, 9, 5, 1958.

complicated than the clinical approach to manifest homosexuality would suggest. The case-history, valuable as it undoubtedly is, constitutes merely a classroom diagram concerning such cases as have been indiscreet (or compulsive) enough to have brought detection and punishment on themselves or at most have felt that their homosexual organization is a distressing abnormality or handicap calling for treatment. It is only when the unconscious roots of manifest homosexuality are examined that we are able to appreciate not only the extensive ramifications of the problem but also the remarkable and indeed indispensable social services rendered by the sublimation of unconscious (infantile) homosexual impulses. Social solidarity between individual males and within male groups, cultural activities of a manifold nature, the transmission of culture from one generation to another, pedagogic ideals, and a not inconsiderable part of religious feeling can be traced more or less directly to the mastery of those powerful bisexual impulses that in large part govern the psychological development of the growing child. Not only so, an as yet unascertained but undoubtedly large part of heterosexual love life (both psychic and physical) is supported and strengthened by contributions from unconscious homosexual sources (identifications). All this tends to be lost sight of in clinical surveys which, even if they do not accept the criminal designation of manifest homosexuality, tend explicitly or implicitly to regard homosexuality merely as a psychiatric disorder in which psychic love, such as is apparently taken for granted in heterosexual relations, plays a relatively minor part. It seems also to be assumed by many clinicians that promiscuity, jealousy and unhappiness are inevitably associated with this form of sexual object-choice. It is a useful corrective to these prejudices to bear in mind that so far most clinical studies are concerned with a small fraction of a special group which in turn represents only a small fraction of the total manifest homosexual population and that in the last psycho-biological analysis manifest homosexuality represents an outcropping of an unconscious psychic stratum on which much of our civilization rests.

XXII. THE CASTRATION OF SEXUAL OFFENDERS*

The specialist in forensic psychology cannot remind himself too often that his particular branch of science differs from other

* Brit. J. Delinq., 1, 5, 1950.

departments of medical psychology, and indeed from most natural sciences, in many important respects. Social factors, for example, play a much larger part in delinquent states than in mental disorders such as the psycho-neuroses; hence sociological criteria figure prominently in the diagnosis, prognosis and treatment of delinquency.

But the social valuation of any one crime is known to vary from period to period and from one culture to another. And in view of modern efforts to establish enlightened policies on an international basis it does seem important to examine these variations with some care, otherwise there is a risk of confusion of international counsel. A policy that is regarded in one country as enlightened may in fact be deemed reactionary in another. It seems all the more reasonable therefore to enquire whether the penal measures or for that matter the therapeutic measures, sanctioned and employed in different countries, exhibit any characteristic variations. In short, since in democratic countries the law represents ultimately a consensus of social feeling, a comparison of penal methods offers an interesting approach to the investigation of differential racial characteristics.

To the sociologist with his techniques of statistical assessment based on conscious criteria, this may appear a comparatively simple issue to be settled mainly by the examination of cultural patterns. But for the dynamic psychologist, the whole question of differential racial characteristics is a quaking bog of uncertainty. Nevertheless the issue cannot be ignored. It was raised in an interesting form on a recent occasion when a film sponsored by the Danish Government and directed by Dr. G. Stürup, the Medical Director of the psychopathic institution at Herstedvester, was shown in London under the joint auspices of the I.S.T.D. and the Howard League for Penal Reform. This dealt with the handling of a selected group of persistent psychopathic criminal and sexual offenders. Three points of socio-legal as well as psychological importance emerged: first, that the governing ideal in treatment is collective rather than individual, namely the need for social adjustment; second, that the patients are admitted on an indeterminate sentence; and third, that a considerable proportion, apparently well over 50 per cent, of the sexual offenders, are castrated. The majority of the sexual offences were committed against children, but significantly enough a number (15 per cent of the total) of exhibitionists were included.

As far as the first point is concerned, it is clear that some difference of attitude must exist as between the sociologist and the psychologist. It is natural that the sociologist should have the health and interest of the community at heart, equally natural that the psychologist's concern should be with the treatment and mental integrity of the individual. The psychologist cannot of course afford to neglect social considerations any more than the sociologist can afford to neglect the criteria of individual psychology, but his primary concern is with the alleviation of the disorder of which delinquent conduct is only the symptom. His social interest is amply satisfied by his efforts to render the individual offender stable enough to accept responsible social regulation. Beyond that point his professional writ does not run.

As for the indeterminate sentence and the treatment of chronic sex offenders by castration, it is appropriate to quote here the opinion of Lord Justice Denning, who remarked on that occasion that whatever might be said for or against these two measures they were against the existing temper of the people of this country. Clearly the indeterminate sentence offends the sense of justice of those who, openly or secretly, believe in the virtue of punishment or that the offender should be allowed whenever possible to purge his offence; and although they are doubtless ready to recognize the social argument that in the interests of public safety the persistent violent offender must be kept under supervision until he achieves self-control, penal reformers are not likely to be mollified by the psychiatrist's special plea that adequate treatment may be prejudiced by the imposition of a too short fixed sentence. The whole subject of the indeterminate sentence, to say nothing of its congener, the 'psychiatric' parole, bristles with difficulties. Whatever may be said in its favour by the psychiatrist or the sociologist, the practice of endowing the psychiatrist with judicial authority, for that in effect is what is implied by the regulation of imprisonment or parole in accordance with medical opinion, is open to the gravest question. Even on therapeutic grounds, the position of the psychiatrist exercising these powers is fundamentally false.

As for the treatment of sexual offenders by castration, this clearly is an issue that calls for objective and dispassionate examination. There is, in fact, good reason to enquire whether the practice is not of the same order as the medieval custom, still practised in some backward communities, of cutting off the hands of certain violent criminals, or, indeed, the habit of some latter-day parents of washing out their children's mouths with soap when they tell lies. Nor can it be only coincidence that a well-defined group of apparently 'normal' people are convinced that the appropriate punishment of any male sexual offender is castration, a prejudice which they usually express in the vernacular. Even if it were clearly established that castration is scientific in the sense that it has acted as a therapeutic agent, it would not follow that practices of this sort have either a professional or an ethical justification. By the same argument we could justify thumb-screws. All of which brings us back to the point originally raised, namely, are the differences between the various penal systems adopted in various countries purely superficial, or do they reflect important cultural differences, (a) in the reaction to systems of punishment, (b) in the valuation of individual as distinct from social 'good' ? It should be the combined task of the sociologist and the psychologist to investigate this problem and to make their conclusions widely known. Otherwise there is a risk that under the protective cover of scientific advancement some obscurantist ideas and practices may continue to flourish, as they did in more superstitious times; and, what is worse, be accepted and approved by well-meaning reformers who are not in a position to recognize their origin.

XXIII. THE GOVERNMENT AND THE WOLFENDEN REPORT ON HOMOSEXUALITY AND PROSTITUTION*

In these stressful times when political and international crises, heightened always by fears of war, tend to absorb public attention, relatively little notice is taken of matters that have been of the greatest moment to mankind since the dawn of civilization. The control of sexual impulses whether by moral, educational, social or penal measures is such a matter. Saving occasions when an unusually sensational case of sexual perversion reaches the headlines, the dark and chequered history of sexual conflict remains buried in anthropological treatises which at the beginning of this century were regarded by legal and social opinion as pornographic works. Under these circumstances the appointment by the Government of a Departmental Committee to consider the legal and social standing of homosexuality and prostitution was an important

* Brit, J. Delinq., 9, 161–3, 1959

decision; it renewed the hopes of those who seek for a humane solution of difficulties that have reduced the authorities to taking measures conspicuously unsuitable to achieve their end. When in addition the Government of the day in full debate enters what is for most purposes a *nolle sequi* to the Report, the time has come for people of scientific temper to take stock of the situation.

In view of the Government's decision to do no more than 'take notice' of the Report's recommendations on homosexuality, we may repeat our regrets that the scientific evidence laid before the Committee was not published. For while the Wolfenden recommendation, viz., that homosexual acts occurring in private between consenting adults should not constitute a criminal offence, would seem to represent a milestone in the progress of instructed public opinion, it was a finding based on a remarkable and long-established consensus of scientific opinion put before the Committee. Viewed from this point of view the Home Secretary's promise of research on the subject, though laudable enough in itself, seems to have operated as a placebo to still the consciences of those who are left with the uneasy feeling that the manifest homosexual is treated as a scapegoat for the homosexual components that exist unnoticed in the community at large. And while it may be argued that after the Wolfenden Report the legal and possibly the social prejudice against homosexuality can never again be so intense, this is possibly an over-optimistic view. It is of course open to the courts to mitigate criminal proceedings by treating the offence as a problem in individual development calling for the most careful scrutiny and where feasible for treatment rather than penal sentence; but it is always possible that some magistrates and judges may be encouraged by the Government's inaction to deal with homosexual cases with unaltered or even more condign severity. Even if such a regressive reaction does not ensue, it must be clear that treatment is appropriate only in cases where homosexuality reflects some mental aberration; it leaves the problem of the so-called 'normal' homosexual entirely untouched. In short, the one indisputable conclusion to be drawn from the Parliamentary debate is that, despite the modern tendency to temper punishment with measures of amelioration, the attitude to homosexuality of our present Elizabethan legislators is in some respects more obscurantist than that of our mid-Victorian forebears.

Turning to the problem of prostitution, the one indisputable conclusion that can be drawn is that never in the history of Departmental Committees or Parliamentary Proceedings has so little been known of a problem that affects so many. The prostitute plying her ancient profession is not a ready subject for investigation; even when apparently co-operative she confesses as a rule with her tongue in her cheek, producing thereby fabrications which do little more than cloud the understanding of her interlocutors. The truth is that the prostitute herself understands the reasons for her choice of profession no more than the bewildered heterosexual knows why he has contracted an unhappy marriage. Despite this drawback or just because of it, the problems of prostitution call for as close and comprehensive investigation as do those of homosexuality. Apropos, it is to be regretted that the Report should give the impression that 'sociology' and 'reform' have nothing to do with 'deliberate scientific investigation'. It is impossible, for example, to assess variations in the incidence of prostitution without a parallel investigation of the rates of premarital intercourse; or to account for different types of prostitute without a social survey of the patrons whose demand the prostitute supplies.

Incidentally the Wolfenden Report itself, though maintaining that its concern is with the problem of street offences, shows a significant inclination towards systems of warning and of early contact with trained social workers and probation officers, thereby giving tacit assent to the view that to concentrate on deterrence of public solicitation is to put the cart before the horse. And although the Committee perforce agreed that prostitution is not a crime, it is clear that its attitude to street offences was to some extent sharpened by the realization that the real problem lies elsewhere, and has so far proved insoluble. If it is to be solved, something more than mere social contact with the young prostitute is essential. The seeds of prostitution are sown during childhood, and, as in the case of delinquent conduct, we must fall back ultimately on child guidance and educational organizations to detect and correct the factors that later on give rise to abnormal or archaic sexual manifestations.

Nevertheless one can sympathize with the difficulties confronting the Wolfenden Committee. Being unable to strike to the roots of the problem they could but gamble on a system of deterrence of street offences, even if by so doing they implicitly confessed the failure of their efforts. To be sure, if fines are deterrent, why not increase these to counterbalance the existing reduction of monetary values? The threat of a three months prison sentence on a third conviction is, however, quite a different matter. The Committee was constrained to justify the suggestion on the grounds that the threat of a prison sentence may induce prostitutes to give assent to a probation order. But this implies that the prison sentence as such is unlikely to prove an effective deterrent. On the other hand, to threaten a prison sentence is a vote of no confidence in the deterrent effect of fines!

Is there then no real solution of this problem of street offences? Judge John V. Barry[1] seems to think that in Australia at any rate there is, although whether this is due to the more systematic application of controlling measures or to the comparative absence of righteous indignation on the part of the general public is not very clear. Incidentally, as in this country, the term 'common prostitute' still applies in Australia – a legal usage which we believe should be abolished. And we are inclined to think that it is desirable to establish 'annoyance' on the testimony of an independent witness. One may well argue that this would make the law governing soliciting entirely unworkable. On the other hand, it reduces court proceedings to a farce to be content with the unsupported testimony of a policeman that the accosted person was 'annoyed'. All in all we must recognize with regret that three years of hopeful labour have ended in a penal anti-climax.

XXIV. CAPITAL PUNISHMENT*

The fact that the most turbulent emotions are aroused in all concerned is itself a clear indication that one of the most fruitful sources of information on capital punishment is not so much the examination of such reliable statistics as exist, as the examination of anthropological evidence. If, for example, it should be a correct interpretation of the habit of blindfolding the prisoner before execution, that it owes less to humane motives of consideration than to an unconscious need to protect the executioner from the (not unnaturally) evil eye of the prisoner, it would amply repay the effort involved were the Royal Commission on Capital Punish-

[1] 'Prostitution: Report from Australia', *Brit. J. Delinq.*, **9**, 3, 1959.
* *Brit. J. Delinq.*, **9**, 1958.

ment to investigate, if not the whole history of atonement, punishment and sacrifice in primitive society, at least the habits and customs of the Middle Ages, when superstition was still a part of natural science and, therefore, less clouded by rationalization. No findings on capital punishment can be regarded as scientific which do not take into account the latest anthropological evidence.

INDEX OF AUTHORS

Abraham, K., 134
Adler, A., 100
Aichhorn, A., 33, 35, 51, 103, 157–8, **164–9**, 306
Alexander, F., 35, 51, 135
Allen, C., 113
Andry, R. G., 276
Attlee, Lord, 62, 352
Baldie, A., 37
Barry, J. V., 396
Batchelor, I. D., 143, 275
von Behring, 24
Bonnard, A., 323–4
Bowlby, J., 42, 143, 314, 323
Braithwaite, R., 63
Bronner, A., 36, 51
Buckle, H. T., 379
Burrow, Trigant, 306
Burt, C., 36, 39, 43
Butler, R. A., 70
Carr-Saunders, A. M., 39
Carroll, D. C., 41, 287–8, 312, 324
Chadwick, M., 43
Coates, S. H., 95
Court, A., 43
Denning, Lord, 392
Devon, J., xi, 34
Dillon, F., 40
Eder, M. D., 36
Eysenck, H. J., 280–2, 291, 319, 323
Ferenczi, S., 133, 137
Forsyth, D., 41
Franklin, M., 41
Freud, A., 42, 55, 301

Freud, S., ix, xi, 7, 11, 13, 17, 33–5, 103, 132–5, 149, 152, 165, 167, 173, 176–7, 197–8, 215, 241, 247, 318, 337, 366–7, 385
Friedlander, K., 41–2, 316–7, 323
Frost, 37
Gibbens, T. C. N., 74, 252, 254, 260
Glueck, E. T., 36, 51, 93, 282, 322–3
Goring, C. B., 43
Gregor, 169
Grey Walter, W., 66, 276, 278, 280
Gruhle, H., 164
Grünhut, M., 64, 74
Grygier, T., 164, 323–4, 354
Hadfield, J. A., 36
Hall Williams, E., 342
Halvorsen, J., 389
Hamblin-Smith, M., 35
Harvey, W., 245
Healy, W., 36–51
Henderson, D. K., 40, 121–2, 355, 381–2
Henriques, B., 43
Hill, D., 355
Hubert, W. H., 37
Jennings-White, H. D., 39
Jensen, E. T., 36
Jones, E., 134, 139
Jung, C. G., 281, 321
Karpman, B., 154, 313, 323
Kinsey, A. C., 187

Kjolstad, T., 389
Klein, M., 42, 57
Kraepelin, E., 121
Kretschmer, E., 321
Krohne, 169
Krout, M., 323-4
Krout-Tabin, J. C., 323-4
Lewis, E. E., 40
Lombroso, C., 33
Low, B., 42
Lynch, G., 72
Maberly, A., 41
McCord, W. & J., 159
Mackwood, J., 37
Maclay, D. T., 370-1, 387-8
MacNiven, A., 40
Mannheim, H., 39, 64, 72, 74, 363
Martin, C. E., 187
Mercier, C., 121
Michaels, J. J., 384-6
Miller, E., 41, 363
Morris, N., 342
Mullins, C., 43-4
Naecke, P., 121
Napier, M. B., 143, 275
Neill, A. S., 45
Norwood East, W., 37, 43
Olivier, Lord, 12
Pailthorpe, G., xii, 35-6, 41
Partridge, G. E., 122, 138
Paterson Brown, W., 41
Pearce, J. D. W., 41
Pomeroy, W. B., 187

Prichard, J. C., 17, 120-1, 148, 314, 354
Quetelet, J., 379
Radzinowicz, L., 42, 74
Rank, O., 217
Reich, W., 35, 51, 135
Reik, T., 35, 51
Roper, W. F., 377-8
St. Loe Strachey, 8
Samuel, Lord, 61
Schmideberg, M., 41, 160, 218, 303, 370, 372, 383-4
Scott, P. D., 96, 283, 365-6
Sellin, T., 62, 353
Sessions Hodge, R., 66, 276, 278, 280
Shaw, O., 45
Spencer, J., 63, 72
Stafford Clark, D., 355
Staub, H., 35
Steinberg, A., 384-6
Stürup, G., 391
Taylor, 355
Templewood, Lord, 38
Thompson, R. E., 93
Torrie, A., 349
Turner, J. W. C., 42
Warren, W., 278-9
Watson, J., 43
Wilkins, L. T., 64, 73-4, 112
Wills, D., 45
Woddis, G. M., 74, 382-4
Woodward, M., 189
Wordsworth, W., 102

SUBJECT INDEX

Abandoning child, 89
Abnormal and 'normal' behaviour, 363-4, 370
Absolution, 4
Accessibility, 105, 168, 306-7, 309
'Acting-out', 151-2
Adlerian treatment, 100
Advanced cases, 376
'Affectionless' child, 86, 143
After-history, 49-50, 52, 108-9, 113
Age distribution and homosexuality, 204-6
Aggression, 57, 108-9, 197, 301-2, 371-2
  and homosexuality, 209, 217
  social, 371-2
  and super-ego, 301 (*see also* Hostility)
Aggressive
  instincts, 173 (*see also* Instincts)
  psychopath, 121, 126, 149, 167
Aim inhibited impulses, 247-8
Alcohol
  and crime, 19
  and guilt, 17, 34
  and homosexuality, 213
  and psychopathy, 121
Alcoholism, 90, 299
Alloplastic reactions, 133-4
Altruism, 7
Ambivalence, 71-2
  in Foreign Offices, x
  of governments, 267

Ambulant
  clinics, 369-70 (*see also* Psychopathic Clinic, Portman Clinic)
  treatment, 73, 112-4, 191, 193, 308-9, 329
  of children, 42, 100, 156
Anal
  character, 134
  -genital perversions, 182, 220, 232
  libido, 179, 245
  phantasies, 146
  sadism, 139, 220
  sexuality, 245
  super-ego, 144
Antagonism to male, 255
Anthropology, 54, 285, 311, 354, 388, 396-7
  and psychopathy, 122, 126, 198
Anti-social character, 317-8
Anxiety, 18, 140
  of castration, 221, 224, 238
  homosexual, 217, 224, 242
  and inhibition, 353
  and psycho-analysis, 240
  readiness, 138
  of separation, 86, 143, 275, 300, 315, 372
  stress, 104
Approved schools, 45, 72-3, 99, 350
Arson, 184
Attempted suicide, 89-90
Attendance centres, 63

SUBJECT INDEX

Attitudes
　to father, 277
　to mother, 277
Auto-erotism, 179, 247 (*see also* Masturbation)
Autoplastic reactions, 133-4

Backward children, 36 (*see also* Mental defect)
Backwardness, sexual, 247, 252
'Bad'
　company, 186
　objects, 157
　parents, 143, 250
Beating, 22, 353
Bed-wetting, 384-6
Behaviour, 83
　disorders, 20, 50, 89-90
　normal and abnormal, 363-4, 370
　'problems', 90
　psychopathic, 125, 127
　sexual, 193-6
　unconscious factors in, 102
Beyond control, 89-90, 92
Bisexuality, 199, 207-8, 211, 223, 231, 236, 247 (*see also* Homosexuality)
Body libido, 179, 245
Borderline
　mental defect, 90-2
　psychoses, 90-2
Born criminal, 8
Borstal, 32, 45, 99, 350
Breaking and entering, 87-90
British Journal of Delinquency, 64-5, 72, 74, 363
British Medical Association, 357
Broadmoor cases, 312

'Broken home', 66, 86, 143, 274-6, 300, 315, 372
Buggery, 22, 220
　and homosexuality, 293

Cambridge University (Law Dept.), 70
Capital punishment, 62, 68, 352-9, 396-7
　abolition of, 353
　age limit, 358
　and deterrence, 352-4
　and reprieve, 356, 358
　and sexual prejudices, 343-5
Car offences, 90
'Care or protection', 89-90, 186, 192, 257, 313
Case
　frames, 374
　history, 84
　records, 374
　selection, 50, 54, 72, 234, 313
Cases
　refractory, 55
　wastage of, 107
Castration, 182
　anxiety, 221, 224, 238
　of sexual offenders, 390-3
Censorship, 12
Character
　anti-social, 317-8
　disorder, 91-2
　-formation, 133, 157
　hysterical, 137
　impulsive ('instinct-ridden'), 118, 135-6
　infantile, 8
　libidinal types of, 134, 135-6
　neurotic, 21, 51, 92, 135-7, 152, 380

Character—*cont.*
  normal, 382
  obsessional, 134, 137
  oral, 134
  paranoid, 131
  and psychopathy, 117–8, 125–6
  psychotic, 121, 137
  traits, 21, 81, 315
  urethral, 134
Characterology, psycho-analytical, 52, **134–47**
Cheating, 16
Child
  analysis, 42, 156
  guidance clinics, 39–40, 60, 162, 297, 315, 350
  psychopathy, 161
  therapy, 100
Civilization and crime, ix,
Classification, 72–3, 81, 91, 336, 377–8
  clinical, 50, 89–90, 93
  and definition, 378–80
  in depth, 132, 297
  etiological, 50, 133, 307
  Friedlander's, 316–7
  of instincts, 173
  of mental disorders, 119, 197–200
  psycho-analytical, 313–4
  of psychopathy, 120–25, 381
  standards of, 123
Classifying school, 276
Clinic, 369, 370
  practice, 106 (*see also* Psychopathic Clinic and Portman Clinic, Ambulant clinics)

Clinical
  aspects, 312
  empiricism, 81
  psychology, 282, 289–90
  recommendations, 98–9
  sociology, 282
  statistics, 89–92
Common prostitute, 396
Common sense, 83, 365–6
Component impulse, 217, 220–1, 240–1, 245–7
Compulsive theft, 16, 93
Conclusions, premature, 303
Concussion, 11, 12
Conditioning, concept of, 281–2, 321–2
Conduct, theories of, 29
Conflict, 7, 104, 273 (*see also* Guilt)
  homosexual, 203
  sexual, 183, 203
  unconscious, 56, 316
Conscience and psychopathy, 303
  social, 293
  (*see also* Super-ego, Unconscious)
Constitutional factors, 22, 84, 133, 138, 260, 278, 304, 315, 347
  and homosexuality, 201
  and psychopathy, 133, 138
  and treatment, 85
'Continuum', concept of, 281–2, 321–2
Control groups, 374
Corporal punishment, 22, 353 (*see also* Beating, Flogging)
Counter-transference, 149, 307–8

SUBJECT INDEX

Court
  contempt of, 194
  prejudices, 176
  reports, 93, 95, 365-8
Courts
  Higher, 44
  Lower, 9, 84, 87, 89, 93
Crime
  degrees of, 344
  and disease, 343
  equivalents, 318
  etiological factors, 278-80
  and homosexuality, 201-3
  or perversion, 372-3
  waves of, 61, 63
Criminal
  and capital punishment, 340-343
  irresponsibility, 342-3, 358
  Justice Act, 61, 63
    Bill, 29-30
  and murder, 340, 343-5
  psychopath, **117-69**, 122 (*see also* Psychopathy)
  responsibility, 5, 6, 11, 13, 80-1, 95, **339-46**, 353, 385
Criminality
  and alcoholism, 19, 121
  and guilt, 17, 34
Criminology and psycho-analysis, **311-24**
Crises, environmental, 153
  pubertal, 298
Cruelty, persistent, 89 (*see also* Sadism, Violence)
Cure, 20, 52-3, 108, 188
  rapid, 158
  standards of, 107
Curiosity, sexual, 180, 246, 310
Cushion slashing, 184

Damaging property, 90
Dartmoor types, 41, 310, 312, 369, 376
Death penalty, 69
  abolition of, 353
Deep analysis, 20
Defect, mental, 90
Defence, mental, 5, 40, 85, 90-1, 208
Definitions, **272-6**, 378-80
Deformities, 71
Delinquency
  and bedwetting, 384-6
  clinical aspects of, **312-20**
  duration of, 377
  episodic, 332-3
  'functional', 298, 316, 385
  juvenile, 9, 36
  latent, 186
  and mental pathology, 27
  neurotic, 50, 90-2, 152, 161, 298, 318-9
  and normality, 23, 196, 314, 381
  and prostitution, 245, 256
  and psychiatry, 330-2
  and psycho-analysis, **292-310**, 311-2, 331-2
  psycho-somatic, 298, 385
  pubertal, 89, 92, 298
  research on, 17, 39-40, 45-7, 50, 62, 66, 70-1, 74-5, 373-5
  social assessment of, 285
  and social psychology, 330-1
  and sociology, 330-1
  a special study, 363
  treatment of, 107-13, **305-10**
  undetected, 295

Delinquency—*cont.*
  varieties of, 293, 298–9, 314
    (*see also* Offences)
Delusions, persecutory, 141
Denial, 225, 256
Departmental Committee on Homosexuality and Prostitution, 11, 62–3, 68–9, 173, 189–90, 389, 393–6
Depression, 14, 124, 145, 379
  and crime, 382–3
Depressive character, 137
Descriptive data, 75
Detention
  centres, 22, 63–4
  preventive, 72, 372
Deterrence, 10, 31, 193, 352–4
Developmental factors, 85–7, 166, 297
Diagnosis, 46–9, **79–96**, 309
  difficulty of, 99
  and magistrates, 23–4
  medico-psychological, 89–92
  research on, 113–4
Diagnostic
  reports, 93, 95, **365–8**
  team, 93–4
  techniques, 47
  theories, 47
Dichotomy, sexual, 248–9
Diminished responsibility, 95, 344, 356
Disappointment, therapeutic, 151
Discoveries, 3
Discretion
  homosexual, 238–9
  professional, 367–8, 372
Disease and homosexuality, 201
Displacement, 13, 140, 184

Disposal of cases, 32, 48–9, 114
'Distributed' transference, 53, 104, 111, 153, 156
Dreams, homosexual, 211
Drug addiction, 90, 124
Drunk and disorderly, 89–90
Duration of treatment, 52, 107

East-Hubert Centre, 62
East London Clinic, 22
Ecclesiastical law, 10, 173, 190
Eclectic psychology, 43
Economic factors, 229
Economics (mental), 140–1
Education, sexual, 264
Educational psychology, 40–1, 60, 94, 296
Ego, 56
  ideal, 12
  modification, 156
  new growth of, 156
  nuclear theory of, 146
  psychopathic, 123, 145
  structures, 303–4
  synthesis, 303–4
Electro-encephalography, 66, 94, 354
Embezzlement, 89
Empiricism, 81, 148–9
Encephalitis lethargica, 11
End products, 82
Endocrinology, 43, 94, 182
Endopsychic factors, 85–6, 109, 133, 142–4, 257, 279, 304, 317
  in treatment, 99
Environmental factors, 85–6, 109, 133, 142–3, 257, 279, 320
  in treatment, 99

Epilepsy, 11
Equivalents
  of crime, 318
  of neuroses, 137, 214–5, 315
  of symptoms, 318
État dangereux, 118, 337
Ethics, of homosexuals, 293
Etiology, 85–7
  of homosexuality, **176–81, 214–29**
  'one-factor', 197–200
  of prostitution, **245–56**
  psycho-analytical, **138–47**
  of psychopathy, **132–47**
  variables in, 315
Evacuation, 8, 39, 48
Evil, 4
Examination
  clinical, **83–9**
  of sexual offenders, 11
  therapeutic effect of, 158
Excretory impulses, 7
Execution, 354
Exhibitionism, 8, 10, 177, 180, 246, 336, 387–8
Exhortation, 150
Experts, rôle of, 267
Expiation, ix, 4
Extenuating circumstances, 83, 95, 98, 335, 357, 379

Factorial
  assessments, **276–80**
  psychology, 321
Failure of treatment, 239, 329
False pretences, 89
Familial
  psychology, 86, 143, 275, 300, 315, 372
  sociology, 22, 86, 143, 279

Family
  influence, 279
  love, 257
Fellatio, 181, 200–1, 221
Fetichism, 184–5, 212–3, 218, 372
Fines, 266–7, 396
Five-year survey (I.S.T.D.), 79
Fixation points, 197, 214, 241–2, 247
Flogging, x, 22, 353
Focal therapies, 106, 150, 156, 237–8, 240
Follow-up, 49–50, 52, 108–10, 113, 236
Food, 14, 305
Forensic psychiatry, x, 33
Forgery, 89
Foster homes, 193
Free will, 80–1
Freudian
  school, 42, 52, 57
  technique, 319–20
  theory, 289
  treatment, 100
  (*see also* Psycho-analysis, Freud, Index of Authors)
Frigidity, 255
Frustration, 8, 17, 85, 87–8, 138–9, 140, 144–5, 228–9, 304
  and homosexuality, 228–9
Functional
  approach, 83
  delinquency, 298, 316, 385
Fusion of instincts, 30

Gain
  primary, 226, 243
  secondary, 226, 243

Gain—*cont.*
  through illness, 108
Gambling, 90
General psychology, 285, 330–1
Genetic psychology, 285
Genital
  development, 134
  impulses, 140, 219–21
  super-ego, 144
Good, 4
Group
  control, 374
  normal, 75
  surveys, 65
  therapy, 100, 150, 159–60, 306
Guilt, ix, 17, 242, 302–3
  absence of, 17
  and alcoholism, 17, 34
  avoidance, 302–3
  and homosexuality, 224, 238, 240, 242
  and psychopathy, 120, 123, 125, 127–8, 142–7, 303, 383–4
  and team research, 288

Hardened offenders, 10, 329, 338, 369
Hate, 301 (*see also* Aggression)
Head injuries, 11
Heterosexuality, 230, 390
  early, 180
  offences, 9
    (*see also* Sexuality)
High Courts, 44
History of study and treatment, **27–76**

Home Office, 21, 27–8, 31–2, 37–8, 43, 61–2, 70–1, 349
  Secretaries, 31, 37, 394
Homosexual, 10
  anxiety, 217, 224, 242
  conflict, 203
  discretion, 238–9
  dreaming, 211
  fellatio, 221
  fixation, 241–2
  jealousy, 210, 390
  love, 209–10
  objects, 207, 211, 221–3, 230
  offenders, 377
  precipitating factors, 226–9
  prostitutes, 226
  regression, 217
  resistances, 240–1
  transference, 241–2
Homosexuality, 8, 68–9, 180, **197–243**, 200–1, 355–9, 393–4
  active, 208, 232
  age incidence of, 204–6
  and aggression, 209
  and alcoholism, 213
  anal genital, 182, 220
  and bisexuality, 199, 207–8, 211–2, 223, 231, 236, 247
  classification of, 206–7
  clinic records, 235–7
  constitutional factors in, 207–8
  criminal, 201–3
  and disease, 201–2, 230
  economic factors, 229
  and ethics, 293
  etiology of, **214–29**
  and fetishism, 212–3, 218
  focal treatment of, 237

Homosexuality—*cont.*
  and frustration, 228-9
  genital aspects of, 220-1, 241
  and guilt, 224-5, 238, 240, 242
  and inhibitions, 213
  and isolation, 228
  and jealousy, 228
  latent, 200
  and the Law, 202-4
  and love, 209
  and neurosis, 202, 213, 233
  obsessional, 241-2
  and Oedipus complex, 215, 222-5
  oral genital, 181
    sadism, 217, 220-1
  parental transferences, 242
  passive, 208, 232
  pathological, 190
  penalties for, 63
  and primary gain, 226, 243
  prognosis of, **230-4**
  and prostitution, 226, 255-9
  and psycho-analysis, 202, **240-3**
  and psychopathy, 213
  and psychoses, 213
  'repressed', 201
  researches on, 293
  roots of, 389-90
  and sadism, 217, 220-1, 241
  and secondary gain, 226, 243
  seduction of minors, 203, 212
  selection of cases, 234
  and social anxiety, 238, 242
    cohesion, 199, 200
  statistics of, 204-6
  and super-ego, 199, 224-5, 240, 242
  and transvestitism, 212-3
  treatment of, 113, 203, 231, **234-43**
  and violent crime, 203
  and war-readiness, 202
Hormone treatment, 92, 182
Hostility, sexual, 183
House of Commons, 29, 68-9
Howard League of Penal Reform, 391
Humanism, ix
Humanitarian approach, 30, 112
Hypno-analysis, 100, 150
Hypnosis, 89, 105, 150
Hysterical character, 137

Id, 12, 135, 138
  resistance, 152
Identification, 140-2, 157, 222
Illegitimacy, 257-8
Imagination in research, 289
Immediacy of response, 56
Imposters, 16
Impotence, 215
Imprisonment, 49, 53, 175, 193 (*see also* Prison)
Improvement, 20, 52, 107-8, 266
Impulses
  excretory, 7
  uncontrollable, 357
Incest, 8
Indecency and homosexuality, 203
Indecent
  conversation, 89
  exposure, 9, 266
Indeterminate sentence, 71-2, 372, 392

Infantile
  character, 8
  sexuality, 10, **176–81**, 245–7
  (*see also* Sexuality)
Inhibition
  and anxiety, 353
  and homosexuality, 213
  and sexuality, 185
Ink-splashing, 184
Insanity and capital punishment, **339–46,** 355
Instincts, 7, 83, 299–301
  aggressive, 173
  component, 217, 220–1, 240–1, 245–7
  fusion of, 30
  and homosexuality, 220
  libidinal, 173
  primacy of, 8
  (*see also* Aggression, Libido, Sexuality)
Instinctual character, 118, 135–6
Institute of Criminology, 70–1
Institute for the Study and Treatment of Delinquency, 21, 36, 44–6, 48–50, 56, 60, 62, 73, 79, 266, 272, 347–8, 351, 354, 391
Institutional
  treatment, 99, 149, 308, 370–1
  types, 369
Institutions, 45, 65, 72, 307
  research on, 285
  (*see also* Approved Schools, Borstal, Prisons, Remand homes)
Intelligence tests, 94 (*see also* Tests)

Interpretation, 158, 273, 321, 374
Introjection, 158, 273, 321
Isolation and homosexuality, 228

Jealousy and homosexuality, 210
Judges, 6
  attitudes of, 31
Judicial tradition, 24, 27, 43
Jungian treatment, 100
Jury, 357–8
Juvenile delinquency, 9, 36
  Acts, 185–6, 366
  and prostitution, 257

Kleptomania, 16, 84, 175 (*see also* Theft, Stealing)
Kleinian school, 57
Kernel complex, 197–200, 215 (*see also* Oedipus)
Kinsey Report, 187, 204–5, 232

Laboratory psychology, 76
Latency period, 176, 178, 245–7
Law
  abindingness, 19
  and criminology, 27
  ecclesiastical, 10, 173, 190
  and medicine, 175
  and prostitution, 263, 266–7
  and psychology, 5, 17, 191
  and social psychiatry, 364–6
Lawyers, 285
League of Nations, x
Legal aspects of sexual abnormality, **173–96**
Lesbian activities, 173
Lex talionis, 342, 356

Liars, 17
Libido, 57
  anal, 179, 245
  cutaneous, 179
  development, 134, 197
  genital, 179
  oral, 7, 179, 245
  primacy of, 8, 246
  urethral, 179, 245
    (*see also* Anal, Genital, Oral)
Loitering with intent, 90
London School of Economics, 72
Lord Chief Justice, 61
Love
  and homosexuality, 209
  and money, 14
  sacred and profane, 248-9

M'Naghten Rules, 6, 13, 18, 31, 62, 80, 98, **339-46**, 347-8, 355-7
Magistrates, 4, 9, 11, 43
  attitude of, 12, 72
  and diagnosis, 23-4
  and psychiatrists, 71
  and psychologists, 4
  and psychopathy, 118-9
  training of, 58, 74
Male homosexuality (*see* Homosexuality)
Manic depression, 124, 302, 332, 382-4 (*see also* Depression)
Masochism, 86, 180, 246
Masturbation, 179, 208-9, 216-7
Maudsley School, 90-3, 324

Mechanisms, mental, 12, 140, 303, 315
Medical psychology, 23, 76, 234, 289
  diagnosis by, 90-3
  Research Council, 375
Medicine and the Law, 175
Medico-legal Society, 175
Mental
  age, 5
  conflict, 7, 104, 183, 203, 273
  defect, 5, 40, 85, 90-1, 208
  defence, 219
  disorders, 197, 200
  function, 295-6
  hospitals, 99
  immaturity, 10
  mechanisms, 140-1, 303, 315
  pathology, 27
  stress, 35-7, 87, 102, 104, 336
  suffering, 76, 273-4
    and perversions, 216
  tension, 87
  tests (*see* Tests)
Metapsychology, 138
Methodology, 373-5
Milieu therapy, 160
Mind
  theory of, 82, 292, 296
  unconscious, 12, 273, 295
Ministry
  of Criminology, 28
  of Education, 28, 80, 349-51
  of Health, xi, 28, 80, 349-51
Minors, seduction of, 10, 203, 212, 227, 231-3
Miserliness, 14, 260
Mixed types, 50-1
Mollycoddling offenders, 167

SUBJECT INDEX

Money
  and love, 14
  symbolism of, 260
Moral
  faculties, 83
  hypothesis of crime, 29–31
  imbecility, 17, 121, 354
  insanity, 17, 121, 354
  obliquity, 121–2
  suasion, 150
  values of criminal, 370
Morality of prostitute, 256
Mores
  sexual, 10
  unconscious, 17, 184
Motivation, 83
Multi-disciplined approach, 87, 235, 271, 311, 328 (*see also* Team research)
Murder, 17, 340, 343, 348
  degrees of, 359
  sexual, 181

Narcissism, 140, 261, 388
Narco-analysis, 100, 156
Narcosis and court reports, 366–8
Need
  for crime, ix
  for punishment, xi, 302
Negative transference in psychopathy, 151
Neurosis, 7, 380
  equivalents of, 137, 214–5, 315
  and homosexuality, 202, 213, 233
  obsessional, 17, 84, 88, 106, 184–5, 241–2, 322, 336
  and prostitution, 261
  and sexual perversion, 183–4, 241
  transference, 151–4
  (*see also* Psycho-neurosis)
Neurotic
  acting-out, 151–2
  character, 21, 51, 135–7, 152, 380
  delinquency, 152, 298, 318
  'equivalents', 50, 92, 137, 214–5, 318–9
  theft, 14–7
'Neuroticism', 281–2, 321, 380
Neutralization and sexuality, 216–7
Non-analytical
  psychiatry, 34
  psychology, 33–4
Non-criminal disorders, 294
Non-delinquents, 89, 99
Normal
  and abnormal behaviour, 363–4, 370
  character, 382
  groups, 75
  mental function, 295–6
  psychology, 34, 38–9
'Normality', 17, 273
  and crime, 23, 196
  and psychopathy, 119, 129, 145, 381
Norwich Scheme, 72
Notification, preventive, 350
Nuclear theory of ego, 146
Nurture, 86
Nymphomania, 230

Object
  in psychopathy, 123

Object—*cont.*
  relation disorder, 316
Observation, 52, 81, 95, 99–100, 309, 320
  of child by mother, 177
  therapeutic, 52
Obsessional
  character, 134, 137
  neurosis, 17, 322
    and delinquency, 84, 88, 106, 184–5
    and homosexuality, 241–2
    and recidivism, 336
Occupational therapy, 305
Oedipus complex, 8, 155, 179–80, 197–200, 212, 215, 222, 224–5, 240, 243, 247–8, 258, 299–300, 316
  and homosexuality, 215, 222–5
Offences
  categories of, 50, 89–90, 104, 173, 285
  indecent, 266
  organization of, 88
  sexual, 9, 89–90, 189, **191–4**, 386–7
  street, 395–6
  of violence, 173 (*see also* Violent)
Offenders, segregation of, 191, 193
'One-factor' etiologies, 197–200
Option of disease, 76
Oral
  character, 134
  -genital perversions, 181
  impulse, 7, 133, 138, 176, 245

sadism, 139, 155, 220–1
  in homosexuality, 217, 220, 287
  in psychopathy, 139, 155
Organic
  physician, 94
  treatment, 99–101
  types, 11, 90
Original sin, 302
Ortho-psychiatry, 320
Out-patient treatment, 73, 79–80 (*see also* Ambulant, Clinic)
Overdetermination, 250

Paranoia, 141
Paranoid character, 131
Parental influences, 86, 109, 143–4
Parliamentary debates, 11
Parole, psychiatric, 392
Pathological
  crime, 6, 10, 18, 82, 103, 336, 377–8, 382–3
  sexuality, 190
Penal
  codes, 4, 7
  institutions, 45, 65, 72, 307
  reform, 30, 38
Penology and psychiatry, 328–9
Performance tests, 94 (*see also* Tests)
'Permissive' treatment, 160
Personality, 133
  psychopathic, 91
  tests, 280, 322–3 (*see also* Tests)
Persuasion, 100, 318
Perversion
  and neurosis, 183–4, 241 (*see also* Sexual)

SUBJECT INDEX

Phallic erotism, 221, 229
Phantasy, unconscious, 180, 265, 367 (*see also* Unconscious)
Pig-tail cutting, 184
Pioneers, 3
Play technique, 42
Police surgeons, 37
Polymorphous sexuality, 8, 10, 176, 207 (*see also* Sexuality)
Portman Clinic (I.S.T.D.), 21, 46, 84, 89–90, 107, 159, 161, 188, 191, 213, 223, 232, 236–7, 239, 313, 351, 382
'Positions', developmental, 57
Precipitating factors, 87–8, 278, 304–5, 315, 347
  in homosexuality, 226, 228
Pre-delinquent phase, 88, 313, 347
Prediction, 64, 72, 93, 282–3, 322–3, 332, 333–4
Predisposing factors, 85–7, 133, 275, 278–9, 285, 297, 304–5, 315, 327, 381
Pregnancy, 107
Prejudice, 4, 69, 177, 189
  sexual, 173, 243, 246, 358
  (*see also* Public opinion)
Prevention, 20, 76, 162, 192, 327, 337, **347–51**
  and notification, 350
  and problem children, 349
  and research, 351
  'screening' project, 349–51
Preventive detention, 72, 372
Primacy of libido, 8, 246
Primary gain, 226, 243
Prison
  Commissioners' Report, 63–4
  medical officer, 34, 37
  and probation, 113
  reform, 307
  sentences, results of, 111–2
  staff, 309
  (*see also* Imprisonment)
Private practice, 106, 113
Probation, 20, 32, 113
  officer, 44–5, 58, 104–5
  service, 44
  and treatment, 154
Problem children, 265–6, 349
Procreation phantasies, 223
Professional discretion, 367, 372
  obligations, 5
Prognosis, 101, 233–5, 283
Projection, 13, 19, 86, 140, 145, 155
Projective psychosis, 140
Promiscuity, 251, 390
Prostitutes
  drab, 254
  emotions of, 248
  fixations of, 248
  juvenile, 252–4
  larval, 186, 254–5, 257–9
  'normal', 261
  professional, 186
  social services of, 249
  types of, 253–5
Prostitution, 9, 68–9, 230, **244–67**, 394–6
  and delinquency, 245, 256–7, 259
  economic factors in, 259, 266
  and environment, 257–8
  and frigidity, 255
  and homosexuality, 226, 255–7, 259

Prostitution—*cont.*
  and intelligence, 252
  laws governing, 263, 266–7
  and marital fidelity, 253
  and mental disorder, 260–1
  and money, 259–60
  and morality, 256
  and narcissism, 261
  and neurosis, 261
  and Oedipus complex, 247
  parental factors in, 258
  and police, 266–7
  prejudice against, 244–5
  prevention of, 262–5
  and promiscuity, 251
  and regression, 246–7, 252
  and sado-masochism, 256
  and sexual ignorance, 258
  and street anxiety, 250
  'tolerated', 261–2
  treatment of, 265–6
Psychiatric
  centres, 64
  factors, 278–80
  pessimism, 148–9
  social worker, 41, 58, 66, 93–4, 105, 265, 286
Psychiatrist, 94
  nature of, 290
  training of, 58
Psychiatry, 34, 39–41, 60–1, 132
  criminal, x, 33, 297
  and penology, 328–9, 364–6
  and psychopathy, 114, 117–9
Psychic patterns, 83
Psycho-analysis, 33–5, 41–3, 75, 101
  'classical', 153–4
  clinical variables in, 314
  and cognate sciences, 370–3
  and criminology, 311–24
  dearth of workers in, 35
  and delinquency, 292–4, 310–2, 331–2
  and homosexuality, 202, 240–3
  indirect studies, 292, 294
  and instincts, 299–301
  and prediction, 93
  and psychopathy, 51–2, 151–5, 294
  rationale of, 150
  recent advances in, **292–310**
  and social work, 93
  and statistics, 206
  and team-research, **274–80**, 286–9
  theories of, 3, 53, 101–2, 292, 296–7
  training in, 58, 312–13
Psycho-analytic
  characterology, 52, **134–47**
  classifications, 313–4
  divergencies in theory, 55–6
  observation, 300–1, 320
  reports, 95–6
  research, **292–310, 311–24**
  surveys, **292–310, 311–24**
  terminology, 271
  training, 312–3
  treatment, 52, 99, 106, 319–20 (*see also* Treatment)
Psychological movement, 30, 33–4
Psychology, 42, 52, 321–2
  clinical, 282, 289–90
  eclectic, 43
  educational, 40–1, 60, 94, 296
  factorial, 321
  familial, 86, 143, 275, 279, 300, 315, 372

SUBJECT INDEX

Psychology—*cont.*
  general, 285, 330-1
  genetic, 285
  laboratory, 76
  and the Law, 5, 17, 191
  medical, 23, 76, 234, 289
  normal, 34, 38-9
  and rationalism, ix
  social, 284-6, 329-30, 330-1
  and sociology, xii, 391-2
Psycho-neuroses, 102, 314 (*see also* Neurosis)
Psycho-neurotic
  character, 92
  delinquency, 50, 90-2, 319
Psychopath
  aggressive, 121, 126, 149
  anti-social, 125, 128
  benign, 122-3
  creative, 121
  criminal, 117-8, 125, 169
  inadequate, 121
  malignant, 122-3
  masochistic, 123
  sadistic, 123, 145
  violent, 128, 158
Psychopathic
  acting-out, 152
  behaviour, 125, 127
  character, 117-8, 125-6
  Clinic (I.S.T.D.), xii, 21, 46, 48-50, 56, 79, 89, 98-101, **107-14**
  conscience, 303
  constitution, 128, 133
  depression, 124, 145
  personality, 91
  super-ego, 123, **142-7**, 383-4
Psychopathology, 244

Psychopathy (criminal), 4, 8, 17-8, 21, 50, 52, 56, 106, **117-69**, 354-5, 380-1
  and alcoholism, 121
  classification of, 119, **120-5**, 381-2
  clinical features of, 125, 131
  a 'cluster' formation, 123-4
  and conscience, 303
  court valuation of, 118-9
  and disease, 385
  and drug addiction, 121, 124
  emotional set, 125-6
  environment, 133
  etiology of, **132-47**
  and Id-resistance, 152
  and instinct, 125-6
  juvenile, 130
  moral faculties in, 120, 123, 125, 127-8
  negative transference in, 151
  and neurotic delinquency, 161
  and normality, 119, 129, 145, 381
  and oral-sadism, 139, 155
  prognosis in, 283
  projection in, 140-1
  and psychiatry, 117-9, 328-9
  and psycho-analysis, 51-2, 117-9, **151-5**, 294
  pubertal, 130
  and reality sense, 125, 127, 129, 146-7
  and recidivism, 129, 148, 336
  and schizophrenia, 130, 162
  and sex perversion, 118, 125
  and sexuality, 126, 139-40, 213, 299
  and social contract, 125, 128

Psychopathy (criminal)—*cont.*
  terminology of, 147
  and theft, 121, 125
  traumatic factors in, 143, 155
  treatment of, **148–63**
  and violent crime, 128, 158
  and working capacity, 125, 127
  and 'working through', 150–3, 155
Psychoses, 102, 137, 318–19, 355
  borderline, 90–2
  and homosexuality, 213
  (*see also* Depression, Paranoia, Schizophrenia)
Psycho-somatic
  delinquency, 298, 385
  discharge, 66
Psychotherapy
  aim of, 98–9
  and observation, 52
  occupational, 305
  vector, 150, 237
  (*see also* Treatment)
Psychotic
  character, 121, 137
  crime, 21, 90
'Psychoticism', 281–2, 321
Pubertal
  delinquency, 89, 92, 298
  stress, 188, 298
  violence, 92
Public opinion, 42, 68–9, 292
  (*see also* Prejudice)
Punishment, ix, xiii, 4, 194, 308, 333, 335
  of sexual offences, 194

Questionnaires, 94, 309, 322–3
Quetelet's law, 379

Racial development, 198
Rapport, 149–50
  (*see also* Transference)
Rationale
  of psycho-analysis, 150
  of treatment, 97–8, **101–5**
Reaction formation, 140
Reactive instincts, 173 (*see also* Aggression, Instincts)
Reality sense, 56, 83, 86–7, 146
  and psychopathy, 125–9, 146
  and sexuality, 218–9
Receiving, 89
Recidivism, 109, 189, 190, 265, **327–38**, 377
  and disease, 324
  and disposal, 327–8
  duration of, 377–8
  juvenile, 337
  and obsessional states, 336
  and prediction, 333–4
  prevention of, 337
  prognosis of, 333–5
  and psychiatry, 117–9, 328–9
  and psychopathy, 129, 148, 336
  and punishment, 333, 335
  and relapse, 322–3
  social bias against, 329
Recovery, spontaneous, 110
Redemption, 4
Re-education, 100, 150, 166, 238–9
Re-examination, 113
Refractory cases, 55
Regression, 140, 182–3, 217, 246
Relapse, 108–9
Remand homes, 45, 350
Reports, diagnostic, 93, 95, 365–8

SUBJECT INDEX

Repression, 13, 135, 140, 245
Reprieve, 356, 358
Research, 17, 39–40, 45–7, 50, 62, 66, 70–1, 74–5, **373–6**, 385–6
  on diagnosis, 113–4
  funds, 67, 375–6
  and imagination, 289
  indirect, 294
  problems, 57–8
  Unit (Home Office), 70
Resistance, 102, 140, 150, 240–1
  and Id, 152
Resistant types, 144
Responsibility
  criminal, 5, 13, 80–1, 95, 216, **339–46**, 353, 369–70, 385
  diminished, 95, 344, 356
  and society, **192–6**
'Responsible' criminals, 6, 10, 11, 79
Results of treatment, 20–1, 23, 52, **107–14**
  in homosexuality, 235–7
  in private treatment, 113
  in psychopathy, 160–3
Roots
  of crime, **3–24**
  of homosexuality, 389–90
Royal Commission on Capital Punishment, 62, 68, 347–9, **352–9**, 396–7
Royal Commissions, 38, 353

Sadism, 8, 86, 180, 246
  and homosexuality, 217–21, 241
  oral, 139, 155, 220–1
  and super-ego, 143, 145

Sado-masochism, 181, 199–200, 221, 256
Scapegoats, ix, 19
Schizoid character, 121, 137, 162
Schizophrenia, 19
  and psychopathy, 130, 162
School
  examinations, 349–50
  medical officer, 349
'Schools' of clinical psychology, 42, 52
Scientific
  Discussion Group (I.S.T.D.), 65–6, 74, 271
  methods, 60
'Screening' system, 73, 375
Secondary gain, 226, 243
Seduction
  of minors, 10, 203, 212, 227, 231–3
  sexual, 251
Segregation of sexual offenders, 191, 193
Selection
  of cases, 50, 54, 72, 234
  psycho-analytical, 313
  of treatment, 101, 105–6
Sentencing policy, 72
Separation anxiety, 86, 143, 275, 300, 315, 372
Sexual
  abnormality, **173–96**
  antagonism, 199
  assault, 191
  curiosity, 180, 246, 310
  education, 264
  fetishism, 184
  hostility, 183
  inhibitions, 185

T.R.C.

Sexual—*cont.*
  instincts, 7
  instruction, 192
  masochism, 246
  masturbation, 179, 208–9, 216–7
  mores, 10
  murder, 181
  offences, 89–90, 386–7
    frequency of, 9
    and mental illness, 192
    and punishment, 189, 194
    treatment of, 189
  offenders, 191, 193
  organization, 100
  perversions, 9–10, 21, 91, 177, 246
    adult, 180
    anal-genital, 182, 220, 232
    and conflict, 183
    curative functions of, 183
    and neurosis, 183–4, 241
    observation of, 182, 192
    option of, 218
    oral-genital, 181
    and psychopathy, 118, 125
    statistics of, 189
    treatment of, 182, 192
  prejudice, 175–6, 178, 190, 358–9
  psychopathy, 125, 299
  re-education, 238–9
  regression, 182–3, 217
  sadism, 8, 86, 180, 246
  zones, 248
Sexuality
  adolescent, 180
  anal, 245
  components of, 176, 245–7
  genital, 245–6
  infantile, 10, **176–81**, 245–7
  and mental pain, 216
  oral, 245
  polymorphous, 8, 10, 176, 207
  'reactive', 173
  and reality sense, 218–9
  and regression, 217
  unconscious theories of, 180, 221, 223
  urethral, 245
Short treatment, 4, 10, 100–1
Shop-lifting, 90, 92
Sin, ix, 4, 10, 312
Social
  aggression, 371
  aspects of sexual abnormality, **173–96**
  cohesion and homosexuality, 199–200
  conscience, 293
  contract, 4, 29–30, 125, 128
  defence, 371
  feeling, 157
  historian, ix
  information, 49
  psychiatry and the Law, 364–6
  psychology, 284–6, 329–30
  reactions, 179, 243
  safeguards, 194
  safety, 81
  work, 66–7, 93
Society, responsibility of, **192–6**
Socio-legal views, 388
Sociology, ix–x, 22, 50, 60, 76, 216, 274, 284–6, 330–1, 369–70
  familial, 22, 86, 143, 279
  and psychology, 391–2
Sodomy, 182

Spontaneous recovery, 110
State
   functions of, 27
   medical service, 45, 47
   medicine and professional discretion, 367–8, 372
Statistical
   boundaries, 335
   method, 51, 301, 321
Statisticians, 329, 334
Statistics, 76, 373–4, 385
   diagnostic, 89–90
   of homosexuality, 204–6
   of prison results, 111–2
   prognostic, 232–3
   and psycho-analysis, 206
   of sexual offences, 186–9
   of sexual treatment, 189
   and team research, 290
   of treatment, 99, 102, 109
Stealing, 11
   frequency of, 4
   and love need, 14
   sweets, 258–9
   (*see also* Theft)
Strap cutting, 184
Street
   anxieties, 250, 361
   offences, 395–6
Stress
   anxiety from, 104
   mental, 35–7, 87, 102, 336
   pubertal, 188
   summation of, 88
Structure, psychic, **142**–**6**, 224–5, 303–4, 316
Sublimation, 140
Suffering, mental, 76, 273–4
Suggestion, 20, 90–100, 105
Suicide, 89–90, 121–2, 379

Summary Courts, 84, 89, 93
Summation of traumata, 143
Super-ego, xi, 12, 31, 56–7, 83, 86, 144, 288–9, 303, 316–7, 383–4
   and aggression, 301
   anal, 144
   analysis, 156
   and homosexuality, 144, 199, 224–5, 240–2
   and psychopathy, 123, **142**–**7**, 383–4
   and sadism, 143, 145
   (*see also* Conscience, Guilt, Unconscious conflict)
Superstitions, 4, 31
Supervision, 49, 62, 99
Susceptibility, 275, 279
Symbolic thinking, 184
Symbolism, 88, 152, 228, 258–60, 283, 305, 372
   of money, 260
Symptom
   formation, 14, 15, 16, 304–5, 315–6
   equivalents, 318
Symptoms, 80, 83–4
Synthesis, mental, 303–4

Tantrums, 17
Tavistock Clinic, 23, 46
Team
   diagnosis, 93–4
   influence, 53, 56
   research, **271**–**91**
   clinical assessments, 280–2
   dangers of, 272
   and definitions, 272
   and guilt, 288
   interpretation of, 273

Team—*cont.*
  research and prediction, 282–3
  principles of, 273–4, 280
  and psycho-analysis, 286–9
  statistics of, 290
  and tests, 283–4
  training in, 286
  surveys, 65
Technique, Freudian, 319–20
Tension, 87
Terminology, 147, 162, 271, 290
Tests
  intelligence, 94
  mental, 66, 94, 283–4, 241–2, 309, 322–3, 349–50
  performance, 94
  personality, 280, 322–3
  prediction, 94, 282–3
  vocational, 94, 349
Theft, 89–90, 175, 299, 385
  compulsive, 17, 93 (*see also* Kleptomania, Stealing)
  neurotic, 14–7
  and psychopathy, 121, 125
Theories of conduct, 29
Theory
  Freudian, 289
  of mind, 292, 296
  and practice, 54–5
Thumb-sucking, 179, 216
Topography, psychic, 142–6
Total function of mind, 82
Training, 58–9, 72, 74, 286, 308, 312–3, 365–6
Transference, 20, 53, 100, 149–50, 167, 294, 306–8
  counter-, 149, 307–8
  distributed, 53, 104, 111, 156
  in homosexuality, 241–2

infantile, 308
negative, 100, 106, 151
and neurosis, 151–4
and prediction, 282–3
in psychopathy, 151
'ring', 159–60
stimuli, 103–4
therapy, 102–3, **156–60**
Transvestitism, 212–3
Trauma, 143–4, 275, 279, 357
Traumata, summation of, 143
Traumatic dysfunction, 57
Treatment, 52, 64, 75–6, **96–114, 305–10**
  Adlerian, 100
  aims of, 101
  ambulant, 73, 79–80, 112–4, 191, 193, 308–9, 329
  of children, 42, 100, 156
  clinical, 19, 23, 46
  compulsory, 307
  conditioning, 98
  duration of, 52, 107
  eclectic, 100
  failure of, 239, 329
  focal, 106, 150, 156, 237–8, 240
  Freudian, 100
  history of, **27–76**
  of homosexuality, 113, 203, 231, **234–43**
  hormone, 92, 182
  institutional, 99, 149, 308, 370–1
  Jungian, 100
  milieu, 160
  moral, 19
  need for, 109
  and neutrality, 153
  occupational, 305

Treatment—*cont.*
  private, 193
  of prostitution, 265–6
  psycho-analytical, 20–1, 101–3, 106, 153–5, 166–8, 240–3, 305–7, 319–20, 324
  of psychopathy, **148–63, 166–9**
  rationale of, 97–8, **101–5**
  research on, 113–4
  results of, 20–1, 23, 52, **107–14**, 160–3
  selection of, 101, 105–6
  of sexual offences, 189–92
  short, 52–3, 100–1, 158, 237
  standards of, 52–4
  technique of, 52–4
  unconscious in, 102
  varieties of, 99–101
Truancy, 89–90
Types, institutional, 369
Typology, 50, 386–7

Unconscious
  anxiety, 18, 104, 138, 140, 221, 224, 238, 240, 353
  conflict, 7, 56, 104, 183, 203, 273, 316
  conscience, 12
  denial, 225, 256
  factors, 273
    in behaviour, 102
  gain through illness, 108
  guilt, 17, 225, 238, 240, 242, 302–3
  homosexuality, 140, 199, 203
  mechanisms, 12, 315
  mind, 12, 273, 295
  morality, 17, 184

  need for punishment, 302
  option of perversion, 218
  phantasy, 180, 265, 367
  predisposition, 297, 315
  symbolism, 88
    in treatment, 102
Uncontrollable impulse, 357
Undetected delinquency, 295
'Unimproved', 108–9
United Nations, x, 376
'Unnatural'
  offences, 187, 204
  violence, 9
Upbringing, 7, 86, 254
Urethral
  character, 134
  sexuality, 245

Valency of factors, 272–3
Variables
  clinical, 293, 298–9, 314
  etiological, 315
Vector therapy, 150, 237
Venereal disease, 256
Verwahrloste Jugend, 164
Viennese school, 42
Violent crime, 9, 17, 61, 89–90, 173, 347–48
  frequency of, 4
  and homosexuality, 203
  prevention of, **347–51**
  in psychopathy, 128, 158
  pubertal, 92
Vocational
  guidance, 94
  tests, 94, 349
Voyeurism, 246

Wandering, 89

War
  fear of, 393
  First World, 3, 39, 263
  readiness and homosexuality, 202
  Second World, 311
  wounds, 11
Wastage of cases, 107
Waves of crime, 61, 63
'Wayward' youth, 164–5
West-End Hospital for Nervous Disease, 36

Wilful damage, 89
'Will to recovery', 188
Wolfenden Report, 11, 62–3, 68–9, 138–9, 173, 189–90, 393–6
Working through, 150–3, 155

X-ray examination, 94

Youth movements, 32–3